E-BUSINESS TECHNOLOGY FORECAST

PricewaterhouseCoopers Technology Centre
Menlo Park
California 94025
U.S.A.

E-BUSINESS TECHNOLOGY FORECAST

May 1999

PricewaterhouseCoopers Technology Centre
68 Willow Road
Menlo Park, California 94025
U.S.A.

Phone: +1-650-322-0606
Fax: +1-650-321-5543

To order copies of the *E-Business Technology Forecast*, order #TC-04-01, please see page ix.

Printing   10 9 8 7 6 5 4 3

CONTENTS

viii | HOW TO USE THIS BOOK

E-BUSINESS OVERVIEW

1 | THE IMPACT OF E-BUSINESS
41 | INTRODUCTION TO E-BUSINESS TECHNOLOGIES

E-BUSINESS ENABLING TECHNOLOGIES

49 | **E-BUSINESS PLATFORMS AND APPLICATIONS**
49 | EXECUTIVE SUMMARY
50 | CATEGORIES OF WEB BUSINESS
50 | E-BUSINESS SOFTWARE
51 | APPLICATION ARCHITECTURE
52 | STOREFRONT COMPONENTS
61 | COMMERCE PLATFORMS
65 | SELL-SIDE PACKAGED E-BUSINESS APPLICATIONS
76 | BUY-SIDE PACKAGED E-BUSINESS APPLICATIONS
79 | NEGOTIATED-PRICE SELLING
81 | PERSONALIZATION
86 | CUSTOMER RELATIONSHIP MANAGEMENT
87 | CUSTOMER-FACING E-MAIL
95 | WEB-BASED CUSTOMER SERVICE
97 | STANDARDS INITIATIVES
100 | MARKET OVERVIEW
104 | FORECAST
109 | **INTEGRATION WITH ENTERPRISE SYSTEMS**
109 | EXECUTIVE SUMMARY
110 | INTEGRATION LEVELS AND METHODS
113 | E-BUSINESS EXTENSIONS TO ERP
117 | ERP PROVIDERS
120 | EVOLUTION AND FUTURE OF EDI
126 | XML AND EDI
130 | EAI: PACKAGED ENTERPRISE MIDDLEWARE
134 | MARKET OVERVIEW
136 | FORECAST
139 | **PAYMENT TECHNOLOGIES**
139 | EXECUTIVE SUMMARY
140 | OVERVIEW
142 | PAYMENT TECHNOLOGIES FOR E-BUSINESS
151 | ELECTRONIC BILL PRESENTMENT AND PAYMENT
154 | DIGITAL CASH
156 | PAYMENT TECHNOLOGY STANDARDS
161 | MARKET OVERVIEW
166 | FORECAST

iv

E-BUSINESS SUPPORTING TECHNOLOGIES

169   **E-BUSINESS INFRASTRUCTURE**

169   EXECUTIVE SUMMARY

170   OVERVIEW

170   HARDWARE: NETWORK INFRASTRUCTURE,
SERVER AND CLIENT MACHINES, SMART CARDS

177   PLATFORM APPLICATION PROGRAMMING

186   BASIC WEB INTERACTIONS

202   E-BUSINESS WEB SITE ARCHITECTURES

208   SECURITY

215   MARKET OVERVIEW

221   LIST OF FIGURES

223   LIST OF TABLES

225   INDEX

Welcome to the *E-Business Technology Forecast*. The *E-Business Technology Forecast* addresses the issues and products in the e-business technology space for both general and technical management. We have tried to put into one volume a general survey of e-business platforms and applications, the technologies that integrate e-business functionality with enterprise information systems, payment technologies, and the technical infrastructure supporting e-business. Our focus is on the use of the Internet for conducting business-to-business and business-to-consumer transactions. However, this focus is not meant to diminish the importance of other (nontransactional) e-business uses of the Internet.

This has not been an easy book to write. Our original idea was to take the *"Electronic Commerce"* chapter from the *Technology Forecast: 1999* and expand it into a full-sized book. We realized very quickly this strategy would not work. Because the velocity and impact of change surrounding e-business had increased dramatically in size, complexity, and importance, we had to return to the drawing board.

Going back to the drawing board entailed more than deciding what additional technologies we needed to cover, which vendors we needed to include, or how to structure the book. We needed to wrestle with a more philosophical question—namely, the difference between e-business activities and the larger subject of business activities that use networked computers.

Only by answering that question in the context of what we wanted to achieve—a comprehensive survey of e-business technology that fit into an easy-to-understand form—could we articulate a working definition of e-business. That definition (found in "The Impact of E-Business") served as the litmus test for deciding which technologies and issues to include. We do not mean to imply that our definition is the single or final definition for e-business. We fully expect that as e-business evolves, so will our definitions.

We feel fortunate to be covering such an exciting subject because we believe e-business is the primary driver for business change for the foreseeable future. Whether from new entrants creating or transforming markets or established companies planning their migration to an e-business environment, we have witnessed blistering creativity in technology, management, and strategy.

This does not mean current e-business implementations are neat, parsimonious, logical, or elegant. Indeed, many of the e-business processes and technical solutions we have seen owe their success more to tinkering than to a straight-line extrapolation of today's business plan. However, the tinkering surrounding e-business is moving toward order—toward business models and technical architectures that are more complex and effective than their predecessors.

As such, we invite the reader to approach this book as a living document—a work in progress that probably will be very different in its next edition. This difference will stem not only from the extraordinary changes we expect to see in technology during the next twelve months, but also to the way e-business is capturing the imaginations of firms, governments, and people worldwide.

Enjoy.

ACKNOWLEDGMENTS

Sponsoring Partner Cathy Neuman

Contributors Joe Fenner, Dan Gordon, Lauren John, David King, Fernando Martinez-Campos, Ann Mueller, Barry Plotkin, Terry Retter, Winfield Treese

Reviewers Yukari Carrie Akiyama, Piers Allison, Doug Baird, Joseph Bellissimo, Robert Benkaim, Saul Berman, Ed Berryman, Jonathan Biggs, Stephen Bingham, Bill A. Bound, Ben Bruggeman, Loren Buhle, Christine Campbell, Joe Casey, Thomas Craighead, Jack Dooley, Lionel Drew, Matthew Faulkner, Klaus-Dieter Floegel, Jens Gastrop, Ed Glister, Philip Gomm, Mark Gribman, Janet Gunn, Kim Hansen, Bob Hatcher, Jan Hauschildt, Bertold Heil, Martin Hemsley, Malcolm Henry, Kerry Horan, Chris Jenkins, Richard Kaczmarek, Gene Katz, Filip Kesler, Stefan Knickel, David Kohn, Toru Koyama, Hendrik Kurz, Marco Langenhuizen, Lawrence Lerner, Chris Lilley, Gareth MacLachlan, Alastair MacWillson, Tom McGonegal, Jeffry Michaels, Francois Moscovici, Masateru Noda, Conrad Nowikow, Grant Nelson, Jeff Nickerson, Rudolf Niehus, Fernando Pardo, Bo Parker, Tim Parsons, Deepan Patel, Ned Pendergast, Robert Pepper, Bernard Plagman, Jeff Pressler, Thomas Preuß, Jim Rafferty, Mark Reed, Frank van Rooij, Klaus-Clemenz Schoo, Monika Seewig, Marc Sel, Khwaja Shaik, Edmond Sheehy, Sandeep Sinha, Steve Sparough, Melissa Spivack, Mark Stringer, Rick Turner, Frank Ulrich, John Velissarrios, Martin van Vessem, Dick Vincent, Marc Voncken, Lars Waltenburg, Gerald Ward, Markus Warnke, Lars Weber, Leo Wisniewski, Jeffrey Zimmerman, Mark Ziskind

Editors John Gauntt, Barbara Jurin

Contributing Editors Eric Berg, Michael Katz

Partner in Charge Paul Turner

Editorial Production Manager Lea Anne Bantsari

Assistant Editors Tanya Langdon, Betsy Schiffman

Marketing and Business Development Gayle Rocklage

Staff Researcher Glorianne Wong

Research Veronica Adams, Paola Lopez, Jim Reed, Karen Scarpelli, Peter Vigil

Graphics and Layout Rick Eberly, Susie Mills

Indexer Lesley Schneider

Copy Editor Lisa Ramos

HOW TO USE THIS BOOK

Welcome to the *E-Business Technology Forecast.*

The *E-Business Technology Forecast* is a publication of the PricewaterhouseCoopers Technology Centre. It is prepared with the assistance of a variety of subject experts. Working with authors' drafts, PricewaterhouseCoopers practice units worldwide collaborate in an extensive editorial review process to produce the final text. Our contributors are recognized in the Acknowledgments section.

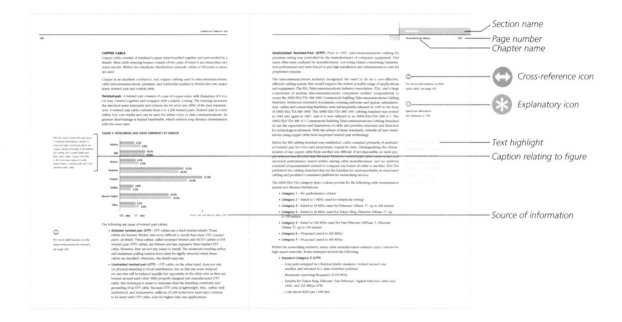

The content of each of the "Enabling Technologies" chapters is organized into the following general sections:

- **Executive Summary**—A brief overview of the chapter's contents.

- **Technology**—Basic background information. This section includes how the technology evolved, how it works, and basic terminology. Recent major events and trends are also discussed.

- **Market Overview**—A summary of products by major vendors in the marketplace.

- **Forecast**—Forecasts for the progress of the technology over the next one to three years (referred to as the "forecast period").

- **References**—A list of references cited in the chapter, plus a bibliography of related reference materials and URLs of selected mentioned companies and organizations that are not intuitive (that is, any URLs that do not follow the standard format of www.companyname.com).

We have chosen the following usage for the *E-Business Technology Forecast*:

- All monetary amounts are expressed in U.S. dollars ($).
- Units of measure are expressed in either metric or U.S. Customary system, depending upon common industry usage.

(Note: A billion is 1,000 million [1,000,000,000 or 10^9].)

As an additional reference aid, the Index makes it easy to locate discussions of specific topics, products, and companies. In addition, the Index defines all acronyms used in the text.

HOW TO ORDER

The *E-Business Technology Forecast* is available both in print and in electronic formats. PricewaterhouseCoopers' clients are invited to request copies from their engagement contact.

The *E-Business Technology Forecast* (order #TC-04-01) is available for US$300 by calling +1-800-654-3387 (U.S. calls only) or +1-314-997-2540, or by sending a fax to +1-314-997-1351. To place an order through the Web, please go to www.pwc-tech-forecast.com or to www.e-business.pwcglobal.com. The price includes shipping and handling. American Express, MasterCard, and Visa are accepted. Payment by check also can be arranged.

PricewaterhouseCoopers partners and staff may request copies of the *E-Business Technology Forecast* by sending a Lotus Notes message to NAC Distribution@Price Waterhouse-US@INTL (request document #TC-04-01) or by accessing the Electronic Business Knowledge Source database.

COMMENTARY AND QUESTIONS

The editors and authors of the *E-Business Technology Forecast* welcome your comments. We also want to hear how you are using the *E-Business Technology Forecast* in your work, and how you might use it in the future. A self-addressed reader response card is included at the back of the *Forecast*.

An electronic mail address has been established for readers to submit comments, questions, or suggestions about the *E-Business Technology Forecast*. PricewaterhouseCoopers users of Lotus Notes can reach the editors at Technology Forecast Editors@Price Waterhouse-US@INTL.

Internet users should send comments to technology.forecast.editors@ pwcglobal.com.

ABOUT PRICEWATERHOUSECOOPERS

Drawing on the talents of more than 155,000 people in 150 countries, PricewaterhouseCoopers LLP provides a full range of business advisory services to leading global, national, and local companies, as well as to public institutions. These services include audit, accounting, and tax advice; management, information technology, and human resource consulting; financial advisory services, including mergers and acquisitions, business recovery, project finance, and litigation support; business process outsourcing services; and legal services through a global network of affiliated law firms.

PricewaterhouseCoopers' depth of experience in electronic business also is industry-centered and worldwide. The firm offers clients the benefit of seasoned expertise, augmented by innovative use of business process and technology to create opportunities for market growth, new sources of profitability, and sustainable competitive advantage. Most important, PricewaterhouseCoopers is a source of holistic insight and support for a company's total e-business needs.

We are committed organizationally to a future where e-business defines the advantages both we and our clients share.

To find out more about PricewaterhouseCoopers, please call your local office or visit our World Wide Web site at www.pwcglobal.com.

The PricewaterhouseCoopers Technology Centre, located in Menlo Park, California, provides PricewaterhouseCoopers engagement teams and their clients with analysis, evaluation, and implementation strategies of emerging information technologies.

The Centre has a staff of more than 40 researchers, technology analysts, and software developers. These professionals have extensive backgrounds in advanced uses of existing technology as well as in the practical application of emerging technologies.

Our Technology Centre staff deliver on-site presentations on technology trends to PricewaterhouseCoopers clients and staff around the world, using the *Technology Forecast* and other proprietary thought leadership publications as references. These presentations supplement our general consulting services, which focus on information technology and business strategy issues.

The Centre also provides fee-based custom research and competitive analysis on information, computer, and communication technologies and industry trends. This research is used to give the firm and its clients a competitive edge in the marketplace.

The Technology Centre engages in research and software development designed to maintain PricewaterhouseCoopers' leadership in delivering professional services. For example, Technology Centre knowledge management initiatives are incorporated in a wide range of audit, business advisory, tax, and consulting services.

THE ROLE OF TECHNOLOGY

There is no question that technology and technology-induced change is at the core of the trend toward e-business. Developments in computing, communications, and content have provided businesses with the power needed to change the rules of competitive engagement in an environment where past performance is no guarantee of future success.

The words "faster, smaller, cheaper" once described only the characteristics of the electronic circuits that comprised the power tools of the information age. As technology went on to permeate every aspect of our lives, these same words—faster, smaller, cheaper—have become the mantra describing e-businesses themselves. As the pace of change quickens, as global markets come within reach, and as new competitors appear with business models never before possible, the world will never be the same again. Simply put, e-business means new businesses within a week, new markets overnight, new products in an hour, new services all the time.

OUR VIEW OF E-BUSINESS

An e-business is an enterprise designed for success in the information age. E-business brings into play an organization's resources and partners in new and innovative ways to create clear strategic advantage. The potential of e-business goes far beyond new technologies to impact and engage all aspects of a business—strategy, process, organization, and technology—to extend the business beyond its own boundaries.

E-business has the ability to create dramatic new sources of shareholder value by enabling organizations to accomplish the following goals:

- Build customer loyalty
- Reach new markets
- Create new products and services
- Achieve market leadership
- Optimize business processes
- Enhance human capital
- Harness technology
- Manage risk and compliance

It is these issues that today's executives are most concerned about as they work to position their organizations for success in an increasingly virtual world.

HOW PRICEWATERHOUSECOOPERS HELPS CLIENTS WIN

PricewaterhouseCoopers' formula for success in the information age is both fundamental and far-reaching. We view e-business as more than just an electronic link in a supply chain or another Web site on the Internet. In fact, we view e-business as even more than the enabling technologies presented here. We approach e-business with our clients as a source of strategic advantage—one that will allow one company to completely outdistance another and, in the process, transform the business rules as we know them today. E-business truly is about "business without boundaries."

E-BUSINESS VALUE

There are three compelling reasons to choose PricewaterhouseCoopers to help provide your e-business solution:

- *Vision and reach*—As a global organization with clients in multiple industries and governments, we are aware of the pervasive effects e-business is having on institutions worldwide. We also understand e-business is more than a technology issue; in fact, it influences the fundamental business strategies and operations of every organization. Based on this vision and our global resources, we are well positioned to empower our clients to achieve the maximum benefits from e-business solutions.

- *Proven results*—Our E-Business Initiative professionals work with clients to create opportunities for market growth, new sources of profitability, and sustainable competitive advantage. Our engagements have covered the range of e-business needs—across dimensions of strategy, organization, business process, and systems. As our case study examples will show, we have helped corporations realize the benefits of e-business solutions—from strategy and design through implementation.

- *Thought leadership*—Our industry and practice teams invest time and resources to gain an understanding of e-business and its implications for our clients. We analyze its impact on government policy, taxation, and legal and commercial operations as well as on the structural and personnel aspects of corporations. Our engagement teams participate in many policy and standards organizations worldwide, and also sponsor studies that address core issues such as privacy and the security of personal information.

We also show our commitment to advancement through investments in groundbreaking technologies, world-class centers of excellence, and industry consortia and alliances.

The following are typical of materials available electronically on the Pricewaterhouse-Coopers e-business Web site: www.e-business.pwcglobal.com.

- *E-Commerce & Privacy—What Net Users Want?*—Discusses your customer expectations with respect to Internet privacy

- *Electronics Business for Managed Care*—Examines e-business for managed care issues

- *Tax and Telecommunications in the E-Business Age, Part I: Infrastructure Issues*—Discusses setting up and expanding a global telecommunications infrastructure

- *Tax and Telecommunications in the E-Business Age, Part II: Basic & Value-Added Services—A Regional View*—Discusses how convergence and the Internet have impacted the telecommunications industry in the provision of basic and value-added services

- *Inside the Mind of the CEO 1999*—Discusses the results of a survey of 802 executives as to their predictions and concerns for e-business

- *Electronic Business Outlook—"A Survey of E-Business Goals, Practices, and Results"*—Provides insight as to where e-business is heading

In addition, PricewaterhouseCoopers' e-business Web site allows you to order the following e-business materials:

- *A Deeper View: Insight into E-Business Internet Privacy and Web Advertising Models*—Discusses new developments in Internet privacy and Web advertising

- *Call Center Live: Call Centers for the Next Millennium*—Discusses the next-generation call center where computer and telephone converge

- *Consumer Technology Brochure: U.S., U.K. Consumers on Parallel Track in Outlook on Use of Technology*—Discusses different views on where the U.S. and U.K. are heading with respect to technology

- *Convergence Scenarios in Media, Telecommunications, and Technology*—Provides insights as to where e-business is heading

- *Electronic Business Outlook: A Survey of E-Business Goal Practices and Results*—Discusses the seven e-business issues that impact some of the clients of PricewaterhouseCoopers

- *Global Convergence Summit: A New Era of Content and Communications*—Overview of the Global Convergence Summit for Content and Communications

- *Entertainment and Media Insider on the PointCast Network*—A CD-ROM with PointCast for the Entertainment and Media Industry, accompanied by a brochure

- *PricewaterhouseCoopers Entertainment Industry Practice Overview*—Discusses PricewaterhouseCoopers Entertainment Industry Practice group

- *The Chief Executive Guide: Beyond the Internet (a supplement to Chief Executive Technology and the CEO: The CEO Tech 100)*—High-level overview of Internet trends and concepts for the CEO

THE IMPACT OF E-BUSINESS

Introduction

The world's leading organizations are reorienting themselves around electronic business, or "e-business," as the term is used in this book. Pioneering efforts are little more than five years old, yet e-business initiatives and startup companies are transforming entire industries and becoming a general phenomenon. Indeed, e-business promises to define what will become the ground rules for commerce in the 21st century.

It is difficult to capture the essence of e-business in a single definition. For example, the World Trade Organization defines e-business as "…the production, advertising, sale, and distribution of products via telecommunications networks." Although these terms are appropriate for an international body created and organized to enhance trade between nation-states, they focus on tangible commodities as opposed to services or content.

Definitions of e-business for services exist. For example, Merrill Lynch defines e-business as electronic transactions of information exchange. "These transactions can include business-to-business electronic trading of goods and services; financial payments; credit-card, debit, ATM, and electronic funds transfer; card issuing and fund processing; bill payment and presentment; and travel distribution along with other information services."

From a corporate perspective, e-business uses information technology to conduct business transactions among buyers, sellers, and trading partners to improve customer service, reduce costs, and increase shareholder value. Technically speaking, e-business extends the use of information technology systems to include people (such as customers, suppliers, distributors, and job applicants) who previously did not have access to the enterprise's information resources.

The *E-Business Technology Forecast* establishes a middle ground between industry-specific definitions that do not span market segments and overarching interpretations that abstract meaning beyond its usefulness. This book focuses on the uses of information technology that cross enterprise boundaries and encompass a transaction or part of a transactional relationship (including customer service, supply-chain integration, or payment processing). The book will not cover purely informational or content-distribution uses of the Web or dedicated, television-like advertising. Although it focuses on transactions that occur via the World Wide Web, the book also covers non-Web forms of interenterprise transactions.

Hereafter, e-business will be defined as the application of information technologies to facilitate the buying and selling of products, services, and information over public standards-based networks. In addition, there must be a computer program on at least one end of a transaction or commercial relationship. At the other end, there may be another computer program, a person using a computer program, or a person using some other network access mechanism. This definition is intended to frame the following technical discussions. As e-business evolves, so will its definitions.

Moving Toward a Customer-Centric World

E-business uses the Web both as a medium and as a market for commerce. The main difference between the Web and other electronic media such as facsimile and telephone is that the Web goes beyond just enabling transactions. The Web becomes an information-rich market space through which buyers and sellers interact. Such market spaces are not fixed in physical territory but are created by the confluence of standards-based networks, Web browsers, software, content, and people. As such, the physical barriers of time and distance between the provider and the customer are minimized.

The elimination of physical elements lays bare the essentials of a commercial transaction. The buyer and the seller "face" each other through an electronic connection. There is no traveling to a physical store, no salesperson, no order book, and no cash register. Instead, there is a Web site. Thus, e-business represents a fundamental shift in how buyers and sellers interact.

Hence, e-business changes the rules of engagement. For the buyer, e-business means the costs of finding an alternative provider are minimal. For the seller, the risks of not engaging a customer's attention and thus losing a customer are high. In this new world, much of the ability to decide how business will be done has shifted from the seller to the buyer.

Before the Web, buyers and prospects depended on people to answer questions, offer advice, provide information, and solve problems as well as take orders. In e-business, the customer is the proactive navigator and the Web site meets the customer face-to-face. It is the site that "listens" to the customer's issues or questions and responds with advice, guidance, recommendations, and pointers to other sources. Transaction capability is taken for granted.

"The primary implication of a customer-centered world is that customer relationship management becomes the core business activity of an e-business."

If the customer's experience in a Web-based e-business interaction is as good or better than dealing with a person, then it enhances the customer loyalty-building process. On the other hand, if the customer is not satisfied and chooses to go elsewhere, it significantly reduces the likelihood of reengaging that customer.

The primary implication of a customer-centered world is that customer relationship management becomes the core business activity of an e-business. Functionally, this shift means the universe of business units and processes that touch the customer—previously limited to marketing, sales, and customer service—need to expand to include engineering, manufacturing, and distribution as well. In the 1990s, many businesses implemented corporate systems that automate these functions at their enterprises.

This expanded scope always has been a key goal. In addition, the costs associated with coordinating business processes across enterprise boundaries tended to limit the ability of firms to integrate their supply chains. However, the Web's potential to engage a global, real-time market with an expanded portfolio of customer-touching business processes and technologies lies at the heart of e-business' compelling vision.

The Impact of E-Business on Cost

E-business affects four broad categories that determine the production and transaction costs of a firm:

- The cost of executing a sale
- The costs associated with procuring production inputs
- The costs associated with making and delivering a product or service
- The cost associated with logistics

THE COST OF E-BUSINESS SALES

One of the biggest impacts of e-business has been the substitution of virtual storefronts for brick-and-mortar infrastructures. Because an e-business Web site is open 24 hours per day, 7 days per week and available to a global market from day one, a business no longer has to build separate physical establishments to attract a larger customer base. A virtual storefront also allows an e-business to manage one store instead of multiple stores, thus eliminating duplicate inventory costs. The convenience of round-the-clock virtual access for customers is an increasingly valuable characteristic of virtual businesses.

A second e-business advantage is that, by providing product or service information online, customers can educate themselves about price and performance attributes. In an e-business environment, prospective customers often arrive at a Web site knowing almost as much as the merchant about product and price attributes. Therefore, subsequent contact between the customer and dedicated sales or support staff tends to be at a higher level.

A third important aspect of e-business is that it enables more efficient order configuration. For example, both General Electric (GE) and Cisco Systems reported nearly one-quarter of their pre-Web-site orders had to be reworked because of errors—a total of more than 1 million orders, in the case of GE. Since adopting a Web-enabled customer interface, Cisco reports an error rate of only 2 percent.

Fourth, the cost savings from processing payments via the Web are dramatic. Although the administrative (marginal) cost of processing a paper check for banks and merchants averages $1.20 and a debit- or credit-card payment averages $0.40 to $0.60, the cost of processing an electronic micropayment made via the Internet can be as low as $0.01 or less.

Clearly, e-business represents a fundamental shift in how the sales process is executed by a company. As a result, e-business compels existing businesses to reexamine how they interact with customers, even as new entrants exploit e-business to reach customer bases previously thought unreachable.

Nowhere has the confluence of virtual storefronts, online information, enhanced order configuration, and transaction cost savings been felt more strongly than in the securities industry. According to The Tower Group, online brokerage is becoming one of the most popular Web activities. In the United States, for example, more than 120 Web sites enable online trading, and the number of online brokerage accounts totals approximately 5 million. As a result, trading securities via the Web has expanded to capture approximately 28 percent of all retail equity trades in the U.S. Considering the online securities market did not exist in 1995, this is an amazing development. (See Figure 1 and Figure 2 on page 4.)

Securities trading is only one area of the financial services sector being redefined by e-business. In 1998, more than 1,200 banks and credit unions in the United States signed with online banking application vendors and providers to build fully transactional Web sites. In 1999, 7,200 banks and credit unions are expected to acquire online banking applications, a 500 percent year-on-year increase in the number of institutions investing in online financial services technology.

At Digital Credit Union in Maynard, Mass., more than 15,000 of its 90,000 customers now access its Web site regularly for information about their accounts. In a given month, its Web site generates between 2,000 and 2,500 loan applications. Two weeks

FIGURE 1: CHARLES SCHWAB'S ONLINE ACCOUNTS AND TRADES COMPLETED (4Q1996–2Q1998)

This figure illustrates the percent of trades completed during the specified period.

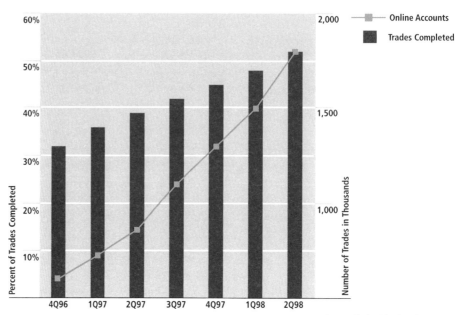

Source: Charles Schwab and IDC, 1998

FIGURE 2: E*TRADE'S ONLINE ACCOUNTS AND TRADES COMPLETED (4Q1996–3Q1998)

This figure illustrates the average number of trades completed per day during the specified period.

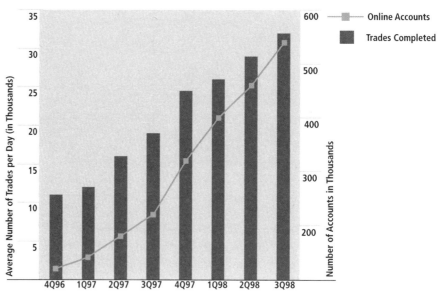

Source: E*Trade and IDC, 1998

after the Spanish bank Bankinter launched its Web site, it had signed up 5,000 users, creating 15,000 transactions. By the beginning to 1999, it had more than 60,000 users, or 10 percent of its customers, generating $100 million of transactions every month.

Relying on the Web, financial services providers can sell products and services in ways that previously required the acquisition of a local bank or the building of expensive branches and ATM machines to create a market presence. Moreover, financial service providers using the Web as their main market channel avoid many of the technology conflicts (such as a separate interface to core systems for ATM, branch, call center, or kiosk transactions) that plague many traditional service providers. Web-based banking and brokerage benefit from a powerful unifying combination of the Internet as a communications standard, a Web browser as a display standard, and a Web server as the access point into back-end operational systems.

See the sidebar "E-Business and Financial Services" on page 6 for more information.

Thus, the Web allows even small financial service institutions to compete more effectively for customers because it does not distinguish between a large bank or securities firm with hundreds of branches and thousands of ATMs and a small firm with a few branches and no ATMs. By eliminating the need for a significant branch infrastructure, institutions of all sizes are able to offer better prices for financial services.

Obviating the need for multiple physical establishments to attract and grow a customer base is a fundamental e-business value proposition. This substitution does not mean physical buildings will disappear, however. Rather, it means many of the previous barriers to market entry based upon ownership of physical facilities in certain industries are falling even as new barriers, such as mindshare (customer awareness of a particular company or organization), take their place.

THE COST OF E-BUSINESS PROCUREMENT

Another area where e-business is making a substantial impact is in procurement. Web-based procurement of maintenance, repair, and operations (MRO) supplies is expected to reach more than $100 billion worldwide by the year 2000. MRO comprises those goods required to run a company that are not raw materials used in the direct manufacture of a product or the provision of a service; generally, MRO supplies are low-cost items purchased in bulk on an intermittent basis.

In the traditional approach to MRO procurement, a corporate purchasing officer would receive a paper-based requisition. That purchasing officer then would need to search a variety of paper catalogs to find the right product at the right price. Not surprisingly, the administrative cost for purchasing indirect supplies often exceeded the unit value of the product itself. According to the Organization for Economic Cooperation and Development (OECD), companies with more than $500 million in revenue typically spend an estimated $75 to $150 to process a single purchase order for MRO supplies.

The goal of many e-business procurement applications, therefore, is to link organizations directly to preapproved suppliers' catalogs and to process the entire purchasing transaction over the Web. Linking to electronic catalogs significantly reduces the need to check the timeliness and accuracy of supplier information.

See the sidebar "All That for a Ream of Paper?" on page 8 for more information.

MRO procurement by large companies previously was done through proprietary electronic data interchange (EDI) applications running on private value-added networks (VANs). Now, the trend is to move these activities to a Web-based environment available to requisitioners (who had no access to EDI in the past) rather than the purchasing department (that may have used EDI but no longer needs to be involved in each transaction). EDI over the Web costs about one-tenth as much as it does over a VAN. Not surprisingly, some of the largest corporate EDI users are migrating their EDI-based MRO procurement to the Web.

For example, Ford plans to move most of its $16-billion-per-year MRO purchases to the Web by the end of 1999. The rollout calls for 500 vendors to be linked via Ford's e-business system by June 1999, with some 3,000 to be signed up by the end of the year. In Sweden, telecommunications equipment maker Ericsson intends to make half of all MRO purchases, including services, via the Web during 1999 and plans to accomplish all its worldwide procurement via the Web by 2001. Similarly, U.K.-based retail grocer J Sainsbury typically processes more than 70,000 MRO-related paper invoices per month. The chain has initiated an Internet-based EDI program with some 20 product suppliers in preparation for moving half its MRO procurement to the Web by 2001.

Dramatically lower transaction costs coupled with the ability to enforce purchasing policy across the enterprise have been instrumental in driving Web-based MRO procurement. Two additional factors have accelerated the trend. The first factor is a defensive reaction by firms that note the cost savings being enjoyed by rivals switching to an e-business procurement mode. The second, and possibly more important, factor is the insistence by large firms such as Ford that their suppliers link into their Web-based procurement systems as a condition of doing business with them.

E-BUSINESS AND FINANCIAL SERVICES

E-business is likely to transform several service-sector businesses, with the strongest impact expected in financial services. Many banks already report a majority of transactions being conducted electronically via ATMs. Electronic stock and currency trading, and electronic settlement of payment, is well established. Rapid growth in Web-based online banking, security brokerage, and insurance services is expected over the next several years.

In financial services, most e-business transactions occur in the retail sector; the proliferation of business-to-business transactions has been slower but is gaining momentum. E-business in financial services is most widespread in Canada and the U.S.; e-business in Europe and Asia is gaining acceptance more gradually. However, the euro may help accelerate the spread of e-business in Europe. Interbank transfers and transactions that use credit cards, debit cards, or electronic purses and checks can be executed in euros.

Banks possess several assets that can help in their e-business endeavors. These assets include the possession of extensive customer information, name recognition and trust, and control of the transfer of value.

E-business' effect on the financial industry is reflected in significant changes in banks' business models rather than in the products offered. These shifts include the following:

- Evolution of the consumer-efficient frontier—The choice of how business is done is shifting from the institution to the customer because of the ease and speed of comparison shopping among different banks' offerings. Banks now must work harder to attract retail customers.

- Rise in disintermediation—New vendors, such as E-Loan and Lending Tree, are winning a large share of the market for certain products, resulting in the commoditization of banks' key products.

- Need for business alliances—Financial institutions now must form and manage alliances with other organizations. Beside the obvious necessity of alliances with technology companies, marketing alliances also are essential.

Because of the commoditization of banks' products, they must distinguish themselves in other ways to be competitive in e-business. One way they can distinguish themselves is through reduced loan underwriting turnaround times. However, this goal requires a new attitude and approach to dealing with risk: To win customers, banks must make decisions in shorter timeframes than in the past.

Security is a fundamental requirement in e-business, and banks are taking advantage of this opportunity by branching into the role of certification authority. (A certification authority is a trusted third party that issues digital certificates as a means of authenticating merchants and consumers in an electronic transaction.) Banks are performing this role primarily on the business-to-business side, where the large transactions require higher security.

On the business-to-consumer side, banks have found customers are willing to conduct online transactions without any certificates.

In October 1998, eight of the world's largest banks joined with CertCo in an alliance called the Global Trust Enterprise to create a digital-certificate-based system for identifying participants in business-to-business e-commerce. Through the alliance, each bank creates and issues digital certificates for its customers, using technology from CertCo, and authenticates digital certificates from other members. The participating banks include ABN AMRO, Bank of America, Bankers Trust, Barclays, Chase Manhattan, Citibank, Deutsche Bank, and HypoVereinsbank.

Banks also are expanding their scope by stepping into the role of commerce service provider (CSP). In March 1998, Fleet Financial Group became the first major bank to offer Web site design and hosting services, called storefronts@fleet. The service has a one-time construction cost that covers reserving a domain name, setting up a secure credit-card processing account, and designing and programming the customer's site. After setup, there is a monthly fee for site maintenance.

This e-commerce offering has a built-in advantage: The bank has proven its ability to handle credit-card processing, fraud detection, and security of money and data—all difficult and expensive processes for any online business. Other banks are likely to follow Fleet. ■

THE COST OF E-BUSINESS SUPPLY CHAIN MANAGEMENT

Even the scope of MRO procurement pales beside the possibilities for reorganizing supply chains around e-business. Rather than increasing production and inventory in advance of actual customer demand, e-businesses are looking to make both their own supply chains and those of their customers and suppliers respond in real time to actual sales.

Visibility of the entire supply chain is necessary so a business can analyze the interplay between interactions such as procuring materials, components, and subassemblies from various suppliers; shifting production between installations or business partners; and moving goods to the final consumer. Understanding relationships between all players in a particular value chain allows an e-business to adjust to new contingencies in real time.

Supply-chain inventory visibility systems such as i2's Global Logistics Manager (GLM) allow firms to track and trace the flow of their goods through a supply chain by, for example, communicating alert messages when a status message indicates that predefined tolerances (such as that a shipment is more than eight hours late) have been violated. Such messages are aggregated and analyzed via data storage and analysis tools to help firms identify bottlenecks, benchmark responsibilities between carriers and suppliers, and better understand actual distribution costs. On the customer side, purchasers are able to track the status of an order in real time via a Web browser.

Realizing the goal of increased visibility means organizations are beginning to merge their enterprise resource management (ERP) systems more closely with customer care and demand forecasting systems as well as external visibility solutions. Vendors, integrators, and analysts have begun to describe this new information technology (IT) process as e-business ERP or Web-based ERP. Regardless of terminology, the ultimate goal is to coordinate data gathered from customers, employees, suppliers, and even competitors with internal, mission-critical corporate data.

Analysts have yet to identify a single killer application driving the adoption of e-business ERP. However, the earliest e-business ERP adopters included large computer manufacturers, retailers, and consumer products companies already accustomed to using traditional ERP systems to manage supply chain operations. In their attempts to capitalize on the real-time communications strength of the Internet, many organizations began leveraging EDI, extranets, and secure Internet connections to enable supply chain partners to share real-time information. Much of this real-time information relates to processes, including product availability, order status, production, and delivery of goods and services.

More than half the 200 IT executives polled in a 1998 *InformationWeek* research survey said they were creating or planning to create a business supply chain using ERP software to enable suppliers, partners, and distributors real-time access to the ERP system. These executives also reported the most strategic advantages afforded by such integration were lower operational costs, better collaboration with partners, and reduced cycle times.

Externally, supply chain optimization requires movement to more standardized cross-business data flows and data definitions. Vendors such as i2, Logility, and Manugistics are offering preconfigured Web clients to link business partners into a company's supply chain. Business partners download the Web client that, with appropriate security, allows access to a company's planning system where the partner can check demand forecasts, available-to-promise (ATP) inventory, and order commitments.

"Rather than increasing production and inventory in advance of actual customer demand, e-businesses are looking to make both their own supply chains and those of their customers and suppliers respond in real time to actual sales."

See the sidebar "Compaq's E-Business Infrastructure" on page 10 for more information.

See the sidebar "Automotive Network Exchange (ANX)" on page 15 for more information.

In that sense, a significant aspect of e-business competition involves a shift away from competition between Firm X and Firm Y and a movement toward competition between the supply chain centered around Firm X and the supply chain centered around Firm Y. The differentiating factor between two supply chains often is which one manages the information "float"—the time between when data is captured in one place and when it becomes available and actionable elsewhere—better than its rival. Although this process is similar to what is taking place in other business segments, e-business enables those supply chains to be configured/reconfigured much more rapidly.

THE COST OF LOGISTICS

E-business transforms logistics from simply packaging and moving goods and turns it into an information business. Introducing online parcel order and tracking via a proprietary network in 1983, Federal Express (FedEx) took nearly 12 years to sign up 50,000 customers. In 3 years, between 1995–1998, after FedEx offered essentially the same service via the Web, the number of customers rose to 1 million. FedEx estimates nearly 70 percent of the 3 million packages it processes each day now are initiated via interactive networks.

E-business changes the logistics business by tying carriers such as DHL and FedEx closer together with product shippers and their customers through electronic load tendering, inventory confirmation, and delivery tracking. Logistics firms are beginning to allow their information systems to be accessed directly by shippers through their ERP

ALL THAT FOR A REAM OF PAPER?

Procurement is one of the hottest areas of e-business. Whether buying thousand-dollar items or reams of office paper, the basic procurement cycle is essentially the same. What e-business enables for procurement is the automation of a time- and labor-intensive process as well as the ability to create and enforce procurement policy across the enterprise through a single buying interface.

Corporate procurement begins with a requisitioner locating and identifying items from supplier catalogs. Once a suitable product and price are found, the next step in the process is to create a requisition. The requisition may include multiple purchase orders and contains data such as line-item details from supplier catalogs or the buyer's cost center or account code information. A requisition may specify delivery locations or adjusted quantities and accounting allocation for each item.

A third aspect of the procurement process involves the mechanisms that ensure the enterprise controls all purchases by defining approval rules for employees and departments. Approval tasks can be assigned on a spending-limit basis, or approval authority can be assigned to specific employees. Once a requisition is approved, a purchase order is readied to submit to a supplier.

The requisitioner must send orders to suppliers in a data format they can handle—fax or electronic data interchange (EDI) formats, for example—and receipt by the supplier often is confirmed in the same way.

Depending on the relationship between the requisitioner and the supplier, payment mechanisms may be invoked at this point, with invoicing information passing directly to accounts payable (AP) and general ledger (GL) systems for payment processing. It also is possible for credit-card information to be passed securely to the supplier. Invoices then may be reconciled against a statement on a per-card, per-supplier basis.

In addition to requisition, order, and payment information processing, procurement entails that goods be addressed to a specified loading dock address and include information about either the employee who generated the purchase order or the employees for whom the goods were purchased. This process assumes the loading dock reported correct receipt of the ordered goods.

Exceptions handling is a major part of procurement. In the case of damaged goods or goods sent in error, both the supplier and the requisitioner must be informed of a problem or a delay.

Finally, goods must make it to the employee's desktop or department floor, and receipt by the end-user must be acknowledged. Only then can an organization conclude it actually has "bought" something. ■

applications. For example, Hewlett-Packard's Medical Products Group has linked its SAP R/3 suite into FedEx's system to offer HP's customers real-time shipping and tracking functions, from order entry through package delivery, all from within R/3.

As more businesses move to build-to-order process models and extremely low inventory levels, increased value is placed on prompt, accurate inbound and outbound logistics. Given the complexity of coordinating fast order fulfillment with the ability to track an order, it is no surprise an increasing number of Web-based e-businesses are outsourcing order fulfillment to parcel delivery firms such as DHL, FedEx, and United Parcel Service (UPS). This outsourcing goes beyond shipping to include warehousing, packaging, and customer support.

Even companies that normally do not worry about tracking parcels because they ship locally or overnight plan to take advantage of the Web to reduce customer service calls, monitor carriers, announce delays, and verify delivery for faster payment. Not only does this capability help maintain customer satisfaction by providing better information, but companies also expect to gain flexibility regarding production scheduling decisions while reducing unnecessary transportation and warehousing expenses.

By changing the basic cost structure of sales, procurement, supply chains, and distribution, e-business introduces new critical success factors. Although, in the past, size and infrastructure were powerful barriers to market entry, e-business technology and organizational principles are turning that notion on its head. Indeed, the triumph of speed over size is becoming more apparent every day.

"By changing the basic cost structure of sales, procurement, supply chains, and distribution, e-business introduces new critical success factors."

The E-Business Opportunity

E-business market forecast figures vary widely among research firms and government agencies such as the U.S. Department of Commerce, which started counting Internet transactions as a distinct category in 1999. Even so, all the research firms and government agencies agree on one thing: The potential of e-business is enormous.

A decade after the "invention" of the Web, some 140 million users access it on a global basis. (See Figure 3 on page 10.) Of those users, nearly half access the Web from their homes, with medium/large and small business access points making up 21 percent and 12 percent, respectively. In addition, by the end of 1998, there were more Web users outside North America (56 percent) than there were in Canada, Mexico, and the United States combined. By year-end 2003, research firms such as IDC predict there will be more than 500 million Web users and more than 700 million connected devices.

During that time frame, the number of Europeans connected to the Internet should increase from 9.9 million to more than 50 million users. (See Figure 4 on page 11.) Europe also is the location of the first permanent "ambassador" to the digital economy. The job advertisement, published on the Web site of the U.K.'s Department of Trade and Industry (DTI), states that the position (known as the "e-envoy") "will spearhead the government's drive to ensure that by the year 2002, the U.K. is the best environment worldwide in which to trade electronically."

The number of PCs connected to the Internet worldwide is projected to rise steadily, from slightly more than 100 million units in 1998 to more than 300 million units in 2002, according to Gartner Group's Dataquest division. (See Figure 5 on page 11.)

Although it remains more an observer than an active participant in the global evolution of the Web, Japan, too, is looking to e-business to move its economy forward. A study by the Japanese Ministry of Posts and Telecommunications (MPT) on communication trends for fiscal 1998 (which ended March 31, 1999) says the Internet is used by

FIGURE 3: USERS AND DEVICES ON THE WEB WORLDWIDE

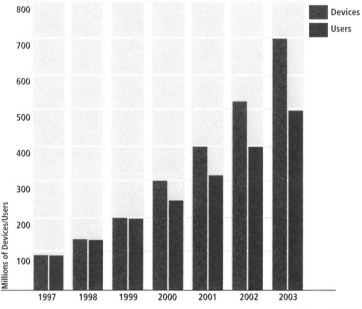

Source: IDC, 1999

more than 11 percent of all households in Japan, an increase from 6.4 percent in fiscal 1997. With more than 40 million households in the country, the study finds more than 4 million households have dial-up Internet access. (See Figure 6 on page 12.) IDC predicts the Japanese Internet commerce market will grow sharply, increasing from $1.5 billion in 1998 to more than $26 billion in 2002. (See Figure 7 on page 14.) However, Japanese observers believe a great deal of improvement is required to change the low consumer confidence in Web transactions. In addition, the country faces more tangible problems such as high shipping costs for physical goods as well as the high cost of local telecommunications service.

COMPAQ'S E-BUSINESS INFRASTRUCTURE

Recently, computer manufacturer Compaq adopted a make-to-order business model to compete more effectively in the marketplace. Compaq's new manufacturing model focuses on three groups: consumers, reseller/partner channels, and preferred business customers.

To better serve these groups, Compaq implemented an e-business infrastructure integrating a variety of products into a common architecture. These reusable common components perform operations, including product configuration, product ordering, pricing, cataloging, and available-to-promise with real-time integration with SAP and multiple existing order-management systems.

More than 1,200 Web sites were built to reach specific customer groups. Although all the sites were customized to specific company needs, they also took advantage of a common infrastructure backbone.

Individual customers now are served through a new Compaq@Home Web site, which enables them to order configurable PCs online. In addition, Web kiosks at stores such as Best Buy, Circuit City, and Office Depot enable customers to configure their own PCs and then have them delivered directly to their homes.

Channel partners such as resellers now are served through the introduction of a partner network application that provides real-time access to product information, ordering systems, training opportunities, and maintenance registration. Channel partners also are served by a new sales leads system, which Compaq uses to monitor sales trends.

Preferred global customers now are given access to customized sites with product and pricing information specific to each organization's individual contract with Compaq.

All these applications have been implemented in 15 different countries with sales exceeding Compaq's expectations. ■

FIGURE 4: THE EUROPEAN ONLINE POPULATION

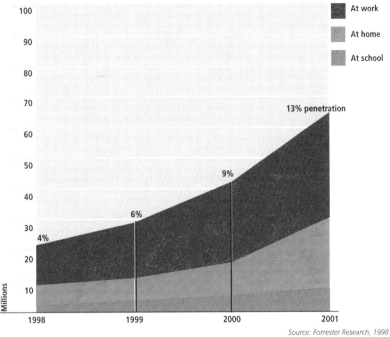

Source: Forrester Research, 1998

FIGURE 5: PCs CONNECTED TO THE INTERNET WORLDWIDE

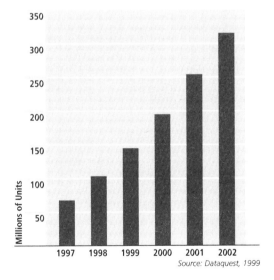

Source: Dataquest, 1999

Even though Asia lags behind Europe and North America in its adoption of e-business, signs are clear that Asian companies are retooling to take advantage of online access to global markets. PricewaterhouseCoopers surveyed 300 chief executive officers from 9 Asian countries in preparation for the 1999 World Economic Forum (WEF) summit in Davos, Switzerland. The survey found nearly 73 percent of the CEOs believes e-business either will "completely reshape" or will have a "significant impact" on competition in their industries. Shenzen Power, based in Shenzen, China, is a typical example. Before going online in 1998, the battery maker had no customers outside China. By the beginning of 1999, it had signed contracts via the Web with customers in India, Israel, and Russia.

FIGURE 6: JAPANESE ONLINE SERVICE PENETRATION: 1996–2000

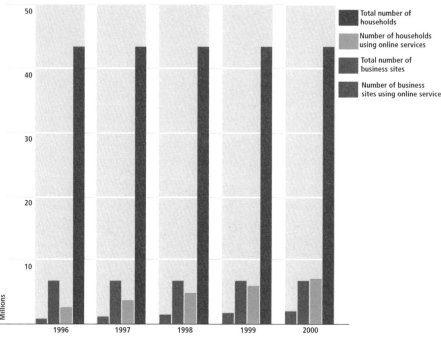

Source: IDC, 1998

E-BUSINESS AND GOVERNMENT

The expression "red tape" often refers to the debilitating amount of paperwork involved in government activity. However, assuming governments can accomplish their technological goals, this term soon may become obsolete. It may be a long time, if ever, before governments are completely digital, but steady progress is being made in establishing online submission of required filings (of tax forms and legal documents, for example) and procurement systems. These changes will reduce the size of the government labor force as well as increase the speed with which governments can achieve results.

Currently, there are many initiatives both on a national and municipal level around the world to submit much of the government paperwork electronically and automate many government services. Most pilot projects involve setting up kiosks in locations that allow the general public to conduct simple transactions electronically. Tasks that may otherwise be time-consuming and tedious for both citizens and public servants

will take moments to complete.

Portugal is one of many countries experimenting with public kiosks that allow citizens to access current government information. Portugal established a public network called Interdepartmental Information System For The Citizen (INFOCID). This project is maintained by state organizations that directly interact with citizens. It was tested initially in 1993–1994 with a few multimedia kiosks set up on the streets of Lisbon. Today, INFOCID covers more than 100 Portuguese municipalities, but it is expected to be available in more than 5,000 locations. The main menu on the kiosks contains information from 15 different agencies not previously centralized. The graphical user interface (GUI) resembles that of the Windows GUI and is said to be relatively easy to use.

For governments to become digital, however, citizens must have a certain comfort level with computers. Most government information systems eventually will be accessible electronically via a range of devices; how-

ever, until then, some training may be required. Currently, there is an economic and social divide between the computer literate and the computer illiterate.

The Singapore government is implementing a comparable project but is employing slightly more aggressive tactics to ensure citizens are computer literate. In Singapore, the majority of the population lives in public housing (by some estimates, up to 80 percent). The Singapore government has opened computer centers in community clubs near all public housing developments. These computer centers come complete with volunteer "cyberguys" to answer any technical questions residents may have. Additionally, kiosks are being installed at transport stations for anyone to access the Internet. The goal of the Singapore government is to make Internet access a basic right for citizens.

In Australia, many pilots currently are underway, some of which can be used by citizens via a telephone. The State of Victoria imple-

Leveraging the explosive growth of the Internet, 1998 saw some $50 billion in worldwide commerce via the Web. This figure is expected to top $1.3 trillion by 2003, with business-to-consumer commerce accounting for $177.7 billion. (See Figure 8 on page 14.) By 2003, the amount of Internet commerce occurring outside the U.S. is expected to exceed the amount that goes on inside the U.S. (See Figure 9 on page 15.)

Currently, the United States is the leader among countries reporting e-business-related revenue, with some 80 percent of the global total, according to the OECD. E-business in western Europe represents around 10 percent and Asia about 5 percent of world e-business trade. Although e-business growth figures of more than a trillion dollars by 2005 have transfixed many observers, others have pointed out that even if these optimistic scenarios are realized, the total amount of commerce on the Web in 2005 would be about the same as the amount of U.S.-only direct mail in 1999.

However, it is mistaken to assume the market size and the overall economic impact of a given phenomenon are synonymous. Even if direct e-business accounts for no more than 15 percent of global gross domestic product (GDP) by 2002, as suggested by the OECD, it already is affecting larger economic sectors such as communications, finance, and retail trade (approximately 30 percent of global GDP) as well as education, health, and government (approximately 20 percent of global GDP) disproportionately.

mented a centralized system that it calls Maxi. Citizens can complete 26 transactions from 7 different agencies on Maxi. Some of the services offered include vehicle and driver's license registration; obtaining driver history reports; ordering birth certificates; changing residential address with multiple agencies; obtaining community information; and bill payment.

Australian citizens certainly will benefit from systems such as Maxi; however, centralized information systems are advantageous to government agencies as well. Often, government ministries and departments fall prey to the "isolated islands of information" syndrome where agencies seldom share information that can be of value to another agency.

Online governments can offer a higher level of democracy to the people for two reasons. First, because legal and policy information is more accessible, the people can gain a higher awareness of government issues and how government decisions directly affect them. Second, the medium opens the lines of communication between citizens and politicians, thereby allowing politicians a greater insight into the public's needs.

On paper, the concept makes sense. In practice, however, it has not necessarily been proven true. In a white paper written by the National Computerization Agency of Korea, the public initially expressed great interest in electronic democracy. The agency therefore believed that bringing democracy online would involve more citizens in the government decision-making processes. However, after experimenting with several political Web channels, the agency found the people remained unresponsive to political issues and unwilling to participate at the level the agency anticipated.

In recent years, members of the U.S. Congress have been flooded with e-mail from citizens responding to political issues or policy decisions. However, according to reports from Congressional aides, although e-mail is taken into account, it is not given the same weight as letters written on paper and sent with a postal stamp.

Technologies that allow electronic government are available; however, the process of implementation has not always been easy. In 1995, the Japanese Council of Government Information Systems submitted a plan to provide online access to as many services as possible (up to 196 different procedures such as various permit and license applications). In 1997, the Japanese Council of Government Information Systems issued the demand that government agencies and ministries digitize all procedures no later than 1998.

Today, 14 of the 196 possible transactions are conducted online; the remaining 182 still are conducted offline using diskettes. According to the Japanese Council of Government Information Systems, the biggest obstacles in bringing the transactions online are choosing a technology to certify identification, ensuring security and integrity of the transactions, and choosing the optimal method for fee payment. ■

FIGURE 7: JAPANESE INTERNET COMMERCE MARKET: 1996–2002

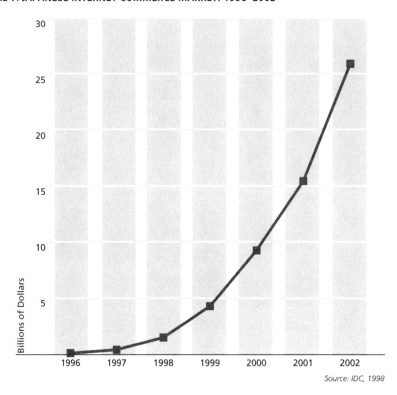

Source: IDC, 1998

FIGURE 8: WORLDWIDE COMMERCE ON THE WEB

This figure illustrates total worldwide sales of products via the Web, excluding securities and brokerage transactions.

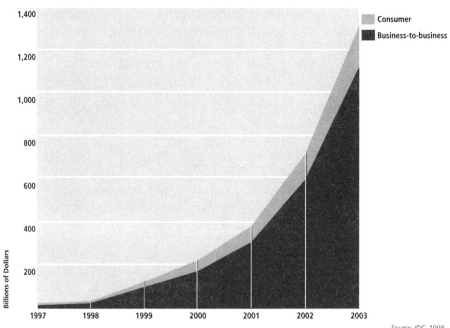

Source: IDC, 1998

There is another multiplier of the Web's impact: Potential customers with the most disposable income have been among the earliest adopters. In the United States, 50 percent of all homes connected to the Web have annual incomes of more than $50,000. Trends

FIGURE 9: GLOBAL VERSUS U.S. INTERNET COMMERCE

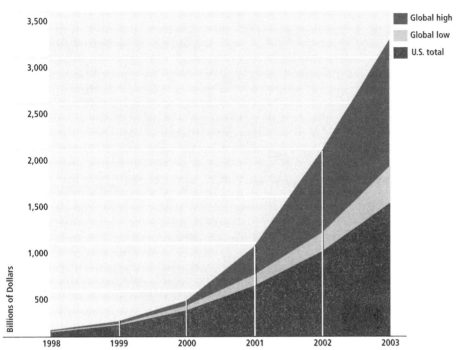

This figure illustrates optimistic ("global high") and pessimistic ("global low") scenarios of the potential for worldwide Internet commerce.

Source: Forrester Research, 1998

are roughly the same in western Europe and Asia. By capturing the largest customers in many industries first, the Web will have a much greater impact than the actual size of the sales transactions conducted on it.

Changes in the buying habits of these customers already has had a significant effect on how business is done. In some segments of banking, such as credit cards, there may be several orders of magnitude difference between the most profitable customers and average customers. It is estimated the top 2 percent of customer accounts produces nearly 100 percent of a bank's profits, and the bottom 2 percent represents a net loss.

AUTOMOTIVE NETWORK EXCHANGE (ANX)

U.S. automobile manufacturers are moving to link original equipment manufacturers (OEMs) of automobiles and suppliers of direct materials and components via the Internet through systems such as the Automotive Network eXchange (ANX).

The ANX system intends to replace the multiple networks and protocols that historically have connected top-tier suppliers to OEMs with a common transport infrastructure based on Internet standards. ANX does not supplant existing EDI standards or technologies, which are used heavily by the automotive industry. Instead, ANX guarantees Internet Protocol (IP) network reliability and enables authentication and virtual private network (VPN) security via IP's security protocol, IPSec.

ANX will use IPSec to provide authentication, encryption, and data integrity between the networks of any two trading partners. Applications intended for ANX Release 1 include computer-aided design (CAD) file transfer, EDI, e-mail, and groupware. Network service providers, which can include Internet service providers (ISPs) and value-added networks (VANs), must meet specific metrics to become ANX-certified service providers.

ANX is expected to become globally operational by the year 2000. It is estimated that if only 20 percent of all U.S. auto parts are sold via business-to-business electronic commerce efforts such as ANX, sales would total $30 billion. More important, companies that do not exploit common infrastructures such as ANX most likely will be unable to do business electronically with the automobile industry in the future. ∎

16

This figure illustrates that total business sales via the Internet will rise from $43 billion in 1998 to $1.3 trillion by 2003.

FIGURE 10: U.S. BUSINESS-TO-BUSINESS INTERNET COMMERCE REVENUE BY INDUSTRY

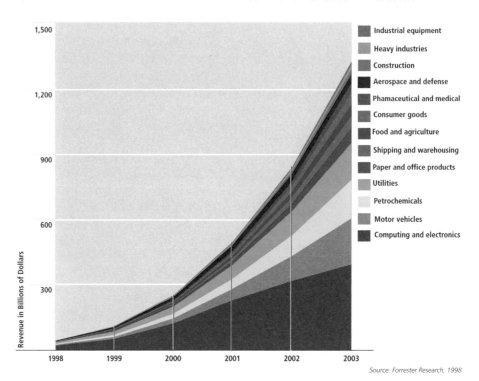

Source: Forrester Research, 1998

FIGURE 11: GROWTH IN INTERNET HOST COMPUTERS AND MAJOR E-COMMERCE DEVELOPMENTS

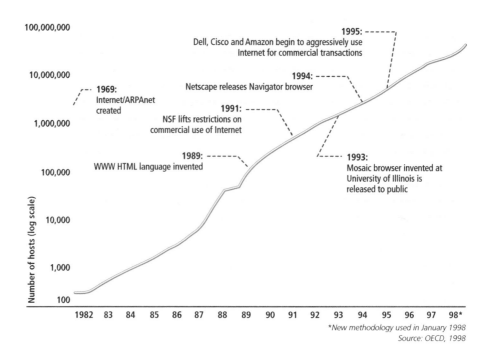

New methodology used in January 1998
Source: OECD, 1998

Although less than 15 percent of U.S. households uses financial software and the Web to manage their affairs, they control a disproportionate amount of total income and assets and account for most of the profitability of the retail banking sector.

Worldwide business-to-business e-business revenue is projected to outstrip worldwide business-to-consumer revenue on the Web by a factor of more than four by 2003. (See Figure 12 and Figure 13 on page 18.)

FIGURE 12: WORLDWIDE BUSINESS-TO-BUSINESS E-BUSINESS REVENUE

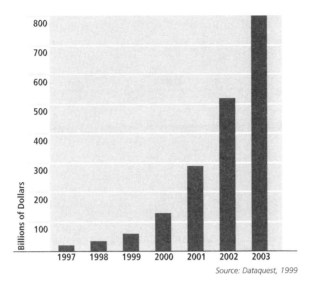

Source: Dataquest, 1999

Thus, the impact of e-business cannot be restricted to the negligible revenue reports by many e-businesses. Perhaps more important than these tangible signs of growth is the growing perception that because of the Web and e-business, many of the commercial

E-BUSINESS AND THE AUTOMOTIVE INDUSTRY

Banking is not the only industry whose profitability hinges on a very small percentage of the total customer base. The same holds true for the consumer automobile industry. Like the banking and securities industries, an increasing number of the auto industry's most profitable customers are changing the way they buy cars.

Since 1996, for example, Autobytel.com has become one of the largest auto dealers in the United States even though it does not own any automobile dealerships. Instead, it matches up dealerships and potential automobile purchasers. Starting out as a telephone and fax-only service, Autobytel.com's move to the Web has taken automotive sales-lead generation to a higher level.

In addition to locating particular vehicles with customized option packages, Autobytel.com lists the estimated cost to the dealer as well as the manufacturer's suggested retail price (MSRP). Armed with such information, potential automobile buyers have far more scope for negotiation. Therefore, customers making purchases through the Autobytel.com Web site buy at prices that generate a 6 percent margin (rather than the usual 10 percent) for the dealer.

Autobytel.com and online rivals such as CarPrices.com, Microsoft's CarPoint, and others are starting to unbundle the sales and service roles of retail automobile dealerships. To date, dealers' service and maintenance functions remain largely unchanged. As customers research more purchasing decisions on the Web, however, the retail auto dealers' role as a marketing channel slowly is being replaced by a sales fulfillment role.

Moreover, the manufacturers themselves are beginning to look to the Web as a means of selling directly to the customer. General Motors (GM) announced in March 1999 that it was launching GM BuyPower—a one-stop Web site offering users access to details about every GM make and model along with vehicle inventory, financing, and the ability to talk electronically to the dealers of their choice.

Previously, customers visiting the GM corporate Web site could only download product information and dealer locations as opposed to picking specific automobiles on a lot. GM BuyPower goes further by including specifics on more than 350,000 vehicles across GM's car and truck lines. So far, GM has signed up around 75 percent of its 7,800 dealers across the United States, signaling a change in the way the company will do business in the future. ∎

FIGURE 13: WORLDWIDE BUSINESS-TO-CONSUMER E-BUSINESS REVENUE

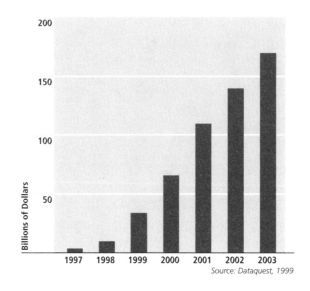

Source: Dataquest, 1999

relationships and business practices that historically defined industry structure and profitability now are up for grabs. Many agree something profound is afoot.

The E-Business Value Proposition

Whenever people are organized for work, they somehow must communicate, allocate resources, make decisions, execute on those decisions, and test them in markets. Whenever people use markets to obtain goods and services, they somehow must search, compare, communicate, negotiate, and buy. The value proposition of e-business is economic coordination that is faster, less expensive, and global.

E-BUSINESS VALUE FOR SELLERS: COORDINATION

E-business decisively lowers the cost of coordinating production and transactions while increasing the speed and quality of both. As a result, e-business is about people coordinating more effectively, coordinating on a far larger scale, and forming new, coordination-intensive business and consumer relationships.

CORPORATE ONE-STOP EXCHANGES

One-stop catalog sites for the corporate buying market are well established. In March 1999, Ariba announced Ariba.com, a private Web site for buyers and sellers to combine their discretionary purchasing activities into a more seamless business process. Ariba's Operating Resource Management System (ORMS) enables corporate buyers to gather content from multiple suppliers over the Web and create dedicated purchase sites within their own intranets. Ariba wants to extend that process even further by organiz-

ing an electronic marketplace for its customers. Suppliers that want to do business with Ariba's customer base do so by passing catalog and pricing information to Ariba.com, accepting orders from the site, and paying a transaction fee to Ariba in the process.

Using ORMS, buyers are able to shop electronically through a single site on their intranet and process transactions over the Web using Ariba.com.

One-stop corporate purchasing sites have

become a heavily contested e-business market. Commerce One launched a comparable Web-based marketplace called MarketSite in 1998. Unlike Ariba, Commerce One wants to provide real-time information exchange among trading partners. Another vendor, TradeEx, has concentrated on more vertical catalog aggregation by organizing private exchanges such as MetalSite and The Plastics Network, which enable companies to buy and sell surplus steel and plastic products, respectively, online. ■

In inventory management for consumer electronics, for example, an electronic product such as a personal computer historically was made by a manufacturer, sat in a warehouse, and found its way to a retailer, where it remained on a shelf until it was bought or returned. This process often took two to three months. In the meantime, the majority of PC production costs are represented by components, which decline in price on average by nearly one-third annually.

See the sidebar "Compaq's E-Business Infrastructure" on page 10 for more information.

Every day that can be shaved off of holding inventory means a manufacturer can use less expensive (and usually more powerful) components and thus maintain a similar profit margin while selling a more powerful product at a lower price. This is the e-business coordination advantage of Dell Computer, which states its PC components sit in inventory for only eight days before being shipped to a PC buyer. The only way Dell can maintain such a low level of inventory is through coordinating each step of its value-creating process at a more detailed level. Internally, Dell has merged its ERP systems with Web-based purchasing, customer support, help desks, and related e-business systems.

The consumer can order a customized product online by defining the desired characteristics (such as processor speed, RAM, disk capacity, and so on) as well as when and how he or she would like it to be delivered. Once the order is placed, it then is relayed up and down Dell's value chain, setting off a stream of parts orders, assembly schedules, shipping notifications, and the financial and accounting processes that underpin the entire transaction.

Although Dell pioneered its build-to-order business model using telephone and fax-based ordering, the Web has enhanced that process by allowing customers to configure different bundles into a more customized package, with the tradeoffs and advantages clearly explained. This capability saves customer service costs by letting customers handle the configuration themselves. It also allows customers to evaluate more options more easily while significantly reducing the chance of error through the guided interaction of Dell's Web site.

"E-business is about people coordinating more effectively, coordinating on a far larger scale, and forming new, coordination-intensive business and consumer relationships."

Coordination efficiencies such as those of Dell Computer generally come in three varieties. The first effect of improved coordination is a direct substitution of e-business technology and processes for physical locations, manual processes, or other expediting functions that necessitate human attention or increase costs but do not add actual value. In this case, the cost of executing a customer order via a Web site versus a dedicated call center or a trip to a physical location can save substantially for both consumer and seller.

A second effect of reducing information processing and communications costs is an overall increase in coordination. For example, online flight reservation systems enable customers to consider many more flight possibilities than previously. Not too long ago, the only way to check flight availability was to work either through a dedicated travel agent or through the airline itself. Travel Web sites not only obviate the need to coordinate with a travel agent over the phone or through a physical site, they also give customers the ability to configure and compare more flights under different value/price bundles.

A third effect is the formation of coordination-intensive business structures that operate across firms and value chains. Dee Hock, the founder of Visa, said Visa's main product was coordination between member banks and the credit-using public. Although

"The very nature of Web-based, two-way interaction, coupled with its communications economies, has shifted the source of competitive advantage away from owning transaction processing assets and toward leveraging customer information and marketing assets."

Visa accomplishes its mission through a vast network of banking relationships supported by one of the world's most sophisticated IT systems, e-business brings much of that same capability to far smaller firms.

For example, Lending Tree is a privately held firm of 20 employees that uses Web-based technology to serve the consumer loan and mortgage market. Consumers visiting the Lending Tree Web site complete a loan qualification form, which varies with the type of loan applicants are seeking but which includes the same basic information as paper-based forms. Running the loan application through its filters, Lending Tree can match lender, loan product, and borrower.

Thus, Lending Tree allows consumers the chance to interrogate a wider base of potential lenders than would have been possible or cost-effective if they used traditional loan agents or direct communications channels to lenders. On the vendor side, Lending Tree screens loan applications so those lenders receive a pool of prequalified applicants for their loan products. Borrowers using the Lending Tree site know any lender from the returned list of institutions will lend money. Lenders, on the other hand, know any borrower referred to them by Lending Tree has been prequalified.

Before the emergence of e-businesses such as Lending Tree, the consumer mortgage situation could best be described as a "butterfly market." On one wing was a large, fragmented, and dispersed group of borrowers who might share certain standard demographics but have almost as many unique features. On the other wing was a group of potential lenders.

Try as they might, the lenders were forced to incur massive marketing and processing costs to find qualified borrowers, let alone try to differentiate their products from those of their rivals. The ability of consumers to compare product and price characteristics of lenders also was curtailed because of factors such as proximity, the variety of loan packages available, and the time involved in trying to examine loan offerings across lenders. Although third-party mortgage brokers existed before the Web, their reach usually was restricted by geography or by contractual agreements with particular groups of lenders. Nationally syndicated mortgage brokers hardly existed.

E-Loan, Lending Tree, and other information brokers are examples of "discovery" e-business models being propagated via the Web. In such cases, previously unstructured encounters between businesses and their customers are being rationalized and aggregated by third parties. These new intermediaries use the Web to coordinate voluminous and complicated information flows that lead widely scattered suppliers and consumers closer to a transaction. This situation runs counter to the conventional notion of disintermediation.

Before the Web, the technical and economic costs of coordinating these information flows over a dispersed population tended to exclude all but the largest firms from participating. However, the very nature of Web-based, two-way interaction, coupled with its communications economies, has shifted the source of competitive advantage away from owning transaction processing assets and toward leveraging customer information and marketing assets.

The impact of improved coordination capability goes beyond enabling price and product discovery business models such as Autobytel.com, however. The longer-term impact of substantial changes in the cost and effectiveness of information processing is the emergence of markets and market principles in areas of economic activity where their application was not feasible before the advent of e-business. Beyond third parties using e-business organization and technology to match dispersed buyers and sellers, other intermediaries actually are creating markets where none existed before.

THE E-BUSINESS VALUE PROPOSITION FOR SELLERS: GLOBALIZATION

The old saying that the world is getting smaller takes on new meaning with e-business. (See Figure 14.) Decision-makers need look merely at two curves—the number of Internet hosts worldwide and the minimum effective size in revenue to appear to be a multinational corporation—to realize that globalization and e-business go hand-in-hand.

FIGURE 14: THE INTERNET MAKES THE WORLD SMALLER

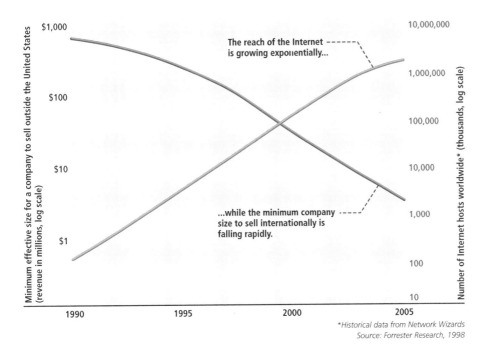

Historical data from Network Wizards
Source: Forrester Research, 1998

Many factors suggest e-business will boost international trade substantially. Although the telephone and the fax machine already allowed much speedier communication between trading partners across borders, before e-business, it was impossible to attract the equivalent of walk-in traffic from another country. The ease with which a user in Japan or Jordan can access the Web site of a vendor in Germany or Mexico to contact, compare, negotiate, and transact for later fulfillment is what e-business is all about. This advantage is limited only by the types of products for which this process works—that is, those products offering a high value-to-weight ratio.

However, globalization throws up new challenges as well as opportunities for e-business. Although English is the global language of commerce, e-businesses are finding multilingual support is important for running successful Web sites. Every Web site should include a literal translation of the terms and conditions of a transaction. In addition, more subtle cultural issues should be taken into account in the creation of any visual or textual content. For example, although a "thumbs up" graphic is considered a positive symbol in many Northern Hemisphere countries, it is considered an obscene gesture in much of South America. Therefore, although e-businesses are able to address a global audience, their success in selling to a specific audience will be influenced by how well they can localize content to appeal to target market segments or even a specific individual's requirements.

Globalization also confronts e-businesses with new complexity regarding how they position their brands on the Web. Before e-business, people saw, heard, read, and some-times dialed a firm's brand in media. Moreover, the brand often was customized for local markets. However, on the Web, brands are used not only for name recognition, but also for messaging and addressing to and from the site itself. As such, domain name reg-istration and brand/trademark issues increasingly have become intertwined.

Many firms invest huge amounts on branding campaigns but are oblivious to registering domain names outside their home country. Even though it is possible to address a global audience from a single point using e-business technology, failure to register interna-tional domain names opens brands to significant time and monetary costs to recover pirated domains as well as to future roadblocks for setting up foreign subsidiaries.

Along with technical and practical considerations for evaluating brand strategies care-fully on the Web, there are perceptual issues. Businesses and consumers have existing perceptions of existing brands that do not disappear when they go online. The tradi-tional strategy of well-produced, often-repeated messages that one brand is better than another, in itself, proves ineffective on the Web. Regardless of their history, e-business brands are defined by the real-time customer experience—in other words, actual deliv-ery versus promise. These brands only are reinforced by offline messages. So while new entrants struggle to get their names recognized in crowded market spaces, established firms face the mixed blessing of existing perceptions and the task of delivering experi-ences that are better than those of competitors as well as complementary to their offline businesses.

In that sense, Web brands—new or transplanted—must reinvent themselves to adapt as quickly as the medium and the market itself. Remember that today's top online brands such as Yahoo! and Amazon.com started out as a Web directory and low-priced book-seller, respectively, to gain relevance as destinations that satisfy a broad range of cus-tomer needs.

Branding is only one of the globalization challenges faced by e-business. Another aspect of the globalization puzzle involves pricing. Historically, multinationals have found they can increase profits by pricing goods independently in each country. However, the introduction of the euro as a pan-European currency promises to make pricing more transparent—and, perhaps, more uniform. This development could accelerate e-busi-ness' impact dramatically in Europe and beyond because consumers and businesses will be able to compare prices from a given vendor in different countries more easily. Observers expect the euro's impact on e-business will be felt initially in the business-to-business sector where there is a pressing need to simplify billing. In the business-to-consumer realm in Europe, however, continued high transportation costs tend to dilute some of the price savings promised by euro-based e-business.

Globalization challenges notwithstanding, the ability of e-businesses to transcend the geographic borders of national markets has been crucial in reducing barriers to market entry. The ability of e-businesses to enter new geographic markets in industries that had seemed impregnable (such as telephony or securities trading) has fired the imagina-tions of would-be imitators even as it has captured the attention of the some of the world's leading business people.

"Globalization confronts e-businesses with new complexity regarding how they position their brands on the Web."

THE E-BUSINESS VALUE PROPOSITION FOR SELLERS: CUSTOMER SERVICE

Service definitely is the business process where the most human contact occurs between a buyer and a seller. Not surprisingly, e-business strategists are finding that customer service via the Web is one of the most challenging and potentially lucrative areas of e-business.

Traditionally, the idea of scaling customer service involved assigning existing staff or adding new representatives to handle an increased volume of inquiries or offering technologies such as interactive voice response (IVR) to help customers navigate to a human expert or to a menu-driven automated response engine.

However, the Web has changed customer expectations about how long it should take to receive a response from an organization. E-business enables customers to help themselves by combining the communications capability of a traditional customer response system with the content richness only the Web can provide—all available and operating 24 hours per day. As a result, conducting business via the Web offers customers the convenience they want while freeing up key support staff to tackle more complex problems.

The Web is a natural medium for automating customer service tasks such as reviewing billing information, finding answers to common questions, checking delivery status, obtaining technical support, or checking account balances. Forrester reports self-service also is the key to success in business-to-customer services. Going forward, Meta forecasts that by the year 2000, 35 percent of customer contact will be via nontraditional electronic means. Meta predicts this situation will drive sales for customer relationship management (CRM) products and services from $1.5 billion in 1998 to $4.7 billion by 2001.

THE SABRE AIRLINE RESERVATION SYSTEM

The SABRE computerized reservation system was launched in 1959 as an internal database for American Airlines. SABRE has progressed through several iterations of technology to become one of the most successful commercial information systems in history. Today, one in three travelers' itineraries worldwide is routed through the SABRE system.

Adapted for outside use in the mid-1970s, SABRE was made available to travel agencies over a proprietary network to provide flight information through a central repository. So successful was the SABRE release that it provided a model for future computerized reservation systems not only for airlines but also for many other segments of the travel and tourism sector.

SABRE extended its reach with the emergence of online services such as CompuServe.

In 1986, EasySABRE was introduced as CompuServe's online travel agent, thus obviating the need for CompuServe members to use travel agents as intermediaries. In addition, SABRE continued operating as a semi-public network.

In 1996, the SABRE Group further expanded its access methods to include the Web. The first instance of this shift was the migration of the command-based EasySABRE to the Web. Next, SABRE launched Travelocity, a Web site offering all the system's features with a more intuitive graphical interface.

Travelocity provides customers with the schedules of more than 700 airlines. Customers can make reservations on 400 of those listed. The Travelocity site also posts last-minute bargains and consolidator fares and provides an e-mail fare-tracking system that can send updates to subscribers immediately

when fares change. Other travel arrangements available through Travelocity include car rental information from more than 60 car rental companies and a hotel reservation system that integrates photographs, location maps, and reviews for more than 35,000 hotels worldwide.

Travelocity underscores the importance of the Web's ubiquitous availability and standardized client software. Now, it is easier than ever before to extend a network directly to end users. SABRE no longer needs to supply hardware or networking functionality because only a Web browser and Internet access is required to access the service.

SABRE is not eliminating its ties to traditional travel agents, however. Providing Web access alongside traditional distribution channels allows SABRE to reach new customers rather than to displace old client networks. ■

Basic e-business customer-service applications can be grouped into either status reporting or frequently asked questions (FAQs); both categories can be integrated with other customer-service infrastructure elements such as call centers. Other e-business tools attempt to move the customer-service process further up the chain of complexity. Web-based response tools from vendors such as Inference employ case-based reasoning (CBR) to attempt to solve customer problems when the information held by the customer is partial or not specific enough. These tools are based on a combination of text-search and similarity measures. Previously solved problems are stored in a file structure called a case base. When a new problem is presented, it is described in text form to the CBR system, which searches the case base for a solution that matches.

The challenges of engaging customers in this new mode of interaction are many, especially when it comes to handling specific customer e-mail requests. When some of the first e-business Web sites were established, Web and customer service managers typically believed support-personnel headcount costs would decrease because customers would be willing to serve themselves when using the Web.

"Depending on the market being served, the ability to hand off most of the provision of service fulfillment between an e-business and its customer base can vary significantly."

The growth of e-mail as a form of customer interaction often outstrips the ability of organizational units to handle it. This problem is compounded by the lack of an e-mail equivalent to the automated call director systems used by call centers to route calls to customer service representatives (CSRs). In response to this challenge, several vendors are offering packaged applications specifically designed to handle customer-facing e-mail. The trend is toward establishing customer e-mail management as a key application to facilitate all phases of communications between companies and their customers. (See Figure 15.)

FIGURE 15: CUSTOMER E-MAIL RESPONSE ARCHITECTURE

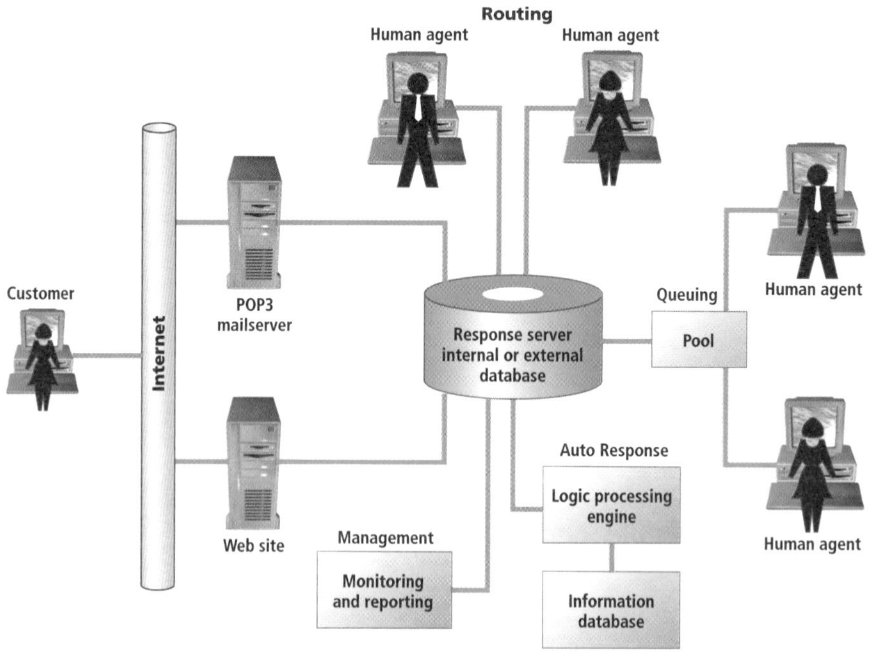

Source: IDC, 1998

Depending on the market being served, the ability to hand off most of the provision of service fulfillment between an e-business and its customer base can vary significantly. For example, industries where product configurations are clear and unambiguous (such as for a book or a music CD) are good candidates for significant customer self-service applications. On the other hand, the more variability involved in a product or service, the more likely it is to require human intervention. The goal of most customer self-service or communications response technologies is to automate the handling of routine tasks and problems, thereby freeing up human interaction to address complex or difficult ones.

In corporate environments, intranet-based self-service packages enable employees to enroll in benefits programs, maintain time and attendance records, schedule vacations, and engage in online learning. A 1998 Forrester Research survey of IT managers in Fortune 1000 firms indicated self-service human resource (HR) systems will account for 79 percent of HR applications in 2001—up from 35 percent in 1998. More than 70 percent of the respondents said they would implement self-service intranet applications even more quickly were it not for Year 2000 projects.

THE E-BUSINESS VALUE PROPOSITION FOR BUYERS: CONVENIENCE

E-business automates and improves many of the activities that make up a buying experience. For the buyer, the convenience offered by an e-business mode of purchasing goes beyond the ability to conduct transactions around the clock. Just as important is the customer's ability to access and display information rapidly and in detail about the product or service lines of an e-business.

Dynamically selecting and presenting information in electronic form is a major differentiator between e-business and its antecedents. Whereas corporate and consumer purchasers previously had to order paper catalogs or travel to a physical facility before they could start comparing price and product attributes, electronic catalogs and other e-business content management systems now present customers with updated information in real time about goods, services, and prices.

E-business catalogs and content also are enhanced by new search and configuration capabilities. Expanded searching functions allow buyers to select relevant sections from potentially large catalogs (such as an automobile parts or construction materials catalog) and concentrate on only the sections they want. Depending on the type of product or service being offered, merchandise can be presented in a rich graphical form with considerably more information than could be made available practically in paper form.

Along with the ability to search and display up-to-the-minute product and price information, buyers benefit from the ability of e-businesses to customize their catalogs. Corporate catalogs can be highly customized to include only preapproved items, prespecified packages, or prenegotiated prices.

Perhaps the most significant change brought about by e-business involves catalog aggregation. E-business enables a buyer to search across multiple catalogs to compare goods and prices of various vendors in a particular market space. E-business also allows vendors from complementary spaces to display their information together.

The movement toward aggregated catalog Web sites is well established. Catalog City positions itself as the world's first catalog shopping portal. On its Web site, shoppers can access information about more than 17,000 catalogs. Of that total, customers can directly browse through more than 2,200 catalogs and can transact through 450 catalogs enabled for direct customer orders.

For buyers, Catalog City provides one-stop shopping from familiar vendors as well as those that are not as well known. Equally important is the ability of shoppers to navigate through catalogs at their own pace or move directly to categories such as clothing, books, gardening, hobbies and crafts, or home improvement supplies.

"Dynamically selecting and presenting information in electronic form is a major differentiator between e-business and its antecedents."

In addition to concentrating catalogs on one site, Catalog City enables shoppers to complete a one-time registration form to order from any catalog on the site. As a result, shoppers need to enter credit-card and shipping information only once. This convenience feature is enhanced further by a single shopping cart icon that can move across different catalogs to compile an order from multiple vendors.

Finally, shoppers can personalize their home pages by adding links to favorite categories or catalogs and be guided to product recommendations by the editors of the site. Specific personalization capabilities include a feature where the shopper can click the Remind Me button to mark any item for purchase later, after noting the date and the occasion. The shopper then receives an e-mail reminder before it is time to purchase the selected item. Another feature involves a gift registry function to help family and friends find desired gifts without duplication for a special event such as a wedding.

Accurate prices and descriptions as well as availability are of primary importance to buyers. However, e-business enables more than just checking product and price information in an interactive setting. The ability to configure different product, service, and price bundles is a major differentiating factor for e-business.

Configuration capabilities at Web sites enable buyers to run through various product or service bundling scenarios before reaching a decision. For example, on the product side, buyers now explore how changing the screen size of the monitor for a PC affects the price. Likewise, on the services side, buyers now considers how deciding to pay extra points on a mortgage affects the interest rate.

A configurator allows buyers to define a product that meets a given criteria or need and whose features and options can interoperate without problems. In the physical product space, there are three basic categories of products, distinguished by how configurable they are: ship-to-order, assemble-to-order, and engineer-to-order products.

- *Ship-to-order products*—Goods with predefined options that have little variability other than a preexisting set of attributes such as color or size. Furniture, computer peripherals, and office equipment are typical examples of ship-to-order products. In this case, an e-business Web site's configuration system tries to find the best match between customer needs and the attributes of available products.

- *Assemble-to-order products*—Products with configuration based on unique customer options. Assemble-to-order products are more variable in their final form but comprise standard components. Computers and certain telecommunications equipment fall into this category. In this case, the e-business system checks the feasibility of a customer request to ensure the specified options are compatible with one another and orders the necessary (though ancillary) parts needed to ensure a correct configuration.

- *Engineer-to-order products*—Products with variable configuration possibilities because the solution is more open-ended. These products require more extensive analysis. An example of engineer-to-order product configuration is on the Cisco Web site where network engineers enter their requirements and the system helps them determine the appropriate configurations. Similar systems can be used to model engineering processes or create complex bills for materials while illustrating the tradeoffs between performance and price to the user.

Concurrent with configuring products or services is the selection of information that provides the context for a transaction. This information includes pricing administration, which enables a firm's selling channels to deploy customized trade promotions and implement complex pricing and discounting strategies for customers based on their profiles and financing alternatives. Related to pricing are financial configurations, which are designed to help a customer calculate different financial justifications—for example, return on investment (ROI) versus life-cycle costs—as well as provide lease versus buy analysis or even generate customized buying plans. The result of dramatically enhanced selection, configuration, and aggregation is a more flexible selection and pricing environment for the buyer.

THE E-BUSINESS VALUE PROPOSITION FOR BUYERS: PERSONALIZATION

Personalization involves tailoring a presentation of an e-business Web site to individuals or groups of customers based on profile information, demographics, or prior transactions. The goal of personalization is to market and sell one-to-one to increase sales and profits and to enhance the user experience to build customer loyalty.

In business-to-consumer commerce, for example, businesses compete for customers on the basis of product attributes such as brand, price, convenience, and service. Because the Web offers customers equal access to all businesses, price and convenience may reach parity quickly across providers. At that point, the primary basis for competition will be service and relationships. The Web provides excellent tools for improving both.

Unlike a broadcast channel such as print, television, or radio where most consumers receive the same content, each Web user has an individual channel to the online presence of an e-business. Instead of providing the same content to everyone, an e-business Web site can provide individually personalized content to each user.

Personalizing a site may be done for business or merchandising purposes. Users of a business-to-business catalog, for example, may see different prices negotiated for their respective companies. In addition to custom prices, product configurations and preapproved packages can be displayed on a Web site customized for a key client. PC manufacturers such as Compaq and Dell have been successful in setting up custom Web sites for their corporate customers.

On the retail side, a consumer-oriented Web site may send personalized electronic coupons to frequent shoppers or use collaborative filtering techniques that display past purchases of customers who indicated a similar interest. Profiling technology developed by companies such as Firefly (acquired by Microsoft in 1998) is based on collaborative filtering techniques. For example, Firefly's Passport profiling software lets users indicate their preferences and receive corresponding Web content; its Catalog Navigator collaborative filtering software compares users' profiles and recommends content based on like preferences. Such techniques are used by Web sites such as Amazon.com, which suggests additional books of interest to shoppers with the tagline, "Customers who bought this book also bought..." followed by the names of several other titles available.

Other consumer-oriented sites, such as those of major media organizations, regularly offer personalized content along with e-mail alerts for new items that match a customer profile. One-stop portal sites such as Yahoo! also enable users to personalize their home pages to reflect search preferences.

Although there are numerous business drivers and presentation formats for personalizing a Web site, the basic process remains the same. The first step in personalizing a site is authenticating the user. In this context, it may not be necessary to know an individual's

"Personalization involves tailoring a presentation of an e-business Web site to individuals or groups of customers based on profile information, demographics, or prior transactions."

true identity. Instead, it is sufficient to ensure that a series of visits by a user represents the same person, even if the precise identity is unknown. In other cases, it is important to have formal authentication.

THE WEB AND THE ENTERTAINMENT AND MEDIA INDUSTRIES

No industry sector has been affected more by the way in which the Web changes information richness and reach than the entertainment and media industries. The Web and e-business influence all aspects of entertainment and publishing—from the way content is distributed to how it is purchased, produced, and consumed. Indeed, the Web and e-business change the role of content itself by allowing users to self-edit content.

The entertainment and media industries historically experience a period of displacement and adjustment whenever a new medium is introduced. For example, radio reinvented itself in the wake of television by changing programming schedules from straight news and entertainment to include local information, music, and talk shows.

The history of the entertainment and media industry has many examples of how one mode of communication and information changes another. However, the unique challenge of the Web and e-business is that this change affects all entertainment and media segments simultaneously. Moreover, the Web has erased the lines between different players in entertainment and media.

News sites such as CNN that offer a combination of print, audio, and even travel reservations are the outward manifestation of a larger convergence that involves content providers and retail vendors. Longer lasting will be the trend toward content as a necessary ingredient to a transaction. (Forrester Research refers to "transactive content" to describe the marriage of transactions, interactivity, and content.)

A quick look at how Web technology and e-business affect the creation and distribution of digital content is indicative of the gathering force that promises to redefine the entire entertainment and media industry.

FILM

In February 1999, the National Association of Theater Owners in the United States met to discuss the implementation of digital projectors. Digital projectors, expected to be installed throughout the U.S. in the next two years, will allow for simultaneous distribution of films. (Currently, most films first are released in major cities and then in less-populated areas; they also are released first in the U.S. and then in other regions as the films become available.) A studio pays approximately $2,000 for a print, and major films require up to 5,000 prints. With the advent of digital projectors, these costs will drop because theaters will receive films on electronic tapes or disks. Eventually, it is expected that films will be delivered via satellite and stored on a server in the theater.

The Web provides a forum for filmmakers to bring their work directly to the public (and increases the chances of having a major studio view the film). This possibility further complicates existing relationships in the industry, such as the one between the filmmaker and the studio. It may be a while before viewers can download complete films from the Web and view them online; however, streaming video technology and Web sites such as iFilm.net and AtomFilms.com (launched in early 1999) provide an outlet for independent filmmakers to post their work. Most of these films are shorts and animations—films that seldom receive wide distribution. On the Web, however, they have the chance to gain greater popularity.

Even so, the studio will not disappear. Most observers believe films available on the Web never will reach the same caliber as films released by major studios. Instead, the Web allows greater visibility for films the major studios buy but the public never sees.

It is unclear how Web distribution of films will change the present system or at what point on the technology-and-price-curve movie audiences will change the way they choose to experience film. This is the same phenomenon as trying to determine the inflection point (when a new technology becomes dominant) for the video cassette market, which was not known until several years after the first video players and tapes hit the market. Nevertheless, the impact of new forms of distribution on industry structure should not be underestimated.

PRINT

Print media organizations wrestle with the dilemma of providing free content over the Web. Many content providers believe that when consumers are not required to pay for content, the value of intellectual property is negated, thus hurting the entire industry. Offering free content, however, has proven a valuable step in creating market presence in the Web medium. Few advertising models have been profitable, however (other than some of the portal Web sites).

New business models emerge frequently. *Salon* magazine, for example, uses a membership plan: Content is free, but profit is made through membership (members receive discounts on merchandise and the ability to access special member areas); advertising revenue; and merchandise sales from *Salon's* Emporium. Most newspapers and magazines also have implemented an information retrieval service as a revenue source. Customers pay a set fee per article retrieved from the publication's archives.

Slate, Microsoft's political/cultural magazine, abandoned a subscription plan after a year and implemented a membership plan similar to that of *Salon*. *Slate* claims to have 30,000 subscribers, but analysts estimate its subscription revenue of approximately $600,000 covers only one-tenth of publishing costs. *Slate's* experience illustrates that content accessed through paid subscription will not necessarily attract Web users.

One major exception in Web consumer behavior appears to be adult entertainment Web sites, for which there has been no shortage of viewers willing to pay fees to access content. In fact, several adult entertainment businesses, including Efox.net and the Internet Entertainment Group, are expected to go public by mid-1999. ∎

Different applications use different techniques for identifying the client software, including browser "cookies," user log-in using a name and password, or personal digital certificates. Most applications today use some combination of log-in information and cookies, whereas digital certificates for individual users are still in the early stages of deployment.

Once an e-business site identifies a user, it can retrieve a stored profile about that user. The stored information may come from several sources, including the forms users fill out when they register for a system, additional information they choose to share with the system through surveys, transaction data about items purchased, or an analysis of browsing behavior (sometimes referred to as "clickstream" analysis).

Once gathered, this information may be stored at a database local to a Web site, shared with other sites (whether part of a single business operation or a collection of business partners), or even stored in a browser cookie if the profile is small enough. More commonly, a cookie is used as a pointer to the information stored in a database.

Given that buyers increasingly are sensitive about what information about them is gathered and how it is used, many e-businesses now post a privacy policy on their Web sites stating how buyers' personal information will be used. The Platform for Privacy Preferences (P3P), a project of the World Wide Web Consortium, provides a framework for managing the flow of personal information and for expressing privacy policies. Although still an early-stage technology, P3P or something similar is likely to gain ground as privacy concerns continue to be a significant issue for consumers and consumer advocates.

THE WEB AND THE MUSIC INDUSTRY

Distribution over the Web presents a monetary advantage for artists. Musicians who sell their works via the Web can take 50 to 75 percent of the sales profit; musicians signed with major record labels take only 8 to 15 percent of retail sales. Some analysts anticipate the birth of as many as 500,000 new independent record labels as a result of the new format.

MP3 (MPEG Audio Layer 3), a digital audio compression format for music files, presents a direct challenge to the recording industry. Typically, a single song on a CD consumes 40 to 50MB of storage. In comparison, one song in MP3 format consumes between 4 to 5MB. MP3 is an attractive distribution option for a number of reasons. Not only is the sound quality comparable to that of a CD, but singles also can be downloaded from the Web very inexpensively or, in many cases, free of

charge. Another attraction is that the listener can download singles from multiple performing groups, thus compiling a personalized mix. Most important, Web users can listen to independent artists who previously needed contracts with major recording labels before they could be heard.

Rather than viewing MP3 as a threat, marketing plans are underway to promote the new format. Some record labels expect to release sneak previews, track-of-the-month subscriptions, and bonus-track rewards.

The recording industry's biggest objection to MP3 is that intellectual property and copyright abuse currently cannot be prevented. However, MP4, the next generation of MP3 technology, is expected to avoid this problem with a watermarking technology that will prevent illegal duplications of recordings.

In December 1998, some of the major record labels (including BMG, EMI, Sony, United Music Group, and Warner) along with the Recording Industry Association of America (RIAA) responded to the threat of music piracy by announcing the Secure Digital Music Initiative (SDMI). They hoped to create a new format to protect artists and record labels from intellectual property piracy. SDMI expects SDMI-compliant products and playing devices to ship by year-end 1999.

A new format, Vector Quantization Format (VQF), was released in early 1999. Although VQF files are being praised for their storage size (files are about 30 percent smaller than MP3), some industry experts believe VQF is too late: Between 5 and 10 million MP3 audio players already have been downloaded from the Web. ■

Once the user's profile is assembled, an application can tailor the information presented to the customer. A selling application may use the profile to select special promotions to offer the buyer, such as a one-time discount, an opportunity to join an affinity program, or information about a product on sale that day. Buy-side applications can employ a user profile to call up previous orders to simplify purchasing the same items again.

If supply chain efficiencies and new ways of executing sales and fulfillment functions represent significant changes in the cost base of e-business, then personalization is where much of the added value is located. E-business leverages two fundamental forces in commerce by combining commoditization of products or services with personalization of them. On the one hand, e-business users are encouraging more channels such as telecommunications to be regarded as pure commodities that should vary mainly in price. At the same time, e-business allows more scope for consumers to obtain products that have been personalized to their needs and tastes.

Examples of how personalization and commoditization can work together can be found in music. For example, consumers might go to CDnow's Web site to save money on jazz CDs because CD distribution has become a commodity on the Web. However, that does not mean the consumers are looking for the lowest-priced jazz CD. Instead, they may be looking for the lowest-priced CD of the particular artist or musical style they prefer. Or,

THE WEB AND THE ADVERTISING INDUSTRY

The online advertising industry has experienced tremendous growth. The greatest challenges for the online advertising industry include the medium itself: Effective methods of measuring advertising visibility have yet to be established, and the visual resolution of a monitor cannot compare with the resolution of a glossy color photo in a magazine.

Web advertising is priced in a wide variety of ways:

- Cost-per-million (CPM) or impression-only (cost-per-thousand of guaranteed impressions)
- Flat fees (HotWired, for example, charges a flat fee for a fixed period of time)
- Click-throughs (fees are levied based on the number of times users click on a banner)
- Sponsorships (package deals of impressions and click-throughs)
- Cost-per-lead (charges are levied for each viewer that registers or submits personal information)
- Cost-per-sale (advertiser pays based on the number of sales resulting from an ad)

- Revenue-sharing agreements (publishers receive a commission, paid upon sale, for sales that result from an ad)

Technical advances are beginning to change the way Web advertising is approached. Streaming video/audio presents new possibilities for online advertising. Rich-media formats allow advertisers to deliver interactive ads where consumers can browse for merchandise, request information, and interact with the advertiser within the ad space. For example, in Blue Marble's interactive ad campaign for Proctor and Gamble's Scope Mouthwash, the banner read, "Get Kissably Close Online"; when viewers clicked on it, they could e-mail a "kiss" to the recipient of their choice. Some Web sites currently will accept certain types of rich media, such as HTML banners, but will not accept other rich-media formats, such as video banners.

In other examples, Red Sky designed a campaign for Hewlett-Packard that let people play Pong, and Agency.com created banners for Metlife that would provide the viewer's ideal body weight. The portal Excite supports and serves rich-media advertising, and according to Excite executives, viewers have a higher rate of response to rich-media than

to traditional banner ads.

Perhaps the biggest challenge facing advertisers on the Internet is the complex question of audience measurement. Popular Web sites being accessed by more than one user on a given ISP's or corporate network may be cached on a local server. Thus, as many as 20 people could be seeing the same page and the same banner, but the tracking software counts it as only one individual (this is particularly problematic in workplaces).

In March 1999, the Future of Advertising Stakeholders (FAST) group published the first set of advertising measurement guidelines. FAST proposes the industry uniformly adopt software that will track individual viewers on cached sites.

Although a variety of options exists for advertising sales, uncertainty still surrounds the effectiveness of Web advertising. The bottom line for advertisers is whether the advertising helps sell the product. For businesses already selling on the Web, the answer is probably "Yes." For companies that have not moved online, the answer is slightly less clear. ■

they may be looking for new artists or titles of which they were unaware previously. Therefore, CDnow has commodified the music distribution channel to enable it to pass on savings to consumers, but the actual added value is related to how CDnow personalizes its service.

Before e-business, the ability of an organization to appear to offer a personal service while driving commoditization and services on a global scale seemed remote. A business could concentrate on commoditization and drive down the cost per unit of a given good or service. Or, a business could concentrate on a more price-insensitive segment of a given market and differentiate itself through personalized service. With e-business, it is becoming possible to do both.

To balance adding value through personalization while maintaining the cost base associated with commodity-based enterprises, e-businesses seek to add information content to a transaction. The goal is to develop a personalized experience coupled with rapid order fulfillment. In this way, a customer may reap an actual or perceived bonus that adds value to transactions involving goods and services, which by all rights should be moving toward commoditization.

Although the balance between the amount of personalization or commoditization differs between e-businesses, the basic lesson remains the same: The Web makes it very difficult to pursue one option to the exclusion of the other. Therefore, many industries that previously competed through price, quantity, or other commodity-oriented factors find e-business requires they now learn more about their customers to remain competitive.

"To balance adding value through personalization while maintaining the cost base associated with commodity-based enterprises, e-businesses seek to add information content to a transaction."

Current E-Business Models

Before embarking on a discussion of how e-business reorganizes existing and Web-only business models, it is necessary to define what is meant by a business model. A business model defines an architecture for the product, service, and information flows surrounding a value-creating activity. A business model also describes the various business "actors" and their roles as well as the potential benefits for the actors, given that they organize in a particular way. Finally, a business model describes the sources of revenue that sustain the model.

According to the OECD, e-business creates new models for organizing production and transacting business. E-business offers intermodality—new environments for migrating existing business models—and complementarity—new forms of business cooperation. The common assumption that e-business directly substitutes or displaces existing business models actually is the most rare instantiation.

The e-business taxonomy falls into two broad categories: traditional business models that have been modified and then transplanted to the Web and those activities that evolved within the Web environment and are native to it.

TRANSPLANTED BUSINESS MODELS

Transplanted activities are the most prevalent e-business examples. E-businesses such as Amazon.com have pioneered Web-based retailing, yet the core business model actually is the same one used by mail-order merchants worldwide. In this case, a Web site is used as a storefront to sell physical goods that then are delivered by a third party. What makes retailers such as Amazon.com unique is their use of e-business technology and techniques to combine the scale of a global book distributor with the convenience and customization of the local bookstore at a cost/performance point that beats both.

Another transplanted business model is advertising-based e-business—sometimes known as the real estate model—where third-party fees support the operation of a free service. In addition to dedicated Web-based publications and the Web versions of print and broadcast media, Web portals such as Yahoo! use this model. In this situation, success or failure is determined primarily by the site's attractiveness to potential advertisers, which varies according to the demographic attributes of a community drawn either by content or by a service.

Running parallel to the advertising model are subscription-based Web sites, in which a user subscribes to gain access to a database of digital products for a specific length of time or for a bundle of search and retrieval privileges. Some of the Web's best-known content sites (in particular, most of its pornography sites) are organized around subscriptions.

In addition, some businesses use the Web to build mindshare in the use of their products (usually software or games). The first instantiation for a given site is targeted toward attracting and retaining customer attention and linkage to a product, while the business involves selling complementary services or support. The second stage often involves the distribution of a trial version of a particular product. For example, although the free client browser strategy was depicted as a revolutionary step in the evolution of a unique Internet economy, browser vendors (and similar businesses such as game developers) merely were following a pattern laid down in the 30-day-free-trial model of standard retail business.

Other traditional activities transplanted to the Internet include direct marketing, which has received a generally negative response because of the indiscriminate use of e-mail (known as "spam") to broadcast unsolicited messages to large numbers of e-mail addresses. The opposite of spam are incentive scheme models (similar to traditional loyalty schemes). So-called permission-marketing competitions or surveys offer free goods or services to entice people to accept targeted advertising or provide personal information.

The fact that many standard business models are being transferred to an Internet environment is not, in itself, negative. Indeed, the new transaction and coordination efficiencies provided by the Web enhance a business' ability to attain critical success factors. These factors, in turn, encourage new forms of market entry and experimentation even as customers realize measurable value in a relatively short time. However, the transition of any business model to the Web is not merely a matter of technology, and each such transition entails a certain degree of risk.

"The transition of any business model to the Web cannot be isolated in technology, and each such transition entails a certain degree of risk."

INTERNET-NATIVE BUSINESS MODELS

Finding e-business models that were inconceivable without the Web is more difficult. However, this is not so much a case of what new business models could be imagined as what new business models would have been impossible unless they enjoyed the cost structure only the Web supported.

The first major e-business segment to grow up around the Internet involved providing access to the Internet or providing services for hosting Web servers, e-mail servers, or other content-oriented services. The emerging commerce service providers (CSPs) are expanding on that trend. These e-businesses assume many of the business processes on behalf of clients that typically are connection-, processing-, or transaction-oriented. However, access and hosting actually are the enabling services that support e-businesses and do not constitute truly new business models.

Instead, the leading candidates for new businesses that would have not been feasible without the Web are a new group of Web-based auctioneers and emerging information intermediaries called "infomediaries." Whether positioning themselves as strictly bid-and-match auction sites, affinity sites that include transaction capability for professionals or consumers, or sites managing trust and value on behalf of clients, these e-businesses are about creating markets.

Auctions. Auction sites can be classified roughly according to the audience and the method through which they make a market on the Web. Certain sites such as eBay or Onsale are targeted toward the general consumer market, although eBay facilitates consumer-to-consumer transactions while Onsale matches consumers with business offerings. The general transaction model for both eBay and Onsale is the Yankee auction format, where one or more identical items are offered for sale at the same time. When the auction closes, bids on items are ranked in order of price, then quantity, then time of initial bid.

These sites also employ Dutch auction models for special cases, where bidding starts at an extremely high price that is lowered progressively until a buyer claims an item by calling "mine." In the flower market in the Netherlands (hence, the name Dutch auction), bids are confirmed by pressing a button that stops an automatic clock.

Another auction model being tested by e-businesses where buyers post a price they are willing to pay for an item or service and the site then facilitates a match with a seller. This is the idea behind Priceline.com, which uses this technique to match unsold airline seats or hotel rooms. Unlike participants in an auction, Priceline.com buyers do not compete with each other for items; each purchase offer is presented by Priceline.com to a cluster of sellers.

For example, nearly 500,000 airline seats fly empty every day. These seats have a wide range of value that drops to zero or even a negative amount (considering the cost of operating an aircraft) the moment a plane takes off. However, an airline's desire to clear excess inventory may be offset by the company's fear of undercutting its fare structure should it announce the existence of these seats publicly. Instead, through intermediaries such as Priceline.com, airlines can accept offers discretely without reporting publicly announced sales.

Although Yankee, Dutch, and reverse auctions are the basic process models for creating markets online, e-businesses are beginning to specialize in targeted business-to-business market segments. These vertical-market e-businesses (sometimes called practical portals) combine the bid/match infrastructure of a dedicated auction site with complementary business process services such as procurement or targeted content. These converged auction/portal sites run the gamut of raw materials, distressed inventory, and perhaps in the future, patented intellectual property. Such sites can focus either on buying (procurement) or selling, depending on whether the process begins with a request for proposal ([RFP], buying) or goods for sale (selling).

Metalsite.com is an information, business services, and auction site for the steel industry, offering secondary or excess hot and cold rolled steel from LTV Steel, Steel Dynamics, and Weirton Steel, among others. Since its launch in mid-1998, Metalsite has signed up some 1,500 registered members—all prospective buyers of steel slabs, plates, and other primary products. Metal producers can access the Metalsite auction service to solicit bids for a particular product, privately review the bids, and then award the sale.

"The leading candidates for new businesses that would not have been feasible without the Web are a new group of Web-based auctioneers and emerging information intermediaries called infomediaries."

Although traditional channels still are being used for payment and logistics, Metalsite plans to facilitate all aspects of the transaction process from order status to claims, order fulfillment, and shipping status reporting.

FairMarket runs a procurement-based Web site that invites potential suppliers to bid on RFPs for industrial inputs. FairMarket's site also uses a rating system under which buyers can comment on sellers' products and on whether those items were represented accurately during the bidding process. Sellers accumulate negative and positive "points" based on buyers' comments, and any that fall below a certain ratings point threshold can be kicked off the site. In addition, FairMarket allows community and business sites to license its customized auction software and hosting services, giving these organizations business-to-business auction capabilities at their own sites.

Basic raw materials are not the only commodities coming under the Web auction hammer. Excess inventory in electronics is the market space for FastParts, an Internet-based spot market that enables members to buy and sell any part that goes onto or into a printed circuit board. Modeled after NASDAQ in the securities industry, FastParts is neither a broker nor a distributor but manages transactions and the physical transfer of traded parts.

Other companies have created private, extranet-based auctions for their dealers and resellers. This is the strategy adopted by Ingram Micro, a leading computer distributor. Previously, Ingram disposed of unsalable inventory at a considerable loss through a network of 50 to 60 computer product liquidators. To improve this situation, Ingram created an auction service called Auction Block. Each week, Ingram runs auctions on 30 to 40 items.

In the past, auctions were limited primarily to high-value goods such as paintings and antiques or to very active markets for financial instruments and true commodities (such as wheat). Today, the improved economics of communication and coordination brought about by the Web allows the auction model to be applied to a much broader range of commodity products than would have been feasible without the ubiquitous, standards-based infrastructure and transaction-processing capability provided by the Internet and specialized auction software.

Moreover, auctions' impact on markets is not limited to the specific markets they create. The existence and expansion of auction-based market-makers open new channels for small to midsized enterprises to reach customers that would have been too widely dispersed to reach before. Previously, the need to identify, contact, and negotiate with a scattered population—coupled with similar costs incurred by buyers—was a formidable barrier to entry. Now, however, e-business auction sites can reach a sizable potential audience.

Infomediaries. Another major e-business segment that qualifies as a new business model is the infomediaries. There are several definitions of an infomediary. One definition of an infomediary is a business whose main source of revenue arises from capturing customer information and developing detailed profiles of individuals for use by selected third-party vendors. (This definition is similar to the functions of a credit bureau in the non-Web world.) Another definition of infomediaries says an infomediary links multiple buyers and seller in vertical niche industries, gathers consistent and comparable information on multiple vendors, and provides tools to help customers evaluate their purchasing decisions.

Aggregating customer information is nothing new. Some of the emerging online intermediaries actually are long-established trade groups. For example, New England Circuit Sales has made markets in excess inventory and components for some 2,000 computer and component manufacturers, resellers, and systems integrators. Another vendor-oriented aggregator segment includes lead generators such as Autobytel.com, which provides a national network of automobile dealers with consumer requests for quotes in return for a fee per lead.

Another content, services, and transactions market-maker for basic materials is Chemdex, which targets the $1 billion market for research chemicals used by universities and biotech and pharmaceutical companies. Before the Web made it possible to aggregate multiple vendor catalogs into a single, searchable Web-accessible database, it was not uncommon for prices of similar items to vary by as much as 40 percent. On the Chemdex site, chemical buyers can search by product and category. Chemdex also is attempting to create uniform product descriptions that make sense of different vendor offerings so customers can comparison-shop. Chemdex reaches some 300,000 researchers working in more than 25,000 institutions via its Web auction site.

WHY THE WEB IS IMPORTANT TO E-BUSINESS

Electronic business as a distinct phenomenon is a product of the 1990s and more specifically, a response to the possibilities created by the Internet. Not only does the Internet provide a near-ubiquitous infrastructure for reaching out to customers and business partners, its value proposition also includes compelling technical and economic factors.

"Not only does the Internet provide a near-ubiquitous infrastructure for reaching out to customers and business partners, its value proposition also includes compelling technical and economic factors."

On the technical side, the Internet provides business with truly converged communications and information handling. Convergence most commonly is discussed either as a network phenomena—both the ability of different network platforms to carry similar kinds of services and the ability of a single network to carry multiple services—or as the coming together of devices such as the telephone, television, and PC. Although the device end of the convergence spectrum tends to occupy popular press accounts, network convergence via TCP/IP is a more realistic concept. A TCP/IP network sends information packets (which are used instead of dedicated circuits) along varying paths to the destination, where they then are reassembled. This packet-switching process is the way the Internet works. In contrast, circuit switching dedicates a circuit to a specific user for the duration needed, which is the way the public telephone system works.

The Internet Protocol enables almost any network to support a range of communications modes that merge broadcast and telecommunications network characteristics such as one-to-one, one-to-many, and many-to-many with content, services, and transactions. Additionally, the Internet's open transport and interface protocols mean network access and communication are vendor- and device-independent.

However, the critical aspect of the Web for e-business involves the network effect, where the value of joining a network increases as more people join. In the same way that fax machines increased in value as they increased in popularity, so has the Web increased its influence as more people have begun to use it. Metcalfe's Law (as enunciated by Bob Metcalfe, founder of 3Com and coinventor of Ethernet) states a network becomes more useful in proportion to the square of the number of users. A primary example of Metcalfe's Law is the Internet because it fostered the development of global e-mail, which becomes more valuable as more users are connected.

Packet Internet Groper (PING) is a program used to monitor Internet performance by repeatedly bouncing a signal (called an echo request packet) off a specified destination and seeing how long that signal takes to complete the roundtrip.

Instead of the imminent collapse of the system some observers predicted would accompany increasing user traffic, the quality of the Web actually is improving. Matrix Information and Directory Services (MIDS) runs an application called the Internet Weather Report (IWR). The IWR uses a network tool called PING to measure the roundtrip times (latencies) from MIDS' Texas-based servers to about 4,000 Internet nodes—hosts, servers, and routers—throughout the world.

MIDS tested a real-world potential Internet crisis on September 11, 1998, when prosecutor Kenneth Starr released a special report on President Bill Clinton's extramarital activities. News agencies had predicted that such focus on a single information event could collapse the network. As it turned out, minutes after the Starr report was released, copies of that information began propagating to other Web servers as people who retrieved a report immediately reposted the file to their own Web sites, thereby coping with the massive information demand.

Another reason the Web has attracted so much interest is that much of its technology is free. On the server-side of the Internet, for example, major Web servers such as Apache were developed and are distributed free of charge. (The earliest Web servers mainly ran on vendor-supplied UNIX products such as Sun's Solaris plus some Macintoshes.) Likewise, on the client side, the first graphical interfaces to the Web—Mosaic and Netscape Navigator—were made available without charge—in some cases along with source code and standards to encourage user-led improvements.

Finally, the Web browser has become a universal client for deploying e-business applications. The user interface metaphors for navigating universal resource locators (URLs), hyperlinked Web pages, embedded graphics, or interactive maps are well established. Moreover, the application programming interfaces (APIs) for tying e-business functionality to Web pages are becoming standardized. Therefore, unlike earlier attempts to reach a mass market through proprietary client software—such as the first online banking packages—the Web allows e-businesses to dispense with the trouble of deploying and updating client-side software and running dedicated dial-in networks.

The Web model of communication and interaction results in a robust set of network services that use telecommunications resources more efficiently and are accessible via technology that is standard and public. Most important, the value of using the Web for reaching customers increases in direct proportion to the number of people joining the network.

Moore's Law was developed by Gordon Moore, one of the cofounders of Intel, who in 1965 forecast that computer chip complexity would double every 12 months for the next 10 years. Ten years later, in 1975, his forecast had proved true. He then forecast that the doubling would occur every 2 years for the next 10 years (through 1985). Again, history demonstrated his accuracy. The average of the two estimates often is stated as doubling every 18 months. In the late 1980s, he again estimated this doubling would continue for another decade.

Thus, the Web provides a ubiquitous piece of client software, the browser, as well as a universal infrastructure—creating a ready-made platform for e-business. More important, the Web has created a self-reinforcing cycle of growth that continually attracts new applications, making it the benchmark for interoperability, scalability, and ubiquity against which future networks will be judged. Consequently, the economic case for organizing an e-business using a Web-based network service has moved beyond whether to adopt Web protocols and procedures to the issue of how, when, and how fast the transition occurs.

HOW THE WEB ENABLES E-BUSINESS

The Web fundamentally transforms the historic information richness/reach tradeoff that determined the basic cost of coordinating product and market activities. The impact of Moore's Law on the price and performance of information processing, communication, and data storage technologies—now connected via the Web—is a critical enabler for e-business. It has bridged the gap between the richness of information—multimedia, amount, degree of customization, and interactivity—and the reach of information—exposure to multiple parties and coverage. Previously, a rich information flow was possible only through the focused use of a few dedicated channels for a select audience, and increased coverage meant sending a more general message through a wider set of channels.

Consider the various information channels through which sellers try to influence buyers as buyers try to find out about the offerings of sellers. Advertisements in newspapers reach a wide range of possible customers yet are limited by their static content as well as by the undifferentiated nature of the audience itself. Direct mail or telemarketing efforts are somewhat richer in their degree of personalization and potential for interactivity but are more expensive. Therefore, in comparison to advertisers, direct marketers sacrifice reach in order to add richness.

Buyers, too, adapt to the same tradeoff of information richness and reach. They can search hierarchically through high-reach/low-richness sources such as the yellow pages in a telephone directory. Or, they may opt for a high-richness/low-reach solution via a salesperson at a physical location.

The information richness/reach tradeoff is central to firms because it heavily influences how they organize their channels to market. Consider the amount of attention that can be paid to a particular customer as a function of the size of a transaction. A consumer buying an automobile or a home or a corporate buyer purchasing in bulk can expect to receive ample attention from a vendor or business partner because the size of their transactions warrant a dedicated communications channel. Yet, for smaller purchases, the cost required to operate an optimized communications channel often is not sufficient.

However, the advent of new and improved technologies at lower price points has enabled a downward shift of attention—that is, an increase in the attention paid to smaller purchases—even as it enables a greater number of individual orders to be addressed. The ability to shift attention downward at an acceptable cost opens new avenues for adding value to transactions or the productive process itself. This opportunity fuels market entry by firms that can organize around e-business technologies to create an information-rich market channel for goods and services at price points previously viewed as not economically feasible.

In the past, for example, Charles Schwab charged $80 for the average trade conducted through a live broker at a branch or over the phone. To compete with other Internet brokerages, however, Schwab dropped commissions to a flat $29.95 for most online transactions—a rate that still remains considerably higher than that of Internet competitors such as Ameritrade or E*Trade, with their cut-rate $8 and $15 commissions, respectively.

Between the Web increasing the value of interaction with a larger customer base and the explosion of efforts to standardize information presentation formats, a further dramatic displacement of the richness/reach tradeoff is possible. This displacement disrupts the existing competitive environment among firms even as it causes a new environment to take shape.

The Web disrupts the current structure of markets not by changing what they are—price-based information structures for exchanging goods and services—but by changing the standards by which timeliness in a market is measured. For example, there was once no question that the fundamental reason for a stock exchange was to provide the advantage of time and place to those who would trade on it and, in so doing, establish the efficiency and liquidity baselines against which other markets would be judged.

"Between the Web increasing the value of interaction with a larger customer base and the explosion of efforts to standardize information presentation formats, a further dramatic displacement of the richness/reach tradeoff is possible."

However, the Web renders the concept of time and place meaningless for trading goods and services. As a result, new metrics such as oversight, fair play, or quality of service are becoming the new baselines for benchmarking markets. Speed and liquidity are taken almost for granted.

Thus, the critical impact of ubiquitous information processing courtesy of Moore's Law combined with inexpensive information transport via the Web is the movement of all markets closer to the dynamics of today's stock exchanges. This shift translates into shorter product and service cycles, more ephemeral competitive barriers, and a decisively lowered cost for firms and consumers to participate in larger, faster, deeper, and more disruptive market spaces. Most important, this is not a transition period but is a taste of how economic life in a Web-based environment is to be organized in the next millennium.

Future Implications of E-Business

"The global impact of the Web and e-business has been compared to the invention of printing, the voyages of discovery, or even the Renaissance."

The global impact of the Web and e-business has been compared to the invention of printing, the voyages of discovery, or even the Renaissance. Like the figures behind those momentous events, today's e-business theorists, practitioners, and even customers have little idea how their actions are creating a new mode of economic life. Until professional historians in 2030, for example, provide some of the first objective commentaries about what happened between 1995 to 2010, e-business will remain far more an art than a science.

Nevertheless, it is probable historians will agree that during this 15-year period, the organization of information and knowledge overtook the organization of physical property to become the prime mover of wealth, culture, and power. More specifically, successful e-businesses organized information and knowledge about customers, rather than information about science or technology, to create competitive advantage.

Historians might note that two institutions—one physical and one organizational—combined to change the way business was done. The physical institution is the World Wide Web, which consists of networked computer hardware and software connected by the Internet Protocol. The organizational institution is e-business, which started as a new way of coordinating transactions more efficiently over the Web but evolves to become a general principle for organizing production and exchange. E-business not only changes the basic cost of executing sales, procuring inputs, and reformulating supply chains and logistics, but it also redefines how business was done by placing a tremendous premium on customer relationship management.

E-business accomplishes this shift by eliminating the historic tradeoff between information richness and information reach. Previously, a rich information flow was possible only through the focused use of a few dedicated channels for a small audience, while increased information reach meant sending a generalized message to a larger base of recipients. However, the Web enables e-businesses to personalize their market propositions to a larger audience. The ability to shift attention downward to the individual customer is critical for reorganizing channels to market.

At the same time, the Web empowers customers to find alternative offerings at minimal cost and effort. Thus, vendors are forced to engage customers' attention or else lose them. As a result, customer relationship management becomes a watchword for e-business. This concept embraces not only classic customer-facing business processes such as sales, marketing, and service, but also expands the universe of customer-touching processes and technologies to encompass engineering, manufacturing, and distribution as well.

However, the way the Web transforms information richness/reach does not stop at enhancing customer relationships with vendors. The dramatically lower cost of coordinating complex information flows among large populations of dispersed users enables markets and market principles to begin operating in areas of economic activity previously thought impossible to attain. Web-based auctions of raw materials, electronic components, or personal items populate e-business market spaces. Buyers begin naming their price and then searching for vendors that will meet it.

Consequently, one of the major impacts of e-business is to disintermediate the traditional involvement of certain intermediaries in business transactions. A human agent, such as insurance or travel agents, previously served a useful purpose in navigating through a sea of complex options. However, with the vast accessibility of this information on the Web, numerous tools can collect and present this data to the customer without the aid of human agents.

On the other hand, new participants called infomediaries emerge to capture customer information and develop detailed profiles of an individual's requirements for use by selected third-party vendors. Infomediaries take advantage of the Web to create discovery-based business models to rationalize and aggregate previously unstructured encounters between businesses and their customers and lead them closer to a transaction.

The end result of the transformation of the information richness/information reach tradeoff via the Web coupled with e-business' concentration on organizing business propositions around customer information is that the routines that shaped 20th century commercial life are being upset profoundly.

The concept of routine is important because business life, like any other, consists mainly of routine work based on experience. It is only within the boundaries of a routine that people function promptly and similarly. It is only to routine processes that most theories and rules about business apply.

Many organizations find it difficult or even impossible to take action either to exploit an opportunity opened by change or to avoid its negative effects. Those businesses able to operate outside established routine—and to survive fundamental changes in many of the competitive conditions that define an industry or even an economic era—are rare.

History is replete with examples of companies that failed to transform themselves as their industries changed. A century ago, railroad executives saw themselves in the rail business instead of the transportation business. As a result, other carriers overtook them using new technologies such as planes and trucks. Likewise, Remington and Underwood saw themselves in the typewriter business rather than in the word processing business. As personal computers became commonplace, many new companies quickly penetrated the word processing market, and the typewriter business withered away.

Although the preceding examples are those of failures, there are just as many stories of reinvention and success. Whenever new things that successfully break established routine are done enough times, others can copy or improve on the actions taken by pioneers to break the spell. More tractable theories and business rules begin to coalesce around the experiences of pioneers. The basic risk/reward tradeoff of the new model starts to become clear. The initial success draws other people, then crowds, into a new way of doing business. A new routine is born.

Nevertheless, it will be some years before e-business reaches the point where it can be called routine. In the meantime, the commercial relationships that have defined the business case for many industries now are up for grabs. Whether decision-makers will see this situation as an opportunity or a threat is unclear. If they want their organizations to be a part of the future rather than a historical example, however, they will be compelled to respond.

The *E-Business Technology Forecast* is an attempt to explore some of the technologies that are empowering organizations to seize the e-business opportunity. It cannot substitute for the willingness of management in leading and emerging firms to reconceptualize how they deliver value in a customer-centric world. For that, there is no technological solution. There is only foresight, innovation, organization, and a healthy amount of luck. Thus, the only useful advice for 1999's decision-makers is to fasten your seatbelts—the ride has just begun.

INTRODUCTION TO E-BUSINESS TECHNOLOGIES

Brochureware to Virtual Organization

Most organizations go through a series of evolutionary steps in transacting business on the Internet. First, they establish a Web presence that represents the company. Often called "electronic brochureware," this presence usually describes the company's basic products, services, and contact information. All major companies have reached this first step because it is relatively simple to create and maintain a read-only file for interested parties.

The second major step is to enable a business function through the Web, such as allowing customers to place orders and track their status using Web browsers. Business partners can tap into a company's information systems using extranets. These business functions are an alternate channel for conducting business, but the Web is not the sole method of doing so. This step is crucial because customers and partners are performing read/write operations with company databases, making issues of data integrity, security, recovery, and system availability very important.

Once a company achieves substantial experience on the Web, it is ready for the third major step: tying a business function to the Web as the primary mechanism of conducting daily business. For example, one industry shifting increasingly to the Web is software sales. Many software vendors are refocusing their business models from physical stores (where shelf space is very competitive) to Web sites. Software distribution by these vendors currently is handled via downloads from Web sites. Some major retail stores have closed in anticipation of the transformation already occurring in this fast-moving industry.

The final step in e-business is to have most mission-critical applications completely available via the Web without an alternate means to conduct business. Most major industries that use electronic data interchange require their partners to conduct business electronically, as is the case in auto manufacturing and banking. Companies in these industries connect most of their major business processes via workflow applications with their partners through all stages of product fulfillment. All partners must design their systems so there is no single point of failure and fast recovery always is available. In addition to this type of intercompany communications, each enterprise will use e-business technologies to integrate disparate business functions on different platforms using a common backbone.

Competing Approaches to E-Business Application Deployment

Enterprises that want to engage in e-business with their customers, suppliers, and other business partners face a spectrum of options when it comes to deciding how to develop and deploy the necessary e-business applications. These choices range from complete custom development on the one hand to complete outsourcing of the function on the other. The major alternatives follow.

COMPLETE CUSTOM DEVELOPMENT

This approach involves building an e-business application from scratch using no vendor-provided e-business-specific tools or platform. However, non-e-business-specific tools certainly could be part of the solution, ranging from development tools such as third- and fourth-generation languages to transaction processing (TP) monitors and other forms of middleware.

BASIC WEB PLATFORM

In this approach, the e-business application uses a Web server platform—although not necessarily one specific to e-business—to provide some of the basic Web functionality. For example, in the simplest case, a commercial or "open source" Web (technically, HyperText Transfer Protocol [HTTP]) server product would be used to provide the basic communications function between the browser client and the e-business site. In this case, all the e-business application functionality would be provided through custom development. That functionality would be invoked by the Web server in response to incoming connections from Web browser clients. This might be done using either the Common Gateway Interface (CGI) or a specific Web server's API set, such as Microsoft's Internet Server Application Program Interface (ISAPI) or the Netscape Server Application Programming Interface (NSAPI). Both methods allow a Web server to communicate with other programs.

See "Server-Side Application Programming" on page 183 for more information on CGI and NSAPI/ISAPI.

A more sophisticated version of this approach would use a Web server that offers greater functionality. For example, a category of products known as Web application servers provides a set of services designed to meet the needs of transactional applications, such as load balancing and high availability. In this case, although the transactional underpinnings for the application are provided by a software vendor, the e-business functionality still is developed by the enterprise.

See "Web Application Servers" on page 204 for more information.

E-COMMERCE SERVER PLATFORM

In this approach, the application is based on a commerce server or merchant server software product. These products go beyond the basic Web server functionality (even that supplied by a Web application server) and provide functionality unique to e-business. For example, a commerce server provides the basic user interface for the buying experience, such as a product catalog; a shopping cart, in which customers accumulate items they wish to purchase; and a checkout function, whereby the purchase can be completed and payment made. A commerce server also may include more sophisticated functionality capable of providing the customer with a personalized shopping experience. However, the enterprise deploying the application still would need to develop (or at least customize) a significant amount of application functionality, probably using an API set provided by the server vendor.

See "Commerce Platforms" on page 61 for more information.

E-BUSINESS PACKAGED APPLICATION

In this approach, the software vendor provides a packaged application that is more or less complete, with minimal or no application development or customization required (or in some cases, allowed). In the limiting case, the e-business enterprise needs only to populate the catalog with its product and pricing information and then is ready to begin accepting orders.

See "Sell-Side Packaged E-Business Applications" on page 65 and "Buy-Side Packaged E-Business Applications" on page 76 for more information.

OUTSOURCING

In this approach, the enterprise neither develops nor operates any e-business system. Instead, it relies on a commerce service provider (CSP), analogous to an Internet service provider (ISP), to provide and operate an e-business Web site on its behalf. The CSPs themselves may be following any of the previously described approaches, and many of the e-commerce servers and e-business packaged applications are designed for use by a CSP that is hosting e-business sites for multiple enterprises. Even in this case, however, some links are required between the e-business application provided by the CSP and the enterprise's in-house applications that are used for order fulfillment, accounting, and so on.

Benefits and Risks of Packaged Applications

The decision regarding the degree of customization versus the degree of third-party product or service offerings is similar to the build-versus-buy tradeoff presented by all enterprise applications. In the e-business case, however, it may be more complex because of several unique factors: the rapid evolution of e-business practices, the relative newness of most of the products and many of the vendors, and the fact that e-business applications are customer-facing and thus may be seen as providing a greater potential for competitive differentiation than back-office applications.

The discussion in this book will concentrate on the two most common forms of e-business application deployment: those using e-commerce server platforms and packaged e-business applications. The discussion will not consider cases that involve primarily custom development of e-business functionality, nor will it include outsourcing of e-business operations.

It also is worth noting that this hierarchy of approaches replicates, at least to some extent, the historical evolution of e-business technology. Early adopters of e-business— in particular, those enterprises that moved beyond the use of their Web sites merely to provide product information and began to offer transactional capabilities as well— often had no alternative but to develop most of the application functionality themselves, typically using a basic HTTP server to handle only communications with the customer's browser. Over time, the software vendors that had been providing basic Web server functionality began to extend their products into the early commerce servers, incorporating functionality specifically designed to support e-business. Meanwhile, they and other vendors developed packaged e-business applications.

Today, the use of packaged applications (as opposed to custom development) is common in specific areas of e-business. A notable example of the foregoing is a buy-side or procurement application designed to handle the purchasing of indirect materials.

The focus of these applications on indirect materials stems from the fact that the items purchased and the purchasing process tend to be fairly common across industries, unlike the purchase of direct materials, which varies considerably across industries. In other words, buying iron ore for a steel mill, buying clothing for a retail store, and buying food for a hotel chain will involve different markets, vendors, and processes. However, the steel mill, the retailer, and the hotel chain all need to purchase office supplies, computer equipment, janitorial supplies, and so on. Thus, by focusing on indirect materials, vendors are able to sell into a much larger market space than if they decided to address purchasing automation in only one vertical industry.

Because enterprise packaged application vendors have focused on a set of processes common across a wide range of companies, they have been able to create packages that have widespread applicability. In sell-side e-business, however, the requirements for a

Indirect materials are items not incorporated directly into the organization's final product; they sometimes are referred to as maintenance, repair, and operations (MRO) materials.

See "Buy-Side Packaged E-Business Applications" on page 76 for more information on e-business and MRO.

successful solution are much more industry-specific: The e-business Web site of a bank, a stockbroker, a retailer, a computer manufacturer, or an industrial parts distributor will not look much like each other, so it is harder to create packaged applications that can be sold into a large market.

Furthermore, many companies see their sell-side Web sites as an important source of competitive advantage. Therefore, the need for innovation and differentiation in sell-side sites means many companies will not implement a generic package because it requires giving up a source of competitive advantage. The same is not true of buy-side packages. Very few companies see buying office supplies as one of their core competencies.

Application Development and Deployment Challenges

As suggested earlier, developing and deploying e-business applications brings with it a number of challenges beyond those found in other enterprise systems. Some of these challenges stem from the characteristics and motivations of the user population. Unlike employees, who may be required to use a particular application as part of their jobs, visitors to a Web site (particularly a business-to-consumer site) can choose to go elsewhere. Furthermore, unlike a situation with employees, training sessions cannot be held for visitors to a Web site to teach them how to use a particular application. At a minimum, this situation puts a tremendous premium on ease of use and intuitive user interfaces. More important, it means a Web site must offer a compelling experience that goes beyond mere usability to draw in visitors and ensure repeat customers.

Another unique characteristic of the user population may be its global nature. A Web site may need to be available in multiple languages, to conform to differing legal frameworks or regulatory environments, and to reflect differing business practices.

See "Personalization" on page 81 for more information. See "Payment Technologies" on page 139 for more information. See "Security" on page 208 for more information. See "Maintaining State and User Activity in HTTP" on page 191 for more information.

An important characteristic of the user population (again, particularly for business-to-consumer Web sites) is that many customers may be unknown to the enterprise. The enterprise may not have done business with them in the past, and the enterprise may not be able to authenticate their identities. This situation gives rise to several issues. An enterprise may want to identify visitors to its Web site and collect information about them so it can offer an individualized experience when they return. This goal requires a user registration process, probably the use of password-protected user logins, and a system for collecting information about each user (either based on what they reveal explicitly or based on what is inferred from their behavior on the site or their purchases). In the absence of a means to confirm the identity of a visitor to a site, there may be risks associated with accepting a credit-card number, and technology may be needed to reduce the possibility of credit-card fraud.

Other unique characteristics of e-business applications stem from the underlying technology itself. Many e-business applications are designed to work over the public Internet and be accessed by Web users with relatively slow (typically, dial-in) access. This setup imposes constraints on the type of content businesses can use on their sites, given the long download times associated with large data objects such as high-resolution graphics and video. An enterprise may need a text-only version of its site that avoids the use of graphical objects for navigation because visitors with slow connections to the Web may turn off automatic downloading of graphics to improve performance.

See "Web Browsers" on page 201 for more information.

Business Web sites cannot control what client software is used by visitors who access the site, so site developers must create applications that can be accessed with all the leading Web browsers, each of which will have multiple versions in use. Depending on the degree to which the various browsers implement HyperText Markup Language (HTML) and other Web protocols in the same way, a business site may need to maintain different versions of the site content for different versions of browsers.

Another technical limitation comes from HTTP itself, the communications protocol by which a Web browser and server exchange information. HTTP was designed for information access applications rather than transactional applications and is missing some of the attributes required for transactions. In particular, HTTP is an example of a stateless protocol, which means the Web server does not maintain any information about the history of its interaction with a particular user. This feature is not a good match for many applications, which are based on the concept of a series of interactions that all constitute part of the same transaction and which also may be based on the concept of many transactions that occur within a given session. Thus, an e-business application must provide the missing attributes, in particular some mechanism that allows transactions and sessions to be superimposed on the underlying HTTP communications.

See "Maintaining State and User Activity in HTTP" on page 191 for more information.

Perhaps the most significant challenge faced in building and deploying e-business applications is the need for integration with other enterprise systems. Although some e-businesses (and many of the most well-known ones) from their inception were created specifically to do business on the Web, the majority involve extending an existing enterprise into the e-business world. Such an existing enterprise already has in place a variety of information systems to which the new e-business applications will now serve as a front end. For example, several points of interaction will exist between an e-business application on a business' Web site and its order management system:

See "Integration With Enterprise Systems" on page 109 for more information.

- The enterprise needs to extract product and pricing information from its order management system to populate the catalog in its e-business system.
- The business must verify product availability in real time, using information from its order management application when orders are submitted via the Web site.
- Those orders need to be passed to the order management system for eventual fulfillment.

Significant Trends and Developments

Although it is impossible to predict the future in detail, several technologies and trends are evident in the pages of this *Forecast* that suggest long-term impact over the evolution of e-business.

XML

The eXtensible Markup Language (XML) is mentioned prominently throughout the *E-Business Technology Forecast*. XML can be used as a standard self-describing mechanism to exchange data between different application systems, both inside and outside enterprise boundaries. XML-based information exchange focuses on the structure of data rather than merely indicating how it should be displayed, which is the only functionality provided by HTML.

We expect XML to play a crucial role in e-business application development during the forecast period. XML is aiming to become the Esperanto of data exchange, a metalanguage that bridges the gap between previously incompatible systems.

What this means for e-business is that there are many more possibilities for organizations to partner and exchange data than before because the need to describe the structure of a document to each participating application is obviated by using the XML tags. If the information systems are XML-compliant, data can be exchanged directly, even between heterogeneous operating systems and data models. Even so, XML still is about the structure of data and not its semantics. Partners must agree on the meaning of the data that they exchange.

It is difficult to predict exactly how XML will affect the development of e-business practice and technology. However, application developers and major e-businesses are looking to XML to provide device and operating-system independence for exchanging data in the same way the Internet Protocol (IP) allowed for network independence for communicating data. As such, we expect a bright future for this World Wide Web Consortium (W3C) standard.

CUSTOMER RELATIONSHIP MANAGEMENT AND PRIVACY

We believe customer relationship management (CRM) is the core activity of e-business. The technology area associated most often with CRM is personalization. Personalization entails tailoring the presentation of a Web site to individuals or classes of customers based on profile information, demographics, or prior transactions. The goal is to market and sell one-to-one and to enhance the user experience so the customer returns to the merchant's Web site.

Heightened emphasis on CRM is a response to the shift in how business is done. The lower switching costs for finding alternative providers via the Web combined with lower costs for market entry make it imperative for an e-business to get to know its customer base at a far more detailed level than in the past.

"We expect to see a host of technologies and techniques to help organizations maintain a balance between customer knowledge and customer privacy."

At the same time, there are countervailing forces (especially in Europe) against organizations manipulating and exchanging information about individuals without their consent. Formal initiatives such as the EU Privacy Directive as well as industry-led efforts such as the Platform for Privacy Preferences (P3P) are seeking to provide frameworks for managing the flow of personal information and expressing privacy policies on e-business Web sites.

We expect to see a host of technologies and techniques to help organizations maintain a balance between customer knowledge and customer privacy. However necessary it may be, such technology and changed business practice will be neither easy nor inexpensive to implement.

NEW INTERMEDIARIES

Although it is true the Web has ignited a significant debate about the future of distribution channels, complete disintermediation will not be widespread. Indeed, we believe that new online intermediaries will proliferate.

Much of the intermediation/disintermediation debate has been depicted as an "all or nothing" decision for firms to make. Although some manufacturers initially tried to use the Web to eliminate the reseller channel completely, they quickly realized the value of their existing market channels could be enhanced significantly by e-business. Instead, many manufacturers are using the Web for presale and postsale interactions with the customer while using partners to facilitate the sales process itself.

As the number of e-businesses grows from hundreds of thousands to millions, the need for advisors, aggregators, guarantors, authenticators, distributors, and even resellers cannot help but grow substantially. The main aspect of these new intermediaries (whether or not they execute the same function offline) is that the value they add to an exchange between a producer and a consumer revolves around their managing information as opposed to managing inventory. Cases in point include Web auctions, mortgage and loan brokering, automobile sales, and industry-specific portals.

The preceding section is a sample of some of the e-business trends we are tracking. It is by no means an exhaustive or exclusive list. We fully expect that as e-business evolves, the relative importance of some technologies and trends will become accentuated even as others fade in importance.

Outline of the Book

The technology section of the *E-Business Technology Forecast* is organized into four chapters: "E-Business Platforms and Applications," "Integration with Enterprise Systems," "Payment Technologies," and "E-Business Infrastructure."

The first chapter, "E-Business Platforms and Applications," focuses on the major software components of e-business and the products available in the marketplace. This chapter will cover both buy-side and sell-side technologies such as Web commerce servers, shopping carts, e-business catalogs, configurators, and personalization engines.

Until recently, many e-business sites were either partially or almost entirely custom-built to provide the functionality because it was not available elsewhere. However, software applications and tools vendors have made significant strides in allowing e-business sites to assemble a selection of best-of-breed applications coupled with custom development to create a strong e-business presence on the Web. Furthermore, packaged applications are available for purchase that provide basic e-business functionality without the need for custom development.

"Integration with Enterprise Systems," the second chapter, looks at the near-term technologies organizations will need as they begin to integrate existing information technologies with new e-business systems. The areas that will see the most activity during the forecast period are e-business extensions to enterprise resource planning (ERP) systems, electronic data interchange (EDI), and enterprise application integration (EAI) technologies.

The integration goal is to link entire sales, production, and delivery processes and systems electronically into one seamless flow of information between an enterprise, its customers, and its partners. Yet, the key technology issue for application integration is how e-businesses get applications that are based on different technologies and with differing business models and data models to work together. These applications must interoperate in a common way on a public network with minimal disruption to everyday operations, not to mention preexisting investment.

The third chapter, "Payment Technologies," surveys how technology vendors are attempting to provide merchants and buyers with secure, reliable, and unobtrusive methods of transferring value. Traditionally, payment information has been transported over private, secure networks. For Web-based electronic business, however, payment methods must address the issues associated with public, insecure networks.

Today, most Web-based payments rely on Secure Sockets Layer (SSL) encryption, which offers cost-effective protection from eavesdroppers but little in the way of authentication. The Secure Electronic Transaction (SET) protocol is more complex than SSL and aims to remedy its shortcomings. SET-based systems are emerging slowly in the marketplace, however. In 1999, no single, widely accepted payment technology exists for e-business. Instead, various technologies firms, financial institutions, and payment brands support multiple technologies and standards. We expect that in two years' time, consolidation will reduce the number of payment alternatives.

"We fully expect that as e-business evolves, the relative importance of some technologies and trends will become accentuated even as others fade in importance."

Finally, there are the key technologies that underline all aspect of e-business and define the infrastructure needed to support e-business' existence, health, and future growth. This is the focus of the final chapter, "E-Business Infrastructure."

This chapter looks at the lower levels of e-business platform technology and then moves to the higher levels of application programming on the Internet. The discussion includes aspects of Web-based interactions such as browsing and downloading, e-business server architectures, and security technologies that affect the e-business arena.

The upshot for transitioning to an e-business environment is that, from a technical point of view, development and deployment of e-business functionality never stops. Firms can expect to constantly reinvent and reinvest in their Web sites to leverage changes in e-business technology, e-business practice models, and the competitive environment. Managing product immaturity, a rapidly changing vendor community, and the migration to the next generation of the Web will test the creativity and resolve of the best management teams. As such, decision-makers are well advised to plan for multiple and more rapid life cycles for their e-business practice models and technology.

Executive Summary

Web-based technology allows companies to emulate or substitute almost the entire physical world experience between the buyer and the seller with computer systems. Retailers use the technology to engage consumers and facilitate transactions. Corporations are embracing the Web as a platform to automate their business-to-business procurement processes. Aggregators use the Web to bring together multiple sellers and buyers in electronic marketplaces.

The Web is being adopted by many economic players, many of which have similar functional requirements. Sellers must attract customers to their online storefronts. Within those virtual stores, sellers need to present their products to potential buyers—a function usually handled by online catalogs. Shopping carts provide a metaphor (and the functionality) for product selection prior to the ordering process. If the final product is the result of combining components and features that work together to meet a specific customer's needs, the merchant must have a way to present the various possibilities to the customer, recalculate prices and options, and display them in an intuitive, interactive fashion. Configurator software most often provides the mechanism for this required interactivity.

The merchant also needs a way to receive the customer's order, process payment, provide shipping instructions, and send confirmation to the customer that these steps have occurred. Some e-business sites must support fixed-price transactions; others need to provide a negotiated-price environment. For many organizations, the ability to integrate these e-business processes with back-office systems is crucial.

Buyers in the business-to-business procurement process need online capability to engage with the seller, search for and select items, and complete the transaction. In addition, a buying organization needs mechanisms to ensure that a purchasing policy is enforced within the organization as well as be able to manage and analyze its approved purchases.

Until recently, many high-end e-business sites either were partially or almost entirely custom-built to meet unique needs and to provide functionality not available elsewhere. However, software, applications, and tools vendors have made significant advances in providing more complete platforms, software components, and standards-based extensions. These advances allow Internet commerce sites to assemble a selection of best-of-breed applications coupled with custom development (whether in-house or contracted) to create a strong presence for business on the Web. In addition, a broad range of packaged solutions now are available.

This chapter focuses on the major software components of e-business and the frameworks available in the marketplace. E-business platforms and applications continue to evolve, and new products appear at a dizzying rate. The vendors and products discussed here represent a sample of the e-business software currently available.

Categories of Web Business

Web-enabled business is an emerging channel for connecting buyers and sellers. This channel is unique because primarily it is electronic, minimizing the physical barriers between the buyer and the seller. As such, this channel also represents a major shift in how buyers and sellers interact to effect an exchange.

Emerging from these considerations are multiple models of e-business. One model is designed to engage and facilitate business-to-consumer transactions. Another model is focused on enabling business-to-business processes (both sell-side and buy-side). A third and more nascent model is an electronic marketplace in which an aggregator brings together multiple buyers and sellers.

SELL-SIDE ELECTRONIC BUSINESS

Sell-side software provides solutions for enterprises to sell their goods and services to consumers or other businesses via the Web. This category includes applications used by sellers for marketing and selling their products on the Web as well as applications used for handling order management and fulfillment. Within this group are several subcategories of software, including catalogs, configurators, shopping carts, requisition or quotation, personalization, order management, and payment. Many software packages provide some level of integration into existing back-end systems for order fulfillment, logistics, inventory management, and financial record keeping. Most recently, certain vertical market applications have emerged that offer banking and other financial services such as online bill presentment and payment to both businesses and consumers.

See "Electronic Bill Presentment and Payment" on page 151 for more information.

BUY-SIDE ELECTRONIC BUSINESS

This category includes applications used by organizations to manage their purchasing. Within this category are systems for managing the purchase of maintenance, repair, and operations (MRO) items (sometimes called indirect goods) and, more recently, for services, capital equipment, and direct goods (materials incorporated into the manufactured product). For corporate-level e-business, buy-side software provides solutions for enterprise procurement and extends the procurement process to the individual corporate desktop. These systems may include applications for workflow approval, user identification and authorization, payment technology (such as purchasing cards), and integration into enterprise resource planning (ERP) systems or budget systems. Buy-side applications often consolidate items from multiple supplier catalogs into an enterprise catalog, use customized catalogs from sell-side suppliers, or provide pointers to preferred supplier catalogs. These catalogs can be hosted by the buying organization, the selling organization, or a third-party provider.

THE ELECTRONIC MARKETPLACE

Marketplace solutions are the newest model of e-business. The Web infrastructure is being used to develop and facilitate online trading communities. These applications create a virtual community that brings together multiple suppliers and buyers. In this case, the marketplace provider supplies the application infrastructure that allows multiple parties to transact business. Auctions often are part of a marketplace solution. Typically, marketplace applications are used by particular types of businesses, such as the health-care industry or industries that manufacture or purchase automotive parts, electronic components, or chemicals.

E-Business Software

E-business software components came to market in late 1995 from IBM, Netscape, and Open Market. However, many transaction-oriented Web sites still are custom-built to meet unique needs and to provide functionality that could not be purchased off-the-shelf. Vendor offerings vary widely in the extent to which they provide a ready-made solution. Some products offer a tools-oriented platform approach that provides a programming, transaction, and database management environment. Other products are out-of-the-box solutions that simplify the creation of a storefront or e-catalog by using wizards (which guide users through the process) or design templates.

Web commerce applications typically target a few parts of a complete Web commerce system, such as a storefront that consists of a catalog, an ordering mechanism, and a payment method. These packaged systems reduce programming and development time and enable less-technical individuals to get an e-business site up and running. Packaged systems provide the basic components and out-of-the-box business logic, and they can be used immediately (with some configuration) to perform useful turnkey Web commerce functions, although those functions may not match the requirements of the business exactly. Such packaged systems employ installation or setup features such as wizards and design templates to achieve this functionality. As these packaged applications evolve and become more mature, they often are marketed in "editions." The system's base edition often is supplemented with a developer's edition that allows custom programming or a hosting edition that allows a third party to host multiple, discrete storefronts on behalf of its subscribers.

Commerce platforms and associated toolkits are intended for e-business sites that require a great deal of customization and flexibility. They provide base-level services such as session management as well as application programming interfaces (APIs) and a framework for building the modules that e-commerce applications require (or for plugging in third-party software components such as personalization, merchandising, or electronic data interchange [EDI] capabilities). Unlike packaged applications, these products typically do not provide business logic or process rules. Although powerful, extensible, scalable, and full-featured, commerce platforms require sophisticated programmers to implement their capabilities.

The common evolutionary path for implementing software solutions is to move from custom, in-house development to the use of platforms and application toolkits, and then to packaged applications. For example, 20 years ago, many companies developed their own accounting applications; today, virtually no business would consider such a project. Web commerce software is such a rapidly developing market that companies often take a combination of these three approaches. Until recently, many high-end e-business sites either were partially or almost entirely custom-built to meet unique needs and to provide functionality not available elsewhere. However, software and applications vendors have made significant advances in offering more complete platforms, software components, and standards-based extensions. These advances allow Web commerce sites to assemble a selection of best-of-breed applications, coupled with custom development to create a strong presence for business on the Web.

Application Architecture

Web computing provides the platform for a new style of application architecture and deployment. Web-based e-business systems consist of numerous components operating in a reliable and secure manner.

Figure 16 on page 52 illustrates how a simple e-business site might be assembled. The primary element is a Web server, which runs a program that implements the HyperText Transport Protocol (HTTP) to exchange messages between the server and a Web browser. The server typically hosts the seller's Web home page, state management procedures, and catalog and order methods. Another element may include a payment gateway or an external service to validate and authorize credit-card transactions or other

"Web computing provides the platform for a new style of application architecture and deployment. Web-based e-business systems consist of numerous components operating in a reliable and secure manner."

See "Maintaining State and User Activity in HTTP" on page 191 for more information.

payment methods. A third element may be integration between the Web storefront and back-office systems and applications. Integration allows traditional retailers and catalog merchants to leverage their existing systems and infrastructure.

FIGURE 16: OVERVIEW OF A BASIC INTERNET E-BUSINESS ARCHITECTURE

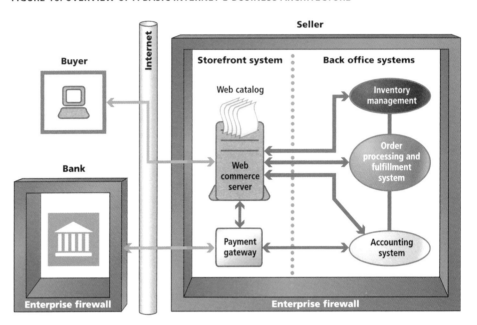

As e-business sites have become more functionally complex and feature-rich, and as traffic to these sites has increased, the simple Web server architecture has expanded rapidly into tiers of application and database servers. This expanded architecture allows high-performance e-business sites to achieve greater scalability and flexibility.

Figure 17 on page 53 illustrates a typical architecture in which the Web server acts as the initial entry point into the site and dispatches appropriate requests (such as a catalog search) to the commerce servers. For sites with many hundreds or thousands of simultaneous users, load-balancing procedures may route requests to various commerce servers that, in turn, respond directly back to the Web browser. These commerce servers typically assume responsibility for conducting the transaction and maintaining state with the Web browser.

Object architectures such as Common Object Request Broker Architecture (CORBA), Distributed Component Object Model (DCOM), or Enterprise JavaBeans (EJB) play two primary roles in Internet commerce applications. First, they may be used for the actual implementation of the application. Second, they may be used to simplify and enhance integration with other systems using the same object model.

Storefront Components

Online catalogs provide a mechanism for sellers to present their products to potential buyers. Configurator software guides customers to define a product that meets given criteria and whose features and options are mutually compatible. Once items have been selected or products configured, the purchase transaction needs to be concluded: selections verified, prices extended, orders totaled, tax calculated, payment method selected, shipping choice determined, rolled-up order presented to the buyer, and order confirmation communicated back to the buyer. In buy-side procurement

FIGURE 17: OVERVIEW OF A MULTITIER INTERNET E-BUSINESS ARCHITECTURE

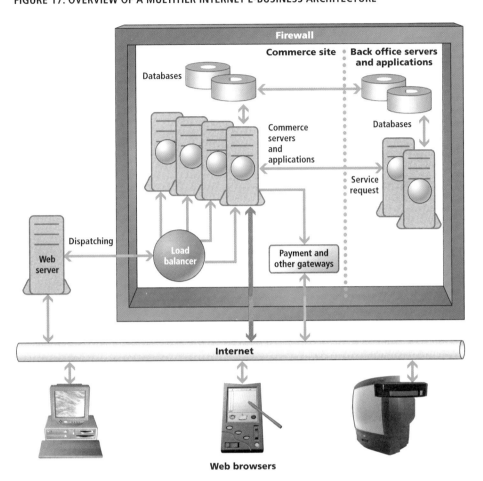

activities, additional steps involving approval, other workflow actions, and managing contract compliance often are introduced into this process. Various software modules assist with these processes.

CATALOGS

Catalogs and other content management systems are used to present customers with information about goods and services offered for sale, bid, or auction. Some catalog applications are designed to manage large numbers of individual items, and search capabilities help buyers navigate quickly to the items they want. Other applications are designed to emphasize merchandise presentation and special offers, much as a retail store is laid out to encourage impulse or add-on buying. As with other aspects of e-business, it is important to match catalog design and functionality to a company's business goals. Although two applications may be called e-business catalogs, one may be completely inappropriate for a particular company, and the other may be a near-perfect match.

Design and Functionality. E-business catalogs primarily are designed to present products to potential buyers as they browse a Web site or use the site's search function. These catalogs typically provide more information about products than paper catalogs. For example, along with traditional attributes such as item number or stock-keeping unit (SKU), item description, and unit price, the e-catalog may provide links to allow customers to access related information such as a photograph of the item, sample color swatches, product or engineering specifications, a material safety data sheet, computer-aided design (CAD) drawings, or a video demonstration. Consumer catalogs also may provide information supplied by other customers (such as book or product reviews) or an opportunity to chat with other shoppers on the Web site.

Electronic catalog software also may present opportunities for cross-selling, such as recommending software, a modem, a leather case, or other accessories when a buyer is purchasing a personal digital assistant (PDA). Or, within the context of a shopper's interaction with a catalog item, the software might suggest a more full-featured version of the desired product that costs more or offers a higher margin to the seller than the original choice. This process is called "up-selling."

More sophisticated catalogs, especially those used primarily in business-to-business transactions, often have real-time inventory status (such as quantity-available), elaborate cross-sell or up-sell cross-references, and incentive structures (such as multiple volume discount pricing tiers or case-lot versus broken-lot pricing). Catalog items also may contain built-in procurement rules that impose limitations on quantity, volume, shipping destination, or shipping method of certain items.

Catalogs may support special customization for corporate clients. These catalogs might include only preapproved items, employee appreciation items, special product bundles (such as a new employee startup kit), or prenegotiated prices. Catalogs focused on the consumer retail market may support special promotional features, branding techniques, or seasonal sale pricing.

Catalog content—that is, individual items and their attributes—typically is stored in either relational or object databases. These databases contain schemas of varying detail to support advanced features and functionality, complex data relationships, and associated multimedia objects. This data then is incorporated into HyperText Markup Language (HTML) pages that are sent to the customer's Web browser in response to a catalog query or search.

See "Connections to DBMSs" on page 205 for more information.

Accurate prices and descriptions—as well as availability or lead time for products—are of primary importance to buyers. Components of an e-business Web site that require frequent updating or involve user interaction most often are created or assembled from databases. Usually, the database that is the foundation for the electronic catalog is populated and updated on a periodic basis from the seller's back-office inventory management system. Alternatively, the catalog system may directly query the inventory system dynamically.

Search Capabilities. The process of searching or browsing a catalog initiates a query to the database. A script running on the server reads the data records returned by the query and then assembles and formats the data according to a predefined (and perhaps personalized) template. This on-the-fly process produces HTML for display in the buyer's browser window. The dynamically generated page display can provide navigational links so that a buyer can drill down to greater levels of product detail. Server-based scripts or client scripting techniques often are employed to enhance the navigation, display, and content manipulation features further.

It is important to consider how a potential buyer will interact with the information presented in a catalog. Some catalog search interfaces work well for buyers who know precisely what they are looking for, whereas other catalog search interfaces are designed for hierarchical browsing or serendipitous discovery.

Electronic catalogs typically include search features such as keyword, full-text, parametric, and associative searches. Keyword searches let customers search using words or phrases that have been predefined by the catalog's author. Full-text searches look for occurrences of the actual text data entered by the user. Parametric searches allow customers to search by characteristics or attributes (parameters) of the item under consideration. Parametric searches often facilitate the acquisition of components, such as those used in manufacturing. Associative searches, conducted using a fuzzy-logic system, retrieve data associated with the searched-for term.

Some catalogs may be structured to provide the ability to group a diverse number of items into a category such as "toys, games, and books suitable for ages 5 to 7." (Items can be part of multiple categories.) Or, a more complex example might be a preassembled aggregation of all items and equipment needed to set up an advanced medical imaging-radiographic facility. The presentation could include interactive visual elements and illustrations of room plans.

In February 1999, the United Nations (in conjunction with Dun & Bradstreet) released a global product classification standard, the Standard Product and Service Classifications (SPSC). The SPSC is a ten-digit hierarchical coding system. The first two digits define a broad category followed by an eight-digit detailed product identifier. The final two digits of the eight-digit code identify the business function (such as lease or rental). For example, Aspect has included the SPSC in its Very Important Parts and Very Important Suppliers databases, which it licenses as part of its data content service. By including this standard, Aspect allows users to correlate internal commodity coding systems with the industry standard, thus allowing procurement professionals to identify commodities easily.

Scope. Catalogs also are expanding in scope. Some catalogs include links to external content such as product reviews and industry news. Some include customer feedback and discussions. Also emerging are aggregate catalogs of products from multiple suppliers associated with a specific market segment such as office products, metals, or laboratory supplies. In addition, specific enterprise procurement organizations have assembled catalogs (or had catalogs assembled for them) from multiple suppliers.

In business-to-business selling, catalogs may be hosted by the buying organization, by the supplier, or by a third party.

CATALOG SOFTWARE VENDORS

Many e-business packaged applications include capabilities for catalog creation and maintenance. In addition, several software products are available to assist developers in creating catalogs for sell-side and buy-side applications. Some vendors may supply both catalog software and content. The following is a representative sample of available catalog software.

Actinic. Actinic's Actinic Catalog guides a merchant through establishing product records that compose a catalog. The software includes fields for product descriptions and services; taxes; graphics or pictures; pricing; the maximum quantity available; and so on. Once created, the catalog can be uploaded to the merchant's Web site. As orders are received, they are collected in a file on the merchant's Web site, and e-mail notification of the orders is sent to the merchant. The merchant periodically checks the site to retrieve and process the orders.

Aspect Development. Aspect Development's CSM Catalog Management can create and manage multilevel electronic component and supplier management (CSM) catalogs. It conducts parametric searches and supports multiple coding schemes, including SPSC. In June 1998, Aspect developed Preferred Catalog, a subscription service in which Aspect creates and maintains catalog content for customers.

Harbinger. Harbinger's Knowbility program helps companies manage and maintain catalogs by organizing, labeling, and centralizing product information. Knowbility converts legacy product data into a Harbinger template where products are assigned new labels and attributes. Once product data has been rationalized (organized and labeled), customers can search a merchant's catalog using natural-language queries. The Knowbility software translates or maps common terms to internal product labels, allowing employees and customers to locate product information easily. In addition, Harbinger supplies catalog content.

Mercado. Mercado Software's Catalog Builder supports natural-language queries and can conduct categorical, parametric, and associative searches. The software also can gather data on customer activity for marketing purposes. Catalog Builder consists of two major components. The Catalog Publisher (used in the development environment) allows developers to select the databases or files to be cataloged. The Catalog Server (used in the run-time environment) links to the catalog and is used to conduct searches and return results. Catalog Builder is designed for use on Microsoft's Site Server Commerce Edition and features APIs to access ActiveX controls.

Requisite Technology. Requisite Technology sells electronic cataloging technology to enterprise software companies to embed in their applications; creates electronic catalogs for suppliers; sells catalog subscriptions; and offers custom content conversion services to organizations. Requisite's BugsEye is a catalog management program that integrates text, parametric, and navigational search techniques. BugsEye is written in Java and can be integrated as a component of third-party enterprise software from companies such as Oracle. Requisite targets distributors and manufacturers in the business-to-business venue.

MERCHANDISING

"Merchandising, sales promotions, or affinity programs are becoming common in e-business and typically are initiated through a seller's catalog or Web site."

Merchandising, sales promotions, or affinity programs (such as frequent-flyer programs, buyer rewards, and so on) are becoming common in e-business and typically are initiated through a seller's catalog or Web site. Some promotions occur beyond that site, however. For example, electronic coupons can be distributed via e-mail to customers to encourage repeat purchasing. Direct mail campaigns can be implemented via e-mail, and software packages to assist that function include e2 Software's SalesOffice and Revnet's UnityMail. Another vendor, Responsys, markets a service called Interact to manage online direct marketing campaigns.

More recently, specialized applications, such as Blue Martini Software's Blue Martini E-Merchandising System, have become available. Its merchandising modules include the following:

- *Merchandise Management*—Allows the site developer to create and manage all content in one place. The developer can build a flexible product hierarchy containing all products and product variations. Using an unlimited number of attributes, each product can be described in full detail. The module allows for multiple price lists and multiple currencies. The module can be used to develop cross-selling opportunities or to create product assortments.

- **Customer Management**—Allows the retailer to collect data on each customer and to develop detailed customer profiles. This data collection includes not only data provided by the customer, but also observed data (such as additions to a shopping cart) or inferred data such as shopping patterns. It also allows for recognition of returning customers and support of loyalty programs.

- **Micro Marketing**—Assists the retailer in analyzing aggregate data about products and customers, matching, for example, customer attributes with product attributes.

- **Tools**—Provides tracking and reporting tools to help the retailer conduct ongoing evaluation and refinement of the operation. A workflow designer is included to help the user fine-tune the processes needed for a particular business.

CONFIGURATORS

If the product being sold has simple features, few or no conflicts between features within the product, few variable components, and straightforward pricing, then a simple catalog may be sufficient to store the product's attributes. An example of such a product is a book.

On the other hand, if the product's feature set is large, maps to a broad range of customer requirements, can be composed of many interconnected elements—some of which are incompatible with each other—and is priced accordingly, then it is unlikely a catalog will be sufficiently flexible to model the various product lines and options. Examples of such products include networking or telecommunications equipment, high-end servers, desktop computers, automobiles, high-performance bicycles, life insurance policies, or mutual fund investment opportunities. In the case of such products, a configurator is the foundation technology to provide the needed functionality.

A configurator is a special-purpose software tool that allows a user to define a product that meets given criteria or needs and whose features and options can be combined to work together. Configurators also may compute the price of an assembled item, calculate payments, or compare the difference between leasing and buying or between buy and repair options.

Typically, a configurator contains a reasoning engine; a configuration model builder; an explanation facility that gives the user a context-sensitive rationale for why a choice is unavailable as well as suggestions for alternatives; and APIs to external languages, applications, and databases. Configuration software needs an underlying component or product database, program logic to define rules or express constraints, and programmed operations that can evaluate combinations based on rules or constraints in concert with the buyer's stated criteria.

Initially, configurators were add-on modules to back-office ERP systems and were used by trained sales specialists or as part of sales force automation (SFA) tools. However, e-business promotes unassisted selling, sometimes called customer self-service, and configurators with intuitive Web interfaces are beginning to be deployed in this environment.

Following is a list of representative configurator vendors and their products:

Calico Technology. Calico Technology's eSales Suite is a set of Java-based applications that guide customers through the purchase process. One of the modules, eSales Configurator, permits customer requirements and requested product attributes to be matched automatically and products and services to be configured accurately. It also provides the opportunity to up-sell and cross-sell by suggesting complementary products and options.

PersonaLogic. PersonaLogic, acquired by America Online (AOL) in late 1998, creates interactive decision guides. The software asks the shopper questions to determine which products might satisfy the shopper's preference. For example, a car buyer can specify features that matter most, such as safety, cost, performance, and size. The software then retrieves items that match the shopper's criteria. Shoppers also can access a quick-compare table that presents a side-by-side comparison of product features.

Selectica. Selectica provides software and tools so software developers can embed configuration expertise into e-business applications. Selectica's ACE Enterprise configuration server application allows the selection and configuration of complex goods and services online. It is a Java application that uses the Java Runtime Environment (JRE).

Trilogy Software. Trilogy Software's SC Config, a component of its Selling Chain Suite, primarily is used by distributors and resellers to deliver quotes based on several product variables. The SC Config also can evaluate product options that would best meet a customer's needs. Trilogy Software's Selling Chain Suite consists of selling applications such as the SC Catalog, SC Commission, SC Pricer, and SC Promotion.

SHOPPING CARTS

In the consumer or retail venue, the shopping cart (also called a shopping basket or shopping bag) is a convenient metaphor into which a buyer can place items selected for purchase. Employing a familiar model from the physical world, the shopping cart holds a record of the selections a buyer is considering for purchase until the buyer is finished shopping and is ready to complete the purchasing process. At any point in the process, the buyer can review items in the cart, remove items, or change the quantity of an item. Some shopping carts can remember the buyer's selection between sessions; this capability is known as a persistent shopping cart. A buyer can leave, then return to the Web site, and still be at the same point in the shopping process.

Most e-business shopping sites use some variant of the shopping cart metaphor to contain and review items or products selected prior to the completion of the order process. Sites optionally may provide one or more shopping aids. For example, an aid might be visibility—that is, the shopping cart always is located in a frame on the current page. This visibility aid can provide immediate knowledge of items already selected for purchase or display a running total of the amount of money spent.

TAX CALCULATION

Business systems often rely on integrated third-party tax calculation software to determine local, state, or other taxes they are required to collect. A niche software industry has developed to provide automated tax calculations and track tax responsibilities of merchants in the U.S. (Similarly, a tax compliance software industry is just beginning to address consumption taxes outside the U.S.) These packages primarily are indexed by the ZIP code (postal code) of the shipping address specified by the buyer. The software also can handle situations in which multiple tax authorities impose different tax burdens across a single ZIP code. The software typically is kept current with monthly updates.

These systems generally also provide additional functionality. For example, jurisdiction-specific logic (discussed shortly) and product or commodity data may be stored along with up-to-date tax rates. This setup allows the appropriate tax computation in a particular jurisdiction in which, for example, a clothing purchase transaction of less than $175

"Most e-business shopping sites use some variant of the shopping cart metaphor to contain and review items or products selected prior to the completion of the order process."

is not taxable, but a clothing transaction of more than that amount is taxable. Where a computed rate needs to be overridden for a specific transaction (for example, because the purchase is being made by an exempt government agency), a reversing transaction is generated. This reversing transaction is given a date and time stamp and a reason code indicating who made the reversing transaction and when and why it was initiated.

Tax software also can capture data from the seller's accounting system, make calculations, and produce audit trails for the generation of reports and returns. For example, the software can produce ready-to-submit sales tax returns for state and local tax jurisdictions. The system can generate a paper tax return or a file for electronic filing programs.

Several vendors of automated tax compliance products are expanding into the international Internet e-commerce market and providing software products with international tax calculation, audit, and reporting capabilities. For example, for more than two decades, Taxware has provided software for sales/use, payroll, and property tax calculations for sales of goods in the U.S. For international e-business, Taxware has built a comprehensive international tax capability that can integrate with either storefront or back-office systems and can be embedded or interfaced with commerce servers or other seller systems. The tax computation is address-driven and comes with a product taxability matrix and six-level jurisdiction logic—ship-to, ship-from, point or port of origin, point or port of arrival, bill-to, and point of title passage—to handle the most complex trade processing. Taxware also interfaces with Web-based e-business servers. (See Figure 18 on page 60.)

The proper operation of tax compliance systems depends upon reliable data about tax rates and regulations being available to the merchant. In addition, uncertainty regarding the classification of the transaction for tax purposes may limit the capabilities of such systems in some instances. However, these potential limitations are a factor in only a small percentage of transactions.

Products to calculate customs duty and perform other shipping logistics to enable international trade are being developed by other vendors. Companies selling on the Web will be able to purchase third-party application software or outsource international logistics and export/import trade compliance.

SHIPPING LOGISTICS

In many order-processing systems, the shipping charge often is set at a fixed fee based on the number of items purchased, weight of the shipment, or the monetary value of the order. With the connectivity of the Web and the interoperability of discrete systems, shipping charges can be determined precisely, in real time, and a tracking number can be assigned to the shipment at the time the order is placed.

TanData's Progistics Merchant module provides global shipping charges in real time, validation of destinations served by major carriers and associated transit times, and tracking numbers for each package. It can use the seller's negotiated rates from the carrier. It allows the buyer to select the speed of delivery and return carrier-approved tracking numbers as hyperlinks at the time orders are confirmed to let buyers track their packages. The low-end version offers United Parcel Service (UPS) shipping. The Enterprise edition allows the seller to add additional carrier modules such as Airborne, BAX, DHL, Emery, Federal Express (FedEx), RPS, USPS, and others as well as to support multiple distribution sites. The product can interface with e-business products from IBM, iCat, Intershop, Microsoft, and Oracle as well as with the seller's back-end warehouse, inventory, or customer management systems.

FIGURE 18: HOW TAXWARE'S SALES TAX SOFTWARE INTERFACES WITH THE COMMERCE SERVER

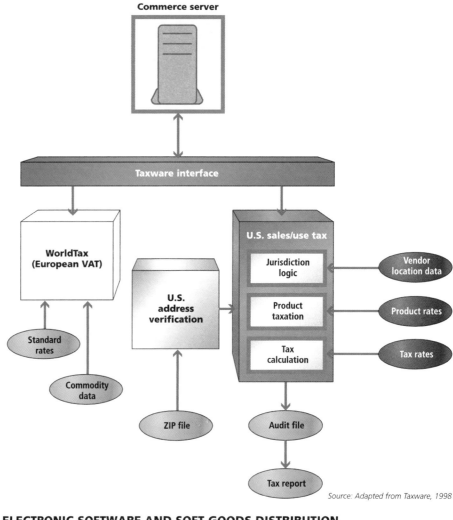

Source: Adapted from Taxware, 1998

ELECTRONIC SOFTWARE AND SOFT GOODS DISTRIBUTION

Another component of an e-business system is the delivery of digital goods to the desktop. The most common item delivered in this manner today is software for direct purchase, rental, or pay-per-use. To facilitate this model of delivery, a niche market of software products is appearing. Typically, these products combine encryption algorithms and compression technologies, and they often are downloaded with files such as a license agreement, installation directions, or marketing materials. Representative vendors in this market space include ClearCommerce, Digital River, Open Market, and Preview Systems. For example, Open Market's Folio publishing products, when integrated with Open Market's OM-Transact, allow publishers to sell content over the Web.

PAYMENT SYSTEMS

Currently, payment in most business-to-consumer e-business systems is handled via credit cards. Credit-card payment systems are common add-on components to e-business systems. Typically, these modules implement Secure Sockets Layer (SSL) or Secure Electronic Transaction (SET) as security standards. E-business sites also can choose to outsource the payment function. ICOMS and Paymentech are two vendors that offer payment-handling services.

See "CyberCash" on page 164 and "IBM" on page 164 for more information.

Other vendors provide fraud detection software or services. For example, CyberSource is a service provider that offers fraud detection using its own technology. It collects more than 30 pieces of data and performs more than 150 calculations, examining factors such as spending trends and where the credit card is being used. Upon receiving an order, the merchant sends a summary of the order, delivery address, name, and credit card number to CyberSource. CyberSource then produces a weighted score that allows a merchant to accept or reject an order. If accepted, the merchant processes the order through the bank (or, alternatively, CyberSource performs the payment-processing services).

Commerce Platforms

One set of vendor offerings for e-business, commonly referred to as commerce platforms, provides software, a framework, and tools for the development of e-business capabilities.

Commerce platforms are intended primarily for midsized and large e-business sites that require a great deal of customization and flexibility. These platforms make it easier to develop e-business applications such as feature-rich catalogs or ordering systems. They provide a well-defined set of APIs as well as integration of common modules that e-business applications require, such as payment methods or shipping logistics. However, these platforms require a high level of technical and programming expertise to implement their capabilities. Deployments are complex undertakings that require application development, integration, and maintenance.

Commerce platform offerings typically bundle the software for an HTTP server, database server, and application servers together with tools to build and maintain the commerce site. The site components usually include a catalog, order-taking and payment functions, security (in the form of SSL or SET), programming methods to manage state and persistence over a session, and basic site-management tools. Commerce platforms also offer some mode of back-office integration (usually via APIs), the ability to populate an electronic catalog from existing data, and the ability to integrate third-party tools and applications. Commerce platforms provide database management facilities, transaction management, scalability, and support for industry standards such as Component Object Model (COM), Distributed COM (DCOM), CORBA, and Java to build distributed systems.

See "Maintaining State and User Activity in HTTP" on page 191 for more information.

Following is a list of representative commerce platform vendors and their product offerings:

IBM. Version 3 of IBM's Net.Commerce is available in two offerings: Start and Pro. IBM's Net.Commerce Pro, a more advanced version of IBM's out-of-the-box Net.Commerce Start product, allows enterprises to develop and manage high-performance e-business sites. Net.Commerce Pro runs on various operating systems including IBM's AIX and OS/390, Microsoft's Windows NT, and Sun's Solaris, and it works with Lotus' Domino Go Webserver (included), Domino Web Server, or Netscape Enterprise Web Server. It includes IBM's DB2 Universal Database 5.0 but also supports Open Database Connectivity (ODBC) connections to Oracle databases. Net.Commerce Pro offers all the capabilities offered in Net.Commerce Start. (See Figure 19 on page 62.)

See "IBM" on page 68 for more information on Net.Commerce Start.

Net.Commerce Pro includes advanced catalog tools to create intelligent catalogs as well as tools for back-end integration with enterprise applications (via EDI and IBM's MQSeries, Customer Information Control System [CICS], and Information Management System [IMS] products). The Product Advisor function is a smart search and filtering engine that lets buyers select attributes to narrow searches. The product

See "EAI: Packaged Enterprise Middleware" on page 130 for more information.

FIGURE 19: IBM'S NET.COMMERCE PRODUCTS

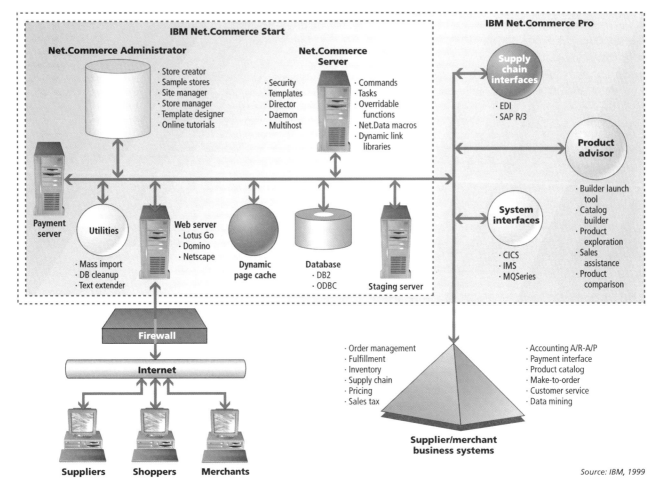

Source: IBM, 1999

exploration, sales assistance, and product comparison features are used to set up rules-based searches through a diverse set of products. The software takes a buyer through an evaluation criteria dialog, and a product comparison feature generates a tabular side-by-side comparison of product attributes. IBM's Catalog Architect content management software is included with Net.Commerce Pro.

Net.Commerce can be integrated with numerous third-party products and software applications to provide an array of e-business functionality. For example, Net Perceptions' Realtime Recommendation Engine can be used with Net.Commerce to direct personalized information to a merchant site's customers. A UPS tracking capability is available. Other third-party products assist with activities such as personalization and target-market merchandising, customer service, automated e-mail response, supply chain management (SCM), payments, and ERP. Most recently, a Java-based auction module was made available for evaluation for selected client installations.

Net.Commerce also supports CyberCash for payment processing through the buyer's financial institution. A provision for the concurrent display of euro and national currencies is included in Net.Commerce.

A group of tools is provided to facilitate the integration of Net.Commerce 3.0 with other enterprise systems and middleware. Net.Commerce interfaces to IBM's IBM Global Services EDI for message translation and delivery. Net.Commerce uses IBM Global Services

See "Net Perceptions" on page 85 for more information.

interfaces to send the information required for an ANSI X12 850 message (purchase order) and to receive the 855 message (order acknowledgment). The acknowledgment is communicated back to the buyer through the Net.Commerce system. Support also is provided for a plug-in interface that allows third-party EDI translation software to interact with Net.Commerce.

For SAP installations, Net.Commerce includes a tool to enable the automated entry of Net.Commerce orders into the R/3 system; order confirmation back to Net.Commerce; price, tax, and shipping calculations in the R/3 system; and order status query.

For the development or integration of more advanced features and functionality, code can be written in C++, Java, or JavaScript. Net.Commerce 3.0 also implements object communication standards, including CORBA, DCOM, and Enterprise JavaBeans.

Net.Commerce Hosting Server allows Internet service providers (ISPs) or commerce service providers (CSPs) to implement Net.Commerce and, in turn, offer application development and hosting services to enterprises that do not want to develop or maintain their own sites.

Commerce service providers are outsourcing businesses that build and maintain commerce sites.

Microsoft. Microsoft's Site Server Commerce Edition (version 3.0) was released in April 1998. Designed for business-to-consumer applications, it contains shopping and buying processes. Site Server Commerce Edition relies on Microsoft's Active Server Pages (ASP) technology, the company's alternative to Common Gateway Interface (CGI) scripts, which allows Web pages to interact with databases and other programs. Web pages are generated dynamically from ASP and sent to the user's browser by Internet Information Server 4.0 (IIS, Microsoft's basic Web server). Site Server Commerce Edition relies on ActiveX components that perform the actual e-business tasks as well as a Microsoft SQL Server database to store content, customer information, and order information. Site Server also can work with any ODBC-compliant database. (See Figure 20 on page 64.)

See "Common Gateway Interface" on page 183 and "Active Server Pages" on page 184 for more information.

Site Server Commerce Edition relies on a set of COM components called the Order Processing Pipeline (OPP) that performs all the buying functions for a Web store. Its first function is the customer's selection of an item to add to the shopping cart; its last function is the acceptance of an order. The OPP has 13 components that can be configured by administrators: Product Information, Merchant Information, Shopper Information, Order Initialization, Order Check, Item Price Adjust, Order Price Adjust, Shipping, Handling, Tax, Order Total, Inventory, and Payment Accept. Site Server Commerce Edition is integrated with Microsoft Transaction Server (MTS) for transaction management. The Commerce Interchange Pipeline (CIP) enables the interchange of structured business data using the Internet or existing EDI systems.

Site Server Commerce Edition has a Buy Now feature with both server and client capabilities (the latter are available as part of Internet Explorer or as a Netscape plug-in). When a shopper clicks on a Buy-Now-enabled link on a Web page, the Buy Now wizard opens a new dialog box within the shopper's browser window. The window shows a title bar containing the name of the store; an expanded product image; an options section for choosing color, size, and quantity; a Next button for continuing the shopping process; and a Cancel button to abort a purchase.

The Buy Now wizard is an ASP application that runs on the client. The Site Server Commerce Edition database can supply product data for Buy Now transactions, and order data from Buy Now transactions can be stored there.

FIGURE 20: MICROSOFT'S COMMERCE SERVER STRUCTURE AND COMPONENTS

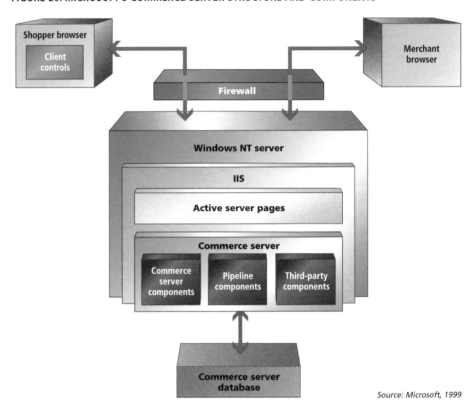

Source: Microsoft, 1999

In a push model of message distribution, the server sends information to the client, although the client may not have requested the information specifically.

A "cartridge" is Oracle's terminology for a program module that plugs into the Web application server through a Web request broker (a CORBA-compliant object request broker that allows plug-and-play of program and application extensions).

See "Shipping Logistics" on page 59 for more information.

Site Server Commerce Edition also includes an ad server that supports ad schedule management and targeted delivery, a push-based content system based on Microsoft's Active Channel, and an auction component.

Oracle. Oracle's Internet Commerce Server 1.1 (ICS) is integrated closely with other Oracle products such as the Oracle8 relational database management system (RDBMS) and Oracle Application Server, and it is built on Oracle Universal Server and Oracle Web Application Server products. CyberCash, Portland Software, TanData, and VeriFone, among others, have created cartridges to extend functionality of ICS for payment services, shipping and handling, tax calculation, and soft goods delivery. (See Figure 21 on page 65.)

Oracle's ICS Store Manager module provides templates for setup and configuration of the store, products, content, and business rules. Store Manager also provides support for product incentives such as coupons, special sale offers, and discounts. ICS can support the marketing and sales of hard or soft goods such as publications, financial data, or software products. The Oracle Universal Data Server is used to generate dynamic Web content, such as price and product descriptions; it uses server-based Java to manipulate and convert data from an Oracle database and format the data into HTML on-the-fly.

ICS provides APIs for integration into back-end enterprise systems such as order entry and inventory as well as for payment interfaces to third-party payment, shipping and handling, and taxation applications. For example, ICS is integrated with TanData's Progistics Merchant software for online shipping and handling.

FIGURE 21: ORACLE'S INTERNET COMMERCE SERVER

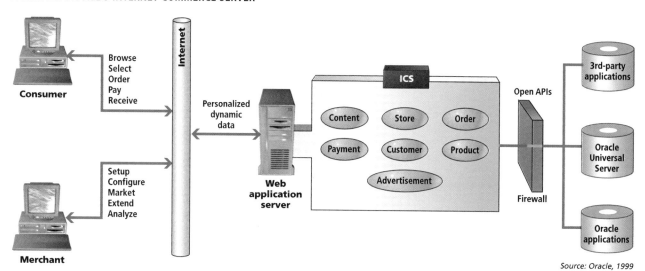

Source: Oracle, 1999

ICS also provides tracking capabilities to capture customer behavior and log the information for analysis and reporting purposes. ICS includes a wide range of predefined reports to analyze store activity. The ICS Staging System is used to create an area for testing new additions and enhancements before their replication to the production version of the commerce site.

In December 1998, Oracle announced the beta release of Oracle Payment Server 1.0, a Java cartridge deployed on the Oracle Web Application Server. It bundles third-party payment systems from CyberCash and ICVerify and supports credit cards, electronic cash, and other payment methods.

Sell-Side Packaged E-Business Applications

Purchasing and implementing a packaged sell-side e-business application is an alternative to developing a custom application using an e-business platform or toolkit product. As the number of organizations using the Web to sell their products has grown, it has created the opportunity for software vendors to sell packaged applications. This situation also reflects a maturing of the technology used for Web e-business sites: The earliest adopters had no choice but to develop their own software (in many cases building on a generic Web server because even basic e-business server platforms did not exist); however, companies today have an increasing range of e-business choices in packaged applications.

The line dividing packaged applications from platform or toolkit products ultimately is an arbitrary one because the distinctions are a matter of degree rather than a difference in kind. Even the most "packaged" of applications may require significant configuration, and even the most basic e-business server platforms will incorporate a range of functionality. This overlap also is reflected in individual vendor's product lines: A single vendor may sell both packaged and platform versions of the same basic application. In this discussion, packaged applications will be defined as those that incorporate the basic functionality necessary to be used out-of-the-box.

Numerous software packages or suites of preintegrated solutions are available for merchants that do not want to build their own e-business solution. These package vendors may target specific market segments such as small to midsized retailers or ISPs that, in turn, may host the software, applications, hardware, and network e-business infrastructure and lease it to their customers.

Personalization involves tailoring a presentation to an audience based on profile information, demographics, or prior transactions.

Today's packaged sell-side e-business applications span a broad range, from basic products to full-featured offerings. However, the market generally can be segmented into entry-level and high-end packages.

Entry-level packages offer easy setup (using vendor-provided templates for basic design and wizards for configuration) and include basic catalog and merchandising functionality. They may be limited in their personalization capabilities, the degree to which they can be customized or extended with custom programming, and their scalability. These packages are designed for rapid implementation and are inexpensive, with prices as low as $500 and typically no more than $25,000. Further customization or integration of entry-level products requires programming, and many vendors offer an expanded, more expensive developer's version of the package, which can be used to develop additional functionality around the core. A significant number of products are available in this area, however, with new ones appearing weekly.

High-end packages typically offer enhanced capabilities in one or more of the major areas of functionality, such as personalization, merchandising, EDI capabilities, or transaction management. They also implement a full set of APIs that can be used to provide integration with other enterprise applications. These packages offer a higher degree of scalability.

GENERAL-PURPOSE SELL-SIDE PACKAGED APPLICATIONS

See "Commerce Platforms" on page 61 for more information.

Because packaged e-business applications are similar to e-business commerce platforms in their basic functionality, this discussion will concentrate on representative products and the additional functionality they provide.

BroadVision. BroadVision's One-to-One Commerce is an application for e-business that can target consumers, businesses, or channel partners and is built on BroadVision's One-to-One Enterprise application (not discussed in this chapter). Its architecture allows both turnkey deployment of an e-business site as well as customization of user interfaces, application logic, and integration with best-of-breed components and existing systems. Information, such as content or customer data, stored in existing external databases can be accessed by BroadVision agents. (See Figure 22 on page 67.)

BroadVision's One-to-One Commerce provides the following:

See "Security Requirements for E-Business" on page 209 for more information.

- Accesses customer data for customized presentation and supports username/password, cookies, and digital certificates for user identification; additionally, the application allows customers to update their profiles and send inquiries to customer service representatives, and it provides real-time integration with call centers for agent assistance.

- Features such as a persistent shopping cart; the ability to save a selection of frequently ordered items for reordering at a later time; on-the-fly product comparison tables; and buying incentives, including percentage discounts, price discounts, price adjustments, and companion incentives for cross-selling.

- The transaction engine handles orders, payment, and fulfillment; provides real-time pricing; uses multiple shipping models such as total weight, total cost, or total items; can restrict shipments based on product or location; and works with CyberCash, VeriFone, or other payment processors.

- Supports order workflow, physical and digital goods transactions and services, pay-per-view digital content and usage-based transactions, and electronic software delivery (ESD) through integration with CyberSource.

FIGURE 22: BROADVISION'S ONE-TO-ONE COMMERCE

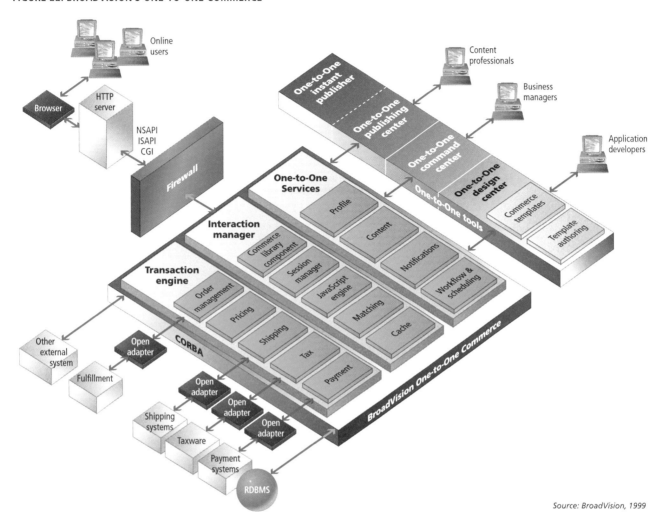

Source: BroadVision, 1999

- Supports integration with enterprise, payment, and shipping systems to leverage existing systems or service relationships. For example, One-to-One Commerce can calculate sales tax in real time (based on Taxware software). It can be integrated with external fulfillment systems or ERP systems including Baan, Oracle, and SAP via e-mail, EDI, flat file, fax, or other data transport mechanisms.

- Site management tools allow businesses to change incentives, advertisements, products, or other content presented to users.

- Content and catalog management tools enable businesses to add, change, stage, and publish content.

In an upcoming release, BroadVision has announced plans to support online Visa purchasing-card transactions as well as electronic integration with the merchant's general ledger.

ConnectInc.com. ConnectInc.com's MarketStream 2.0 is a buy-side and sell-side solution that provides supply-chain management support for business-to-business e-business. MarketStream supports browser-based application configuration and administration. It also includes integrated cross-supplier catalog searching, product-specific attributes, customized pricing, buyer profiling and personalization, fulfillment tracking information, ERP system integration, and reporting capabilities.

MarketStream 2.0 interoperates with CORBA, COM, JavaBeans, Enterprise JavaBeans, and MTS. It can be integrated with ERP and middleware solutions from Baan, Cognos, Fulcrum, Informix, MQSeries, Object Design, Oracle, PeopleSoft, Rational, SAP, Sybase, TSI Mercator, and Tuxedo. MarketStream uses IBM's WebSphere Application Server Advanced Edition and WebSphere Performance Pack, and it integrates with IBM's MQSeries transaction middleware. MarketStream functions on OS/390, many UNIX platforms, and Windows NT. It uses any Java Database Connectivity- (JDBC-) compliant database, Fulcrum search engine, or any browser implementing ActiveX, Dynamic HTML (DHTML), eXtensible Markup Language (XML), HTML 2.0+, Java, or Virtual Reality Modeling Language (VRML).

iCat. iCat originally was formed to develop software for building interactive catalogs on CD-ROM. The product then was expanded to create commerce-enabled online stores. Electronic Commerce Suite 3.0 Professional Edition allows the creation of a storefront using a wizard for the selection of templates and functionality. The storefront has a shopping basket for order aggregation and can be configured with CyberCash, IBM Payment Server, and VeriFone payment methods; FedEx and UPS for shipping; and Taxware for tax calculation. It comes with a Sybase SQL Anywhere 5.5 database to implement the catalog function, and its Commerce Publisher tool allows for administration of the catalog. However, it can be integrated with any existing ODBC-compliant database. The suite also includes hooks for integration to back-office systems.

In November 1998, Intel announced it would acquire iCat and operate it as a division of the company; the transaction was completed at the end of 1998.

IBM. Net.Commerce Start is the packaged version of IBM's Net.Commerce product offering; Net.Commerce Pro offers more advanced capabilities. (See Figure 19 on page 62.) According to IBM, Start is designed for midsized or larger companies that want to implement an e-business site quickly at a low entry price. It also can be used by a CSP to host up to 51 separate stores on a single hardware server.

Key features of the Start version of Net.Commerce include the following:

- *A store creation wizard*—Guides the store administrator through the configuration process. The wizard covers store type, layout, and style; creation of Web pages and templates; catalog navigation; and pricing, shipping, tax, and payment functions. The wizard then generates the necessary templates, macros, and configuration information. Three prebuilt sample stores are included and demonstrate the complete shopping process (catalog search, user registration, order form/shopping cart, checkout, and payment).

- *A library of graphical elements*—Can be used in the design of the store Web site.

- *IBM's Payment Server*—Allows secure credit-card processing via the use of the SSL or SET protocols. In a multistore hosted environment, each store can select which credit-card brands it accepts and with which financial institutions (acquiring banks) it wants to work.

- *Integration with IBM's Lotus Domino*—Provides outgoing e-mail capability (for order confirmation to the buyer, for example) as well as the ability to host discussions among customers.

Net.Commerce Start is available in various European and Asian languages and runs on several operating systems, including IBM's AIX, Microsoft's Windows NT, and Sun's Solaris.

Inex. Inex offers three versions of its Inex Commerce Court product: Inex Commerce Court Publisher (enables catalog creation), Inex Commerce Court Lite (provides storefront design and online order and payment processing), and Inex Commerce Court Professional (provides standard and custom storefront functionality). (See Figure 23.) Inex provides a suite of applications that extend Microsoft technologies to provide e-business solutions. Inex runs on top of Microsoft Site Server Commerce Edition (version 3.0) for self-hosting or Microsoft Commercial Internet System (MCIS 2.0) for hosting at an ISP or CSP.

FIGURE 23: INEX'S COMMERCE COURT

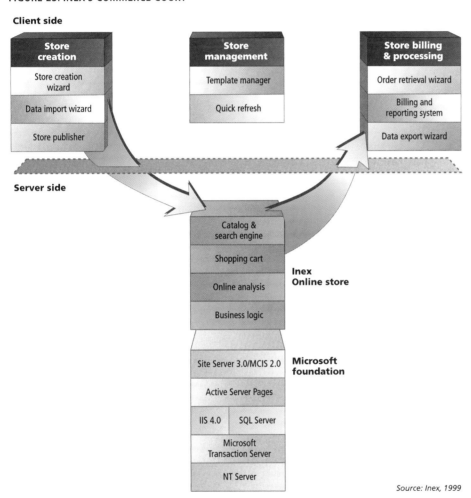

Source: Inex, 1999

The Inex Commerce Court Server Extensions provide the necessary tools to establish and maintain a site. They include the following:

- *Installation Manager*—Assists in configuring a system to meet specific network requirements. It requires Windows NT 4.0 running Internet Information Server, ASP, and SQL Server 6.5.

- *Database Management System*—Assists in managing and maintaining databases, including the processes of setting up directories, creating a data source driver to point to SQL databases, and configuring ODBC drivers for SQL databases.

- *Remote Store Builder*—Assists ISPs or CSPs in creating user names and passwords for each customer as well as creating logical connections that tie together the remote access permissions with user login, the Web store, and database.

- *Customer Store Wizard*—ISP/CSP tool that runs on a merchant's local machine, takes the user's name and password, and uses that information to modify a template to point to the proper database with the appropriate security rights. The Customer Store Wizard modifies the Web store, retrieves orders, and updates the store database.

Intershop. Intershop's Intershop Merchant Edition 3.0 allows the creation and maintenance of a storefront using these template-driven components: Catalog Manager, Product Manager, Customer Manager, and Inventory Manager. It also includes Sybase System 11 as its database. Merchant Edition comes with two application servers—one to handle administrative requests and one for storefront requests—to separate the workload between the administrative and storefront functions. (See Figure 24.)

FIGURE 24: INTERSHOP'S MERCHANT EDITION

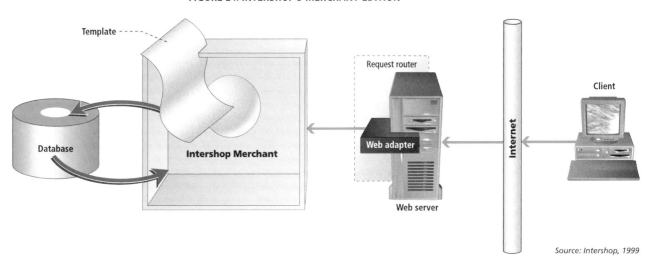

Source: Intershop, 1999

Intershop's cartridge family of products allows integration with many third-party software modules. Cartridges are available for payment methods (Automated Transaction Services, CyberCash, VeriFone's vPOS SET, and WorldPay) and order management and logistics (Open Market's OM-Transact, SAP [Intershop Enterprise Edition only], and TanData's Progistics). Other cartridges provide extended functionality, such as a language pack for Spanish and a cartridge for electronic software distribution.

In addition to the Merchant Edition, Intershop offers a Hosting Edition targeting ISPs and telecommunications providers (telcos). The Hosting Edition includes a Search Accelerator Cartridge (SAC), an expanded search tool built on Fulcrum's SearchServer and SearchBuilder software. SAC helps ISPs and telcos offer site-wide search capabilities for customers.

A Developer Edition offers a toolset that works with Java so developers can design software that connects with Intershop and can customize databases. The Enterprise Edition is designed to provide high-performance, high-end integration, and it includes a choice of Oracle8 or Sybase as its database. Also included are the Intershop Developer Kit and the Intershop Search Accelerator Cartridge, which allows customers to perform searches throughout all stores on an Intershop site.

InterWorld. InterWorld's Commerce Exchange is a high-end business-to-consumer or business-to-business solution that includes three primary modules:

- *Product Merchandising*—Provides tools to create catalogs that can be tailored to the buyers' processes, including pricing, promotion, and presentation.

- *Account Management*—Allows customers, in self-service mode, to review past order history or check the status of specific orders.

- *Order Management*—Covers browsing and item selection, including a shopping cart metaphor, order entry and payment authorization, and shipment and delivery.

Commerce Exchange includes a set of visual tools for developers to use when building or managing applications, including content and customer administration or the specification of merchant policies and business rules. (See Figure 25.) Commerce Exchange provides a full range of order processing, inventory management, accounting functions and reporting capabilities. It is designed for high-volume sites, including large enterprises, ISPs, CSPs, telcos, and financial services providers.

FIGURE 25: INTERWORLD'S COMMERCE EXCHANGE

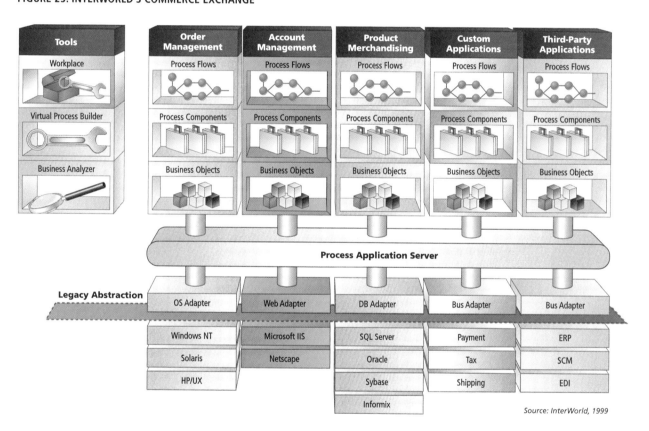

Source: InterWorld, 1999

InterWorld's adapter modules allow the product to work with multiple operating systems, on multiple Web server platforms, and with a variety of databases and third-party plug-ins for payment methods, tax calculation, and shipping logistics as well as interface with back-office ERP, SCM, and EDI systems.

Mercantec. Mercantec's SoftCart 4.0 provides store creation tools and templates to simplify the process of building an e-business site. Designers can customize the look and feel of a site further using content-creation tools from various vendors. SoftCart's API-based architecture can accommodate a range of databases, Web servers, browsers, order delivery options, tax and shipping models, and payment methods. Mercantec's

SoftCart Suite includes a drop-ship fulfillment module, a link to Intuit's QuickBooks accounting system, a choice of several online payment systems, and ANSI X12 850 (EDI purchase order) support.

Microsoft. Microsoft's Complete Commerce is a bundle of software, hardware, and services for ISPs and CSPs. The software is based on Microsoft's Site Server Commerce Edition and includes CyberCash and other systems for secure payment processing, TanData's Progistics for shipping and logistics, and Taxware for sales tax calculation. Several ISPs and CSPs currently offer the Complete Commerce package.

Netscape. Netscape's CommerceXpert suite includes its SellerXpert sell-side packaged application and its ECXpert application, which provides the order-processing functionality and linkages to enterprise systems (particularly via EDI). ECXpert can be used to communicate orders to trading partners using a variety of EDI message formats. (Netscape's CommerceXpert suite also includes BuyerXpert, a packaged application for procurement, discussed later.) SellerXpert provides an Open Buying on the Internet- (OBI-) compliant catalog and is designed to support advanced business-to-business selling over the Internet. MerchantXpert is an online merchandising solution that enables enterprises to establish high-end business-to-consumer sites rapidly. The CommerceXpert Suite runs on Sun's Solaris. ECXpert also has been ported to Windows NT.

See "Open Buying on the Internet (OBI)" on page 97 for more information.

Open Market. Like Netscape, Open Market's sell-side packaged application offering consists of two linked products. LiveCommerce is the catalog component, and OM-Transact handles the ordering process (including shipping, tax calculation, and payment processing). LiveCommerce has strong catalog functionality, including the ability to generate catalog entries automatically from lists of product attributes. Customization and personalization can be applied to page appearance, product categories and attributes shown, cross-selling, discounts, and marketing promotions and can be done for individual users or groups of users. Its newest release, LiveCommerce 2.0, includes inventory, pricing, and product information APIs that link with ERP systems. OM-Transact includes a variety of payment capabilities, including partial payments, micropayments, and generation of credit memos; it can accept payments via purchase order or secure credit-card payment processing using SSL or SET. Open Market has a rules-based fraud prevention module that can monitor credit-card "hot" lists and can limit the number of times a credit card is used per day.

Pandesic. One of the most highly integrated e-business packaged applications is the Pandesic E-business Solution from Pandesic, a company formed by Intel and SAP in 1997. Pandesic's software, which builds upon and extends SAP's R/3 ERP software suite, handles not only the e-business server functions (such as catalog, shopping cart, order processing, and payment acceptance), but also the major back-office functions (inventory management, warehouse operations, shipping, financial accounting and reporting, and electronic links to suppliers). Thus, Pandesic is designed to provide the complete suite of information systems required when selling products over the Web. An e-business could run entirely on Pandesic without requiring a separate set of back-office systems.

As a result of this integration, when a customer places an order on a Pandesic-enabled Web site, it automatically sets in motion the processes resulting from that order, including generating a packing slip and shipping label; instructing the delivery carrier to pick up the shipment; notifying the customer (via e-mail) that the order has been shipped; arranging for any necessary replacement of inventory (if the order has caused inventory to fall below preset levels); initiating payment to the supplier (if the merchandise was on consignment rather than owned by the merchant), the delivery carrier, and the sales tax authorities; and updating the general ledger and accounts payables and receivables systems.

From a technical point of view, Pandesic is built around a subset of SAP R/3 (primarily functionality from the Sales and Distribution, Materials Management, Warehouse Management, and Finance modules), which has been extended with a series of COM objects that implement the additional e-business functionality. The Web server functionality is provided by Microsoft Site Server Commerce Edition, which uses ASP technology to generate the Web pages accessed by the customer and merchant dynamically by pulling data from the R/3 database. Pandesic provides credit-card processing (using Cyber-Cash's software), tax calculation (using Taxware), shipping management (using Tan-Data's Progistics), and electronic payments (using Citibank's Worldlink). Pandesic also provides its own set of APIs to customize and extend the functionality of the system. (See Figure 26.)

FIGURE 26: TECHNICAL ARCHITECTURE OF THE PANDESIC E-BUSINESS SOLUTION

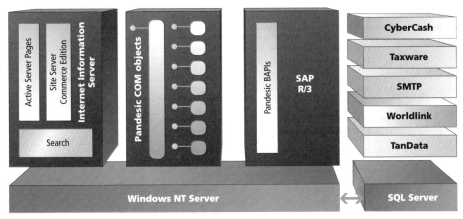

Source: Pandesic, 1998

Pandesic does business with its customers based on providing an integrated offering that includes software, hardware, installation, and hosting services. The software is provided on an "evergreen" (that is, continually updated) basis, and the hardware is upgraded as necessary to keep up with the transactions volume. Pandesic provides this functionality in exchange for a relatively low initial charge and then earns a percentage of the revenue generated from the site.

VERTICAL MARKET PACKAGES
In addition to packages that implement Web storefronts, several packages are available for industry-specific Web sites, particularly in the area of financial services. Following is a list of representative vertical market package vendors and products:

BroadVision. BroadVision's One-to-One Financial enables banks, brokerages, mutual fund companies, and other financial institutions to deploy personalized financial services applications. Building on the One-to-One Command Center found in BroadVision's Enterprise and Commercial versions, the core components of One-to-One Financial include the following:

- More than 50 out-of-the-box financial services functions for the rapid deployment of applications

"In addition to packages that implement Web storefronts, several solutions are available for industry-specific Web sites, particularly in the area of financial services."

- Quote services that enable institutions to offer personalized stock tickers to their customers for tracking their individual stock portfolios on a real-time basis
- Customer service functions
- Transaction engine and security features for transaction and data security
- Extensible profile database and intelligent matching agents for personalization and protection of privacy
- Financial server for integration with financial components and existing financial systems
- Integration with Integrion
- Comprehensive bill payment, including integration with CheckFree
- Alerts on quotes and bank balances

Brokat Infosystems and MeTechnology. Brokat Infosystems and MeTechnology offer the Brokat Twister and Me/4 financial services e-business platforms, respectively. In March 1999, the companies announced plans to merge and currently are working on ways to combine the two existing packages.

Twister is an application package that supports financial services functions such as e-banking, e-brokerage, and e-payment. It allows customers to complete banking transactions online with a high degree of security. The Twister e-banking solution contains Java-based encryption software that can be used in all browser and Web server environments.

Brokat's X-Presso gateway that communicates with Twister consists of Java banking transaction classes and Java Security classes. It supports a variety of authentication modules including smart card certificates and personal identification number- (PIN-) based systems. The Short Message Service (SMS) Gateway allows Twister to send and receive SMS messages to and from mobile phones. This gateway is used for functions such as stock quotes or account balances, but it also can be used for more advanced functions such as creating digital signatures. Twister components communicate through CORBA/Internet Inter-ORB Protocol (IIOP).

Me/4 is an integration and transaction platform that enables financial institutions to operate multiple sales channels uniformly over consistent interfaces, regardless of the underlying protocols or authentication mechanisms. The Me/4 platform enables banking transactions to be completed electronically 24 hours per day and supports a variety of security mechanisms and standards, including PINs, smart cards, SET, Open Financial Exchange (OFX), SSL, and homebanking computer interface (HBCI). Transactions can be completed from a variety of Internet devices, including kiosks, set-top boxes, mobile phones, or PDAs. Among Me/4's banking solutions are the following: Corporate Banking, Finance Partner, HBCI Banking, Internet Banking, Mobile Banking, Retail Banking, Stock Broker, and Terminal Banking.

Edify. Before its entrance into financial services applications, Edify was known for its customer service system, the Electronic Workforce, released in early 1992. In May 1996, Edify established a presence in the financial services industry with its Edify Electronic Banking System, an application development run-time platform (a packaged solution that automates numerous transactions, allowing customers to complete the banking transactions via the Web or the phone). The Edify Electronic Banking System integrates back-office applications with bill payment processors such as CheckFree and TransPoint.

The Edify Electronic Banking System contains a "call-me" option to request support; an agent then responds to the request by calling the customer back rather than responding via e-mail. The Edify Electronic Banking System is accessed by customers via telecommunications devices such as phone, fax, pager, e-mail, or Web browser. It can be used independently or in conjunction with the Edify Open Finance Server. The Open Finance Server supports most banking customer-service functions, such as wire transfers, interbank funds transfers, returned check notifications, downloadable bank statements, and so on.

IBM. IBM offers the Interactive Financial Service (IFS) platform. Similar to the Edify Electronic Banking System, the IFS platform allows consumers to connect to financial institutions' systems through devices including personal financial management (PFM) software, Web browsers, voice response units (VRUs), and the telephone.

Security First Technologies. Security First (referred to as S1) began as the technology division of Security First National Bank, an Internet-only bank. S1 offers a suite of products known as Virtual Financial Manager (VFM), which includes Virtual Bank Manager (VBM), Virtual Credit-Card Manager (VCCM), and Virtual Investment Manager (VIM), with the planned addition of Virtual Loan Manager. VBM, the initial product, allows customers to perform secure banking transactions over the Web. The VBM user interface allows the account-holder to pay bills, including the ability to categorize payments made within the system or by check and view pending payments; transfer funds between accounts; view transaction details (known as "registers"), check images, and periodic statements; open new accounts; and purchase certificates of deposit. The administrative interface allows CSRs to administer all account types and create or modify product attributes. Release 4.0 is capable of supporting up to 250,000 customers per installation.

VCCM provides similar functionality to VBM for credit cards rather than deposit accounts. It allows credit-card holders to view transactions posted to their accounts and their monthly statements; categorize their expenditures; and make payments on their accounts.

VIM allows customers to manage their brokerage accounts, including buying and selling securities and mutual funds; initiate margin transactions; view their portfolio position; and manage their individual retirement accounts (IRAs). In addition to their portfolio summary and details of securities held, customers can view their recent transactions and open orders and can obtain real-time market quotes. The product can handle a wide range of financial instruments, including stocks, options, rights, warrants, mutual funds, variable annuities, U.S. government securities, corporate and municipal bonds, mortgage-backed securities, commercial paper, and limited partnership interests. Transactions are passed via electronic links to the clearing institution that handles the actual trading.

The VFM products run on the HP-UX operating system and use the Informix RDBMS, the Tuxedo/T transaction processing (TP) monitor, and Netscape's Enterprise Server as the underlying technology.

Security First's customers include major banks and financial institutions such as the Australia and New Zealand Banking Group, Citibank, Huntington Bancshares, The Principal Financial Group, and Wachovia.

Buy-Side Packaged E-Business Applications

Buy-side packaged e-business applications are designed to automate corporate purchasing processes. The major focus of vendors has been on the procurement of MRO items. These items sometimes are referred to as indirect materials because they are not incorporated directly into the organization's manufactured product. Typical examples of indirect materials would be office supplies, computer equipment, and maintenance and repair services and supplies.

A typical example of a buy-side application is an intranet site that enables employees to purchase office supplies. The application provides a list of products from an office supply vendor or an aggregated list of products from multiple vendors. The employee selects the supplies needed, and the application places the order with the lowest-priced vendor or determines whether the goods already have been purchased and can be delivered from another location. Because most users of procurement systems are infrequent users, ease of use becomes important.

One reason for the focus on indirect materials stems from the fact that the items purchased and the purchasing process tend to be fairly common across industries, although the purchase of direct materials will vary considerably. In other words, buying iron ore for a steel mill, buying clothing for a retail store, and buying food for a hotel chain will involve different markets, vendors, and processes. However, the steel mill, the retailer, and the hotel chain all need to purchase office supplies, computer equipment, janitorial supplies, and so on.

FUNCTIONAL COMPONENTS OF BUY-SIDE PACKAGED APPLICATIONS

A typical buy-side e-business packaged application will have the following major functional components:

- A multisupplier catalog
- A rules-based workflow system for routing purchase requisitions through the steps needed for approval
- A mechanism for transmitting approved purchase orders to vendors and possibly querying their systems for product availability, pricing, and order status
- A set of management and reporting tools

Multisupplier Catalog. The catalog is designed to allow employees to compare products from all the organization's approved suppliers. It offers extensive search capabilities, allowing employees to find products through various methods, including moving through a hierarchy of product categories, full-text search on the catalog description, and parametric search that allows a product to be specific in terms of desired attributes. The catalog typically allows for the inclusion of photographs and detailed product information.

The catalog may reside on a server located in the buyer organization's network. Buyers also may connect directly to a supplier's catalog over the Internet and see a personalized view. This view will be a result of their company's specific catalog and their own access rights and personalization. Alternatively, the catalog may be hosted by a third party.

The interface to the catalog and the management tools for a buy-side catalog may be different from those for a sell-side catalog. For example, unlike a catalog maintained by a single organization, a buy-side application catalog needs a mechanism to allow multiple suppliers to enter or update information. Furthermore, catalog updates initiated by a supplier may need to go into a queue for review and approval by the purchasing department before they take effect.

Workflow System. Because much of the benefit of the buy-side package comes from automation of routine transactions and better enforcement of company purchasing guidelines, the workflow system plays a critical role. It allows individual employees to create purchase requisitions, which then are routed through a series of approval steps, if necessary. These steps might include approval by the employee's manager, by a higher-level executive, by the finance organization (for budget control), and so on. The specific routing taken by any given transaction will depend on the contents of that transaction, as expressed by a set of rules that encode the company's policies. These rules might include stipulations such as "purchases of more than $100,000 require vice presidential approval" or "purchases of items designated as hazardous materials require approval by Health & Safety."

In some cases, the buy-side application may interface with the workflow module of the organization's ERP system, allowing the ERP system to handle the routing and approval process.

See "E-Business Extensions to ERP" on page 113 for more information.

Interface to Suppliers. A buy-side application not only automates the company's internal purchasing process but also takes advantage of electronic links to its suppliers, including the ability to transmit approved orders to a supplier. Depending on the supplier's information systems, this transmission might take place via a traditional EDI message, by a real-time network link (over the Internet or a private network) to the supplier's order entry system, or (at a minimum) by an e-mail message sent to the supplier.

See "EDI" on page 113 for more information.

However, the company's employees also need to access information about product availability, delivery dates, and so on. This information may not reside in the catalog itself because it is so volatile. In the ideal case, the buy-side application package would take advantage of a network connection to the supplier's information systems to access real-time information. In cases where such access is not possible—typically because suppliers' systems are not capable of handling that kind of inquiry directly—the supplier may need to create a separate database that is updated periodically from its operational systems.

Many buy-side e-business applications also provide a receiving interface that buyers use to indicate that goods have been received. This ability is important particularly in the acquisition of indirect goods shipped in small packages that may not be logged at a receiving dock. Receiving information then can be passed to internal systems to authorize payment and track the location and disposition of physical goods.

Management and Reporting Tools. Management tools allow the administrator to define and update the workflow, grant various levels of access to the system to employees and suppliers, control updates to the catalog, and monitor the status of transactions as they move through the system. Reporting tools provide summary information about purchases, allowing for analysis by supplier, by item purchased, and so on. This information allows an organization to assess the performance of its suppliers (for example, what percentage of orders were unable to be fulfilled within a 48-hour period), negotiate better prices with its suppliers (based on better information about the aggregate volume of purchases), and track where its money is being spent.

Internal procurement or buy-side applications also may need to support cost accounting by maintaining relationships between the purchase order and a cost account. This relationship can be used to determine how to allocate the cost of goods and return that information to internal accounting systems.

"Many buy-side e-business applications also provide a receiving interface that buyers use to indicate goods have been received—an ability important particularly in the acquisition of indirect goods shipped in small packages."

BUY-SIDE E-BUSINESS PACKAGED APPLICATIONS

Representative buy-side packaged applications are discussed below. Other buy-side applications include Clarus' Clarus E-Procurement (formerly marketed as Elekom Procurement), Elcom's PECOS Procurement Manager, Fisher Technology Group's Corner-Stone, and Sterling Commerce's Gentran family of products.

Ariba. Ariba's Operating Resource Management System (ORMS) is a packaged application that helps organizations set up central procurement of indirect goods and services. These include MRO, capital equipment, services, and travel and entertainment. In addition, ORMS provides an architecture for managing workflow approvals as dictated by a company's internal business processes. The system uses a Java-based user interface and runs on UNIX.

Ariba.com Network is a standards-based Internet service that connects buying organizations using Ariba ORMS with suppliers. The network provides support for catalog and content management as well as order transaction routing. The network also supports multiple protocols to allow the exchange of content and transaction information.

Commerce One. Commerce One's BuySite is an application that automates the internal procurement process. The user interface is a Web-based requisitioning system that resides on a company's intranet where it is directly accessible to individual desktop users. BuySite allows users to browse for products and services from a multisupplier catalog. The catalog works in conjunction with Commerce One's MarketSite (an electronic market) to deliver real-time price and availability information. Buyers then may order online by selecting the items and submitting the requisition form.

Requisitions that require approval are routed automatically to the appropriate personnel, and any enterprise buying policies are enforced through BuySite's business rules. When the requisition has been approved, BuySite automatically converts it to an electronic purchase order and transmits the order to the supplier via Commerce One's MarketSite. BuySite supports standard Microsoft Windows NT computing environments. MarketSite comprises software and commerce services that enable trading partners to exchange business information and provide access to value-added services, including a supplier catalog content management system.

Intelisys. IEC-Enterprise, the focal point of the Intelisys Electronic Commerce (IEC) solution, is an intranet-based purchasing system that automates the procurement process. Buyers can access supplier-managed catalogs to select and purchase goods over the Internet from preferred suppliers. The system also provides administrative controls to manage the process. IEC-Enterprise places orders via ANSI X12 EDI documents and XML. The system complies with the OBI standard. Other elements in IEC's commerce suite are designed for suppliers:

- *IEC-Link*—Works with a supplier's existing electronic catalog or electronic order processing system to bring them into compliance with the OBI standard. The supplier then can communicate with an OBI-compliant corporate buyer.

- *IEC-SupplyNet*—Provides Internet-based catalog management and supports the electronic exchange of documents such as purchase orders and requisitions, invoices, advance shipping notices, and acknowledgments.

Netscape. Netscape's BuyerXpert (part of Netscape's CommerceXpert family) allows enterprises to streamline internal procurement processes, execute transactions with suppliers, and manage broad aspects of supplier relationships. BuyerXpert operates as a stand-alone application. It uses Netscape ECXpert for commerce exchange and integration with existing systems and infrastructure. BuyerXpert provides a user-configurable rules engine that supports more than 200 rules to allow customization of all aspects of the BuyerXpert application. BuyerXpert executes external transactions via both EDI and Internet commerce, and the software manages aspects of supplier relationships from product discovery to delivery.

Trade'ex. Trade'ex Electronic Commerce Systems' product suite comprises three applications, two of which are relevant to corporate procurement:

- *Procurement for the Enterprise*—A packaged buy-side application that manages the internal procurement of indirect goods in a workflow process.

- *Marketplace for the Enterprise*—Combines the capabilities of the buy-side and sell-side products into a single solution, managing multiple buyers and sellers. The system also includes online capabilities for online negotiations and auctions.

Trade'ex Procurement for the Enterprise is built around a catalog designed to integrate multiple suppliers into a common structure. The system allows a particular product to be purchased from any one of a number of suppliers, and intelligent filters determine which supplier has the best price, availability, or delivery time. New features in the latest release include keyword and attribute search capabilities; a regional catalog management system that controls the product and supply sources from which users may choose based on their delivery location; a workflow display that shows required workflow steps and a document's status in the workflow; drag-and-drop utilities for designing workflow diagrams; the ability to set up user groups; a requisition dialog to initiate, find, and track requests more easily; and support for XML.

Trade'ex applications are written in Java and JavaBeans. The software runs on Microsoft and Netscape Web servers, Oracle Application Server 4.0, Microsoft 4.0 and Netscape 3.1 browsers, and any JDBC-compliant database. The applications can be integrated with many ERP systems, including Baan, Oracle, PeopleSoft, and SAP.

Negotiated-Price Selling

In the physical world, auctioneers, brokers, purchasing agents, or traders using well-established rules and procedures mediate environments in which the price for goods or commodities is determined through negotiation or dynamic pricing. Rules and procedures are represented easily in software, and systems for negotiated-price commerce transactions are becoming more common on the Web. The Web enables ease of communication and the ability to bring together a large, geographically dispersed audience of buyers and sellers, thus providing a cost-effective mechanism to expand the use of auctions, bid systems (such as sealed bids for awarding contracts), and exchanges.

AUCTIONS

Web auction sites enable the sale of a variety of items, ranging from toys to commodity supplies, perishable inventory, and raw materials. Specialized auction sites are available for categories of goods, such as electronic components, consumer electronics, and used automobiles. To date, most interest has focused on individual sites that offer auctions as a service (such as eBay and OnSale). Most of these sites use an auction management system developed in-house; however, application vendors are beginning to offer products that include the technology. The availability of such software effectively lowers the cost of entry into this commerce channel. Some vendors license their auction software, customize their core software for very large enterprises, or host a commerce service that runs their software.

"The Web enables ease of communication and the ability to bring together a large, geographically dispersed audience of buyers and sellers, thus providing a cost-effective mechanism to expand the use of auctions, bid systems, and exchanges."

Auction software registers buyers and sellers and manages user accounts. The system generally requires a deposit, credit card, or other business relationship before a buyer may participate in the bidding. As a convenience for buyers, the software may offer automatic bidding, which increases each bid to a preestablished maximum if other bids come in. Some auction software notifies bidders via e-mail of the current state of the bidding so they can increase their bid without checking the Web site frequently. Auction software may be integrated into existing order management systems, which handle the remainder of the processing (tax, payment, shipping, logistics, and so on)—just as they do for any other sale.

BID SYSTEMS

Web-based bid systems allow corporate buyers to place open orders to purchase particular items. Sellers on the system are notified of the buyer's interest and then have the opportunity to bid for the business. Auction software vendors are expanding the capabilities of their products to support Web-based bid systems.

Another model supports more complex specifications, such as for items that need to be fabricated or machined. Bid systems allow purchasing agents to submit requests for quotations (RFQs) for materials or components used in the manufacturing process. Most bid-system software vendors offer a hosted service.

FreeMarkets OnLine is a vendor that hosts a bid-system service. The company's BidWare software enables suppliers to submit bids in an interactive marketplace to compete for business. Buyers on FreeMarkets are material purchasers from large enterprises; the sellers on FreeMarkets are fabricators that manufacture or supply custom components and materials to buyers' specifications. In 1998, FreeMarkets created online markets for more than $500 million of industrial parts and supplies using its proprietary online bidding technology. The company has expanded its services and has entered into an arrangement with the Commonwealth of Pennsylvania Department of General Services to arrange and conduct a Web-based bid system for state purchasing contracts. Prescreened and prequalified suppliers will be able to view the specifications of supplies needed and submit bids online.

EXCHANGES

More than $50 billion of excess inventories and assets being disposed of are traded annually in the U.S. alone, by some estimates. In the semiconductor, component, and computer markets, the value of excess goods is estimated to reach $18 billion. Because of the cost incurred by carrying excess or stale inventory, suppliers need to create a market for that inventory. The Web allows them to announce they have excess goods or capacity, and Web-based auction technologies provide a way to sell the excess supply.

One organization, FastParts, operates an exchange in which the needs of buyers and the excess inventory of computer-electronics sellers can be matched. In the FastParts model, there is no charge to buy or post lots to the site; instead, the buyer and seller share the charge of a small transaction fee based on the value of the completed trade. All transactions are anonymous; FastParts handles all funds processing and component shipping.

Spot markets also can use Web-based auction technologies. Spot-market exchanges exist for commodities such as natural gas, electricity, or crude oil. For example, Southern California Gas sponsors the Energy Marketplace, a Web-based exchange that lets customers shop for the best gas prices. Small to midsized providers list their prices, and residential, small business, commercial, and industrial customers can shop for the best price or lock in long-term rates when prices are low. Gas providers receive access to a broader market at a lower price; Southern California Gas receives a subscription fee from each provider and increases its distribution volume. Because of the recent California state deregulation of electricity, consumers can use the Energy Marketplace to shop for electricity provision as well.

AUCTION SOFTWARE VENDORS

Following is a representative list of auction software vendors and their products:

Moai Technologies. Moai Technologies' LiveExchange is an application that can be used by companies to liquidate inventory or to sell consignments, collectibles, or distressed merchandise. It is written in server-side Java and supports both Java and HTML clients. APIs are provided to facilitate integration with ERP systems. Its latest version, 2.2, also interfaces with CyberCash to provide credit-card authorization and processing.

Moai's LiveExchange is integrated within computer distributor Ingram Micro's Auction Block. Auction Block is a bidding service that allows Ingram's registered reseller partners to purchase new, unopened products, which are sold subject to the condition that they cannot be returned to the manufacturer.

OpenSite Technologies. OpenSite Technologies' OpenSite Auction 4.0 is an entry-level software product that allows businesses to host auctions on their Web sites by automating the setup, operation, and maintenance processes. Businesses can customize auction rules, page displays, customers, items, sellers, commission rates, and bid increments. The product runs on either OpenSite's proprietary database or an Oracle database.

WebVision. WebVision's WEBtropolis provides a commercial auction package that includes additional modules for catalog sales and for legacy database integration. WEBtropolis tools are written as extensions to Netscape's Enterprise Server and run on top of UNIX. WEBtropolis allows multiple auction formats and handles third-party merchant product submissions. It supports multiple payment types so credit cards can be verified and processed in real time via several industry-standard solutions such as CyberCash, First Virtual, and VeriFone.

In partnership with True Software and using technologies such as C++, Java, and Visual Basic, WebVision is working on integrating XML-based technology into its WEBtropolis Application Development Framework.

Personalization

Unlike a broadcast mechanism such as print, television, or radio, where the entire audience or readership receives the same content, each Web user has an individual connection to the online presence of a business. To take advantage of this new mechanism, instead of providing the same content to everyone, a site can provide personalized content to each user.

Personalization entails tailoring the presentation of a site to individuals or classes of customers based on profile information, demographics, or prior transactions. The goal of personalization is to market and sell one-to-one and to enhance the user experience and build customer loyalty so the customer returns again to the site.

USER PROFILES

In its simplest form, personalization is achieved through user registration—when users initially visit a site, they are asked to provide demographic information and indicate preferences or categories of interest. The user profile information is stored in a database

A cookie is a block of data that a Web server stores on a client system. When a user returns to a Web site, the browser sends a copy of the cookie back to the server. Cookies are used to identify users, to instruct the server to send a customized version of the requested Web page, to submit account information for the user, and for other administrative purposes.

along with a unique user-ID and password. When users revisit the site, they are prompted to log in using their unique user-ID and password, which initiates a query into the profile database and retrieves the information previously entered.

Different applications use different techniques to identify the individual. These techniques range from a user log-in (described earlier) to browser "cookies" to personal digital certificates. Most applications today use some combination of log-in information and cookies, whereas digital certificates for individual users still are in the early stages of deployment.

A profile also can contain additional information a user chooses to share with the system through the registration process or ongoing surveys. These methods sometimes are referred to as explicit profiling. Building profiles from transaction data about items purchased or analysis of browsing (clickstream) behavior are examples of implicit profiling. Implicit profiling automatically tracks user behaviors and attempts to draw inferences about individual users.

Clickstream data coming into a Web site from an unknown user can be compared with patterns of clickstream behavior from previous visitors to the site and used to guide the creation of targeted Web pages. Additionally, a data warehouse repository with this clickstream data can be analyzed with data mining pattern recognition software to devise the rules that govern which message to offer the anonymous prospect, how to counter points of resistance, and when to attempt to close a sale.

Given the profile, an application then can tailor the presentation to that user. A selling application may use the profile to select special promotions to offer the buyer, such as a one-time discount, opportunity to join an affinity program, or the product on sale that day. Buy-side applications can use the profile to call up previous orders to simplify purchasing the same items again.

Of course, the profiles can be used in many other ways, especially as systems become more sophisticated. In particular, the use of profiles combined with general demographic information is becoming more common as a tool for merchandising and one-to-one marketing efforts on the Web.

COLLABORATIVE FILTERING

Collaborative filtering takes advantage of previous decisions made by other people with whom a given individual shares common characteristics to select information likely to be relevant to that individual.

Collaborative filtering applications collect observations of user preferences and then make recommendations based on correlation matrices of users' tastes and preferences. This information can be collected explicitly or implicitly. In some situations, collaborative filtering engines explicitly ask users to rate their choices; in other situations, the engines passively track the pages users view, the products they purchase, and other choices they make and use this information to create an implicit profile. Collaborative filtering engines then seek to predict what products individuals or groups of users will be likely to purchase, based on their similarity to other individuals and groups. Thus, if two individuals have shown (through their past choices) their preferences are correlated highly, then new books one of them enjoys likely will be enjoyed by the other as well. These new books can be suggested for purchase to the second person based on the first person's judgment.

A common example is found at e-business sites selling books or music CDs. Such sites often use collaborative filtering to recommend to customers additional titles they are likely to enjoy. This recommendation comprises items selected by other customers who made the same previous purchase.

The more individual information a collaborative filtering database contains, the more useful recommendations or suggestions can be. By capturing user behavior characteristics automatically and thus increasing the number of profile attributes without requiring users to respond to requests for information, the accuracy of collaborative filtering can be improved.

RULES-BASED PERSONALIZATION

Unlike collaborative filtering, where the choices of previous users influence the options presented to an individual, rules-based systems match user profile data to a set of pre-defined rules or assumptions. A content-matching engine is the means by which these rules are used to identify content to be received by profiled users. Several different types of rules can be applied effectively. A content rule may say something like, "Show all Event_announcements whose region is Midwest to anyone whose Customer_region is Midwest." A customer rule might say, "Include anyone whose Past_purchases includes one transaction in excess of $10,000 in the Big_spender group." A profiling rule might say, "If customer indicates Home_equity greater than zero, set Home_ownership = true."

CASE-BASED PERSONALIZATION

Case-based personalization software translates user-supplied freeform text into a query that can be run against a database. This software most often is used to automate query-handling interactions. Typically, software that supports this process combines natural language processing and case-based reasoning to retrieve answers to questions using either a decision-tree model or fuzzy logic. The query is sent to a database of cases, which then may retrieve records of past solutions. Case-based personalization often is found on help desks, call centers, or automated e-mail response systems. More recently, it is being deployed in e-business venues when a user is engaged in a question/answer dialog and unsure of the exact item desired. Case-based personalization software matches a user with a short list of products or services.

See "Responding to Messages" on page 91 for more information about how this technology is used.

PERSONALIZATION VENDORS

Following is a representative list of personalization vendors and their products:

Art Technology Group. Art Technology Group's (ATG's) Dynamo suite utilizes artificial intelligence to personalize the online relationship between the merchant and the consumer. The core of the application is the Dynamo Personalization Server. The Dynamo commerce applications provide tools for storefront customization, transaction support, and targeted promotions. Although originally built in C++, all Dynamo applications now are built in Java.

Any interaction the consumer instigates, such as conducting a search for a specific product, marks the beginning of a customer profile. As data is gathered about the customer, specialized promotions targeted at the individual can be delivered.

ATG's Ad Station manages customer profiles, tracks customer behavior, and delivers targeted ads across large-scale sites and ad networks. It is capable of tracking and reporting customer behavior in real time and reports can be exported into spreadsheets for further analysis.

Brightware. Brightware's Advice Agent for customer assistance on the Web is an example of case-based personalization being applied to interactive e-business situations. Advice Agent provides assistance to customers by learning their needs and showing them relevant information and solutions. It uses an automated Web dialog to provide the personalized advice and targeted content. (See Figure 27.)

FIGURE 27: BRIGHTWARE'S ADVICE AGENT ARCHITECTURE

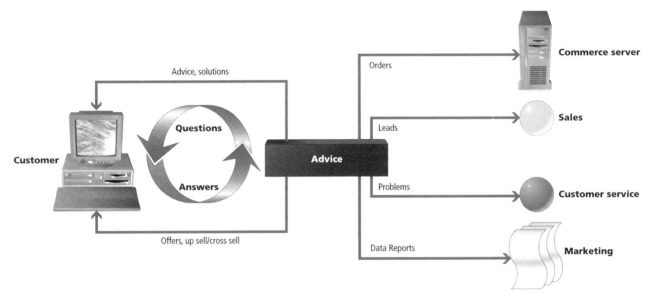

Source: Brightware, 1999

BroadVision. One of the leading vendors in rules-based e-business applications is BroadVision. Its One-to-One Command Center (integrated into BroadVision's One-to-One Enterprise and three vertical versions: Financial, Knowledge, and Commerce) allows sellers to develop business rules that evaluate user information gathered during previous interactions and use it to target products and services during subsequent interactions. One-to-One Command Center lets sellers define the rules that match content to users based on profile information, transaction history, session behavior, and other data.

Engage Technologies. Engage Technologies' ProfileServer 4.0 provides several profiling options to allow selling sites to choose the type and depth of profiling that best matches each site's needs. Profiles can be developed using observed behavior, answers to survey questions, or declared data (such as registration data), which can be aggregated or tracked across domains such as business units, channels, partners, or sites. Advanced profiling techniques are based on observed behavior of visitors across multiple Web sites that use Engage's software. As a visitor browses through Engage-enabled sites, the software builds an individual profile based on the type of content viewed, the time spent viewing, and other factors, including the frequency and recency of visits to a particular interest category or site.

See the sidebar "Platform for Privacy Preferences" on page 85 for more information.

Information is processed into profiles that include a user-ID number, an interest category code, and an interest score to indicate a level of interest in a particular category. Each individual profile can be associated with more than 800 attributes. These profiles can be used by other applications to deliver targeted offers, personalized pages, or profile-based advertising. ProfileServer subscribes to standards initiatives such as the Platform for Privacy Preferences (P3P), and sites that use Engage can display the TRUSTe Trustmark to display their commitment to privacy standards.

Firefly Network. Firefly Network, acquired by Microsoft in April 1998, provides personalization technology based on collaborative-filtering techniques. To encourage consumers to provide profile information, Firefly also became an advocate of individuals' privacy protection. The Firefly Passport, although no longer sold as a separate product, allows users to see a log that indicates how their data has been used, to change profile information, and to request data not be used in the future on those sites that used Firefly personalization technology. In its acquisition of Firefly, Microsoft gained the personalization technology and Firefly's involvement in P3P, Open Profiling Standard (OPS), and Information and Content Exchange (ICE). The P3P technology allows individuals to specify what personal data they choose to share when they visit a Web site. Microsoft, assisted by TRUSTe, is developing a privacy wizard that can automate part of the P3P implementation process.

MultiLogic. MultiLogic's Exsys expert system software provides an application development environment to capture knowledge and experience in a rules-based method. Exsys Web Runtime allows a merchant to deploy the expert system directly on a Web site. Exsys' inference engine takes the expert system rules and combines them with user data to determine the best recommendation for the user's specific situation. The inference engine also enables the system to consider the probability of competing recommendations. The engine can explain why a question is being asked, how the data will be used, and how it arrived at a particular recommendation.

Net Perceptions. Net Perceptions' Realtime Recommendation Engine infers customer preferences from observed behavior and suggests items for purchase. For instance, it can make inferences between the length of time one spends reading a news article and one's level of interest in that article. Other actions that may indicate interest level in an item are bookmarking, printing, saving, scrolling, and making a purchase decision. The Realtime Recommendation Engine resides on a Web server. Other applications that create or use customer data can feed data to the server or request predictions through API calls. In addition to making complementary recommendations, it also provides cross-sell table support and serendipity control.

Vignette. Vignette provides many Internet relationship management tools. Its enterprise products include StoryServer 4.0, which has a component called Lifecycle Personalization. This component provides the ability to present content appropriate at each stage of the customer life cycle: from initial visitor to long-term customer. The software

Serendipity control lets a seller increase recommendations for low-volume items when users otherwise might not know about them and decrease recommendations for high-volume items when most users will know about them.

PLATFORM FOR PRIVACY PREFERENCES

The Platform for Privacy Preferences (P3P) provides a framework for Web users to manage the flow of personal information and for Web sites to express their privacy policies. The Open Profiling Standard (OPS), now absorbed into P3P and pioneered by Firefly, is supported by both Microsoft and Netscape browsers. With OPS, the user completes a personal profile that controls what information is transmitted and to whom via browser settings. Still an early-stage technology, it (or something similar) is likely to gain ground as

privacy concerns continue to be an issue for consumers and consumer advocates.

P3P is under consideration by the World Wide Web Consortium (W3C). However, the proposed standard does not meet the European Union's Privacy Directive (October 1998) that requires companies to obtain individuals' consent before gathering personal demographic or marketing data about them.

Several companies engaged in software or service provision for electronic commerce

over the Web are working to establish the Information and Content Exchange (ICE) Protocol. Adobe Systems, CNET, Microsoft, Sun, Vignette, and others plan to create a set of specifications that will allow the rapid exchange of information including profiles, prices, and products across a variety of Web servers. The ICE protocol utilizes XML and conforms with the Open Profiling Standard that specifies only the transmission of data about customers that they themselves had approved for dissemination. ■

can use behavior data to infer visitors' interests and update navigation and content accordingly. StoryServer software also lets merchants recommend content based on the choices of visitors with similar interests. Another component, decision-support services, provides a business-level analysis of customer behavior to help gauge how effectively content attracts and retains visitors. It can generate reports based on custom criteria to determine what content is accessed, how often, and by which type of visitors.

Vignette's Syndication Server leverages digital assets such as product content, media, and self-service information. It helps establish distinct affiliate groups and build targeted packages for distribution across multiple, affiliated Web sites. One component, Subscription Manager, is used by affiliate sites to subscribe or unsubscribe to syndication offers. Another component, the Syndication Agent, is a small Java-based application that lets affiliates download these packages automatically and remotely, process the content of the packages, and remotely manage them over time. It is built on the XML-based ICE protocol.

Vignette is working with technology companies including Adobe, Channelware, Microsoft, National Semiconductor, and Sun, as well as a group of content providers, to develop ICE. The protocol describes content syndication relationships between Web servers and provides for the automatic, controlled exchange and management of online assets between business partners.

Customer Relationship Management

The heightened emphasis that e-business places on customer relationship management has created a market for software packages that assist organizations in carrying out this function. Such packages are designed to be used by employees who interact with customers. Siebel and Vantive provide two examples of customer relationship management software.

Siebel. Siebel 99, a Web-based application suite, supports sales, marketing, and customer service. Its enterprise resource management solution includes the following applications:

- *Siebel Sales Enterprise*—Supports multitiered distribution and allows for data exchange between laptops, hand-held computers, and the corporate server. This feature is useful particularly for sales representatives who need to access data from remote locations.

- *Siebel Service Enterprise*—Used for customer relationship management (CRM). It features tools to support service request management, service environment profiling, and problem resolution (using case analysis, product specifications, FAQ databases, and customer service solutions).

- *Siebel Call Center*—Integrates sales and customer-service functions. It supports on-demand sales or service assistance to customers. Customer service representatives (CSRs) can access customers' histories and accounts and then recommend products and services based on customers' historical purchases. Siebel Call Center offers computer telephony integration (CTI) that supports dialed number indexing service (DNIS), automated number identification (ANI), and interactive voice response systems (IVR).

- *Siebel Field Service*—Supports field service operations such as maintenance schedules, repair requests, and parts exchanges and returns. The software also can provide detailed instructions regarding what materials are required for a given service order.

- *Siebel Marketing Enterprise*—Includes a prebuilt datamart and an online analytical processing (OLAP) server for data analyses. It also includes market segmentation, campaign, call scripting, and workflow management tools.

- *Siebel InterActive*—Uses agent technology to gather personalized information automatically about potential customers, industries, and so on. Customized information is then delivered to the user's desktop.

- *Siebel Product Configurator*—Supports marketing, sales, and customer service operations. It manages product configurations to ensure product and service pricing is accurate, and it allows product and marketing departments to create promotional product configurations that can be distributed to the appropriate sales and customer service channels.

Vantive. Vantive 8 is a suite of Web-enabled applications that supports inventory, customer service, procurement, sales, field services, and marketing. Vantive 8 is composed of five major applications:

- *Vantive Enterprise*—A suite of Web-enabled CRM applications. It can be integrated with back-office and legacy systems and is designed for use by employees who directly interact with customers.

- *Vantive Support*—A CRM application that supports customer service operations via phone, fax, e-mail, and the Web.

- *Vantive Sales*—Contains quote and proposal software as well as forecasting and enterprise reporting software. The application has mobile capabilities.

- *Vantive FieldService*—Supports operations such as tracking and logging service requests, assigning service orders, tracking the time and materials spent on a given order, and managing inventory.

- *Vantive HelpDesk*—Helps merchant sites establish a customized technical assistance system. It can route or respond to problem reports submitted over the Web or a corporate intranet.

Customer-Facing E-Mail

Companies that establish a Web presence often are surprised by the large volume of incoming e-mail that results. This influx can occur even when a company is not selling its products or services actively via the Web and even when it does not solicit communication via e-mail. The Web-using public seems to act on the principle, "If you have a Web site, obviously you also are prepared to accept communication via e-mail."

One problem has been the lack of clearly defined organizational responsibility for handling incoming e-mail. Another obstacle has been the lack of automated tools with which to handle it. These tools would be the e-mail equivalent to the Automated Call Director (ACD) systems used by call centers to route incoming telephone calls to CSRs. The lack of such tools is changing, however, with several packaged applications now available that are designed specifically to handle customer-facing e-mail.

The e-mail automation market is moving toward establishing customer e-mail management as an application used to facilitate all phases of the communication between companies and customers. Major vendors are moving to make their systems encompass both response and proactive (that is, outgoing) e-mail correspondence. Most vendors also are adding COM, CORBA, or Java interfaces to facilitate the integration of e-mail management into other customer-facing applications. Some also are offering business intelligence capabilities and can add customer e-mail response to a company's existing knowledge management systems.

Partnerships with vendors in related fields such as artificial intelligence could prove beneficial in stimulating growth in the marketplace. For example, Kana Communications partnered with Inference, a provider of case-based reasoning tools, to create its intelligent auto-response e-mail package. An emerging trend is for companies (such as eGain Communications) to offer both e-mail management applications and hosted services in addition to software.

The following discussion refers to e-mail from "customers," which could be any member of the public contacting the company via e-mail. As some of the following examples will illustrate, the person sending the e-mail message could have some other relationship to the company besides current or prospective customer; for example, the person might be a prospective employee, a prospective distributor of the company's products, a shareholder, and so on.

BASIC FUNCTIONALITY OF CUSTOMER-FACING E-MAIL PACKAGES

A typical customer-facing e-mail package includes the following basic functionality:

- The ability to receive incoming e-mail messages and route them to the appropriate destination—the Automated Call Director functionality referred to earlier

- A workflow mechanism for moving the incoming messages through the series of steps necessary to generate a response

- Some type of knowledge- or rules-based system capable of creating or suggesting an appropriate response to each message

- A case-management system that allows incoming e-mail messages that are continuations of previous interactions to be associated with the history of that interaction

- A set of tools for managing the process of responding to e-mail and for use by the site administrator in configuring and administering the e-mail system

Therefore, in its simplest form, a customer-facing e-mail package can be seen as a hybrid of a workflow system that manages the process of responding to e-mail messages with a knowledge-based system that manages the content used in those responses.

USING WEB FORMS AS AN ALTERNATIVE TO FREE-FORM E-MAIL

If a company expects a significant volume of its inbound e-mail communications to originate from visitors to its Web site, then it may prefer to encourage those visitors to use a Web form rather than e-mail as the vehicle for incoming messages. The advantage is that a Web form requires the customer to communicate in a structured fashion unlike e-mail, which essentially is freeform. Some of the specific benefits of using a Web form include the following:

- The customer can be required to complete certain fields of the form using pull-down menus, thus limiting the range of allowable entries into those fields to keywords the form designer has specified in advance. For example, the form might have a field that asks "What product are you contacting us about?," with a list of the company's products in a pull-down menu. Requiring the customer to pick from among valid product names makes it easier to route the message to the appropriate destination.

- In addition to improving message routing, the structured nature of the form— the fact that data is received back in designated fields rather than in a freeform e-mail message—also makes it easier to process the information in the message automatically. For example, if a customer has checked a box saying "Send product catalog for Dishwashers" and filled in a field on the form with a postal mail address, it is easier to extract that address and pass it to a mail fulfillment program with instructions to send the appropriate catalog than if the customer's request had to be inferred from the text of an e-mail message.

- Because the form consists of a series of fields to be completed, it encourages the customer to include certain information that will be relevant to responding to the message but that might not be included if the customer were just sending an e-mail message. For example, if a software company is receiving messages requesting assistance with its products, it probably needs to know what version of the product is in use and what operating system it is running on. Including these fields in a Web form is much more likely to result in that information being collected than if the customer was relied upon to include it. This requirement also can be enforced by the Web server through a validation process when the form is submitted. If fields designated as mandatory have not been filled in, the form and an error message is returned to the customer.

- The information generated from the Web form will be formatted correctly. For example, currency signs and non-English characters such as accents and umlauts frequently are corrupted by e-mail gateways, and many users do not understand the limitations of the Simple Mail Transfer Protocol (SMTP) with regard to formatting issues such as tabs, bold text, and spaces.

Using Web forms as an alternative to incoming e-mail has several drawbacks, however. A company is more likely to receive incorrect information about the customer's e-mail address, thus making it impossible to respond to via e-mail. (This error occurs not because the customer is giving out an incorrect address intentionally but because the address was mistyped or an incorrect address syntax was used.) In contrast, messages received by e-mail typically have a return address that is generated automatically by the customer's e-mail server, making it more likely to be correct.

By its nature, a Web form requires the user to have a Web browser and Internet connection. This assumption is not always true. Many users have e-mail only. Corporate policies or other reasons may make the Web site unavailable. The user may be working from a PDA with no Web capability at all. E-mail messages can be created offline, perhaps during an airline flight, and sent later. Finally, a Web form may not be designed to allow for all contingencies. If users are reporting a software problem, they might provide a screen image, but the form designer may not have provided for that functionality.

A hybrid method is the auto-responder. The user sends e-mail to a given address and receives a template for response. However, even this approach is difficult unless the user is aware of the limitations of Internet e-mail formatting and how to work around them.

ANATOMY OF A CUSTOMER-FACING E-MAIL PACKAGE

Receiving and Categorizing Incoming E-Mail. The first task to be performed in handling incoming e-mail is to receive it into the system and route it to the appropriate initial destination. As incoming messages are received into the system, they need to be categorized or sorted. For some messages, this process will be simplified because the message bears an explicit address the package recognizes. This address might be one of a set of addresses the company has announced, either to a specific group of customers or to the public in general. In other cases, the address might be a generic term the package recognizes, such as `Employment@Mycompany.com`.

If the application package does not recognize the e-mail address as one it has been programmed to handle explicitly, it then must attempt to categorize the message by looking at its contents (including both the subject line in the message header and the body of the message itself). In the simplest case, the package would look for the occurrence of specific keywords—for example, those that match the names of the company's products. There also might be generic words that indicate the content of a message; for example, terms such as "résumé" or "employment" would identify the message as one from a prospective job applicant. Typically, more weight would be given to words in the subject line of the message than in the text itself on the assumption that the subject line is a better indication of what the message is about than arbitrary words in the message text.

The application package also might recognize certain incoming messages as continuations of prior e-mail exchanges that were handled through the system. For example, an outgoing e-mail response generated by the system might include a case number in the message subject line, along with some instructions to the recipient saying "If you respond to this message, make sure this case number appears in the subject line of your response." The package then would recognize the case number and be able to associate the new message with the history of previous e-mail exchanges, thus making it possible to route the new message more accurately than if only the incoming e-mail address were used.

This set of procedures for categorizing and routing incoming messages typically is expressed as a set of rules (which might take the form "IF To-address equals 'Toaster-Service' THEN Take-Some-Action"). The rules are searched sequentially until one of the IF statements is satisfied, at which point the appropriate action is taken. If none of the IF statements is satisfied, then some default behavior is invoked. These rules are developed and maintained by the site administrator for the application package.

Initial Routing of Incoming Messages. Once an incoming message has been categorized using the foregoing set of rules, it is routed to the appropriate initial destination. This destination might be another module of the application that generates an automated response, or into a CSR's work queue, or into some external application. In practice, more than one of these actions might occur. For example, the system may be set up to acknowledge each incoming message that relates to customer service automatically, perhaps giving the sender a case number to be used for tracking purposes, at the same time the message is being routed to a CSR.

Automated responses typically would be used when the incoming message is a request for standard information. For example, a message sent to New-Subscription-Info at a magazine might result in an automated response telling the sender about the various ways to order a new subscription, with another e-mail address to use for specific questions not answered by the generic response. In other cases, an automated response may be used when the sender's message has been transferred to another application for subsequent processing. For example, a résumé sent to `Job-Applications@Mycompany.com` might be routed automatically to an external file from which it can be imported into the company's human resources (HR) or recruiting system, with an automated response to the sender that says "Thank you for submitting your résumé. If we have a position that matches your qualifications, we will contact you within 30 days."

If all messages could be handled with an automated response, however, customer-facing e-mail packages would not be necessary because the automated responses could be handled by the company's basic e-mail system. The real benefits of these systems come into play when incoming messages need to be handled on an individual basis. In that case, a message would be routed into a work queue for response by a CSR.

Managing Message Workflow. The system for managing message workflow is at the heart of the customer-facing e-mail package. The workflow system is built around a set of work queues defined by the application site administrator. Incoming messages are assigned to one of these work queues based on the THEN clauses of the message-categorizing and message-routing rules described earlier. These rules assign a message to a specific queue depending on various factors, such as the type of response needed, the urgency of the response, and the characteristics the CSR will need to have in order to respond. For example, at the coarsest level of granularity, there would be separate queues for different functional areas such as sales and customer support. Within each functional area, there would be specific queues according to product type or type of problem. Within customer support, for instance, there might be separate queues for different kinds of problems such as new purchasers who are having trouble getting the product to work initially versus products that have failed. There also might be different queues for different classes of customers or different queues for the levels of skill needed to respond.

Each queue then would have one or more CSRs assigned to service it. These CSRs access messages waiting in the queue to which they are assigned. In practice, a given CSR might be assigned to service multiple queues, in some sort of priority order; for example, the CSR might be directed to "Handle messages from the queue for Platinum-level accounts; if there are none, then handle messages from Gold-level accounts." Once the CSR has accessed a message, the application would present the relevant information and possible actions, as described later.

In addition to handling the initial assignment of a message to a CSR, the workflow component of the application typically would provide additional functionality. Some of this functionality would relate to the handling of specific messages. For example, there might be a rule that says "All responses to messages from Platinum-level accounts must be copied to the customer's sales account manager" or "Copies of all messages assigned to 'Escalated' status should be sent to the Team Leader."

Other functionality would relate to monitoring and managing the overall workflow. This process would allow customer service managers to view status information such as the number of messages waiting in each queue in the system, the length of time the average (or oldest) message in each queue has been waiting, or the average length of time it is taking the CSRs to process messages in each queue. Based on this information, the manager could reassign CSRs to queues where response time did not meet the organization's service level objectives. The system also would notify team leaders or managers whenever there were unanswered messages in a queue older than a predefined threshold value for that queue.

Responding to Messages. Once a CSR has accessed messages from the queue(s), the application package provides relevant information and possible actions. Relevant information includes the history of messages associated with this case (if this is a follow-up message to a previous e-mail exchange) or with this customer, links to information relevant to the product or problem that the message is about, and so on.

"If all messages could be handled with an automated response, customer-facing e-mail packages would not be necessary."

The application also provides one or more template responses, which the CSR then could select and edit before sending. These templates could contain data fields that would be populated with information from the incoming message and from the customer information database. For example, a raw template might say "We apologize for the difficulty you are experiencing with your **<name of product>**. Unfortunately, our records show your warranty expired on **<warranty-expiration-date>**. We will be happy to service this item out of warranty for an estimated repair cost of **<repair-cost-for-this-product>**." The missing values for product name, warranty expiration date, and estimated repair cost would be filled in automatically by the system before the suggested response is presented to the CSR. All these features are designed to reduce the time and effort it takes for a CSR to handle each message.

If none of the template responses is appropriate, there also may be tools to allow the CSR to search the application's knowledge base or an external information repository for information that would be helpful in composing a response.

In addition, the application can provide the ability for the CSR to run an external program and insert that program's output into the response. For example, to respond to a message from a customer questioning a billing statement, the CSR might need to call up that customer's account detail from the company's accounts receivable system. Rather than having to summarize the detail and manually compose response to the customer, the relevant detail could be inserted by the CSR into the outgoing response. Accessing the external program could be automated by presenting the CSR with a script to be run as one possible option.

Besides replying, other actions the CSR could take include reassigning the message to a different CSR or queue, escalating the message to a higher priority or assigning it for special handling, or closing the case associated with that message.

Managing the Knowledge Base. If the workflow system is the heart of the customer-facing e-mail packaged application, then the knowledge base is its brain. It contains the template responses presented to the CSRs, with each template tagged to indicate the relevant set of questions for which it is appropriate. As mentioned earlier, the template responses can include automatically populated data fields and scripts.

The knowledge base is maintained by the site administrator using a series of tools provided by the application package. New template responses could be developed by the administrator, or CSRs could forward new responses they have created to customer messages for possible inclusion in the knowledge base.

Management and Reporting Tools. In addition to the tools for managing the message-categorizing and message-routing rules and the knowledge base, the customer-facing e-mail application package typically also includes a variety of other management tools such as tools for handling the workflow (by assigning CSRs to queues).

The application also would include the capability to generate various types of management reports. Some of these reports would summarize information based on the incoming message traffic—for example, frequently asked questions, products generating the most installation difficulties, and so on. Other reports would be based on the response process, such as average time to respond to messages in each queue, or CSR productivity statistics.

TECHNICAL ARCHITECTURE OF CUSTOMER-FACING E-MAIL PACKAGES

Although the basic functionality of customer-facing e-mail packages generally is similar across the major products, the details of how this functionality is implemented can vary widely. Some of the major differences include the following:

- *Implementation*—How the client software (particularly the client software used by the CSR) is implemented. Some vendors have chosen to use a browser-based interface in the belief it makes their applications easier to deploy and support. Other vendors have chosen to develop Windows- or Java-based client software in the belief it allows them to offer richer functionality in the client side of the application.

- *Integration*—Whether the application server is self-contained or is designed to integrate with an existing e-mail package.

- *Degree of customizability*—Whether the application has a set of APIs that allow custom-developed applications to integrate with it via DCOM or CORBA.

- *Degree of modularity*—Whether the application server is implemented as a single application program with multiple functional components or whether each function is implemented as a different application task (which may offer greater flexibility in deployment).

- *Data architecture*—Whether the application provides its own data storage mechanism or stores its data in standard RDBMS products and how accessible the data is to other applications.

- *Scalability*—How the application scales to larger volumes of message traffic and larger numbers of CSRs (for example, whether the application server can be split across multiple computers in a clustered environment).

PACKAGED E-MAIL VENDORS AND PRODUCTS

Following is a representative list of packaged e-mail vendors and their products:

Acuity. Acuity's WebCenter Enterprise solution uses the WebACD (automatic call distributor) to route customer queries to the appropriate CSR. Besides channeling customer queries, it analyzes the queries for possible automatic responses and can push the customer history and profile to the CSR's desktop before the CSR responds.

Adante. Adante's e-mail management software, Adante 2.1, analyzes the content of incoming e-mail (scanning for keywords) and determines whether the available auto-responses might satisfy customers' queries. If an autoresponse will not suffice, the program routes the e-mail to the appropriate agent, depending upon the content of the e-mail. CSRs that use Adante 2.1 can access message queues, contact histories, account profiles, and so on, through a standard Web browser client interface. Adante features a three-tiered architecture and an API that uses Microsoft's COM. It also provides call centers with a direct upgrade path to an integrated CTI suite from Genesys Telecommunications Laboratories so users can manage e-mail and phone calls in a blended media environment. (Adante is a wholly owned subsidiary of Genesys.) Adante uses Microsoft's SQL Server and Internet Information Server.

Aptex Software. Aptex's patented context vector technology is a context-sensitive information-retrieval system that discovers relationships not able to be detected by other technologies. This system can respond automatically to customers with the appropriate information retrieved from a corporate database, or it can route customer inquiries received via e-mail, Web pages, or call centers to the appropriate CSR. It also includes an enhanced Java-based graphical user interface (GUI), enhanced learning capabilities to allow the reply generating agents to fine-tune their answers, and the ability to have targeted sales pitches tacked onto replies via an add-on called Virtual Sales Force. Version 3.0 adds queuing and routing to existing automatic response capabilities through integration with Adante's e-mail workflow application. SelectResponse is server software that runs on Windows NT or Solaris and works with any Java-enabled Web browser.

Brightware. The company's original automatic intelligent response technologies— Answer Agent and Advice Agent—were based on its knowledge management development environment. Contact Center (its e-mail-based call center module) extends existing Lotus Notes and Microsoft Outlook e-mail clients by providing availability status, message histories, and rapid response. Contact Center uses a push model of message distribution to route messages to the appropriate CSR. Contact Center stores message data in IBM's DB2, Microsoft's SQL Server, Oracle7 and Oracle8 Server, Sybase, and other database servers that support ODBC. (See Figure 28.)

FIGURE 28: BRIGHTWARE'S CONTACT CENTER

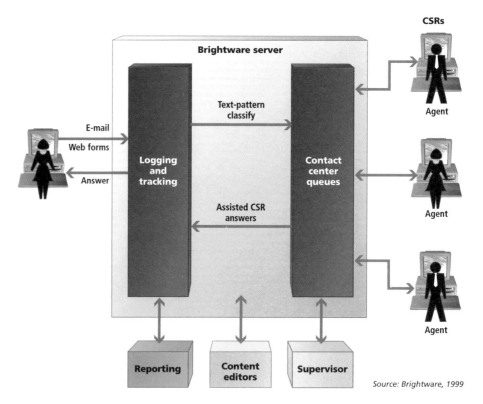

Source: Brightware, 1999

eGain Communications. eGain Communications' Email Management System (EMS) includes the standard packaged e-mail application features discussed previously, which are accessed via a standard Web browser. EMS runs on Windows NT with Microsoft's SQL Server and Internet Information Server. (See Figure 29 on page 95.)

ErgoTech. A unique feature in ErgoTech's WebLeader E-Mailroom product is a collaboration tool that lets users create a draft and circulate it to others for comment before sending out the response. E-Mailroom runs on Windows NT and uses SQL databases from IBM, Microsoft, or Oracle to store transaction records.

Kana Communications. Kana Communications' Customer Messaging System (CMS) version 3.0 has several add-on modules to help mine e-mail messages for additional information. Kana Direct extracts e-mail addresses from specific message categories to

FIGURE 29: eGAIN'S EMAIL MANAGEMENT SYSTEM

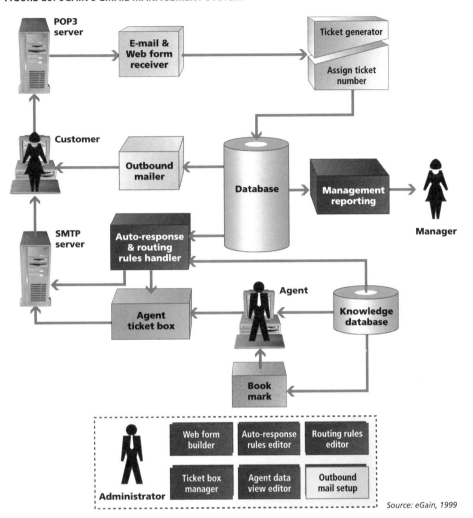

Source: eGain, 1999

create lists that can be used for outbound e-mail marketing; Kana Classify uses artificial intelligence to analyze inbound messages and classify them; and Kana Link lets companies connect CMS to other customer data repositories and exchange information.

Mustang Software. Mustang Software's e-mail management software, Internet Message Center (IMC) Enterprise Edition, is designed for companies that receive a high volume of e-mail. IMC includes features such as content analysis and automatic mail routing. After the content of a customer's e-mail is analyzed and routed to a CSR, the CSR can draw from a library of company documents and drag and drop the information relevant to the customer into the outgoing e-mail. The software also allows CSRs to access customers' profiles and history before composing a response. Version 2.3 features a new interface to the Response Library (the part of the client software that CSRs use to find scripted responses) that categorizes subjects and allows full-text searches on responses. IMC includes both a browser-based client and a Win32 client. IMC uses Microsoft's SQL Server and Internet Information Server.

Web-Based Customer Service

Use of the Web for customer service is not limited to e-mail or Web forms. Web-based customer-service technologies have expanded to include Internet telephony and alternatives such as interactive text chats and call-back requests.

The use of IP telephony in Internet call centers allows customers to speak directly with call center agents while they are using their browser to access the organization's Web site. It is frequently integrated into preexisting call centers and is composed of several core technologies. The gateway software, which runs on the server, provides the connection between the packet-switched Internet (ultimately, the customer's PC) and a circuit-switched connection to the CSR's telephone. The server software is installed as a front end to an ACD or Private Branch eXchange (PBX).

For an individual consumer to use IP telephony, the only components required are a single installed telephone line (such as a residential line); a multimedia PC (or an IP phone set); and Internet phone software, which is available for most operating environments.

IP telephony can be used in call centers when, for example, a user is on a corporate Web site and requests technical support. The user would click on a call button displayed on the page. The call button is a hypertext link that activates the IP telephony software that would then connect the user with a call center agent. Some call buttons might first ask for a customer ID. This data allows the call center agent to access the customer's history, which products the customer is using, and what problems the customer has encountered previously. Allowing the call center agent to access the customer account history also can enable the agent to sell upgrades or new products based on the customer's purchasing history. This capability is enabled by CTI technology and is available as a feature of high-end CRM software packages.

See "E-Business Extensions to ERP" on page 113 for more information on CRM software.

As an alternative to IP telephony, customers with two telephone lines can supply their secondary phone number to the merchant. While online, the customer can submit a request for support and expect a call on the secondary line. Call-backs also are used in situations where the customer is protected by a firewall that does not permit IP telephony. The Web site delivers a page to the customer's desktop that requests pertinent information from the customer (such as phone number, the nature of the query, or a convenient time to receive calls), and the agent then calls the customer back on the telephone.

For customers using slower connections, CSRs are using Web-based text chats. Customers can request support via the Web and then begin a "chat" with a CSR. Some software products, such as eBridge, allow for escorted browsing, in which the agent can escort the customer through Web pages containing information relevant to the customer's query. The agent and customer will move from Web page to Web page in sync with one another. This technology likely will quicken the resolution time of any given query and make customers more self sufficient in the future.

WEB-BASED CUSTOMER SERVICE VENDORS

The major telecommunications providers have become players in this software arena. MCI's Click'nConnect service places a button on corporate Web sites that will launch an IP telephony call via an Internet gateway that is routed to a call center agent's telephone. This service supports Web browsing and Voice-over-IP (VoIP) over a single telephone line. AT&T's InteractiveAnswers and Sprint's Give Me A Call service, however, require two lines—one telephone line for Internet access and another line for sending and receiving regular telephone calls. Some vendors currently offering customer relationship management IP telephony packages include the following:

eFusion. eFusion's IP Push to Talk mechanism allows customers to place calls to merchants while simultaneously browsing the Web on the same telephone line. eStream is an application gateway that provides a call-waiting service—when a new call comes in, a screen appears to notify the user of the incoming call. The user then can choose whether to receive the call. The user can accept and receive the call without closing the Internet connection.

eFusion's eBridge can be integrated as a front end to a preexisting call center. The call center agent and the customer must both click to browse, but the call agent decides the focus of the browsing session and determines which screens are active on the customer's desktop based on the customer's query. Both the customer and the call agent must have the Internet Call Assistant running on their desktop system. The Internet Call Assistant is an application that works in conjunction with the IP phone client and is responsible for registering users at the eFusion application gateway.

Ericsson. Ericsson's IPT solution is an Internet-based application package that allows phone-to-phone, fax-to-fax, PC-to-phone, or PC-to-PC connections over IP networks. It is the core hardware system that enables the following applications: The Phone Doubler provides a call-waiting service; Phone Doubler Quick Call (PDQC) allows customers to place calls to a call center while maintaining an Internet connection; and IP Telephony Solution for Carriers (IPTC) is a scalable application for large- or small-sized telcos or ISPs which uses compression techniques that support connections (such as those just mentioned) over an IP network.

Sitebridge. Sitebridge's CustomerNow software allows a CSR to communicate with a potential customer by presenting information proactively (or "pushing" it) to the customer's browser window. The information thus presented can consist of Web pages, Microsoft PowerPoint slides, other files or documents (such as sales collateral material in Adobe Acrobat form), or even a live product demonstration. The CSR can give a customer a "guided tour" of a Web site, moving through a series of pages in sequence, with each page being displayed simultaneously in both the CSR's and the customer's browser window. These pages will be "live," allowing the CSR to help the customer generate a product configuration or quotation, or complete an online order form.

One component of CustomerNow, the Profile Agent, obtains pertinent information about the customer prior to connection with a CSR. This information can include the customer's profile, the purpose of the call, or a case or order number. The application also automatically collects information about the shared Web session while it is in progress and allows this information to be downloaded into a SFA or contact management application.

Standards Initiatives
Several initiatives are underway to develop a set of standards or protocols to facilitate and enhance the growth of e-business. Most of these are proposed by consortia or groups of loosely affiliated vendors. Some, however, are sponsored by standards groups such as the Internet Engineering Task Force (IETF) and The Open Group.

OPEN BUYING ON THE INTERNET (OBI)
OBI is designed for business-to-business purchasing over the Internet and is aimed at standards-based procurement of high-volume, low-value transactions. The specifications are based on the 850 (purchase order) transaction sets defined in the ANSI X12 standards for EDI. Version 1.0 of the specification, released in July 1997, contains architectural as well as technical specifications and guidelines. The OBI standard is the result of work by the Internet Purchasing Roundtable, which included software vendors such as Netscape, Open Market, and SupplyWorks and buying organizations such as Apple, National Semiconductor, and Office Depot as well as American Express. The OBI Consortium of more than 60 members (taken under the umbrella of CommerceNet in June

See the sidebar "Key Internet Organizations" on page 178 for more information.

1998) now is in charge of the standard, and version 1.1 was completed in June 1998. The next version is expected in mid-1999. Planned enhancements include international support and XML. XML adoption should facilitate interoperability between different companies' systems for purchase orders, invoices, and other business documents that are critical to the procurement process.

The OBI version 1.1 specifications focus on the following processes:

- *Access*—The process by which a requisitioner accesses a specialized catalog at a selling organization

- *Ordering*—The data format for order-related information that is exchanged between trading partners

- *Transmission*—Methods for transmitting order-related data between organizations

- *Security*—Security mechanisms for authentication, secure communications, and nonrepudiation

The OBI architecture is based on the premise that process "owners" should be responsible for information associated with their business processes. For example, buying organizations are responsible for requisitioner profile information, account codes, tax status, and approvals. Selling organizations are responsible for electronic catalogs and the associated price, order entry, and inventory mechanisms. The OBI protocol ensures the two formats are able to interoperate. (See Figure 30 on page 99.)

The OBI architecture can be viewed as the interaction of four entities:

- *Requisitioner*—The person who actually wants the merchandise. This person accesses online catalogs of authorized suppliers and places the order (essentially a requisition) directly with the supplier.

- *Buying organizations*—The purchasing management and the information systems that support purchasing. These systems include an OBI server for receiving OBI Order Requests (requisitions) and generating OBI Orders as well as systems for handling the requisitioner profile information, trading partner information, workflow, approvals, and account and tax status information necessary to complete an order. The buying organization also negotiates and maintains contractual relationships with preferred selling organizations.

- *Selling organization*—Maintains an electronic catalog presenting product and price information that can be tailored for each buying organization. The selling organization's catalog must be integrated with inventory and order management systems (collectively referred to as "fulfillment systems") and an OBI server for sending OBI Order Requests to the buying organization's OBI server and for receiving OBI Orders.

- *Payment authority*—Provides payments to the selling organizations and an invoice or debit to the buying organization. Payment authorities may include financial institutions, or selling organizations may assume the responsibilities of a payment authority.

See "Catalogs" on page 53 for more information.

The OBI standard uses SSL to secure communications over the Internet. Digital certificates based on the X.509 standard are used for authentication of requisitioners as well as servers. Digital signatures can be applied to OBI Order Requests and OBI Orders to

FIGURE 30: OBI 1.0 PURCHASING PROCESS

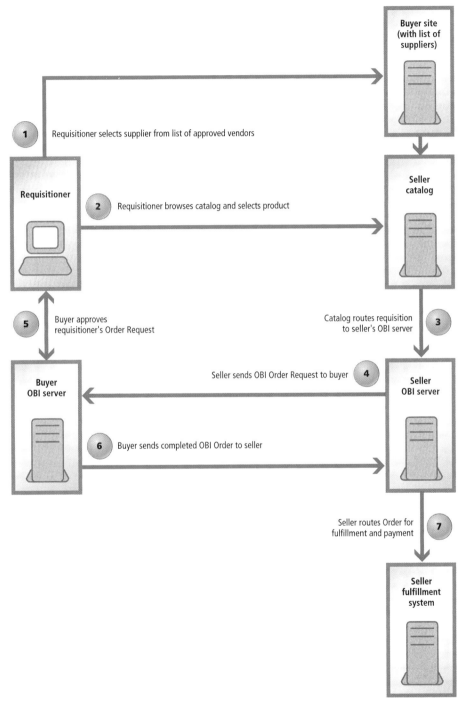

1. The OBI purchasing process begins with the requisitioner, who selects a potential supplier (seller) from a list of vendors that the purchasing department has approved and accesses that supplier's OBI server.
2. After making a product selection, the requisitioner submits a requisition directly to the supplier, rather than to the company's purchasing department.
3. The supplier's catalog server routes the requisition to the supplier's OBI server.
4. The supplier's OBI server then sends an Order Request to the purchasing department's OBI server, requesting authorization to proceed with the transaction.
5. The purchasing department reviews the Order Request and approves it.
6. To authorize the approved transaction, the purchasing department's OBI server sends an Order to the seller's OBI system.
7. The supplier's OBI server routes the approved Order to the fulfillment system.

Source: Designing Systems for Internet Commerce, 1998

provide high levels of assurance on the identity of the order originator. Exchange of OBI Order Requests and Orders is accomplished with HTTP. Within OBI, HTTP also is used for transmission of Order documents between servers.

Netscape's Xpert server is OBI-compliant, Commerce One provides an OBI-compliant solution, IBM has announced support for OBI in its Net.Commerce solution, and SupplyWorks has an OBI-compliant purchasing system.

OPEN TRADING PROTOCOL (OTP)

The Internet Open Trading Protocol (IOTP, or more commonly, OTP) was created by a global consortium of more than 30 vendors, financial institutions, and payment system organizations as a framework for implementing e-business. Global consortium members that played a direct role in creating OTP include Canadian Imperial Bank of Commerce, CyberCash, Fujitsu, Hitachi, HP/VeriFone, IBM, MasterCard, Mondex, Netscape, Oracle, Sun, Universal Card Services (formerly AT&T Universal Card Services), and Wells Fargo.

Unlike OBI, which is designed for business-to-business transactions, OTP is aimed at facilitating business-to-consumer transactions. This vendor-neutral protocol is designed to ensure that e-business transactions take place securely and efficiently, regardless of the method of payment used. OTP is extensible, meaning new trading features or approved payment mechanisms can be added if needed without disrupting any OTP protocol already in place. OTP works in conjunction with SET and other protocols. In October 1998, IOTP version 1 was introduced as a draft specification to the IETF. The IETF will take the responsibility for further development. In February 1999, the OTP working group of the IETF submitted version 2.0 of the specification as a draft. The group expects to submit OTP for IETF consideration as a proposed standard in mid-1999.

See "XML" on page 195 for more information.

OTP aims to standardize purchase agreements, product offerings, the transfer of goods and services, the delivery of purchase receipts, and problem resolution. By using XML to define components, OTP can provide interoperability among catalog and order systems, payment systems, and customer support systems.

OTP spans the entire e-business transaction life cycle by specifying clearly understood rules and methodologies that perform the following:

- Communicate the terms and conditions of a transaction, including offers for sale, agreements to purchase, and receipts for purchases.

- Acknowledge orders and arrange for delivery of goods and services digitally or physically.

- Support different payment mechanisms by complementing rather than replacing existing payment systems. In addition, OTP will enable users to process payments from debit/credit cards using smart card technology from Europay, MasterCard, and Visa.

- Provide support for problem resolution.

- Enable all parties in e-business transactions to keep detailed records of purchases. Such records could be used, for example, for audit purposes or to make expense claims. The records also could be used to send a claim back to a merchant to solve a problem. In addition, transaction data could be fed into financial management software programs for analysis and planning.

Market Overview
INTERNET COMMERCE APPLICATIONS

The market for Internet commerce applications experienced robust growth in 1998 and likely will continue through 2003, according to IDC. In 1998, the market for e-business applications reached $444 million; IDC estimates that figure will grow 280 percent to $1.7 billion in 1999. By 2003, the market is expected to top $13 billion. (See Figure 31 on page 101.) A significant factor behind the steep growth is the increased availability of these products since early 1998.

FIGURE 31: WORLDWIDE INTERNET COMMERCE APPLICATIONS MARKET: 1998–2003

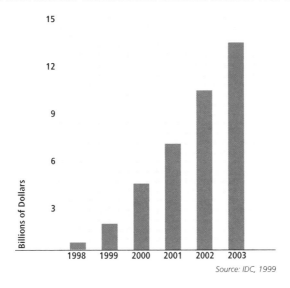

Source: IDC, 1999

IDC reports that in the U.S., the majority of the growth in the Internet commerce applications market will occur from now through early 2001. In Europe, demand for the software will peak about one year after the U.S. Meanwhile, the Asia Pacific region will overtake Europe in 2002 as the second-largest market for Internet commerce applications as China and Japan incorporate the Web into their business infrastructures.

The business-to-business Internet commerce applications market is extremely fragmented. Netscape was the leading vendor in 1998, with 15 percent market share; it was followed closely by Ariba, with 14 percent, according to IDC. Sterling Commerce was in third place with a 6.7 percent share. (See Figure 32.) Following AOL's acquisition of Netscape, AOL and Sun have formed an alliance headed by a Sun executive and seconded by an AOL executive; employees report to both companies. The Netscape name has been retained on the e-business server products.

FIGURE 32: TOP BUSINESS-TO-BUSINESS INTERNET COMMERCE APPLICATIONS VENDORS: 1998

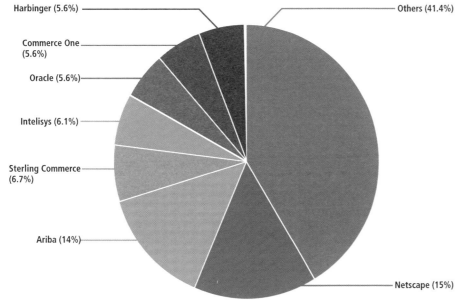

Total = $178.3 million   Source: IDC, 1999

IDC reports the business-to-consumer Internet applications market remains highly fragmented as well. The four leading vendors—BroadVision, Netscape, Open Market, and Oracle—had a combined share of 32 percent; each of the 30 other developers had no more than a 5 percent share. (See Figure 33.)

FIGURE 33: TOP BUSINESS-TO-CONSUMER INTERNET COMMERCE APPLICATIONS VENDORS: 1998

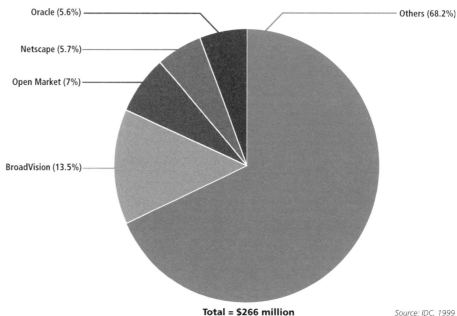

Oracle (5.6%)

Netscape (5.7%)

Open Market (7%)

BroadVision (13.5%)

Others (68.2%)

Total = $266 million

Source: IDC, 1999

SELL-SIDE PACKAGED APPLICATIONS

Dataquest estimates the sell-side e-business software market reached $155.8 million in 1998, a 93 percent growth over 1997 revenue. Figure 34 shows Dataquest's sales projections for sell-side software through 2003.

FIGURE 34: SELL-SIDE SOFTWARE MARKET: 1998–2003

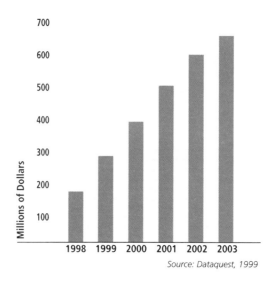

Source: Dataquest, 1999

In 1998, BroadVision and Open Market dominated the sell-side software market, with 16.6 and 20.2 percent market share, respectively. (See Figure 35 on page 103.)

FIGURE 35: TOP SELL-SIDE SOFTWARE VENDORS: 1998

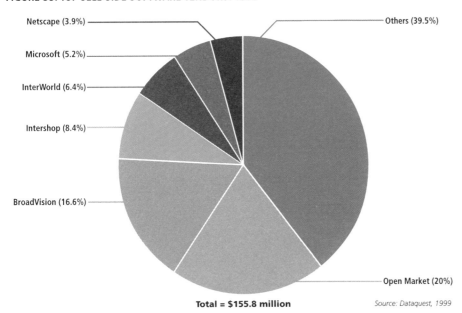

Netscape (3.9%)

Microsoft (5.2%)

InterWorld (6.4%)

Intershop (8.4%)

BroadVision (16.6%)

Others (39.5%)

Open Market (20%)

Total = $155.8 million   *Source: Dataquest, 1999*

Online Banking Applications. According to IDC, the market for online banking applications in the U.S. will be $326 million in 1999, doubling to $653 million in 2000. The online banking application market also will grow relative to the total banking/finance application market, from 17 percent in 1999 to 31 percent in 2000. Like other areas of e-business, the market is highly fragmented, with the top three vendors—Edify, Integrion, and Security First—accounting for less than one-third of total industry revenue in 1998; the next 15 vendors accounted for one-third, and vendors with revenue in this market of less than $1 million accounted for the remaining one-third. (Total industry revenue includes both software and services.)

FIGURE 36: WORLDWIDE WEB-BASED PROCUREMENT SOFTWARE SALES

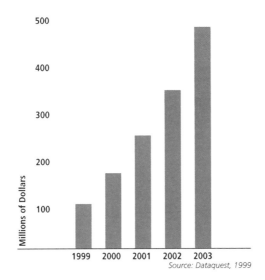

Millions of Dollars

500

400

300

200

100

1999 2000 2001 2002 2003
Source: Dataquest, 1999

BUY-SIDE SOFTWARE

Figure 36 illustrates Web-based procurement software sales projected through 2003 by Gartner. In a January 1999 study, Forrester Research reports that 65 percent of survey respondents currently use a Web-procurement solution that was built in-house; only 22 percent use a commercial product. The survey respondents cited two major future purchasing criteria for packaged Web-procurement software: better integration and improved functionality. (See Figure 37.)

FIGURE 37: FUTURE PURCHASING CRITERIA FOR WEB-PROCUREMENT SOFTWARE

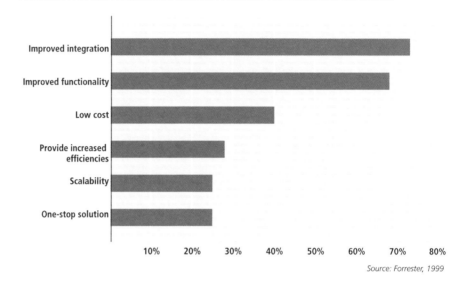

For a January 1999 study, Forrester Research interviewed 40 companies that were early adopters of Web-based MRO purchasing. Survey respondents indicated two major future purchasing criteria for packaged Web-procurement software: improved integration and improved functionality. Multiple responses were accepted.

Source: Forrester, 1999

CUSTOMER-FACING E-MAIL

Due to the ubiquity of e-mail, companies that today received 500 e-mail inquiries per day will receive 2,000 per day by the year 2000, according to Forrester Research. Although the market for e-mail response management software is not very large today, Gartner estimates it will reach $500 million by 2002.

Forecast

Sell-Side Applications

Companies doing e-business increasingly will buy (rather than build) their sell-side applications, except for situations in which the application itself is a significant source of competitive advantage.

XML will have a big impact on catalog vendors because proprietary catalog systems will be dropped as companies adopt open standards.

Configuration technologies linked directly to ERP systems will be available on manufacturers' and retail Web sites.

Through links to real-time inventory systems, customers will know immediately what items are in stock, which are on order, and how quickly items will arrive.

Use of shipping logistics and tax compliance software and services will proliferate during the forecast period.

The focus of e-business application software will shift away from narrowly defined commerce platforms toward a broader vision of managing customer relationships.

Outbound marketing will continue to mature, evidenced by increased targeted e-mail marketing, personalized Web sites, and more sophisticated tracking and trend analysis.

Buy-Side Applications

Buy-side (procurement) applications increasingly will be integrated with ERP systems. The procurement application will handle catalog, configuration, and availability and inventory status, and then will hand off the order to be placed through the buying organization's ERP system.

In the buy-side software market, companies will emerge that blend transactions, interactivity, and content based on buy-side platforms and catalog technology.

As more potential participants access the Web, the use of negotiated pricing mechanisms will grow. The special-purpose technology available today to implement negotiated and auction pricing will be integrated into enterprise and specialty Web sites.

Independent procurement applications vendors will offer complete internal process solutions for full-service purchasing. They will facilitate the integration of procurement applications with HR, ERP, and financial systems; manage directory-based authorization; and ease data aggregation and analysis.

Web-Based Customer Service

Tools that integrate video with call centers will mature. Examples include one-way video for customer instruction and two-way video interaction with customer service representatives. However, the applicability of these solutions will be limited until Internet infrastructure significantly increases the bandwidth available over today's dial-up speeds.

IP telephony increasingly will be incorporated into corporate applications as a standard feature. Call centers increasingly will use the Web as an additional communications facility.

Customer-facing e-mail systems will be extended to handle outgoing e-mail marketing campaigns and will become integrated more tightly with other forms of Web-based customer service.

Vertical online communities will develop, such as a value chain with multiple participants in which a retailer could pass a Web session to the product manufacturer for technical service.

Standards

Internet standards including OBI and OTP will grow in importance as the number of enterprises doing businesses on the Internet increase. Involvement of Internet standards organizations will speed up development and acceptance.

REFERENCES

ARTICLES

Abbott, Shawn. The debate for secure e-commerce. *UNIX Review's Performance Computing.* February 1999: 37.

Andrews, Whit. Startup aims to build better online catalogs. *InternetWorld.* October 12, 1998: 16.

Dorobek, Christopher J. Group demos way to shop multiple e-catalogs. *Government Computer News.* December 14, 1998: 8.

Dragan, Richard V. iCat Electronic Commerce Suite 3.0 Professional Edition. *PC Magazine.* January 5, 1999: 172.

Dugan, Sean. OBI connects buyers and sellers. *InfoWorld.* January 25, 1998.

Frook, John Evan. Blue collar business on the Web. *InternetWeek.* September 14, 1998: 43.

Hayes, Garrett Michael. E-commerce gets easier. *Computerworld.* August 3, 1998: 60.

Hoffman, Richard. Four solutions to rev up your e-commerce business. *Network Computing.* December 15, 1998: 75.

Indermaur, Kurt. At your service: electronic commerce agent technology. *DBMS.* September 1998: 31.

Kerstetter, Jim. Mercantec diversifies e-commerce products. *PCWeek.* September 21, 1998: 28.

O'Malley, Kevin and Terence Kelly. An API for Internet auctions. *Dr. Dobb's Journal.* September 1998: 70.

Shachtman, Noah. Get personal—business sites are trying to match products and services more closely to customers' needs. Is it working? *InternetWeek.* November 2, 1998: 36.

Shankar, Gess. Inex builds stores fast. *InfoWorld.* September 28, 1998: 52.

Strom, David. E-wallets: not the right solution for e-shopping. *Computerworld.* January 11, 1999: 30.

Tools for growth in e-commerce: the future is bright for business-to-business electronic commerce. *InformationWeek.* December 7, 1998: 91.

Watson, Weyman and Douglas Bailey. OBI: up close and personal. *e-Business Advisor.* October 1998: 44.

Weil, Nancy. Giga: few online profits in next 12–18 months. *Network World.* January 11. 1999.

PERIODICALS, INDUSTRY AND TECHNICAL REPORTS

Bell, Steven, Stan Dolberg, Shah Cheema, and Jeremy Sharrad. *Resizing online business trade.* Forrester Research. November 1998.

Chatham, Bob, Stan Dolberg, and Tripp Ritter. *Beyond online order taking.* Forrester Research. October 1998.

Chatham, Bob, Stan Dolberg, and Tripp Ritter. *Buy-side market realities.* Forrester Research. January 1999.

Cooperstein, David M. and David Goodtree. *E-mail outsourcing.* Forrester Research. December 22, 1998.

Dolberg, Stan, Stuart D. Woodring, Shanta Puchtler, Elizabeth W. Boehm, and Tripp Ritter. *Sizing commerce software.* Forrester Research. May 1998.

DuBois, Erina. *Business to business electronic commerce reaches into the supply chain.* Dataquest. May 4, 1998.

Hagen, Paul R. *Best practices of highly effective personalizers.* Forrester Research. November 12, 1998.

Hagen, Paul R. *Dell taps Ask Jeeves for self-service search.* Forrester Research. November 24, 1998.

Hagen, Paul R., Carl D. Howe, and Debra Berman. *Pragmatic personalization.* Forrester Research. May 1998.

Hagen, Paul R. and Donald A. DePalma. *Better customer service propels personalization.* Forrester Research. July 31, 1998.

IDC. *Anatomy of a cyber sale: the components of an Internet commerce transaction.* IDC. May 1998.

Kadison, Maria LaTou, David E. Weisman, and Ketty C. Lieu. *New retail competencies.* Forrester Research. June 1998.

Levitt, Mark. *Automated e-mail and Web response software: bringing better service to your organization.* IDC. October 1998.

Levitt, Mark. *E-mail/Web response software market review and forecast: 1997–2002.* IDC. May 1998.

Lief, Varda, Mary Modahl, Waverly Deutsch, Gordon Lanpher, and Michael Putnam. *Dynamic trade.* Forrester Research. June 1998.

McCarty, Meredith. *Worldwide Internet and e-commerce services market and trends forecast, 1998–2002.* IDC. October 1998.

McClure, Steve and Barry Plotkin. *Brightware: automating customer interaction on the World Wide Web with intelligent agents.* IDC. August 1998.

McQuivey, James L. and Christopher Mines. *Personify enters the commerce personalization fray.* Forrester Research. June 19, 1998.

Meta. *From outsource to cybersource.* Meta. December 18, 1998.

Meta. *Interbusiness commerce infrastructure models.* Meta. July 8, 1998.

Meta. *Organizing for EC.* Meta. September 28, 1998.

Meta. *Organizing for EC: getting started.* Meta. October 26, 1998.

Meta. *The ROI of buy-side electronic commerce.* Meta. July 23, 1998.

Meta. *The ROI of sell-side electronic commerce.* Meta. July 10, 1998.

Moore, Cynthia and Susan Cournoyer. *Electronic commerce services in vertical markets: the demand side.* Dataquest. August 17, 1998.

Purchase, E. and M. West. *Electronic commerce platforms and applications.* Gartner. January 13, 1999.

Satterhwaite, R. *Introducing the BTB "Sell side magic quadrant."* Gartner. September 3, 1998.

ONLINE SOURCES

Woods, Bob. *Lycos joins the auction gang.* Newsbytes News Network. November 2, 1998.

URLs OF SELECTED MENTIONED COMPANIES AND ORGANIZATIONS

Art Technology Group www.atg.com

Aspect Development www.aspectdv.com

Calico Technology www.calico-technology.com

Firefly Network www.firefly.com

FreeMarkets OnLine www.freemarkets.com

FairMarket www.fairmarket.com

Information and Content Exchange www.w3.org/TR/1998/NOTE-ice-19981026

Internet Engineering Task Force www.ietf.org

Kana Communications www.kana.com

Mercado Software www.mercado.com

Moai Technologies www.moai.com

National Semiconductor www.nsc.com

Open Buying on the Internet www.openbuy.org

OpenSite Technologies www.opensite.com

Platform for Privacy Preferences www.w3.org/P3P

Security First National Bank www.securityfirst.com

Trade'ex www.tradeex.com

TRUSTe www.truste.org

United Nations Standard Product and Service Classifications www.unspsc.org

Executive Summary

Integration is critical to e-business because it is the bridge that connects an organization's e-business systems with its preexisting enterprise applications. This chapter focuses on the near-term technologies companies will need as they begin to integrate existing information technologies with new e-business systems.

The technology candidates that will see the most activity during the forecast period are e-business extensions to enterprise resource planning systems, electronic data interchange, and enterprise application integration technologies. The goal of these systems is to link entire sales, production, and delivery processes and systems electronically into one seamless flow of information between an enterprise, its customers, and its partners.

Integration is not a trivial undertaking, however. Organizations are discovering e-business requires them to integrate formerly disparate systems and applications at a higher level of interactivity than was previously the case.

Assuming organizations work in tandem with partners, there also is the need for information flows to follow the physical flows associated with production and distribution. The increased use of electronic data interchange on the Web to supplement electronic data interchange's traditional use on proprietary networks is a parallel trend to increased integration of business processes across enterprises.

Finally, there is the need for organizations to support a range of distinct business processes both inside and outside of enterprise boundaries. Enterprise application integration often is defined as the sharing of data in support of shared business processes among any connected applications or data sources. Moreover, such sharing is accomplished without massive changes to existing applications and data structures.

Therefore, the key technology issue for application integration is how e-businesses get applications that are based on different technologies and with differing business processes and data models to work together in a common way on a network. More specifically, how does an organization integrate an e-business "stack" on top of what already exists? How is integration accomplished quickly and with minimal disruption to everyday operations, not to mention preexisting investment?

Answers to these questions are neither trivial nor inexpensive; however, they are crucial for scaling e-business functionality. This chapter will focus on enterprise application integration in three main areas: the movement of enterprise resource planning systems to an electronic business environment; the extension of electronic data interchange messaging over value-added networks to enterprise data interchange over the Internet; and emerging enterprise application integration middleware designed to connect applications without the need for custom programming.

Integration Levels and Methods

With e-business, more applications will touch customers and business partners directly than ever before. As a result, the need to flex or change supply chains rapidly, collaboratively plan and schedule with partners, and personalize customer treatment will compel tighter integration between the various applications used by a single enterprise as well as integration between the applications used by trading partners. The challenge, therefore, is for organizations to understand how best to accomplish the appropriate degree of integration.

The reality of e-business is that most organizations will be adding e-business functionality to an already-existing information technology (IT) infrastructure, rather than starting from a "greenfield" situation. As a result, organizations are faced with the challenge of integrating the new e-business systems with their preexisting applications. The technologies for doing so are the focus of this chapter.

Integration can occur in various forms, which vary along multiple attributes. For example, the level of functionality provided by different integration solutions varies, as does the degree of transparency (that is, how nonobtrusive or seamless the integration is to a user of the system). In general, integration methods that provide the highest level of functionality and the greatest degree of transparency also are the most complex to implement.

In its simplest form, integration can mean the ability to export data files from one application and import them into another application, possibly after undergoing some translation between different data formats. The data could consist of transactions (for example, orders placed via an e-business server that are being imported into a fulfillment system) or of other types of data (for example, part numbers and descriptions that are being exported from an order entry system into an e-business server's catalog). This type of integration often occurs in batch mode, meaning that changes to data in the source system accumulate over time, and then are applied periodically (for example, every 24 hours) to the target system.

More sophisticated forms of integration can differ from this simple form in several ways. Rather than exporting data files from the source application and importing them into the target, the source system may be able to invoke actions in the target system. This invocation can occur either synchronously, using a remote procedure call (RPC), or asynchronously, using message queuing. This invocation can be event-driven, meaning that it happens in response to actions in the target system rather than via a periodic batch update. In some sophisticated forms of integration, different data formats can be reconciled automatically in one of the applications or they both can use the same data formats in the first place, rather than needing a separate translation process. For example, an e-business server could invoke functionality in an enterprise resource planning (ERP) suite to check on product availability before accepting an order over the Web.

In reality, integration between two applications typically occurs at multiple levels simultaneously. Figure 38 on page 111 depicts seven different levels of integration; each level relies on services provided by the levels below it. The lowest four levels, application connectivity, provide basic data movement between applications. They encompass the functionality provided by traditional middleware.

The next two levels, content transformation and business event processing, concentrate on application integration. Content transformation includes data format translation services as well as matching and validation of data semantics (that is, the meaning of data elements) between applications. Business event processing allows the source

"Middleware" describes several different types of software, all of which sit in the middle and provide connectivity between two or more types of software. It also can translate information between the software.

FIGURE 38: APPLICATION INTEGRATION HIERARCHY

Business Integration	**Business Process Development** Business process design/modeling, real-time decision support, state management
Application Integration	**Business Event Processing** Automatic event notification, flow control, content routing, transactional integrity
	Application Content Transformation Format translation, data semantics, validation, pre-built templates
Application Connectivity	**Application Bridges & Gateways** For legacy, Web, database, and packaged applications
	Application Interaction Styles Publish/subscribe, publish/reply, file transfer, request/reply, conversational
	Message Handling Services Queuing, security, message management, administration
	Basic Communications Point-to-point, reliable broadcast, IP multicast, IIOP/ORB, database, Web, 3270 SNA

Source: NASG, 1999

application to invoke actions in the target application in response to events such as changes in the values of critical data, the expiration of timers, the arrival of control signals, or the completion of transactions. This integration often is provided by the various components of an ERP vendor's application suite. Providing this integration between applications from multiple vendors is the objective of an emerging class of products known as enterprise application integration (EAI) middleware.

The highest level of integration shown is business integration. This category describes an ideal state where systems enable such tight integration among multiple business processes that a change in one process is propagated automatically into related processes. The tools to create this degree of integration do not yet exist.

In addition to these multiple levels of integration, approaches to carrying out the actual integration differ. These approaches roughly follow a four-layer taxonomy. (See Figure 39 on page 112.) The lowest-level technical response involves complete custom integration between multiple applications. The custom-developed integration would need to handle everything from the basic details of moving data reliably from one application to another, to the business logic that implements the integration of the two applications' functionality.

The next approach relies on classic middleware—including RPCs, message-oriented middleware (MOM), and transaction processing (TP) monitors—to handle some of the "housekeeping" details of the integration. Using middleware would free developers from writing their own routines to handle reliable transfer of data between the two applications or from worrying about enforcing transactional integrity when multiple systems are being integrated. Developers still would be responsible for writing the business logic.

See "Application Servers as TP Monitors" on page 206 for more information.

Another approach uses vendor-supplied toolkits, known as EAI middleware, to provide the business logic as well as the data transfer aspects of application integration. The EAI middleware vendors supply prebuilt adapters or connectors that can be used to link the functionality of leading enterprise packaged applications. The vendors also supply tools to build adapters for custom-developed software. Some EAI middleware packages also operate at higher levels of the integration hierarchy shown in Figure 38, with an emphasis on integration between business processes rather than just integration between information systems. Such a package would provide business process

FIGURE 39: APPROACHES TO APPLICATION INTEGRATION

interfaces for typical functions such as order entry, so that a new order placed via an e-business Web site could contact and update all the applications involved in the order-entry process.

In the final approach, a single application vendor provides integration between multiple components of its application suite. The result would be similar to that described for EAI middleware but without the need to purchase third-party software to connect the applications. Furthermore, an application vendor typically can provide integration between its own applications that is tighter and more seamless than is possible with applications from multiple vendors because fewer inconsistencies must be bridged between the underlying data elements and logic of the two applications.

The choice of integration levels and approaches is not an either/or proposition for firms; they likely will use multiple types. The remainder of this chapter focuses on three specific areas of integration:

- *E-business extensions to major ERP suites*—Allow an organization to purchase e-business functionality from their ERP vendor with the expectation that it will integrate tightly with their existing systems.

- *EDI*—Historically has provided integration between the applications of multiple trading partners using standardized message formats and specialized network services, and is being affected in several ways by the use of the Internet for e-business.

- *EAI middleware*—Allows for integration between different applications operated by a single enterprise as well as between those applications operated by multiple enterprises.

ERP

For the many companies that use major vendors' ERP suites as the center of their applications architecture, integration of new e-business systems primarily means integrating those systems with the existing ERP package. All the major ERP vendors have established e-business strategies that include the following:

- How the functionality in their packages can be accessed through standard Web browsers as opposed to application-specific client software

- How their packages will interoperate with e-business systems that are being implemented, or can themselves encompass e-business functionality

- How their packages fit into a less enterprise-bounded e-business world, where information and transaction flows within the enterprise remain important but flows beyond the enterprise assume equal importance

EDI

Although EDI has been used heavily in certain industries for the last 20 years, the explosion of Internet-based e-business is beginning to change the EDI world in several ways. Providing Web-based interfaces to classic EDI systems expands the scope of EDI usage by allowing smaller companies, that might not have been able to afford the cost of modifying their systems to make them EDI-compliant, to participate in an EDI-enabled trading community. At the same time, using the Internet to transport EDI message traffic has become an alternative to using traditional value-added networks (VANs), although the Internet does not provide the full functionality offered by a VAN. Meanwhile, efforts are underway to reimplement traditional EDI message formats in the eXtensible Markup Language (XML).

See "XML" on page 195 for more information.

More generally, the entire e-business world is faced with the challenge of ensuring that desirable features of traditional EDI, such as security, reliability, and authentication, become universal in Internet-based e-business.

EAI

A third important area of enterprise system integration is packaged middleware for connecting e-business systems to other enterprise applications. EAI software, as this category usually is called, is a product that facilitates the integration of multiple applications that otherwise could not be integrated without custom software development. Unlike traditional middleware, EAI software is designed to provide prepackaged connectors that integrate commonly used enterprise applications. In addition, EAI software attempts to effect integration at a higher level than traditional middleware—creating integration at the application or business process level rather than at the data level. EAI software vendors and their customers believe this layer is a more natural candidate for enterprise integration, and efforts at this level will result in lower-cost, more robust integration solutions.

E-Business Extensions to ERP

The Internet's initial impact on the major ERP suites was the addition of Web-browser interfaces, which allow employees to access an ERP system via an alternative client than the native ERP software. This setup had several benefits: The learning curve required for users to access ERP functions via a browser interface is lower than if they must use the myriad forms-based screens that typify most ERP user interfaces. Furthermore, because Web browsers are installed on virtually every computer in use today, adding a browser interface provided the mechanism for universal self-service employee access to enterprise systems such as benefits enrollment or time and expense reporting. However, providing a browser interface does not by itself add any e-business functionality to an ERP system.

Once the browser interface had been added, the next step was to allow access by non-employees to selected information within an ERP system. For example, customers could check the status of a pending order or verify that a payment had been credited to their accounts; these actions could take place even if the order and the payment were made via traditional (non e-business) methods.

Adding full e-business functionality to an ERP suite goes well beyond providing read-only access to customer data, however. It can include providing an e-business Web server that implements an electronic storefront and provides tight linkages between the Web site's catalog, order-entry system, customer database, and other elements and the corresponding ERP suite functionality. It also can include Internet-based supply chain integration; one organization's ERP suite can communicate electronically with the corresponding systems of suppliers, distributors, and other business partners.

The functionality of ERP suites can be divided into several broad areas:

- *Back-office operations*—Areas such as manufacturing, financials, inventory and order management, and human resources (HR) were the first to be covered by ERP systems, which integrated these previously disparate functions into one package.

- *Supply chain management (SCM)*—This function enables companies to optimize the entire logistics, production, and distribution process, from acquiring raw materials from suppliers to scheduling and shipping products to customers.

- *Sales force automation (SFA)*—Some ERP vendors also are providing SFA functionality to manage aspects of the sales process such as contact management, sales forecasting, and order management.

- *Customer relationship management (CRM)*—One theme of CRM (as opposed to SFA) is to connect the various experiences a customer has with a company—marketing, product selection, purchasing, receiving, and post-sale support—into a managed relationship, where a company is able to identify which customers it should focus its limited resources on and how to do so effectively. The other theme of CRM is to provide a seamless customer experience to encourage customer retention.

Ultimately, packaged vendors want to provide total business solutions and have their package serve as the corporate information backbone.

Vendors, integrators, and industry analysts have begun to describe the integration of e-business functionality with ERP systems as e-business ERP or Web-based ERP. Other terms used by the technology press include ERP/Web-extension and e-business backbone.

For some organizations with well-established ERP systems, the challenge will be to coordinate Web activities with internal information systems implemented well before the rise of the Web. However, other organizations will need to implement new ERP systems that include e-business functionality. Meanwhile, ERP vendors, enablers, and integrators are working to deliver new products and solutions to help organizations meet these challenges. Their efforts range in complexity from Web-enabling ERP functions via a browser interface to integrating ERP functions between business partners.

WEB-ENABLING ERP FUNCTIONS

Because the usual business purpose of Web-enabling is to allow a larger group of users to access a specific function, the Web interface typically is simpler than the application-specific ERP client software; for example, it may allow only the more common interactions, include more built-in defaults, and so on.

One area where many companies have working systems today is in the self-service HR intranet area. These applications range from simple viewing of HR policies through display of individual employee HR status to self-service benefits selection and enrollment.

LINKING E-BUSINESS SERVERS TO ERP FUNCTIONS

A more demanding application involves linking e-business servers to core ERP functions. The trend is for ERP vendors to supply both application programming interfaces (APIs) for order entry or catalog front ends and ready-made catalog or electronic storefront modules that conform to those APIs. Customers can choose the ERP vendor's own e-business server or can integrate one from a third-party software vendor that calls on the ERP suite's APIs.

INTEGRATING ERP FUNCTIONS WITH OTHER ERP SYSTEMS

The scenario for supporting browser-level business partner access—that is, access by a member of the business partner's staff—to core ERP functions is not much different from the scenario for consumer access. The same kinds of APIs and prebuilt applications for those APIs can be used for business-partner integration where the partner is a user responding to information displayed on a browser.

The vision of directly linking two business partners' ERP systems is a more demanding form of integration. Most important, the two ERP systems must be able to communicate transactions directly, without human intervention. For example, SAP's Business-to-Business Procurement package can communicate between buyer-purchasing and supplier-catalog modules from different sources. Similarly, PeopleSoft offers a free downloadable Supply Chain Collaborator application for integration with PeopleSoft's supply chain modules. Although today's ERP integration solutions are vendor-specific, increased movement toward multivendor integration scenarios is anticipated during the forecast period.

INTEGRATING ERP FUNCTIONS WITH E-BUSINESS VIA APPLICATION SERVERS

Web application servers—special-purpose Web servers that provide the functionality needed for transactional applications—can be used to connect Web-based e-business applications with an ERP suite. Typically, the application server hosting the e-business application is integrated with the ERP package by using connectors written by the application server vendor that call on APIs supplied by the ERP vendor. (See Table 1.) The functionality of these APIs also may be exposed to application server developers, although the level of detail of existing APIs is somewhat coarse-grained compared with other kinds of application-server objects.

An application programming interface (API) is a message format used by an application program to communicate with the operating system or other programs such as a database management system.

See "Web Application Servers" on page 204 for more information.

TABLE 1: ERP/APPLICATION SERVER INTEGRATION SOLUTIONS

Vendor	ERP/Application Server	Description
Apple	Apple WebObjects	WebObjects has created Adaptors for both SAP and PeopleSoft. These interfaces were designed prior to the SAP Java RFC (JRFC) and are custom solutions for the Windows NT and Sun Solaris platforms. WebObjects also maintains an ability to interface with pure Java but does not have specific Java-based ERP connectors.
Bluestone	Bluestone	Bluestone is the first all-Java Web application server to provide an SAP connector using SAP's new JRFC. Bluestone also has created its own Java-based connector to PeopleSoft, shipping it in late 1998. Bluestone claims several wizards and highly graphical views of fine-grained SAP data tables make it easy to add business logic objects to applications developed in its environment.

TABLE 1: ERP/APPLICATION SERVER INTEGRATION SOLUTIONS (CONTINUED)

Vendor	ERP/Application Server	Description
HAHT Software	HAHTsite	HAHTsite was the first with a customized connection to SAP. HAHTsite is not a Java-based server, but it does have wizards and class libraries that give the application developer drag-and-drop access to all SAP variables. Its latest release, which became available in February 1999, allows rapid application development (RAD) access to nonrelational data sources. HAHT claims its server development environment can talk to any ERP system that has a published API; however, for ERP systems other than SAP, the burden of programming the ERP connection falls to the customer.
IBM	IBM WebSphere	IBM has connectors to MQSeries, CICS, IMS, and DCE Encina; Lotus Domino has a connection through LotusScript eXtensions (LSX) for SAP's R/3. As a committed supporter of Enterprise JavaBeans (EJBs), IBM also will benefit from the EJB 2.0 ERP plug-ins, once they become available.
NetDynamics (division of Sun)	NetDynamics	The Platform Application Component (PAC) for SAP is about two years old and is based on a combination of BAPIs and RFCs, resulting in tight integration with SAP. The PeopleSoft PAC is a little more than a year old. Both provide what NetDynamics describes as "coarse grain" business objects within the NetDynamics application programming environment. Having been purchased by Sun almost a year ago, NetDynamics is in the process of realigning its technology toward the full spectrum of Sun's Java APIs, but that is a major transition from its previous platform-specific C/C++ coding.
Netscape	Netscape Application Server (NAS)	Formerly Kiva, the NAS for SAP R/3 had its first customer shipment in January 1999. According to Netscape, the SAP Java RFC was not sufficiently mature when the SAP-oriented connection was developed, so it uses BAPIs and other RFCs. Netscape currently is working on a JRFC upgrade to the NAS for SAP R/3. A NAS for PeopleSoft is expected to be released by mid-1999.
Persistence Software	PowerTier Web Server	Persistence Software, another all-Java Web application server, has developed no ERP plug-ins of its own but claims third-party SAP and PeopleSoft connection modules from Active Software work with its PowerTier Web Server.
WebLogic (acquired by BEA Systems)	BEA Connector Series	WebLogic is a pure-Java Web application server company acquired by BEA Systems in 1998. The company reports it recently has achieved integration with BEA's Connector Series, which includes a BEA-to-SAP connector (done by TSI Mercator) and a BEA-to-PeopleSoft connector.

Source: Zona Research, 1999

THE OPEN APPLICATIONS GROUP

The Open Applications Group Inc. (OAGI) was founded in 1995 by a group of ERP vendors seeking to develop interoperability standards in ERP software. Today, OAGI membership has expanded to include a wide range of ERP technology vendors and associated organizations. Current members include the leading ERP and EAI vendors as well as other software vendors and PricewaterhouseCoopers.

See "Data Type Descriptors" on page 195 for more information on DTDs.

In August 1998, OAGI announced full support for the industry-standard meta language, XML, approved by the World Wide Web Consortium (W3C) in February 1998. The data type descriptors (DTDs) necessary to define integration content to XML were published on the OAGI Web site in January 1999. The XML DTD files, expressed in machine-readable format, provide the common model for business software application component interoperability contained in the Open Applications Group Integration Specification (OAGIS). OAGIS describes the major components, their integration dialogs, and the content of those dialogs for many key enterprise business applications, including financials, human resources, manufacturing, logistics, and supply chain components.

ERP Providers

Following is a representative list of leading ERP vendors and their initiatives to provide e-business functionality.

BAAN

Baan has announced plans to release a series of Web-based applications called Baan E-Enterprise. Although still in the early stages of development in May 1999, the applications are designed to extend an enterprise's supply chain by sending mobile agents over the Web to search key suppliers for materials, check product inventory, place orders, notify accounting systems, and handle shipping arrangements. Baan says the system's first module, called Purchase Order Push, will be released in late 1999.

Currently, BaanERP delivers Web e-business capabilities to employees primarily for managing the back-office sales order fulfillment process from product selection to product feedback. BaanERP uses both Java and ActiveX to deliver access to Baan functionality through desktop browsers. Baan reports that by using the Web-enabled functionality in the BaanERP suite, users can manage the sales order entry and tracking process entirely via a Web browser.

J.D. EDWARDS

The December 1998 release of J.D. Edwards' OneWorld ERP software included Java and HyperText Markup Language (HTML) clients for Web and intranet deployment. These new options allow employees to use a Web browser to initiate OneWorld Financial, Manufacturing, Distribution/Logistics, and Human Resources applications. OneWorld runs on both UNIX and Windows NT Web servers.

Moving forward, J.D. Edwards is working toward the following goals:

- Universal availability of access to browser-based OneWorld applications
- Java-enablement for its WorldVision AS/400 solution

ORACLE

Oracle has announced its intention to move its entire suite of enterprise applications to the Web. Oracle Applications 11, released in mid-1998, includes Web applications for more than 20 new business processes. Examples of Oracle's Internet-enabled applications now available include these:

- *Oracle Strategic Procurement*—Released in November 1998, Oracle Strategic Procurement is a self-service, intranet-enabled ERP application that automates the entire purchasing life cycle from planning, to procurement, to payment. Using Oracle Strategic Procurement, buyers can concentrate on analyzing supplier performance and procurement opportunities and creating and maintaining key supplier relationships.

- *Oracle Field Sales Online*—Released in September 1998, Oracle Field Sales Online is a browser-based solution for intranets that automates the full sales cycle from account and contact management, to opportunity management and pipeline analysis, to order management and sales compensation. Oracle reports sales representatives can use the system intuitively—accessing summary information such as booked orders, purchases, and sales transactions. Sales representatives then can export the information to their preferred spreadsheet.

PEOPLESOFT

In November 1998, PeopleSoft introduced a comprehensive e-business strategy comprising three key components:

- *Transform the ERP backbone into an e-business backbone*—PeopleSoft is enhancing its ERP offering by integrating it with full EDI, electronic funds transfer (EFT), and messaging agents and by exposing an appropriate collection of APIs in the core software for add-ons.

- *Provide e-business extensions*—PeopleSoft will provide (in-house or with partners and acquisitions) a set of business process modules that can be used by employees, customers, and business partners. The set of processes includes sell-side applications such as Web order entry, Web bill presentment, and online bill payment and buy-side applications such as coordinating and managing supply and demand among trading partners.

  PeopleSoft already has a line of self-service applications for simple Web-enabled access to core functions. PeopleSoft supplies applications for use by employees (benefits, training, and procurement), vendors (invoice, payment, and delivery information), and customers (order status and payment status tracking).

- *Construct the PeopleSoft Business Network (PSBN)*—PeopleSoft intends to offer an enterprise intranet solution to bring together a set of functions that will make PSBN the home page for enterprise users. PeopleSoft and Microsoft announced in March 1999 that key design and software for PSBN would come from Microsoft.

  Among the initial functions to be included in PSBN are these:

  - An employee benefits community that enables employees to self-select benefits with the help of online guides to the various benefits options available.

  - A recruiting and training community where company recruiters can use PSBN for job postings, interview scheduling, and employee evaluations while prospective job candidates can use the system to get directions to company headquarters.

  - Other functions that share the employee self-service orientation, including Payroll and Procurement, Telecom Services, and Travel and Expense Management.

SAP

SAP has had EDI and EFT capabilities for many years. Now, SAP is integrating Web e-business capabilities for employees, suppliers, and customers into its R/3 ERP suite via Releases 3.1 and 4.0.

Release 3.1 (which shipped in December 1996) delivers e-business functions including product catalog access and online store building. Release 3.1 also provides employees with Web browser access to a variety of functions, including sales order creation and status, inventory queries, and customer account management.

With Release 3.1, SAP enhanced the R/3 system for a more seamless integration with the Web through four key features:

- The SAP Internet Transaction Server (ITS)

- Business Application Programming Interfaces (BAPIs)

- Internet Application Components (IACs)

- Remote Function Calls (RFCs)

SAP's R/3 Release 4.0 expands the Internet functionality of its ERP applications. For example, Release 4.0 includes more than 40 R/3 IACs and hundreds of new BAPIs. 1998's Release 4.5 has more than 80 IACs and additional new BAPIs.

Organizations not in a position to upgrade to SAP Release 3.1 or higher can use other Web integration methods. These methods include using a third-party tool, such as the NetDynamics Web application server, to access the SAP BAPIs. In addition, BAPIs in SAP also can be accessed directly using Java, C++, and Visual Basic (ActiveX).

ITS. SAP's ITS is the gateway between a user's Web browser and R/3. ITS implements a Web interface to R/3 that enables employees to access R/3 transactions with a Web browser instead of the SAP client software. (See Figure 40.) The server runs on Windows NT 4.0 using Netscape's Enterprise Server or Microsoft's Internet Information Server, or it runs on HP-UX, IBM's AIX, and Sun's Solaris using Enterprise Server.

FIGURE 40: SAP'S INTERNET TRANSACTION SERVER

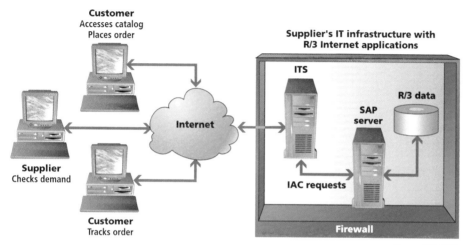

Source: SAP, 1999

BAPIs. With the cooperation of Microsoft and other third parties, SAP created BAPIs to enable customers and third-party vendors to integrate their software components with R/3. (BAPIs have e-business applicability but are not e-business-specific.) By using BAPIs, programmers can continue to use their preferred development language without having to be experts in ABAP, SAP's proprietary language. In addition, the BAPI interface is published (available to anyone) and stable (it will not change between SAP releases). To date, SAP BAPIs accommodate CORBA, Java, and Microsoft's Component Object Model (COM)/Distributed COM (DCOM) programming.

IACs. IACs are Internet-enabled SAP business applications; they provide the business logic as well as the Web page design. They are built upon BAPIs and require the use of SAP's ITS.

IACs execute transactions within R/3 in response to requests from ITS. Each IAC is designed to provide an Internet-enabled solution for a specific business transaction (such as Create Sales Orders).

SAP R/3 Release 4.0's IACs can be customized to fit client needs. These IACs include a Product Catalog application, an Online Store, Available to Promise (ATP) functionality, Order Entry, Service Requests, Financial Electronic Correspondence, and Interactive Requests, including the ability to query a bank for interest rates or account balances. Additionally, Release 4.0 provides order status checking, stock replenishment, and bank data transfers.

RFCs. RFCs are a series of interfaces implemented as class libraries. BAPIs are a type of RFC. In late 1998, SAP released a Java RFC aimed at interfacing with Java-based Web application servers that support Enterprise JavaBeans (EJBs).

Evolution and Future of Electronic Data Interchange

This section covers various changes underway in the world of EDI. These include the use of the Internet to carry traditional EDI message traffic as a replacement for a traditional VAN; the use of Web interfaces to traditional EDI functionality as a means of allowing a broader range of businesses to participate in EDI; and the reimplementation of existing EDI message standards in XML. Among the lessons being learned by e-business practitioners is that EDI will remain a critical infrastructure for Web-based commerce, given that EDI provides users with security (that is, trading partners can be assured that an EDI document is routed without modification) as well as audit trails, acknowledgments (important for document tracking), and authentication.

In that sense, although certain technologies and emerging standards such as XML are changing how EDI is presented and used, the business case for EDI remains unchanged. Consequently, the point of many of the following technologies and emerging standards is to map desirable EDI functionality to a Web environment, either by using the Web to transport EDI message traffic or by reimplementing EDI functionality in new forms via the Web.

TRADITIONAL EDI

EDI refers to the exchange of electronic business documents, such as purchase orders and invoices, between applications. The exchange involves no paper or human intervention. EDI requires a network connection between the two companies exchanging business documents, called trading partners. Traditionally, this connection has

> *"Among the lessons being learned by e-business practitioners is that EDI will remain a critical infrastructure for Web-based commerce given that EDI provides users with security, audit trails, acknowledgments, and authentication."*

QUEUING

Although traditional EDI essentially is a batch store-and-forward process, the rise in functionality and sophistication of queuing systems in the last decade creates new opportunities for EDI.

This evolution of queuing systems will shorten message turnaround times significantly because transactions can be sent continually instead of waiting for later batch transmissions. The most popular use of queuing in this manner is for internal company systems. However, analysts expect substantial use of queuing across enterprises during the forecast period.

Fundamentally, queuing systems follow the same approach as store-and-forward systems: If both the sender and receiver are online, transactions flow through both sides. If the receiver is unavailable, the system stores the transactions and forwards them

once the server is ready. Servers can consume requests at a rate different from clients. For example, the clients could have queued up 10,000 transactions slowly over a 2-hour period. The other partner can start 5 servers to consume these transactions in a 15-minute period.

As compared with RPC, the main disadvantage of queuing comes from the fact that the transaction may not be processed immediately. The application must have less-critical data concurrency needs. The original client must check later or receive an acknowledgment for transaction results. This procedure is acceptable in some applications—for example, when entering online orders. In other applications, such as airline reservations, updates must be done synchronously.

Messages can be placed in a queue using a variety of mechanisms: first in, first out

(FIFO) is the most common system, with messages consumed in the same order in which they were sent. Prioritized messages can be inserted in front if they are marked with high-priority codes.

Messages can be postponed using timed-release functions to be processed at special batch periods during the night. Messages also can be chained (linked so they are dependent upon one another for operation) when there are transaction dependencies.

Although queuing has many advantages, major challenges must be solved. Currently, there is no MOM standard among queue product vendors. This lack of a standard means queues are not interoperable across different products because their APIs and message formats are different.

Popular queuing products are IBM's MQSeries, Microsoft's MSMQ, Netweave's required a dedicated leased line or a connection to a VAN. In theory, by defining a standard way to describe business transactions, EDI allows all vendors and their customers to link their computing infrastructures without worrying about the differences in their respective organizations and systems.

Initial successes with EDI were in markets where a large number of suppliers sold products to a small number of buyers, such as the automobile parts industry. In these cases, large purchasing companies chose to invest in proprietary systems that permitted them to do business more efficiently with other industry participants. The dominant purchasers dictated to the dependent suppliers that all transactions would use EDI. EDI has provided great value to trading partners, especially those in heavily EDI-enabled industries such as retail, automotive, transportation, and manufacturing.

EDI has resulted in significant competitive advantages and benefits to its users, including lower costs, better responsiveness to customers, and improved channel management. EDI also reduces cycle times, allows better access to transaction status, and reduces monetary float by submitting bills and payments faster. As a result, many companies in these EDI-enabled industries are finding that they must use EDI to compete effectively, maintain business relationships, and win new contracts.

EDI exists in the high end of the market where large players send and receive large numbers of EDI documents on a regular basis over a VAN, doing enough volume to justify the substantial cost. However, these larger firms have been prevented from doing business with smaller companies that cannot afford EDI. For many small and midsized companies, the necessary investments in EDI hardware and software and monthly VAN connection fees make EDI cost-prohibitive. More recently, the advent of

Netweave DS, PeerLogic's Pipes, and Suite Software's DOME. A special category in this arena is publish-and-subscribe products. The functionality required for this type of integration involves applications expressing interest in certain events (subscribing); applications signaling that an event has occurred (publishing); applications monitoring for the occurrence of business events (brokering); and notification of event occurrence to subscribers (messaging). One or many subscribers may be dependent on the publishing of a particular event. One subscriber also may express interest in multiple events. (See figure.) IBM's MQSeries Publish/Subscribe and Tibco's Rendezvous are examples of publish-and-subscribe products.

There are two basic methods for applications to register their interest with a message broker. First is subject-based addressing, where a message broker uses the definition (subject) of a message, such as fin.exp.new, to distribute information (such as employee number, expense amount, and date) to every application tasked with processing an expense report. Whenever an event triggers a particular message type, the publish/subscribe message broker engine is activated.

Another subscription method is to base application interest on the contents of fields within a message. For example, an approval application could subscribe to all purchase orders over a specified dollar amount. Purchase order messages below this amount are routed according to a different set of approval rules. ■

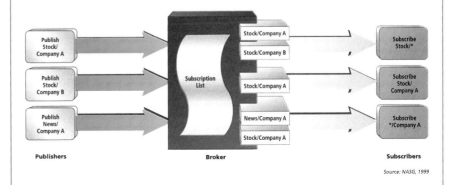

Source: NASG, 1999

the Internet has created a common communications infrastructure that provides the communications capabilities of a VAN (but not the value-added services that a VAN provides) at a much lower price.

Although traditional EDI requires complex interfaces to applications and a significant financial investment, Web-based EDI requires only a PC, an Internet connection, and a standard browser for a company to participate in an existing EDI infrastructure. Although this approach does not provide full end-to-end automation, businesses can substitute manual interaction and not implement the complicated EDI translation sets when using Web-based EDI.

EDI first was used more than 25 years ago, but the slow development of standards and numerous proprietary formats made a complex process even more unwieldy. Many industries developed their own standards, which further confused the marketplace. By the 1980s, however, more generic EDI standards had emerged.

Current EDI standards are maintained by two groups. The Accredited Standards Committee X12 standard (ASC X12) was developed by the American National Standards Institute (ANSI), based in the U.S. The other standard, the Electronic Data Interchange for Administration, Commerce and Transport (EDIFACT), was developed by the United Nations Economic Commission for Europe (UN/ECE).

Both X12 and EDIFACT define a common set of business forms, data elements, and protocols that allows business applications in different organizations to exchange information automatically and securely. EDIFACT has been proposed as a worldwide standard that would merge with the X12 standard. At the same time, CoreStates Financial and the Royal Bank of Scotland are pioneering new techniques that offer end-to-end EDI capability between the European and North American standards. This end-to-end capability enables automatic translation of an EDIFACT standard transaction into an X12 standard transaction.

The content of electronically transferred data has evolved into very sophisticated EDI formats. Standards organizations and major companies have focused intensively on developing transaction sets for their high-volume interactions. Thousands of data elements have been defined across a variety of applications. The more popular applications focus on the product supply chain from procurement through the order fulfillment process. EDI standards have been adopted by hundreds of thousands of companies. These formats cover most of the data needed among partners to interact.

EDI has hundreds of transaction types because the standards cover many industry applications. Some examples of these ANSI X12 transaction sets are shown in Table 2.

TABLE 2: ANSI X12 EDI TRANSACTION SETS

Transaction Set	Transaction Type
104	Air shipment
204	Motor carrier shipment
251	Pricing support
270–277	Health care inquiry, notification, status request
304	Shipping instructions
350–355	U.S. customs inquiry, status, arrival, manifest

TABLE 2: ANSI X12 EDI TRANSACTION SETS (CONTINUED)

Transaction Set	Transaction Type
404–431	Rail carrier shipment, freight details, waybill, shipment weights, settlements
466	Rate request
561–568	Contract abstract, status, management report
812	Credit/debit adjustment
837	Health care claim
838	Trading partner profile
840	Request for quotation
847	Material claim
850	Purchase order
855	Purchase order acknowledgment
856	Ship manifest
859	Freight invoice
860	Purchase order change request
869	Order status inquiry
875	Grocery purchase order
879	Price change
894	Delivery/return
940	Warehouse shipping order

TRADITIONAL EDI PROCESSING

The basic problem to be solved when implementing partner-to-partner EDI is the incompatible data formats used by the two partners' internal systems. The data formats for a retail procurement system are different from those of a clothing manufacturing system. When establishing a new EDI relationship, partners enter into a formalized Trade Partner Agreement (TPA), which sets up the rules by which they will conduct business electronically. The next step is to select a VAN and to use translator software. This EDI translator software is needed to convert an organization's internal formats into an EDI format to be transmitted. The receiving partner will have EDI translators that convert from a standard EDI format to the target organization's internal format.

The biggest cost in EDI involves developing a translation process from internal company systems to EDI formats. The more files and resulting transaction formats, the greater the cost. Another major cost is integrating translation software to company systems. Many vendors provide translators that can be purchased, but some additional coding will be needed to extract and condition files for the translator. Finally, companies face the ongoing cost of incorporating program changes when adding new fields and messages to applications.

Rigid transaction sets and fixed business rules are implemented internally in applications. When the business rules of a partner change (perhaps as the result of a merger or acquisition), great effort is spent in revising the translation, data conditioning, and exception handling processing.

THE ROLE OF THE VAN

Data transfer in EDI most commonly is done using a VAN, which provides the necessary infrastructure to bridge incompatible networks and keep track of transaction flow. VANs also provide the basic infrastructure to transmit the data securely through a store-and-forward mailbox facility. Most EDI data is transmitted from one partner to another as file transfers during off-peak periods, with data stored at the VAN and forwarded to the recipient.

VANs support data encryption, compression, audit trails, statistics gathering, and data recovery. In addition, some transaction types acknowledge the receipt of data. An extremely important feature of VANs is the concept of nonrepudiation: EDI data transmitted from one partner to another is legally binding if contested in court. VANs have elaborate tracking and verification mechanisms to ensure partner authenticity.

Traditional EDI services connect EDI partners to a VAN hub using mailboxes. (See Figure 41.) The main advantage of a VAN is that it stores, sorts, and forwards messages to other partners even when both sides may not be ready simultaneously for communications. The transmissions usually occur in batches preceded by headers and followed by trailers, charging either by the number of characters transmitted or by the number of messages. VAN accounts must be set up for every trading partner and can be expensive—$20,000 to $50,000 per month for a typical medium-sized partner. The benefits are security, performance, and reliability that far surpass basic Internet services today.

FIGURE 41: THE EDI PROCESS USING A VALUE-ADDED NETWORK

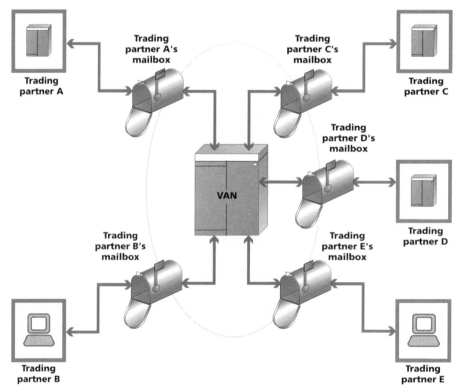

Source: Dataquest, 1998

Many major companies have set up hub-and-spoke arrangements with their VANs, as opposed to using direct point-to-point links with their trading partners. The hub-and-spoke topology means the VAN can bridge communication incompatibilities and server availability for all connected partners. VANs will support incoming bisync, X.25, TCP/IP, Systems Network Architecture (SNA), and X.400 communications and shield partners from needing to connect using protocols besides the ones they commonly use.

TRADITIONAL EDI OVER THE INTERNET

Traditional EDI systems require a network connection between the two organizations exchanging documents. Typically, this setup requires a dedicated line running between the two companies or a connection to a VAN. However, the advent of the Internet has created a common communications platform upon which business can be conducted. The universal connectivity provided by the Internet allows multitudes of additional parties, particularly small and midsized businesses and consumers, to utilize EDI technology at a lower cost. In addition, Internet-based EDI reduces transaction cycle time by using direct transfer instead of mailboxes.

However, these technologies raise critical issues that have been solved in VAN-operated data networks. Security in a public network such as the Internet, with hundreds of millions of access points, presents many challenges of authentication and authorization. Site availability also becomes more important as the Internet is used for more business-critical functions. The scalability to handle sudden bursts of message traffic caused by large numbers of users arriving on a site simultaneously has been a problem on some sites. Therefore, the very nature of the Internet requires different planning and implementation for application-to-application communications from proprietary networks.

Conducting EDI transactions on the Internet has many potential benefits, but the Internet was not created with the intention of conducting transactions securely and reliably. Trading partners subscribing to a VAN can be assured an EDI document will be routed to its recipient without any modifications. However, this level of assurance is not provided when connecting to the Internet via an Internet service provider (ISP). A public network, by its very nature, is susceptible to information being viewed, copied, or altered while en route to its final destination.

Although the Internet does an efficient job of routing packets to their final destinations many different intermediate network nodes handle packets between the source and the destination. It is at any one of these nodes where anyone with a network protocol analyzer could capture, view, or reassemble the data packets that make up a message. If data packets contain sensitive information, measures must be taken to prevent such threats from occurring when an EDI document is sent over a public network such as the Internet.

Authentication is the process of determining that trading partners are who they claim to be. Authentication eliminates the possibility of "spoofing" the identity of a trading partner while a document is in transit. In the case of a VAN, a trading partner can send or receive a document only after it has been authenticated by the VAN. This process usually consists of the user logging into the network with the appropriate user-ID and password.

Several parties are developing and implementing measures that will make the Internet a more secure and reliable communications network. The Internet Engineering Task Force's (IETF's) proposed Internet EDI (EDI-INT) standard, in draft form as of mid-1999, defines the standards for using encryption and digital certificates to secure EDI transactions over the Internet. In addition to these drafts, many industries are developing their own industry-specific protocols for using EDI over the Internet. For example, the Automotive Industry Action Group and the Gas Industry Standards Board each have developed a set of standards above those specified in the EDI-INT.

Audit Trails and Acknowledgments. VAN subscribers also can track an EDI document through the VAN. An example of this tracking involves notifications sent to the trading partner upon the download of the EDI document by the recipient. Document tracking and functional acknowledgments offered by the TCP/IP protocol suite or supplied by an ISP do not meet the level of service provided by a VAN. This tracking information is very important in designing an application as well as in meeting the approval of financial auditors and legal counsel.

Although direct transfer of EDI is attractive, facilities must be built to store and forward data if the target site is not available. In the end, many of these value-added services today are being supplied by VANs using the Internet as the transmission medium.

XML and EDI

X12 and EDIFACT-based transaction sets use fixed-length fields and positional meanings. The applications that interpret these transaction sets have built-in rules indicating how the various fields are to be interpreted.

The fixed nature of the record-oriented X12 and EDIFACT standards reduces flexibility in extending formats. Extending such a data format can be done only by "field stuffing," where existing fields in the transaction set are reused or overloaded, or by special transaction formats agreed upon by each partner pair. This situation leads to volumes of special program code that specifically looks for these extensions on both ends of the transaction.

It is not unusual for a large customer to need to support industry-specific versions of X12 formats. For example, an automobile manufacturer must support the Chemical Industry Data Exchange (CIDX) for its industrial chemicals as well as the Electronics Industry Data Exchange (EIDX) for its electrical components. To complicate matters further, specific business rules for each partner must be programmed into the applications in the receiving end of transmission. A system engineered in this way is cumbersome to maintain and revise.

These difficulties are facilitating a growing interest in a more flexible way of defining transaction sets based on the XML standard of World Wide Web Consortium (W3C). More flexible formats such as XML offer a transition from EDI fixed formats to self-identifying data.

Using an XML-based language for EDI overcomes many of the problems of X12 and EDIFACT-based approaches. In an XML-based language, data does not occupy fixed-size slots. Instead, variable-length fields are delimited by tags such as **<PRICE>** or **<PRODUCTID>**. Deleting a field from a transaction set does not require redefining the set or recoding applications on either end of the EDI connection if the field is not being used. This procedure allows more flexibility in defining new formats that can be rendered by a variety of tools and platforms.

There is a natural mapping between XML tags on the one hand and objects on the other, where a computational object can be defined for each tag in an XML-based language. Interpreting a particular XML-based transaction set requires a compact and general-purpose XML parser and a set of objects for interpreting the particular tags found in that language. Such an architecture opens up many possibilities that are difficult to invoke with traditional EDI, such as the following:

- Each EDI partner can have a set of objects for interpreting the same XML-based data.

- One set of XML-defined tags can reformat the data for storage in a database, and another set can display the data in a Web browser as part of a purchase-authorization application.

- The tags for interpreting a particular XML-based transaction set can be sent with the transaction set to update the message recipients dynamically.

XML EXAMPLES

In the financial world, there have been several standards to exchange data. The Integrion Gold standard currently is being merged with the Open Financial Exchange (OFX) standard to become IFX. The OFX standard is migrating from a standard used for batch exchange of files between client desktop software (such as Intuit's Quicken) and financial services providers to an online messaging standard that service providers can use to communicate with each other. Combining the new IFX with XML can allow numerous service providers to interact with consumers about recurring events such as paying a bill. For example, along with a bill for telephone calling-card service, a consumer's Web shopping agent could discover one company charges $20 per month for cellular phone service while another company charges only $15. Figure 42 and Figure 43 on page 128 illustrate how this process might work.

See "Open Financial Exchange" on page 160 for more information.

FIGURE 42: OFX BILLING AND PAYMENT PROCESS

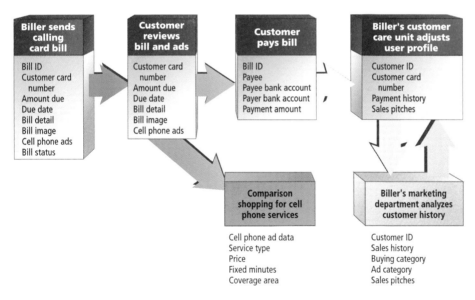

Source: Gartner, 1999

DRAWBACKS TO XML-BASED APPROACHES

XML-based approaches to exchanging data are not without drawbacks. The current enthusiasm for XML obscures the fact that adopting XML does not obviate the requirement for extensive transaction-set design. Furthermore, XML-based messages are bulkier than their classic EDI predecessors.

The design issue is not well-enough understood by technology decision-makers. XML is not a data description language; rather, it is a specification for creating data-description languages. Without appropriate attention to the requirements of the application, it is

FIGURE 43: OFX BILL PRESENTMENT IN XML NOTATION

Source: Gartner, 1999

just as possible to build a bad design in an XML-based language as it is in an X12 format. The years of effort that have gone into defining existing EDI formats need to be preserved in the transition to XML.

The widespread perception that the DTD for an XML language will be comprehensive enough to serve as a specification of an interchange language needs to be revisited. A DTD supplies limited syntactic information about the structure of an XML language and has no provisions for storing semantics. A DTD can prescribe, for example, that each **INVOICE** has one and only one **INVOICE_NUMBER**, but it cannot state the requirement that an **INVOICE_NUMBER** has to lie within a certain range, have a certain layout, or match with a **VENDOR_NUMBER** in some way. These kinds of constraints are as important to a data specification as the kinds that can be expressed in a DTD, and some structure is needed to express them.

More important, XML does not provide a universal lexicon of transaction sets automatically. The ease with which new data languages can be designed in XML makes it hard to agree and standardize on any one.

One way in which e-business may solve this problem is to establish repositories where XML specifications can be stored and publicly accessed. If specifications can be searched, then a specification can be retrieved by index from a repository. Although the repository approach is attractive intellectually, it is doubtful such a strategy will work unless there is agreement (both industry-specific and cross-industry) on a broad category of XML specifications.

Actual repositories just are coming into existence. CommerceNet purchased the XML Exchange from XML Solutions in July 1998, intending to create a public repository that would allow developers to discuss and distribute XML tag sets and DTDs. Independent expert panels would assess and control the quality of DTD submissions to ensure downloads were usable. The site still is gathering momentum.

The Graphic Communications Association (GCA) announced the formation of a DTD repository in May 1998. The initial focus of this repository is less on XML-based DTDs and more on traditional Standard Generalized Markup Language (SGML) DTDs for applications such as describing the structure of a conference proceeding.

One virtue of the transition to XML-based data may be that it is starting to focus attention on the relationship between data and the business rules used to manipulate it. Existing design practice made it easy to ignore this relationship because the data and rules were separate.

EDI applications currently in place can migrate to XML in one of three ways:

- **Complete XML replacement**—In this case, both source and target applications are changed to use XML-based data streams.

- **Replace source EDI format with XML**—In this case, one organization may adopt XML-based data formats internally but may transact with a partner that does not wish to change. The XML-based partner uses a translator to map the XML-based data onto X12 or EDIFACT data, which then is transmitted. The translation step can be removed whenever both partners are ready for XML.

- **Create new transaction sets in XML**—In this case, the partners agree that new applications and transaction sets will be done in XML. Existing EDI applications remain in X12 or EDIFACT format.

The last strategy may be the predominant adoption path for XML-based EDI. Enterprises that already have EDI systems view them as critical aspects of business function and will want to see how the new architecture pans out on prototype and small-scale systems before embarking on expensive retrofitting projects. In addition, business-to-consumer uses of XML are expected to grow before any business-to-business uses because consumer applications (such as catalog presentation and ordering) do not require the kinds of deep negotiations about messages and structures as EDI.

Efficiency of the new representations also is a concern. Tagging and interpreted flexibility come at a cost. XML tags are thought to add as much as 35 percent overhead to the sizes of messages. However, the justification argument is that computer and network technology has dropped in price and increased in performance so dramatically that the additional overhead for tags can be justified. There also are tag-aware data-compression algorithms that can Huffman-code all tags to a fraction of their uncompressed size.

XML-based messages do not need to use the HTTP protocol for transmission. Any of the application protocols used in EDI (File Transfer Protocol [FTP], Simple Mail Transfer Protocol [SMTP], X.400, or LU 6.2) can be used as well.

Understandably, traditional EDI vendors have been slow to embrace XML-based EDI. Vendors such as Harbinger and Sterling Commerce have no announced plans to release XML support in any of their EDI products, and it is not clear when they will begin to embrace this standard.

"One virtue of the transition to XML-based data may be that it is starting to focus attention on the relationship between data and the business rules used to manipulate it."

Huffman coding is a method of compressing a given set of data based on the relative frequency of the individual elements. The more often a specific element, such as a letter, occurs, the shorter its corresponding code in bits. Being one of the earliest data compression codes, Huffman coding, with modifications, remains one of the most widely used codes for a wide variety of message types.

OTHER USES OF XML

XML has many uses beyond EDI as it relates to electronic business. Two developments in particular are indicative of the flexibility of XML as both a commerce language and a communications language.

1. XML will become the main mechanism for interoperability across applications. Major application suites need to have their data available to other systems. XML will be used as the primary format for this exported data, which then can be imported to internal company systems or transferred across networks. This setup eliminates the need to marshall data types across different platforms or publish record layouts for emitted data formats. It also provides extensibility.

2. There is a World Wide Web Consortium (W3C) proposal for the eXtensible Query Language (XQL), which is intended to query XML data in different ways. The proposal—submitted by Microsoft, Texcel, and web-Methods—offers unique solutions beyond what the SQL language can support. ■

Despite these difficulties, XML-based business languages are proliferating rapidly, and several are proposed or are in use for e-business:

- *OFX*—A specification for financial transactions developed jointly by CheckFree, Intuit, and Microsoft in 1997.
- *FIXML*—An XML rewrite of the FIX financial transaction interchange standard, released by the FIX Organization in late 1998. The group cited XML's flexibility and extensibility as reasons for the change.

FUTURE XML DEVELOPMENTS

One of the fastest-growing areas of XML use will be in the business-to-consumer market. Consumers will be able to order and make payments from XML-generated messages from their browsers. Later, they will be able to query databases stored as XML data for items related to their original orders. The Internet itself will provide the backbone to connect millions of consumers and businesses together.

There are many possibilities for XML to standardize any kind of data interchange among companies. One such development is the publishing of company product and services information in standard XML-based catalogs. These catalogs then can be accessed on demand or by scheduled extraction. A company can have all its relevant product data in a database consisting of XML-tagged content for all interested customers to see. Then if a purchasing department is studying product lines from many vendors, eXtensible Query Language (XQL) queries are initiated to extract this data from the different vendor databases. This data then can be aggregated, categorized, and placed in the customer's database for detailed analysis.

EAI: Packaged Enterprise Middleware

"The key e-business issue for application integration is how e-businesses get applications based on different technologies and with differing business models and data models to work together."

The key e-business issue for application integration is how e-businesses get applications based on different technologies and with differing business models and data models to work together. These pieces must interoperate in a common way with minimal disruption to everyday operations, not to mention preexisting investment.

Enterprise application integration (EAI) software represents a new approach to middleware, the software that helps to integrate applications. By packaging together commonly used functionality—linking popular enterprise packages and legacy applications in relatively predefined ways—EAI software promises to reduce the time necessary to develop solutions that integrate applications from multiple vendors, to keep pace with rapid changes in the supported applications, and to perform at an acceptable level to be used in mission-critical settings.

Interest in EAI solutions is the result of several factors. Foremost is pressure arising from more competitive business environments, where shorter application life cycles are becoming common. Instead of repeatedly creating the same logical processes and data repositories, developers are attempting to reuse existing applications and services. This process becomes important especially when information systems are coping with the effects of a merger or acquisition.

EAI is designed to allow developers to choose different levels of integration (for example, data-level, application-interface level, or business-process level) between legacy and new systems. The result is that many older systems that still perform valuable tasks are able to continue. Indeed, it is often the case that the return on an EAI investment is measured by how little of the installed base needed to be changed to leverage a new system.

Another driver behind EAI deployment involves sharing information between disparate applications that never were designed to work together. Business process automation (as it is sometimes called) is the automation of tasks an organization already may be doing manually to leverage two or more applications. For example, a business may print a sales report from an ERP system to use it to cross reference customer information for credit checks in another system. EAI would transform this from a manual to an automated process.

HOW EAI SOFTWARE SIMPLIFIES INTEGRATION

The promise of EAI software—that enterprise integration can be plug-and-play—is a challenge to achieve.

Vendors of the major ERP suites are separating their applications into components so users can mix and match human resources, financials, or SCM modules. Componentization is an impressive concept, but integrating pieces from multiple vendors can be daunting.

Using middleware standards such as CORBA and COM/DCOM to integrate vendors' software and components has not been straightforward. Even with interfaces such as SAP's BAPIs or specialized middleware, linking heterogeneous applications is a complex task that many organizations do not have the in-house expertise to undertake. Organi-

See "BAPIs" on page 119 for more information.

THE SAN FRANCISCO PROJECT

For years, application class libraries have provided many infrastructure services for security, directories, data access, and messaging. They also standardized common functions in business processing by callable routines. In the last few years, there has been an extension of this concept into frameworks.

A framework defines the collaboration of components at run time. Unlike class libraries in which driver programs call the necessary components, a framework has a predefined flow of control. In essence, the framework calls the company programs usually written as extensions to the framework. There are default behaviors for objects in a framework as well as custom-built behaviors.

The San Francisco Project, sponsored by IBM, is a Java-based framework that was developed by more than 100 independent software vendors (ISVs) to accelerate the development of corporate business applications. (See graphic.) The objective is to create a system that is highly mobile and interoperable, and Java was chosen as the standard for this framework.

The foundation layer of this framework provides the basic infrastructure services: nam-

ing, security, messaging, and persistence. The common business objects execute on top of this layer. These objects are shared by all applications regardless of industry. An employee object in a payroll system can be used in a benefits application with the same data attributes and method processing. The core business process layer addresses the business flow needs of traditional company applications such as accounting and inventory. All these lower layers have a common goal: to increase component reusability across all applications.

Custom-developed applications then are created to form the top layer, extending functionality by additional Java classes into actual products. Currently, the San Francisco Project has more than 3,000 classes and 500,000 lines of code, and several applications are being offered. The elusive goal of standardizing processing across applications and enterprises may be reached using this approach. ■

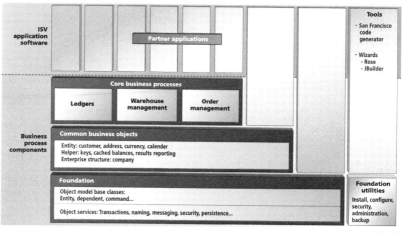

Source: IBM, 1999

zations still often hire system integrators or consultants to help with the integration, and they even may outsource the management of these systems entirely. The EAI package attempts to select a manageable but comprehensive set of requests. A package will fail in its application if the enterprise's needs cannot be mapped onto that request set.

THE ARCHITECTURE OF AN EAI SYSTEM

An EAI package attempts to simplify interfacing by eliminating the need for custom interfacing software to be developed. The EAI vendor (or third party) supplies a connector that translates a fixed set of requests from the EAI package to and from the software being interfaced. By providing prebuilt connectors, the EAI package supplier can shield the enterprise developer from numerous, low-level interface details.

Connectors (also known as adapters) are the interface to the applications packages supplied by the EAI vendor. Each supported application needs a connector, and all connectors must be upgraded when the set of requests that can be handled changes. (See Figure 44.)

FIGURE 44: ARCHITECTURE OF AN EAI SYSTEM

The transport system moves data between connectors and other components of the system. Typical EAI transport systems are asynchronous and provide transactional integrity. Synchronous, broadcast, multicast, and publish-and-subscribe transports also could be used, but many applications are better-suited to the asynchronous model. A rules engine processes events and possibly triggers new events in the connected applications in response, including notification of subscribers. Some EAI systems such as Frontec use a proprietary transport system, but most EAI suppliers use existing messaging systems such as IBM's MQSeries.

A data transformation engine converts data from one application format to another. For performance reasons, it would be best if data were converted directly from a source format to a destination format, but often the data is converted into an interchange form first, one proprietary to each EAI vendor.

The EAI category received much attention in 1998 and attracted many vendors. The following companies are among those offering EAI solutions.

Active Software. Active Software's ActiveWorks is used to integrate diverse business environments and information sources, including Internet applications, legacy systems, databases, and so on, and is suited particularly for integrating front-office applications into enterprise systems. The ActiveWorks adapters enable communications between applications. and support software from many major application vendors, including Baan, Calico, Clarify, InterWorld, Kenan, Microsoft, Oracle, PeopleSoft, Pivotal, SAP, Siebel, and Vantive. ActiveWorks has an architecture with a central broker managing an event loop. Events are added to the queue by package adapters, which connect with integrated applications and agents or clients that reside on servers. (Agents are developer-customized clients in Active parlance.) Adapters, agents, and clients can publish events from their applications or servers and can subscribe to events. Version 3.0 of ActiveWorks shipped in December 1998.

CrossWorlds Software. CrossWorlds' approach depends on high-level business-process models called "collaborations." Its Customer Interaction application, for example, contains 21 collaborations linking customer-management functions such as pricing, quote generation, and order status with ERP applications. Connectors link collaborations with other applications. Current available applications are Customer Interaction, Supply Chain Interaction, and ERP Interaction.

Extricity. Extricity specializes in business-to-business integration using Java, XML, CORBA, and DCOM. The Extricity Alliance Process Manager defines and maintains EDI process definitions using XML with a graphical user interface. The Alliance product suite focuses on collaborative planning, forecasting, logistics, asset management, and ERP systems. Customers use these applications to collect and distribute company internal data to partners, pass manufacturing line data to the supply chain, and coordinate shipments.

Version 2.0 of Alliance shipped in December 1998. One feature of the Extricity offering is a suite of adapters for products from other middleware vendors, including Active Software, IBM, NEON, Oberon, Tibco, TSI, and Vitria.

Frontec. Frontec enters the EAI marketplace from a background in EDI and message brokering. Frontec Group's AMTrix system connects only to IBM's MQSeries and SAP's IDoc and ALE interfaces, although Frontec has announced plans for connectors to Baan, J.D. Edwards, Manugistics, MFG Pro, Oracle, and PeopleSoft. The Frontec system is more of an integration framework than an application. It is intended to be used by a knowledgeable systems integrator. Version 4.1 shipped in January 1998; the current version is 4.2.

New Era of Networks (NEON)/IBM MQ Integrator. MQ Integrator, released in April 1998, is IBM's entry into the EAI marketplace. MQ Integrator uses a combination of IBM's MQSeries messaging system and NEON's rules and data transformation engine.

NEON has focused on the rules and data transformation engines rather than a complete package. NEON's partnership with IBM is intended to supply lower-level transport services, whereas its relationship with Oberon (discussed below) adds business-process modeling and ready-built interfaces.

Oberon. The Prospero system focuses on high-level interfaces that do most of the detail integration work internally. Prospero links commonly used front-office applications (such as databases, groupware, Internet, and desktop applications) and enterprise functions (such as supply chain management software) with back-office ERP applications. Oberon's Prospero Building Blocks are prebuilt blocks of code used to interface to a variety of disconnected corporate applications. Building Blocks currently are available for many J.D. Edwards and SAP modules; additional Building Blocks for Baan, J.D. Edwards, Oracle, PeopleSoft, and SAP are under development.

Vitria Technology. Vitria Technology's BusinessWare is a framework for developing EAI solutions rather than an out-of-the-box application. BusinessWare supports analyzing and building business-process models, but few predefined models currently are available. Vitria Technology plans to support Clarify, PeopleSoft, and SAP applications. Version 2.0 was introduced in June 1998.

> *"The business advantage of integration between enterprise resource planning systems and e-business will lead to increased demand for products and services that provide such integration."*

See "Commerce One" on page 78 and "Pandesic" on page 72 for more information.

Market Overview

E-BUSINESS ERP

The business advantage of integration between ERP systems and e-business will lead to increased demand for products and services that provide such integration. During the forecast period, as organizations meet Year 2000 challenges, analysts expect Fortune 1000 IT executives to shift their attention to e-business-enabling their ERP systems. In January 1999, Zona Research reported that between 1998 and 1999, transaction-enabled Web application servers tied to ERP systems had doubled their influence in the marketplace. *Fortune* reported in December 1998 that the current $23 billion enterprise software business may be an $84 billion industry by 2004, enhanced, in part, by Web-extension offerings.

According to Giga, the movement of ERP vendors into e-commerce will affect the leading commerce server vendors, including BroadVision, IBM, InterWorld, Microsoft, Netscape, and Open Market. IBM will continue its focus on Web sites that integrate into back-end legacy systems. Netscape will emphasize Web sites for business-to-business procurement. However, Netscape is more likely to be a partner with ERP vendors rather than a competitor because of its ownership by America Online (AOL), its partnership with Sun, and its strength in Web site front-end systems. BroadVision, with its strengths in Web site personalization, and Open Market, with its expertise in creating custom, high-transaction-volume Web sites, also likely will partner with ERP vendors.

Examples of ERP vendors that have partnered with or purchased other companies to take advantage of e-business opportunities include the following:

- Baan has acquired Aurum's sales force automation and financial applications and Caps Logistics' transportation planning and scheduling software.
- PeopleSoft is partnering with Siebel and Vantive to integrate their sales force, marketing, and field service automation with PeopleSoft's ERP applications.
- SAP is partnering with several software providers, including IBM, which will offer merchandise planning and retail applications for R/3. SAP also has an equity stake in e-business software providers Commerce One and Pandesic.

Part of ERP vendors' approach to e-business is to automate internal corporate processes using standardized, best practice models. However, those models still are being formed and involve many intercompany (rather than just internal) processes. Because of these factors, the ERP vendors' e-business solutions will be attractive primarily to their existing customers during the forecast period.

EDI

The EDI market is in a period of dramatic transition. After several years of annual growth exceeding 30 percent, the EDI services market began to slow in 1997. IDC predicts the EDI services market will expand at a compound annual growth rate (CAGR) of at least 22 percent, reaching nearly $2.4 billion in 2002. As vertical markets such as grocery, manufacturing, transportation, and retail approach EDI saturation, many providers are beginning to target new industries such as high technology, health care, and government.

The EDI services market is fueled by three major providers: GE Information Services, IBM, and Sterling Commerce. Figure 45 on page 135 shows the market share of the leading EDI services vendors for 1997 (the latest figures available).

FIGURE 45: WORLDWIDE EDI SERVICES REVENUE BY PROVIDER: 1997

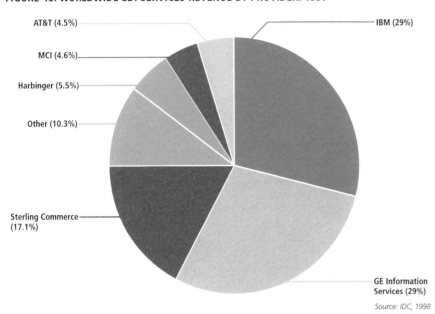

AT&T (4.5%)

MCI (4.6%)

Harbinger (5.5%)

Other (10.3%)

Sterling Commerce (17.1%)

IBM (29%)

GE Information Services (29%)

Source: IDC, 1998

Several major vendors are in the EDI translator marketplace. Harbinger, with its Trusted Link Enterprise, takes the translation one step further: It integrates with Baan, Oracle, PeopleSoft, and SAP R/3 applications. In 1998, Harbinger also acquired Premenos, maker of the Templar product, which encrypts and digitally signs each message for transmission over the Internet. Other vendors and their EDI translation solutions include GE Information Services' Enterprise System 5.1, St. Paul Software's WEB EC, and Sterling Commerce's Commerce Now.

Some of the major VANs in the EDI arena include Advantis, AT&T Easylink, GE Information Services' TradeWeb, PSINet IntraNet (which uses virtual private networks for EDI), and Sprint. These VANs provide data encryption, EDI conversions (to e-mail, X.400), authentication, document conversion, key management, trading partner implementation support, and 24-hour help-desk support. They also bridge incompatible communication protocols and provide special mailboxes for different time zones and processing cycles.

Rather than replacing traditional EDI with new Web-based solutions, many EDI-enabled businesses will move EDI to extranets. This shift will occur differently among industries depending on how EDI is used in each industry. For example, in industries with trading groups that have fewer than a few hundred partners and high transaction volumes, companies can reap significant savings by moving EDI to extranets. Nearly all companies in such industries (including petroleum and computing) will make this move by the end of 2000, according to Forrester.

Led by the automotive industry, manufacturing industries with multiple tiers of suppliers will shift EDI trading to extranets layer by layer. EDI between manufacturers and first-tier suppliers will move quickly, but Forrester predicts the full transition of all layers will not be completed until between 2002 and 2004.

Finally, in industries such as consumer goods and grocery, where retailers long have used EDI for vendor-managed inventory, reluctance to move to extranets is high. In these industries, the current process works effectively, suppliers bear the brunt of costs, and EDI VANs manage the electronic interfaces to the trading partners.

XML will change the face of EDI within the forecast period. By year-end 1999, both EDI-FACT and ANSI will operate XML repositories; by year-end 2000, these organizations will synchronize their global repositories, according to Gartner. Although Gartner predicts existing EDIFACT, ANSI, and industry-specific data flows will experience minimal impact from XML through the end of 2000, these data flows will migrate to XML at a rate of five to ten percent annually beginning in 2001. By the end of 2003, XML-based EDI will account for 30 percent of e-commerce transactions, with another 30 percent supported by XML EDI-to-EDI gateways. The remaining 40 percent of transactions will be supported by traditional EDI.

EAI

According to IDC, the overall middleware market is expected to grow from $2.2 billion in 1998 to $5.2 billion in 2001. The Yankee Group predicts more rapid growth for EAI software—from $270 million to $780 million over the same period. (See Figure 46.)

FIGURE 46: EAI SOFTWARE REVENUE GROWTH: 1998–2001

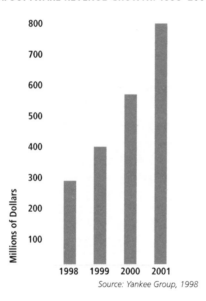

Source: Yankee Group, 1998

EAI software is offered for sale directly to enterprises, but EAI vendors also enter into partnering arrangements with ERP vendors and other enterprise application suppliers. When Siebel and Vantive, rival customer relationship management providers, entered into preferred front-office partnerships with PeopleSoft at the end of 1998, Active Software formed partnerships with both Siebel and Vantive to supply adapters for integration between the systems.

Forecast

ERP

The major ERP vendors will continue to add e-business functionality to their product suites throughout the forecast period.

Having an enterprise's ERP suite extend its functionality to encompass suppliers, distributors, and customers will become the norm.

Infrequent users of corporate systems or those who do not require the full functionality of the ERP system will use the Web browser to access these systems because the Web is cheaper (reduced software license costs), less complex and easier to use, and can become a single interface for multiple applications.

New, easier-to-use devices to access the Web will mean a greater user base for e-business ERP as users communicate via interactive television, personal digital assistants (PDAs), and in-vehicle devices.

EDI

EDI will continue to merge with Internet-based e-business during the forecast period. Many new EDI users will start by using the Internet (rather than a VAN) as a message transport particularly as companies that already are heavy EDI users incorporate smaller suppliers into their EDI networks.

XML will play a major role in facilitating the movement of EDI activity to the Web as well as the creation of industry-specific e-business standards. Specific industries or trading communities, such as the computer industry or automobile spare parts dealers, will develop their own standard data definitions and message formats for Web-based e-business outside the traditional standards processes.

Traditional EDI traffic using VANs as service providers will continue to grow throughout the forecast period but at a slightly lower rate than in previous years.

XML use in business-to-business communications for new applications will increase dramatically. Exporting data from application suites and developer tools using XML will become standardized.

EDI via the Internet will replace a portion of the current EDI volume over VANs.

Queuing products will proliferate for a variety of EDI transmissions.

The replacement of VAN proprietary networks will be an evolutionary process.

EAI

As the EAI marketplace matures, proprietary interface standards will be replaced by XML or other standards that will be part of the conversion process.

Consolidation among EAI vendors will occur as they are acquired by corporate application or classic middleware vendors.

REFERENCES

ARTICLES

Carnell, Michael. NetDynamics. *Intelligent Enterprise*. November 1998: 64.

Carr, David F. Enterprise resource planning broadens definition, faces interoperability woes (standardization desirable among ERP vendors). *Internet World*. November 16, 1998: 24.

Carr, David F. Market narrows with BEA purchase of WebLogic. *Internet World*. October 5, 1998: 1.

Copeland, Lee and Pedro Pereira. Self service on the information superhighway. *Computer Reseller News*. November 16, 1998: 7.

Cox, John. BEA creating middleware buzz. *Network World*. November 9, 1998: 40.

Dalton, Gregory. UPS tests Bluestone—software deals with heavy transactions. *InformationWeek*. March 16, 1998: 90.

Dyck, Timothy. Almost enterprise-ready: Bluestone app server lacks manageability. *PCWeek*. June 22, 1998: 35.

Holt, Michael and Stannie Vizard. Netscape foots the bill: reworked e-commerce strategy relies on app server. *InfoWorld.* October 5, 1998: 1

Kirkpatrick, David. The E-ware war. *Fortune.* December 7, 1998: 102.

McKie, Stewart. ERP meets Web e-commerce. *DBMS.* July 1998: 39.

Nerney, Chris. They're not start-ups anymore. *Network World.* February 16, 1998: 26.

Porter, Jack and Jeetu Patel. Make the Web work for you—Doculabs tests nine Web Application development tools to see which one is the best for your business. *InformationWeek.* June 22, 1998: 63.

Schreier-Hohman, Robin. Netscape opens up PeopleSoft apps. *Network World.* November 9, 1998: 40.

Schwartz, Jeffrey. SAP embraces Java and XML. *InternetWeek.* December 11, 1998.

Seltzer, Larry. Battle for the middle tier. *PC Magazine.* October 20, 1998: 40.

Stein, Tom, Gregory Dalton, and Jeff Sweat. PeopleSoft's e-business—ERP vendor aims to become a hub of Internet business activity. *InformationWeek.* November 9, 1998: 26.

Stein, Tom. Extending—Companies that don't use enterprise resource planning software to share information may regret it. *InformationWeek.* June 15, 1998: 75.

Swoyer, Stephen. Cloudscape, WebLogic ally for developers. *ENT.* October 7, 1998: 50.

Tiazkun, Scott. Oracle applications target Web-based ERP solutions. *Computer Reseller News.* October 5, 1998: 126.

Tadjer, Rivka. Enterprise Resource Planning. *InternetWeek.* April 13, 1998: 40.

Vizard, Michael and Matthew Nelson. Netscape vows ERP integration, pushes I-commerce. *InfoWorld Electric.* June 4, 1998.

Wong, Wylie. WebLogic rolls out its new Tengah Application Server. *Computer Reseller News.* June 15, 1998: 94.

PERIODICALS, INDUSTRY AND TECHNICAL REPORTS

Duvall, Mel. *Meta Group: Net forcing new issues.* Inter@ctiveWeek Online. January 11, 1999.

ERP to Web app servers: why should we care? Zona Research. January 1999.

NetDynamics 4.0 PAC for PeopleSoft. NetDynamics White Paper. February 16, 1998.

Open Buying on the Internet. OBI Consortium White Paper. Release V1.1. June 1998.

Terhune, A. *SAP leads ERP players into electronic commerce.* InSide Gartner Group. August 12, 1998.

Zona Assessment Paper. Zona Research. Issue 12. January 1999: 5.

ONLINE SOURCES

Capturing electronic commerce opportunities. February 1999.
    www.oracle.com/database/oracle8i/solutions/ecommerce.html

E-business enabling business on the Internet. November 1998.
    www.peoplesoft.com/en/whitepapers/1407-1198.pdf

URLs OF SELECTED MENTIONED COMPANIES AND ORGANIZATIONS

American National Standards Institute www.ansi.org

Automotive Industry Action Group www.aiag.org

Commerce Banker www.sterlingcommerce.com/pdsv/ploc/comm/bnk1/index.html

Ecommerce Innovation Centre www.cf.ac.uk/uwcc/masts/ecic

Electronic Commerce Canada www.ecc.ca/About/Description.html

Financial Exchange Protocol (FIX) www.fixprotocol.org

Gas Industry Standards Board www.gisb.org

GE Information Systems www.geis.com

Graphic Communications Association www.gca.org

IBM Net.Commerce Hosting Server www.software.ibm.com/commerce/net.commerce/chsweb.html

IBM Content Hosting Server www.ibm.com/globalnetwork/contntbr.htm

Kerberos: The Network Authentication Protocol web.mit.edu/kerberos/www

Minerva www.minerva-is.com

Oakland Electronic Commerce Resource Center www.ecrc.ctc.com/oakland

Open Applications Group www.openapplications.org

The Electronic Commerce Guide e-comm.internet.com/e-comm

Trusted Link Commerce www.harbinger.com/products/edi/tlc

Trusted Link Templar www.harbinger.com/products/edi/templar

United Nations/Economic Commission for Europe www.unece.org

Wireless Application Protocol www.wapforum.org

World Wide Web Consortium www.w3.org

Executive Summary

The objective of payment technologies is to provide buyers and merchants with secure, reliable, and unobtrusive methods of transferring value. Purchasing goods and services in an electronic medium should be as easy, or easier, than traditional face-to-face transactions. To meet these objectives, a payment infrastructure must be put into place. Traditional financial services providers and new electronic business enterprises will compete to provide new payment frameworks.

Payment types include cash, checks, credit and debit transfers, payment card transactions, automated clearing-house transactions, and wire transfers. These methods differ on several important dimensions. Some methods—cash, for example—are more appropriate for occasional or ad-hoc transactions of relatively small value. Other methods—such as automated clearing-house transactions—are more appropriate for regular transactions of medium value. Credit and debit transfers, also known as giros, are more common in Europe, while checks are more common in North America. Each of these types of payment has an electronic analog.

Payment methods are the processes used to transport payments electronically. Traditionally, payment information has been transported over private, secure networks. For Web-based electronic business, however, payment methods must address the issues associated with public, insecure networks. Today, the most common payment methods rely on Secure Sockets Layer encryption, which offers protection from eavesdroppers. This method has several drawbacks, however, including that critical information—such as credit-card or debit account numbers—is distributed more widely than desirable and that authentication of both parties is weak. The Secure Electronic Transaction protocol is more complex than Secure Sockets Layer and aims to remedy its shortcomings. Systems based on Secure Electronic Transaction are emerging slowly in the marketplace.

In 1999, no single, widely accepted payment technology infrastructure exists for e-business. Various technology firms, financial institutions, and payment brands (such as MasterCard and Visa) support multiple technologies and standards. Moreover, each collection of technologies is in a different phase of design, construction, and deployment. Factors influencing deployment include the maturity of technology elements, the relative strength of the competing vendors, and the rate of consumer acceptance. In 1999, more solutions are proposed than necessary; in two years' time, consolidation will reduce the number of payment alternatives.

Although a few dominant payment technologies will emerge, no single method or type is expected. The payment type and method best suited to occasional purchases is not expected to meet the needs of larger, more regular purchases. Instead, businesses and consumers will choose payment products on the basis of cost, efficiency, convenience, and trust.

Overview

Payment technologies are the collection of techniques that enable value to be transferred from one organization or individual to another—most commonly, for buyers to compensate sellers when purchasing goods and services. Governments, financial institutions, and businesses have cultivated these technologies over many centuries to make compensation streamlined and safe for all parties involved. Whether a payment is made electronically or by way of cash or even barter, the same key requirements are involved. These requirements are as follows:

- *Authentication*—Buyers, sellers, and any intermediaries that may be involved (for example, a bank) need assurance the players are whom they claim to be.

- *Authorization*—These same players also must be sure that each is acting within his authority when offering, transferring, or accepting payment.

- *Nonrepudiation*—The payment transaction must be constructed in a way that binds all players and does not allow any one player to deny or back out of the transaction.

- *Data integrity*—Agreements surrounding the payment transaction must be constructed so these documents cannot be altered without detection.

- *Privacy*—Ethics and good business practice dictate that players in a financial transaction keep the details confidential under most circumstances. In addition, transaction details in the wrong hands provide the information needed to create fraudulent transactions.

"Repudiation" is the refusal to acknowledge a contract or debt.

The five key requirements are not difficult to satisfy in the vast majority of payment transactions. In the United States, for example, approximately 80 percent of all payment transactions are made with cash, with customer and merchant face-to-face and with the value of an average payment about $11. Buyers walk into stores, inspect merchants' products, choose what they wish to buy, and exchange cash for goods directly with the storekeeper. No intermediary is involved in the transaction, the players each understand their roles, and anyone with cash is authorized to spend it. Because these transactions involve the immediate exchange of cash for goods received, repudiation is unlikely to occur. For most purchases, there are receipts, and there may be other printed materials stating conditions for return, guarantees, and so on.

In addition to these five requirements, other key issues differentiate among payment mechanisms:

- *Liability*—Different schemes assign the risk of a failed transaction to different parties. In most cases, the liable party is either the merchant or a financial services company.

- *Transaction costs*—Although large payment transactions can afford transaction fees, purchases of less than $10 are practical only when fees are quite small. Also, systems vary in assigning fees to parties of the transaction.

- *Infrastructure*—Some payment systems depend on a collection of new services, such as trusted certificate providers, while others demand far less infrastructure.

- *Anonymity versus auditability*—The degree of payment privacy usually varies inversely with auditability and is a problematic issue for payment systems due to the need to detect and track inappropriate transactions.

- *Interoperability and portability*—New payment systems must mesh with traditional payment systems, be supported on common computing platforms, and integrate easily with other financial applications used by individuals and enterprises.

- *User acceptance*—All users must trust a payment method and find it easy-to-use and convenient. Users include individual and corporate customers, merchants, billers, government agencies, and financial institutions.

TRADITIONAL PAYMENT TYPES

Although approximately 80 percent of payment transactions in the U.S. are cash based, the cumulative value of these transactions is relatively small. For larger transactions not made face-to-face between trading parties, governments and financial institutions have created alternatives to cash. Checks, credit and debit transfers (called giros), payment cards (both credit and debit), automated clearing-house (ACH) payments, and wire transfers facilitate payments without the need to exchange cash directly for goods and services. Although each of these payment systems works differently, they all involve additional intermediaries—institutions necessary to satisfy the five payment system requirements mentioned previously.

Check. A check is defined as an instruction traditionally written and printed on paper and given to the payee that asks a financial institution to transfer funds to a named party. The check can be exchanged for cash by presenting it at the payer's bank or (more commonly) having the payee deposit it to his or her bank account. Signatures of the parties serve to authorize and authenticate the transaction, and the integrity of the check is ensured to some degree by the difficulty of making undetectable modifications to an ink-on-paper artifact. One or more trusted intermediaries (the financial institutions themselves, not other intermediaries) are needed to make a transaction complete. These intermediaries maintain an audit trail and ensure the check draws upon available funds. If funds are not available, the check is returned to the payee, who then must reconcile the problem.

Credit Transfer. A credit transfer, also called a giro, is similar to a check in the sense that it is an instruction to transfer funds. Unlike a check, however, giro payers submit credit transfers to their financial institutions requesting that funds be forwarded to the payee's bank account. This process is simpler than a check because funds must be available and verified in real time for the process to move forward. Credit transfer is more common in Europe, where all consumer banks commonly offer this service.

Debit Transfer. Direct debit transactions typically are used when a payer and payee (such as a utility provider) regularly exchange value. The payer authorizes the payee to draw direct payments from his bank electronically. Direct debits are common in most European countries.

Payment Card. A payment card (which includes credit, debit, and purchasing cards) is a plastic card designed to facilitate payment by a cardholder to a merchant preregistered to accept payments using that card. Credit cards provide payment to the merchant while extending credit to the cardholder; debit cards draw against available funds on deposit. Purchasing cards are issued to employees of a business typically to facilitate autonomy in acquiring items such as office supplies. Card companies, notably Master-Card and Visa, license the cards, which are provided to customers by the "issuing bank." Merchants register with a bank, called the "acquiring bank," which accepts credit- and debit-card transactions, and pays the merchant. Transactions are authorized and settled through a clearing-house managed by the card companies. Payment card information commonly is carried on magnetic-stripe or smart cards.

"Although checks, credit and debit transfers, payment cards, and automated clearing-houses each work differently, they all involve additional intermediaries—institutions necessary to satisfy key payment system requirements."

Automated Clearing-House. Automated clearing-house (ACH) payments provide both check and credit/debit transfer functionality between banks without paper documentation. The most common ACH payment is a payroll or benefits payment. For example, in the United States, many retired people receive monthly Social Security benefits deposited directly to their bank accounts by way of an ACH system. ACH also can be used to debit funds from the payer's account on a regular basis. ACH debits are useful when the amount owed varies, for example, as it would with a utility or telephone bill. ACH systems are implemented in different ways in different countries. In the U.K., the Bankers Automatic Clearinghouse Systems (BACS) essentially provides the same service as ACH in the U.S. As of January 1999, a system called TARGET began providing bank-to-bank settlement for euro transactions. To transfer funds between countries when two currencies are involved, it is common to use the Society for Worldwide Interbank Financial Transactions (S.W.I.F.T.) system.

Wire Transfer. The final method, wire transfer, is used for relatively large monetary transactions. Users of wire transfer are ordinarily banks, corporations, and governments. With an average transaction value of more than $4 million, wire transfers account for a small proportion of transaction volumes and a large proportion of total transaction value.

A global initiative is in place to implement real-time gross settlement (RTGS) systems, initially for high-value transactions. RTGS systems are designed to eliminate systemic risk that may arise from the default of one or more participants in interbank settlement processes. It is worth noting the difference between clearing and settlement, with clearing relating to the sending of transactions from the originating to the paying institution, and settlement referring to the netting of the outstanding transactions between participants.

In summary, conventional payment types provide useful models and existing trusted infrastructure for new techniques developed to enable electronic business.

Payment Technologies for Electronic Business

When buyers and sellers meet in an electronic medium (including the telephone) with the intention of transacting business, new challenges emerge. First, buyers and sellers need to carry out a payment that is both immediate and does not require physical interaction—in other words, buyers and sellers do not conduct business face-to-face. Because the payment mechanism typically is a credit card, both parties must find ways to authenticate their identities to ensure neither is engaged in credit-card fraud. (Once digital cash becomes widely used, the willingness and ability to conduct "anonymous" transactions may supplant the need for such authentication.) Second, when transactions occur over networks that are inherently insecure, new possibilities arise for a third party to eavesdrop when financial information is exchanged (thus breaking the privacy). Other problems, such as dispute resolution, also take on new complications when business is electronic.

Other issues affect the design of payment technologies. Here are several key factors to consider:

- When the size of a payment is relatively small, for example, then lowering the cost of the transaction will be crucial. Payment-card transaction costs are in the neighborhood of $0.50, and several suppliers are experimenting with micropayment techniques that may be able to reduce this cost to a fraction of a cent.

- When buyer/seller relationships are long-lived, then efficiency and convenience will take precedence over matters of risk. For example, sellers will be content to provide goods and services and then dispatch an electronic invoice, thus exhibiting confidence the buyer will pay.

- Customers will want choices among a portfolio of payment options. To meet this need, suppliers offer "wallets" of different kinds. A wallet is an electronic file containing the purchaser's financial information for multiple payment alternatives along with encryption and certification information for each.

- Businesses aim to keep in direct contact with their customers and to have access to information about them. They are unfavorable about payment schemes that insert third-party providers between customers and merchant.

Payment technologies for electronic business mirror the conventional methods described earlier. There are methods that replicate the role of cash, systems that enable checks and giros to be issued electronically, and ways for customers and businesses to use payment and credit cards. According to Giga, the most prevalent Internet payment method by far is the use of payment cards (99 percent in 1998, projected to be 90 percent in 2002), followed by electronic checks or giros and electronic cash (both less than 1 percent in 1998, 2 to 5 percent in 2002).

PAYMENT CARD TRANSACTIONS

Payment card transactions follow the stages shown in Figure 47 on page 144. Cardholder Alice provides her card number as part of the sales voucher to Merchant Bob. Although historically Bob would have taken an impression of the card on a paper voucher, today he ordinarily swipes the card through a magnetic reader. Bob may have a policy of checking on transactions above a certain amount with his bank, which is called the "acquiring bank." The acquiring bank may provide a simple check against a list of stolen cards or may complete a check that reaches all the way to Alice's bank, which is called the "card-issuing bank." Assuming the checking process completes successfully, Bob then submits the transaction to the acquiring bank, and the settlement is made through the card association clearing-house. Alice's account is debited, Bob's account is credited, and the transaction is considered complete. In the U.S., virtually all payment-card transactions in stores are authorized in the foregoing manner.

Payment card technology encompasses different categories of accounts at Customer Alice's card-issuing bank. Alice's card may represent a credit account that she must settle partially or entirely on a monthly basis, or it may represent a debit account that draws on funds on deposit. Alternately, Alice may use a payment card issued by her employer to conduct purchasing under prenegotiated terms that routes the transaction to her company's card-issuing bank. Although the payment technology remains the same, Alice's banking relationship can vary.

The manner in which disputes are resolved may vary as well. Merchant Bob's account may be credited for Customer Alice's purchase immediately and adjustments made later if she disputes the purchase when she receives her monthly statement. If the transaction is fraudulent—that is, if Alice reports that she did not make the purchase at all—then different policies are instituted by Bob's acquiring bank that assign the liability. For example, it is customary for acquiring banks to accept liability when the payment card is presented to the merchant and the signature verified and to assign the risk to the merchant for transactions where the card is not present.

Initially, payment card transactions handled over the Internet were conducted using standard e-mail or Web forms to send payment card data to the merchant without any special security. Customer Alice simply mailed her payment card information to Merchant Bob, who sent it onward to his acquiring bank. In an Internet environment,

See the sidebar "Electronic Wallets" on page 156 for more information.

Animating Customers, Merchants, and Other Parties

Inspired by Bruce Schneier's 1996 book Applied Cryptography, *a cast of characters has been assembled to demonstrate how payment technologies work.* **Alice** *is a customer who wants to make a purchase,* **Bob** *is a merchant who provides goods and services, and* **Carol** *is another customer who manages purchasing for her company.* **Trent** *is a trusted third party, and* **Pauline** *manages a payment gateway between the Internet and conventional payment clearing-houses. To balance out the cast,* **Eve** *is an eavesdropper who intercepts messages when she can, and* **Mallory** *is willing to launch a malicious attack to disrupt commerce.*

See "Secure Electronic Transaction" on page 157 for more information about liability and fraud protection.

FIGURE 47: TYPICAL PAYMENT-CARD PROCESSING

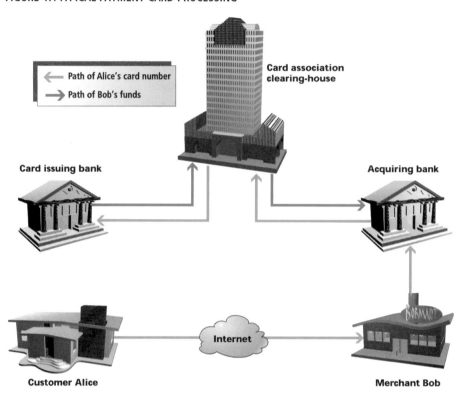

however, it is possible for an eavesdropper such as Eve to listen in on the communication between Alice and Bob. (See Figure 48 on page 145.) Payment card data has a consistent pattern that Eve can exploit to seek out Alice's data automatically. Because most payment cards do not use authentication such as a personal identification number (PIN), Eve then would be able to launch transactions with Alice's payment card data that will be paid by Alice's card-issuing bank. In short, sending sensitive information such as payment card data in plain text over the insecure Internet is not advisable.

DEBIT CARD PAYMENT VERSUS ELECTRONIC CHECKS

Payment cards that debit from an account are similar to electronic checking systems. Both draw on the payee's available funds rather than accumulating debits and providing short-term loans to the payer. However, the two payment technologies differ in several important ways:

1. Debit cards and checks use different clearing-houses. Although the two dominant credit-card suppliers (MasterCard and Visa) provide debit clearing in the U.S., it is the traditional banking community that provides infrastructure for both paper and electronic check handling. This situation is different in Europe, however.

2. Debit cards are associated more closely

with the immediate purchase of goods or services, whereas checks often are written in response to invoices or monthly bills. Particularly for consumers (versus businesses), sending checks in response to bills is more familiar than providing a debit account number with which the merchant can draw the amount.

3. Checks often are issued in a batch by the drawer to several different payees, whereas debit transactions occur in single episodes—for example, when making an online purchase or a purchase at a brick-and-mortar store.

4. Personal identification numbers (PINs) authorize debit transactions, whereas a

digital signature authorizes an electronic check. This distinction is important because a digitally signed electronic check authorizes the transfer of a specific amount of value; in contrast, anyone with access to a debit-card number (and PIN, if one is used) potentially has unlimited access to the complete balance on deposit.

As e-business matures, it increasingly will be difficult to distinguish between these two payment technologies. Their architectures are similar, and, in the end, any differences reflect segmentation and competition in the financial services community rather than functionality. ■

FIGURE 48: EAVESDROPPING ON INTERNET TRANSACTIONS

Secure Sockets Layer. The most popular process in use today to protect sensitive information such as payment data uses the Secure Sockets Layer (SSL) protocol, which was developed by Netscape and is now a de facto standard. SSL encrypts data sent between Customer Alice's browser and Merchant Bob's server. SSL constructs a communication connection where all data is encrypted before being transmitted over the Internet. Handshake routines at the onset of an SSL session share identifying information between the two parties, select one of several encryption algorithms to be used, and create the necessary session-specific encryption keys. Alice's browser, for example, must locate Bob's public key, which is stored at Bob's Web commerce site. Using Bob's public key, Alice's browser can create an encrypted message only Bob can read containing a unique, session-specific key that will be used to encrypt messages exchanged between the two parties for the duration of this transaction. After the handshake is completed, Alice's browser and Bob's server exchange data that is encrypted using conventional secret-key encryption before being transported over the insecure network. The entire process is transparent to Alice and Bob because the complex SSL technology has been embedded successfully in browsers and servers without burdening users with the need to understand or be involved in the setup of the secure data transfer.

See "Confidentiality" on page 210 for more information about public- and private-key encryption.

The SSL protocol has some disadvantages, however. Although SSL encryption provides reasonable protection for confidential data transport over insecure networks, it does not address the question of whether Customer Alice is indeed the owner of the payment card number she uses nor that Bob is in fact a bona fide commerce merchant. Both players in the transaction are vulnerable to impersonation on the part of the other party. As Figure 49 on page 146 illustrates, SSL protects Alice's communication from Eve. However, although Alice may think she is transacting business with Bob at www.BobMart.com, she is in fact communicating with Mallory, who has constructed a Web commerce site that looks like Bob's site but is located at www.Bob-Mart.com. Having obtained Alice's payment card information, Mallory now can masquerade as Alice to make purchases at other merchant sites or even at Bob's site.

As Figure 49 on page 146 shows, the primary purpose of SSL is to make pair-wise communication secure. The limitations of SSL as a payment protocol include the following:

See the sidebar "Digital Signatures" on page 211 for more information.

- SSL has no mechanism to support a customer's digital signature, and so merchants cannot later prove the customer authorized the transaction. This limitation is the reason card companies classify SSL transactions as mail-order/telephone-order (MOTO) or "card not present" transactions and place the liability for fraudulent transactions on the merchant.

FIGURE 49: SSL PROHIBITS EAVESDROPPING, NOT MASQUERADING

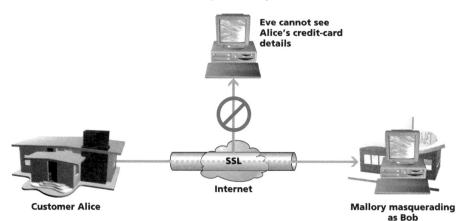

- SSL passes payment-card information to the merchant, who then must secure this data on his server as well as in transit to the card clearing-house. In other words, SSL provides secure transport between two parties, but payment transactions necessarily require secure communication among three (or more) parties.

- SSL uses third-party certificates, although not exclusively from a trusted third party, to verify the validity of the merchants' public keys. Browsers accept certificates from many sources, thus weakening the ability of customers to detect fraudulent merchants. Most consumers do not have their own public-key/private-key pairs or certificates, thus weakening the ability of merchants to detect fraudulent customers.

To reduce risk, merchants often conduct one or more checks to increase the likelihood their customer is trustworthy. For example, Merchant Bob may ask for Customer Alice's billing address and verify it matches the billing address in Alice's credit-card provider's database. However, the lack of third-party authentication mechanisms for payment-card transactions, combined with the fact that the card physically is not present during an electronic purchase, limits the merchant's ability to verify it really is Alice who is making the purchase using her card. If the merchant verifies Alice's billing address and only sends goods to the same address, it can reduce the chance of fraudulent transactions.

As the level of Web sales grows, however, merchants' concerns regarding fraud on the part of the buyer will increase. To identify both buyers and sellers, the two-party protocol with encryption (such as SSL) must evolve into a three-party protocol, with a trusted third party certifying the identity of the buyer and the seller through techniques that validate and authenticate both parties.

SSL version 2.0 (developed by Netscape and released in 1995) supports strong authentication of a Web server; however, some of the functional shortcomings of SSL 2.0 combined with the discovery of some security flaws prompted further development. SSL version 3.0 (developed with public comment and released in 1996) added client-side authentication as well and is considered a reasonably secure protocol.

SSL 3.0 has been adopted by the Internet Engineering Task Force (IETF) as part of what it calls Transport Layer Security (TLS) version 1.0. Extensions to TLS that allow for third-party certification have been drafted and were published in January 1999 when the IETF issued a Request for Comment (RFC 2246). Work is underway to address other important needs such as secure time stamping. Two possibilities are on the horizon:

- The Secure Electronic Transaction (SET) protocol, which includes a method for authenticating all parties with third-party certification, could replace SSL in some situations, for example, in higher-value transactions. (Note that SET involves much more than simply a more robust certification.)

See "Payment Technology Standards" on page 156 for more information about SET.

- SSL could be extended to include trusted third-party certificate-based authorization mechanisms to address the weaknesses noted herein. In so doing, SSL could address some of the concerns leveled against it, while remaining simpler than SET. (Note that adopting SET requires significant investment by all e-business players.)

ELECTRONIC CHECKS

An electronic check works much like a traditional check. Customer Alice prepares a check, either in electronic or paper form, which is an instruction to her bank to pay Merchant Bob a certain sum. More specifically, as shown in Figure 50, Alice's check instructs her bank to "pay to the order of" Bob, which makes her check a negotiable instrument. Alice signs the check and sends it to Bob. Bob endorses the check and sends it to his bank, which is called the "payee's bank," and the check moves on to a clearing-house and then to Alice's bank, which is called the "drawer's bank." Funds are drawn from Alice's account and transferred back to the clearing-house, on to the payee bank, and finally into Bob's account.

FIGURE 50: TYPICAL CHECK PAYMENT PROCESSING

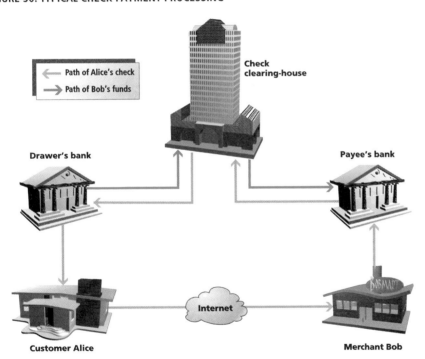

Disputes are resolved by moving the paper check to the source of the problem. If Alice's checking account lacks sufficient funds, then her check is returned to Merchant Bob, who must contact Alice to resolve the problem. In addition, because banks often credit the payee immediately, Bob's account may be debited the amount of the returned check. In the case of paper checks, a good deal of cost and delay is associated with physically moving the paper check through each of these steps.

Of course, Customer Alice cannot sign an electronic check in the same manner as a paper check. Instead, she prepares a digital signature by creating a digital "hash" of her instructions (the information on the check) and encrypts that hash with her private key.

See the sidebar "Digital Signatures" on page 211 for more information.

Merchant Bob, the banks, and the e-check clearing-house are assured the check is from Alice because they can decrypt the hash with Alice's public key, thus verifying the message is from Alice. In addition, they can use the hash to verify the instructions have not been modified. (Note that like a traditional paper check, every e-check has a distinct serial number, which prevents it from being submitted for payment multiple times.)

See "Electronic Bill Presentment and Payment" on page 151 for more information.

Three other models are used for electronic check handling, each a variant on the traditional check processing flow: cash and transfer, lockbox, and checks used with bill presentment systems. Cash and transfer and lockbox models will be discussed here; bill presentment models will be discussed in a subsequent section.

Cash and Transfer. In a cash-and-transfer model, as shown in Figure 51 on page 150, Alice issues a check to Bob, who forwards the check directly to Alice's bank rather than to his own bank. Alice's bank then initiates an electronic cash transfer through the clearing-house and on to Bob's bank. The cash-and-transfer model exploits the

HOW SECURE ELECTRONIC TRANSACTION (SET) WORKS

The SET protocol is invoked after Customer Alice has completed browsing, selecting, and ordering a product or service from Merchant Bob, her provider. Before the SET transaction begins, Customer Alice will have approved the completed order form and selected one of her payment cards.

1. Alice sends a message to Merchant Bob, indicating which payment card is to be used and requesting a copy of the certified public key for the appropriate payment gateway.

2. When Bob receives the request, he assigns a unique transaction identifier to the message and transmits that identifier to Alice along with his certified public key and the certified public key for Pauline, who operates a gateway between the insecure environment of the Internet and a secure communication channel with issuing banks for the payment card of choice.

3. Alice verifies with Trent, a trusted third-party certification service, that the certificates attached to Bob's and Pauline's public keys are authentic, and she stores those keys for future use. Alice's software creates the order information (OI) and payment instructions (PI). Her software places the transaction identifier assigned by Bob in both the OI and the PI; this identifier will be used by Pauline to link the OI and the PI when Bob requests payment authorization. Alice signs the OI and the PI with her private key, encrypts the digitally signed PI and her payment card account number with Pauline's

public key, and sends this information to Bob.

4. Bob receives the order and verifies Alice's identity with Trent. Next, Bob uses Alice's public key to check the digital signature on the OI to ensure that the order really came from Alice and that Alice's message has not been changed in transit.

Notice that Bob cannot decrypt the PI containing Alice's payment-card number because it was encrypted using Pauline's public key. In a SET transaction, the buyer's payment-card number is not shared with the merchant.

5. Bob begins filling Alice's order. At the same time, Bob also requests payment authorization by generating and digitally signing a payment authorization request, which includes the amount to be authorized, the transaction identifier from the OI, and Alice's PI. Bob encrypts this information and the PI with Pauline's public key and sends it to her.

6. After the OI has been processed, Bob generates and digitally signs a purchase response message (which again includes Bob's certified public key). The response then is transmitted back to Alice.

7. When Alice receives the purchase response message from Bob, she can again verify Bob's public key with his digital certificate and then use Bob's key to verify his digital signature. Alice knows Bob has received and now processed her order.

Rechecking with Trent guarantees Bob's certificate has not been revoked.

8. Pauline receives Bob's authorization request and Alice's PI. She decrypts it using her own private key and then verifies certificates that authenticate Alice and Bob. Next, she uses Alice's public key to check Alice's signature on the PI. Pauline now is sure Alice and Bob are authentic and the messages are unaltered.

9. Pauline also verifies the transaction identifier received from Bob matches the one included in Alice's PI. She then formats and sends an authorization request to the card-issuing bank via a non-Internet-based secure payment system and awaits a response. The issuer processes the authorization request and sends a response back to Pauline via the secure payment system.

10. On receiving authorization, Pauline generates and digitally signs an authorization response message, which includes the issuer's response and a copy of her own certified public key. The response is encrypted using Bob's public key and transmitted back to Bob.

11. When Bob receives the authorization response message from Pauline, he decrypts it using his private key, verifies with Trent the digital certificate attached to Pauline's public key, and verifies her digital signature on the authorization response message. Bob stores the authorization response for use when requesting payment after the order has been filled completely.

opportunity for the payee to communicate directly with the drawer's bank, due to Internet connectivity. Although the clearing and settlement are needed in this model, they are needed only once.

Lockbox. In the lockbox transaction, as shown in Figure 52 on page 150, Alice issues a check directly to Bob's account at his bank. The payee's bank then directs the check by way of the clearing-house to the drawer's bank for settlement and notifies Bob that Alice has made a payment. The lockbox model is aimed at improved cash management for the payee. Rather than accumulating and forwarding checks to his bank after some period of time, Bob arranges for his bank to receive the checks directly and handle them immediately. In doing so, funds are transferred more quickly to Bob's account. (Note that the term lockbox originally referred to the technique of establishing local repositories for paper checks to decrease their time in transit.) Again, this process is exactly the same in the physical world as in the digital world.

12. Bob then completes processing of Alice's order by shipping the required goods or performing the requested services. When the order is fulfilled, Bob requests payment.

(Note: Bob may request payment in minutes for some transactions, in weeks for others, and perhaps in months on some occasions.)

13. To request payment, Bob generates and digitally signs a "capture request," which includes the final amount of the transaction, the transaction identifier from the OI, and other information about the transaction. Bob encrypts his payment request using Pauline's public key and sends it to her.

14. When Pauline receives Bob's capture request, she decrypts the request using her private key. She then uses Bob's public key to verify his digital signature on the capture request. Bob's capture request is matched to the previously processed authorization request using the transaction identifier. Pauline then creates a clearing request, which she sends to the issuer via a non-Internet secure payment network.

15. Pauline generates and digitally signs a capture response message, which includes a copy of Bob's own certified public key. The response then is encrypted using Bob's public key and transmitted back to Bob.

16. When Bob receives the capture response message from Pauline, he decrypts it with his private key, yet again verifies the digital certificate on her public key, and then uses

Pauline's public key to check her digital signature. Bob then stores the capture response so he can later reconcile his total capture requests submitted with the payments received.

The SET transaction is complete. The important issues are as follows:

- All participants are authenticated using third-party certification.
- All participants reconfirm authenticity throughout the exchange.

- All communication is encrypted using certified public keys.
- The merchant does not have access to payment card data for the buyer; it is passed on in an encrypted form.
- The protocol is complex and depends on detailed communication among four players: customer, merchant, payment gateway, and trusted third party. ■

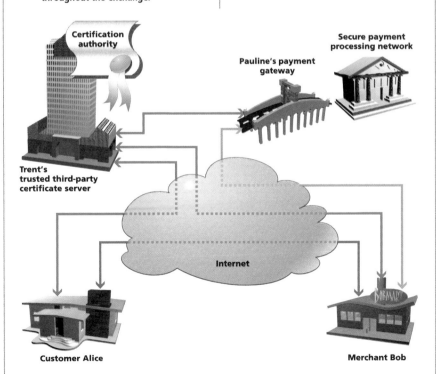

FIGURE 51: CASH-AND-TRANSFER MODEL FOR ELECTRONIC CHECKS

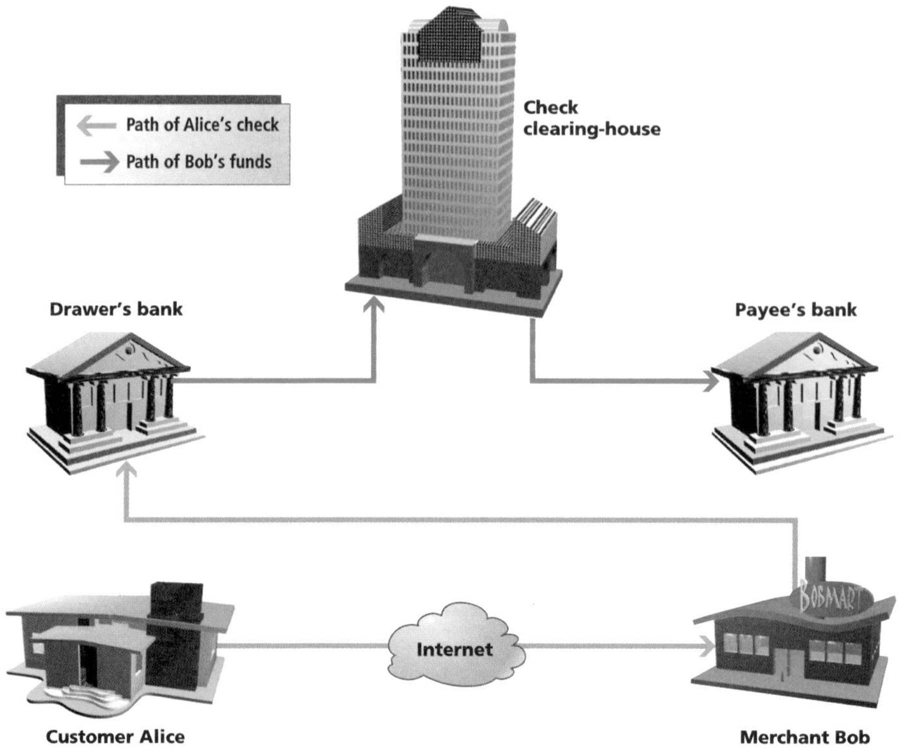

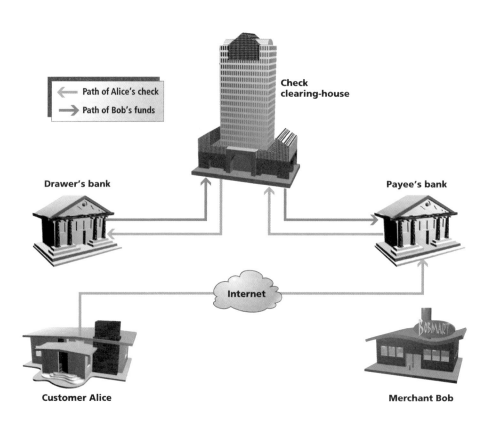

FIGURE 52: LOCKBOX MODEL FOR ELECTRONIC CHECKS

All the methods for handling electronic checks have the potential to reduce "float" and to change its beneficiary. Without the need to ship paper checks from one place to another, these electronic transactions can take place in hours rather than days. If consumer behavior remains constant, then the primary beneficiary would be Bob, who would receive Alice's funds earlier. Alice's check no longer would languish in the mail, which provided Alice with the float. However, if Alice is a sophisticated consumer, she is likely to request last-minute delivery of her e-check, thus effectively regaining the float.

Consider the case of Carol, who is an accounts payable manager for a U.S. corporation. Even though Carol has set up electronic data interchange (EDI) relationships with primary trading partners to trigger electronic payments, she still manages purchasing agreements with many other suppliers. Thus, Carol still must create many checks to pay the rest of the company's bills. As a sophisticated cash manager, Carol is likely to develop a payment function that issues electronic checks on a scheduled basis just prior to payment becoming due. From Carol's point of view, a shift from managing paper to performing electronic transactions will reduce costs and gain efficiency.

The shift to electronic payment is less dramatic in Europe, where corporations already use direct credits to a large extent. Similarly, direct electronic payments or credits are adopted and used easily by consumers familiar with the giro.

In the U.S., most observers believe electronic checks will be adopted quickly by businesses and less quickly by consumers. Observing that the first electronic check was issued in June 1998 by the U.S. Treasury to GTE as payment for internetworking services, Forrester Research suggests government will be an early adopter of electronic check technology. For example, the U.S. Department of Defense is issuing more than 1,000 electronic checks per day to its suppliers in an aggressive pilot program. Meta analysts identify large corporations as leaders in this area, arguing that small and mid-sized businesses operate more like consumers and have grown used to the float built into conventional check processing. Meta forecasts the onset of mass adoption of electronic checks to begin in 2001 for major corporations. This adoption will be enabled in part by support for Web-based payment technology by enterprise resource planning (ERP) vendors. E-checks probably will not prevail in Europe, however, due to the dominance of giro payments (especially in business-to-consumer settings).

ELECTRONIC CHECKS VERSUS ACH PAYMENTS

Electronic checks differ somewhat from ACH payments, although both authorize electronic instructions asking for a transfer of funds:

- For businesses and governments that wish to credit their customers' accounts on a regular basis, ACH credits already have replaced paper checks. The ACH technique commonly is used for benefits, payroll, and other regular payments to individuals. For customers wishing to pay businesses the same amount on a regular basis, ACH debit relationships compete with electronic checks.

- Unlike the automatic credit and deposits provided by ACH, electronic checks are used by consumers to pay varying amounts to different providers as needed.

Electronic Bill Presentment and Payment

Electronic bill presentment is the distribution of bills and invoices to customers over the Internet. The primary motivation for billers to use electronic bill presentment either is to reduce the cost of sending a bill or to reduce the cost of handling receipt of payments. In the U.S., it typically costs from $0.75 to $1.25 to print and mail each bill to a consumer. In contrast, the cost of electronic bill presentment is estimated to be $0.35 each. These estimates suggest that enterprises serving millions of customers—for

"Float" is the time when a payment is in transit, for example, after a check has been deposited by the merchant in his or her account and before the funds have been withdrawn from the customer's account. The funds have not yet moved from customer to merchant. Benefiting from the float (at the expense of someone else's float) is a goal for all parties in a payment transaction.

See "Web-Enabling ERP Functions" on page 114 for more information.

example, regional or national telephony providers, regional energy utilities, or large health care providers—quickly could save millions of dollars even if only a modest percentage of their customers could be encouraged to accept electronic bills.

In the U.S., electronic bill presentment services commonly are paired with corresponding electronic payment schemes. Although it is likely that individuals and enterprises will issue electronic checks in response to paper bills, most observers believe customers are unlikely to respond to online bills with cash or paper checks. Furthermore, the ability to review a bill and then simply pay it with a click on an icon is one of the most significant benefits for customers. As a result, those who provide bill presentment services also provide electronic payment processing. In examining this emerging market, SRI Consulting concluded that although major competitors vary in their approaches, all are aiming to provide integrated electronic bill presentment and payment (EBPP) systems.

In Europe, many bills already are settled by direct debit transfers. For example, utility providers offer a discount for subscribers using this payment method because it improves debt collection significantly.

HOW EBPP WORKS

There are three basic models for electronic bill presentment and payment: biller direct, consolidator, and the e-mail approach.

FINANCIAL ELECTRONIC DATA INTERCHANGE (FEDI)

Financial electronic data interchange (FEDI) is a business-to-business payment system that has existed for 20 years but only recently has started to gain momentum. Essentially, FEDI is the electronic exchange between business partners of payments and remittance information. (FEDI handles only monetary transactions, however, as distinct from electronic funds transfer [EFT], which is used to pass monetary transactions as well as letters of credit and other financial instruments between banks or between businesses and banks.) Because all funds transfers must be made through the banking system, FEDI transactions always involve at least one bank and generally include two—one for each trading partner.

Paper-based bill payment systems are labor-intensive, slow, prone to human error, and costly. The National Automated Clearing House Association (NACHA) estimates the average cost of a paper payment between companies at $8.33, compared with the cost of an electronic payment at $3. FEDI payment systems are beneficial for several reasons:

- Automatic reconciliation of remittance details—Suppliers receive the payment advice together with the related remittance information, enabling them to automate the accounts-payable function.

- Higher quality and speed of information processing—Incoming data can be processed by the receiver's application automatically and immediately without employees rekeying data.

- Fewer errors in documents—Because transaction information is processed automatically, potential administrative mistakes and misunderstandings are reduced.

- Improved cash-flow management—Future cash flows and commitments can be planned precisely.

- Lower processing costs—Businesses have one channel for all payments; this simplicity and efficiency result in lower operation and maintenance costs.

- Certainty of payment date—The date the funds are to be debited from the buyer's account and credited to the supplier's account is readily accessible to both parties.

- Use of public standards—Users are not locked into one service provider because FEDI uses the international Electronic Data Interchange For Administration, Commerce and Transport (EDIFACT) standard.

Despite FEDI's benefits, it does not offer quick return on investment; rather, it should be considered a long-term solution. FEDI usually relies on a value-added network (VAN) for message transport.

Unlike EDI and ACH funds transfers, FEDI integrates a remittance advice with the fund transfer itself. Although this method offers reliability and security, its high costs have been a significant barrier to adoption for smaller companies. Currently, FEDI is used primarily by companies with annual revenues of more than $100 million. FEDI payments make up about 10 percent of these large companies' total payments volume, while smaller companies use FEDI for less than 0.05 percent of their total payments.

In January 1998, the Chicago Clearing House Association (CCHA) and Electronic Data Sys-

- **Biller direct**—In this model, a merchant prepares and presents bills directly to customers on the merchant's Web site. Merchants thus retain a direct channel of communication to their customers and are well positioned to provide additional products and services and to integrate electronic billing with conventional billing systems. Customers can be offered incentives to use the EBPP option, for example, with price discounts. However, consumers who want to pay some or all of their bills at one central location are not served well by this model.

- **Consolidator**—This model addresses the perceived consumer need to pay many bills at a common location; however, in doing so, the merchant's objectives often are compromised. If the bank is the consolidator, for example, then it is able to push money from a customer's account to the merchant. When a bank operates as a consolidator, then it is in position to serve its customers better, and the merchant potentially loses direct customer contact.

In an attempt to reconcile this imbalance, the consolidator approach has two variants: "thick" consolidation and "thin" consolidation. When a consolidator such as a bank steps between a merchant and the customer and blocks all direct communication, this action is termed "thick" consolidation. In contrast, "thin" consolidation means a consolidator presents a summary of the bill and accepts payment while routing the customer to the merchant for billing details. Clearly, merchants tend to favor thin consolidation.

TYPICAL FEDI MODEL

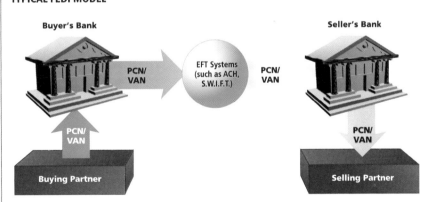

Source: Elsevier Science, 1998

tems (EDS) signed an agreement to provide intranet-based e-business services, including FEDI capabilities, to small and midsized businesses. The services enable businesses to transmit payment and remittance data electronically, plus exchange key documents with their trading partners. The services are provided over an intranet with authentication, encryption, and acknowledgment features.

Factors encouraging the growth of FEDI

include increased electronic payments by the U.S. federal government (and its initiative to convert all its payments to electronic ones) and the overall growth of e-commerce encouraging companies to use electronic payments.

The U.S. Department of Treasury's EFT '99 mandate, which required all banks that process ACH payments to be FEDI-capable by September 1998, created a large increase in

FEDI transactions in 1998. FEDI transactions over the ACH network totaled 64.5 million in 1998, an increase of 42.7 percent, compared with the 45.2 million transaction made in 1997.

In 1998, the U.S. Federal Reserve System made low-cost FEDI software from Bottomline Technologies available to the 12,000 financial institutions connected to FedLine, its electronic payment transaction connection. ■

FEDI TRANSACTION GROWTH

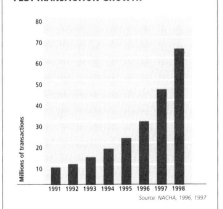

Source: NACHA, 1996, 1997

- **E-Mail**—The key idea of the third model (sometimes known as "invited push") is that merchants send graphically rich electronic bills directly to their customers. This process contrasts with the alternate models, both of which invite the customer to a Web site to view the bill. The e-mail approach should be simpler for customers, who can receive bills along with other e-mail, and it also allows direct communication between merchant and customer. However, by bringing customers to a central site, direct billers and consolidators make authentication, tracking, and auditing significantly easier, so the e-mail method is the least developed in the marketplace.

Regardless of which EBPP model is followed, there are three basic steps that someone such as a merchant or a consolidator must undertake to make EBPP systems work:

Bill Data Extraction and Transformation. Billing data must be extracted from legacy billing systems and transformed in preparation for electronic presentment. Even the most aggressive estimates of the uptake of EBPP suggest that the vast majority of bills will be printed on paper and mailed by post for years to come. Therefore, the first task is to tap into the biller's system, locate just those customers who request electronic billing, and reformulate a data stream currently aimed at a paper printer.

Bill Presentment. The bill must be presented on a Web server or via e-mail and enhanced with features customers and merchants value. For example, bills from telecommunication and utility providers include important details both merchants and customers will want to study. A shift in telephone calling patterns may signal the need to reconfigure the customer's billing arrangement. A sharp rise in energy consumption may indicate the customer's heating system has a fault or, when plotted against local temperature, may be explained by an unusually cold winter.

Bill Payment. A convenient payment method must be available. For the customer, convenience may be a scheduling function that will trigger payment instantly, at a future date, or perhaps on recurring dates. For the merchant, payments need to be aggregated, deposits to the bank managed, and updates provided for enterprise accounts-receivable systems. For customer convenience, support for payment cards, electronic checks, and electronic funds transfer (EFT) will be needed.

"Electronic, or digital, cash is an analog for paper currency and coins. The central idea behind digital cash is that buyers possess electronic tokens that can be exchanged immediately for goods and services."

From a payment technology viewpoint, EBPP is a repackaging of existing payment types and methods to apply electronic payment to incoming bills. For the consumer, paying a telephone bill and purchasing a product online may be very similar experiences. The consumer will choose a payment type—such as a credit- or debit-card account or an electronic check—and dispatch it using SSL or SET.

As subsequent discussions of the market indicate, EBPP is an emerging market that will be hotly contested by all players. From the supplier side, the major drivers will be continuing access to and control of information that flows to the customer. Billers, financial institutions, and consolidators will compete in this market. For consumers, the major drivers will be convenience and other perceived values that encourage a shift from paper to electronic payments. Critical mass—that is, the availability of most or all bills to consumers and of enough customers to billers—will be a key indicator to watch.

Digital Cash

Electronic, or digital, cash is an analog for paper currency and coins. The central idea behind digital cash is that buyers possess electronic tokens that can be exchanged immediately for goods and services. In some cases, these tokens are used anonymously; that is, buyers use digital cash in the same way as ordinary cash, and no audit trail connects the buyer to the purchase. Digital cash accomplishes two goals: First, because there is no need to authorize and process each transaction, the transaction is less expensive to execute. Therefore, digital cash opens the door for small online purchases, such as an issue of an electronic newspaper—something not economically feasible with e-check or electronic credit-card payment. (Micropayments are small payments, and to support micropayments, transaction costs must be reduced. The cost of a payment-card or check transaction commonly is estimated at $0.50 or more, so payment types other than card and check are favored. The most common way to provide for micropayments is with a digital cash solution.) Second, some digital cash implementations protect the privacy of the buyer, who may be reluctant to have an electronic record created for every purchase made online.

Minting electronic coins and currency is a straightforward process. A token is created that contains a monetary value paired with a unique serial number. Tokens are purchased by customers and are given to merchants in exchange for goods and services. Tokens are stored on the customer's computer or, often, on portable devices such as a smart card. For example, Customer Alice, who resides in the U.K., may purchase 500 Deutsche Marks and store them on her smart card for use on her holiday in Germany. Although she likely will use other payment methods for high-value transactions (for example, her hotel bill), Alice purchases snacks, newspapers, and gifts with her electronic purse. When Alice's holiday is over, she can exchange her unused digital cash for local currency.

Simpler schemes are possible. A stored-value smart card may be used to carry unsigned, unserialized tokens. The card, often used in applications such as transit, can be recharged by placing it in a card-accepting device and providing a path to traditional payment systems. Reloading the card can be as simple as depositing coins and cash or drawing against a payment-card account. Rather than providing all the functions of traditional cash, digital cash can be offered as "scrip," which means it is redeemable only at certain locations.

See "Smart Cards" on page 176 for more information.

The challenge for digital cash schemes is to construct a system that disallows the counterfeiting or duplication of currency, that is, that guarantees a coin is authentic and is spent only once. At the same time, digital cash transactions must remain simple and inexpensive to preserve their ability to support small transaction amounts. Finally, in many cases, digital cash transactions need to occur when both customer and merchant are not connected to a network. Solutions to these challenges take several forms, but the two basic categories are as follows:

- Digital cash providers that utilize special hardware devices to prevent counterfeiting and will not spend tokens more than once. Stored-value cards are smart cards that carry a certain amount of digital cash stored directly as a balance on the card. The integrity of the balance information is maintained by the smart card's hardware and software design. On-board encryption precludes manipulating the digital cash data.

  Stored-value cards do not require online verification and thus help reduce transaction costs by allowing consumers to purchase items without a credit card and without the merchant needing to verify each transaction. This approach allows users to gain the portability necessary to shop from any device equipped with a compatible smart-card reader. However, because smart cards and smart-card readers are only used in a few countries, this way of protecting e-cash probably will not become available during the forecast period.

- Digital cash providers that maintain a currency server that contains the serial numbers of all coins currently in circulation. When a customer exchanges a token (available in a range of denominations) for products or services, the merchant submits the token to the currency server where it is immediately validated, the token is removed from circulation, and an electronic payment is returned to the merchant. Notice that, unlike traditional coins and currency, tokens are not returned to circulation but rather are spent only once.

Despite the common intuition that digital cash should be as prevalent as its real world analog, the market for digital cash products has not flourished. There are several reasons for this. First, for digital cash to be used offline, customers and merchants must equip themselves with a new generation of cards and readers. For online systems utilizing smart-card technology, customers must purchase card readers; merchants must have card writers as well as readers. Second, it remains unclear whether and when electronic shoppers will be attracted to micropayments and, in turn, when merchants will begin to offer them. Third, trials of electronic cash alternatives to date are characterized by a clumsiness not associated with traditional, coin-based transactions.

Payment Technology Standards

There are a multitude of protocols associated with payment technologies. Virtually every provider of payment services has assembled a collection of encryption techniques, Web protocols, interfaces to legacy payment systems, and so on.

Two large standards efforts emerge as the most critical for payment technologies in the next two years, the SET protocol and the Open Financial Exchange (OFX) standard. SET and OFX are complementary standards. SET offers authentication services currently

ELECTRONIC WALLETS

An electronic wallet is a collection of customer data necessary for completing payment transactions. In its simplest form, the wallet contains customer account information, that is, payment-card numbers for different accounts. More complex wallets, for example the SET wallet, also contain the customer's private key and third-party certification data.

Electronic wallets can reside in different places. Site wallets store personal profiles at an individual Web site. Remote or server-side wallets store financial information on the Web so it can be used with a community of merchants. Distributed wallets divide information between the customer's access device and a Web site. Finally, personal wallets store all information on the customer's computer or on a smart card and can, in principle, assist purchasing at any merchant site.

Each deployment model of an electronic wallet has its own strengths and weak-

nesses, as follows:

- Site wallets—Provide convenience when conducting business with individual merchants but offer no support to the consumer conducting business at many different sites.

- Remote wallets—Provide cross-site support but interpose a new player between customer and merchant; they may be provided by a bank or portal.

- Distributed wallets—Shrink the size of the application but at the cost of requiring a third-party player.

- Personal wallets—Operate to a public standard (such as the SET standard) and have the potential to enable payments to any and all merchants without interposing another player directly—if they can be made simple to install and valuable to use.

The challenges for personal wallets center on deployment, added value, and critical

mass. In addition to providing a repository of financial and security information, these wallets also provide transaction tracking and interfaces to personal financial management software, such as Intuit's Quicken or Microsoft Money. Suppliers of wallets emphasize convenience to encourage customers to install and use wallets. Schemes involving a third party are not expected to be popular with merchants.

Marketing, not technology, dominates the design and distribution of wallets. Electronic wallets contain data and perhaps encryption, but not payment technology per se. Wallet suppliers offer tools for financial institutions and other payment companies to brand the wallet with their own trademarks. Successful e-business payment companies will be those that convince customers to adopt their particular wallet. Competition among companies deploying consumer wallets is expected to be fierce. ■

lacking in SSL transactions. OFX enables financial data to be tagged in a standard manner; these uniform descriptions (in OFX format) then can be sent wherever necessary, perhaps using the SET protocol. In this manner, OFX provides for selective sharing of financial information, which is important as merchants, financial institutions, and consolidators wrestle over access to customer information.

SECURE ELECTRONIC TRANSACTION

SET is a standard describing a complex authentication mechanism that makes it extremely difficult to commit fraud. The most widely used card-acceptance mechanism over the Internet, SSL, only has a weak built-in feature for authenticating customers and merchants. Consumers should be concerned because they provide payment-card information and hope the merchant will guard that information and use it appropriately. Merchants should be concerned because they accept payment-card information without any guarantee the customer is the true owner of the card. These weaknesses have been outlined earlier and are summarized in Table 3.

See "Open Financial Exchange" on page 160 for more information.

TABLE 3: SSL VERSUS SET

Characteristic	SSL	SET
Certification	Pair-wise sharing of certificates; consumers may not have certificates	Certification of all parties by trusted third party
Authentication	No mechanism exists to authenticate parties	Both customer and merchant are authenticated
Nonrepudiation	No mechanism to capture customer's commitment	Customer digitally signs commitment to purchase and pay
Risk of merchant fraud	Customer gives key financial data to the merchant	Customer gives key financial data to the payment gateway
Liability for customer fraud	Merchant liable in case of fraud	Financial institution liable in case of fraud
Infrastructure	In place in browsers and Web servers	Proven in pilot demonstrations; available as packaged software or software tools; not widely deployed
Anonymity versus auditability	Allows each party to certify itself at the onset of a transaction, but assurance of the identity is weak	Requires all parties to be certified repeatedly throughout the transaction
Interoperability	Standardized by the IETF	Standardized by SETCo
User acceptance	Widely used by customers on the Web	Not yet in widespread use

A Brief History of SET. In 1995, the leading credit-card associations, MasterCard and Visa, were faced with a dilemma: Software vendors in the fledgling e-business market were creating competing standards for accepting credit cards over the Internet. In one camp was Microsoft, and in the other camp, IBM. Seeing this schism as a potential block to widespread adoption of credit-card use over the Internet, the credit-card associations agreed to put competition aside and persuaded the software vendors to do likewise. The result was the SET Consortium, an international initiative which eventually included other credit-card companies such as American Express and Novus-Discover as well as nearly every major e-business software and security vendor.

See the sidebar "How Secure Electronic Transaction (SET) Works" on page 148 for more information.

"Chargebacks" are items on a credit-card bill that are disputed by the cardholder.

After nearly two years of work, the Consortium published the preliminary SET 1.0 specification in June 1997, with a final version released in September 1997. In December 1997, MasterCard and Visa founded Secure Electronic Transaction LLC (referred to as SETCo) to manage the SET specification, oversee software compliance testing through its agent, Tenth Mountain Systems, and address issues related to the adoption of the SET global payment standard.

SET 1.0 automates the authorization, verification, and settlement processes of a credit-card transaction conducted over the Internet. The first SET pilot projects were conducted in 1997 at a variety of sites. Since then, more than 100 European and Asian banks have begun working on SET pilot projects. As of early 1999, MasterCard and Visa report successful pilot projects and anticipate more widespread deployment will occur soon. Visa highlights 65 Web merchants, all in Europe and Asia, that have adopted SET technology. However, most of these pilot projects were launched in 1997. The adoption of SET appears to be slower than expected, even in Europe and Asia.

In January 1998, MasterCard and Visa each announced merchants using SET-compliant software no longer would be responsible for chargebacks that result from a SET transaction. In a traditional credit-card setting, if a mail, telephone, Web-based, or other "card not present" purchase is found to be fraudulent for some reason, the merchant assumes the cost of that purchase, and the consumer's liability legally (in the U.S.) is limited to $50. In a SET transaction, however, a merchant has assurance that a customer is legitimate because of the built-in authentication mechanism. To encourage merchant use of SET, the credit companies have relieved the merchants of this liability.

E-business software vendors seem more enthusiastic than merchants and banks about the possibilities offered by SET. Vendor gatherings are scheduled throughout 1999 as interoperation testing continues. The four key SET components tested for interoperation are wallets, merchant servers, payment gateways, and certificate authorities. As of April 1999, 23 software vendors have enrolled in the SET certification program, and 6 of these suppliers have been granted use of the SET-MARK, a certification trademark, for some or all of their products. SETCo participants are a mixture of traditional system providers (such as Fujitsu and IBM), major e-business vendors (such as CyberCash and VeriFone), and niche vendors focused on SET (such as GlobeSet and Trintech Group).

SET developers are working on SET 2.0. An April 1999 SETCo overview identifies six areas where enhancements are under discussion. SET 2.0 will support the transport of PINs to enable debit transactions, for example. Other enhancements include the ability to cancel or renegotiate an order and to assign multiple payment instructions to a single order. Payment enhancements include the ability to negotiate payments and support for purchasing cards. SET 2.0 also will include a way to encrypt credit-card data using smart cards. There are plans to reduce the size of certificates as well. Release 2.0 is scheduled for release in late 1999.

SET Prospects. SET so far has enjoyed support by European and Asian banks. IBM alone says it has more than 100 SET customers outside of the U.S. In the U.S., however, analysts estimate that no more than a dozen banks have embarked on SET pilots, although many of the country's largest banks—including Bank of America (which merged with NationsBank in October 1998 under the name BankAmerica), Chase Manhattan, Mellon Bank, and Wells Fargo—have been among those pilots. Many e-business merchant sites in the U.S. already have implemented SSL-based merchant servers and have shown little interest in migrating to SET.

Several other concerns have been raised about the use of SET. Because SET does not allow the merchant access to credit-card numbers, processes such as customer profiling, handling disputes, and chargebacks are complex. Concerns also have been raised about the performance of SET. Encryption technology is, by rule, processor intensive, and a SET transaction includes several encrypted and digitally signed message exchanges with the consumer and the payment gateway. Several accelerator card vendors, such as Rainbow Technologies, are trying to fill this void with hardware devices that allow the processing-intensive cryptographic aspects of a transaction to be offloaded to a processor designed specifically to handle SET. General-purpose cryptography coprocessors such as those on IBM mainframes also speed up SET.

In November 1998, Gartner issued an analysis of SET performance issues. The report concluded that for small and midsized commerce applications, SET would require no more server resources than an equivalent SSL-based system. For large-volume commerce servers, a modest 5 to 6 percent increase in resources would be required. The report also forecasts hardware support for cryptography functions that would reduce the load on the server's processor as well as improved cryptographic algorithms that would have the same effect. Gartner concludes that SET provides significant improvements in security and trust with only minor performance penalties that can be addressed in an affordable manner.

As Web merchants and their processing systems mature, it also will be difficult to convince them to migrate to SET. Many merchants that were waiting for SET in 1997 have given up on the protocol and moved ahead instead with SSL encryption and reliance on fraud detection services that solve most of the e-business issues SET attempts to solve. Furthermore, debit cards, which require the consumer to enter a PIN, are not supported in the current version of SET (1.0).

EUROPAY C-SET AND E-COMM

Two French consortia are supporting competing smart-card-based electronic payment implementations: Europay C-SET and e-COMM. (See Table 4.) The consortia say they developed SET alternatives because of two concerns: authentication, which still is not regarded as being sufficiently robust for online credit-card transactions in France, and nonrepudiation, which consortia members argue is not strong enough in SET.

TABLE 4: C-SET VERSUS e-COMM

Technology	Europay C-SET	e-COMM
SET compliance	Requires software at merchant site to convert SET transactions to C-SET, allowing interoperability but adding cost and time.	Supports SET but has no provision to convert transactions to C-SET.
Portability	Certified identity and address of C-SET's translator is stored on a smart card, thus allowing portability.	Currently not portable; plans are to support future Europay, MasterCard, and Visa standards-compliant smart cards with cryptographic functions including SET, enabling portability.
Functionality	Uses POS terminal to present the PIN to the smart card for identification; software is inside the terminal.	Uses POS terminal to present the PIN to the smart card for identification; software is inside the PC.
Hardware and software requirements	Requires a personal reader (developed by Groupe Bull), attached to a PC into which the Europay smart card is inserted when a customer makes a purchase. C-SET-equipped sites also allow customers to use magnetic-strip credit cards for purchases.	Requires a PC, the e-COMM software, a card reader (developed by Gemplus), and browser-enabled access to the Internet.

Source: Gartner, 1997

OPEN FINANCIAL EXCHANGE

OFX is a specification for the exchange of financial data between financial institutions, businesses, and consumers via the Internet. It currently covers home and small business banking, bill payment, and presentment as well as transactions in investment areas such as stocks, bonds, and mutual funds. OFX originally was developed by Check-Free, Intuit, and Microsoft.

OFX is a particularly important standard due to the increasingly complex relationships among merchants, financial institutions, and electronic commerce companies that are vying for access to customers. OFX is the strongest contender for standardizing payment transactions and, in particular, for providing information selectively to different players in the value chain. Without OFX, consumers will be forced to choose one supplier of financial services; with OFX, transactions following the standard may be processed with several suppliers.

The OFX standard defines a set of tags that identify common elements of financial data. OFX is a derivative of the Standard Generalized Markup Language (SGML). SGML provides a flexible means of tagging and delimiting data, which is exactly what OFX accomplishes. In a typical OFX message, for example, tags such as **<STMTRQ>** identify elements of data—in this case, a statement request. Using the OFX markup standard, a stream of data such as **<BANKID>12109999<ACCTID>9998888<ACCNTTYPE>Checking** can be created and dispatched from a customer using any OFX-compliant product to any bank. By accommodating standards such as SGML, OFX is neutral with respect to operating systems and provides a blueprint anyone can implement to share financial data.

One area where OFX provides leverage is in support of home banking and investment management. Vendors such as Intuit can aggregate information on behalf of their home-banking customers and ship out OFX payments as well. Customer Alice may ask her telephony provider to send a line item debit to her Quicken account, for example, and OFX provides the common standard for communication. Alice's telephony provider may be willing to send the total amount due while providing billing details to Alice only when she logs into the carrier's Web site.

OFX sets no requirement about what information is shared. OFX is expected to provide a meeting place for merchant billers and consolidators, each of whom has a different interest in the customer. Consolidators intend to provide value by bringing most of Alice's bills to a common location. Merchant billers can respond to consolidator requests for the total amount due while retaining item line details that identify specific products and services. Customer Alice should have the best of both worlds—a single place to pay bills as well as the ability to visit merchants for a detailed view of her transactions.

Integrion Financial Network/GOLD. Soon after OFX was launched, a second consortium was formed to launch a competing standard. Integrion Financial Network is a banking industry network service provider comprising major North American banks and IBM. The competing exchange specification is called the GOLD standard. In April 1998, however, the Banking Industry Technology Secretariat (BITS, a division of The Bankers Roundtable and an organization comprising more than 125 of the largest banks in the country) facilitated the convergence of the Integrion Financial Network's GOLD and the OFX specifications.

"The Open Financial Exchange is a particularly important standard due to the increasingly complex relationships among merchants, financial institutions, and electronic commerce companies that are vying for access to customers."

See "Electronic Bill Presentment and Payment" on page 151 for more information.

The converged standard, known as the Interactive Financial Exchange (IFX) specification, will be based on the two original specifications and be independent of any particular network technology or computing platform. It will have two alternative implementations: OFX's implementation will be based on SGML, and Integrion's implementation will use application programming interfaces (APIs). The public review and comment period on the IFX specification ended in March 1999. The final standard is expected later in 1999.

COMMON ELECTRONIC PURSE SPECIFICATION

The Common Electronic Purse Specification (CEPS) is a standard for the behavior of smart cards. Driven by Europay, Sermepa, Visa, and ZKA (Zentraler Kreditausschuss), CEPS published the first version of its specification in March 1999. (Sermepa is the technology subsidiary of Visa Espana, which represents more than 150 financial organizations and operates the world's largest Visa Cash program.) CEPS will unify the systems already deployed by Europe's major smart-card providers. CEPS formalizes a common protocol without specifying the smart-card operating system. CEPS will compete with the Mondex system and will provide similar services in different ways. For example, although Mondex supports anonymous transactions and transfer of value between cards, CEPS implements a more typical model, which provides an auditable track of purchases and value stored. Although version 1.0 of the CEPS standard is finished, deployment is not expected until after 2001. When 75 million Geld-Karte, 30 million Proton-based cards, and 10 million Visa Cash cards are unified under the CEPS standard, there will be an installed base of more than 100 million cardholders. As a result of this strategy of migrating a large population of current card users to CEPS, Giga forecasts that CEPS will become the global standard.

BANK INTERNET PAYMENT SYSTEM

The Bank Internet Payment System (BIPS) is an initiative by the Financial Services Technology Consortium (FSTC), a cooperative effort by several U.S. banks, technology firms, and government agencies to increase system security and thereby encourage companies to initiate payments via the Internet. (FSTC members include BankAmerica, Chase Manhattan Bank, Citibank, and Wells Fargo bank as well as organizations such as the U.S. National Security Agency, the U.S. Department of the Treasury, and the U.S. Postal Service.) The BIPS project also will produce a specification for a secure server, which banks will use to provide payment transaction services on the Internet. The first BIPS specification was released for comment by the FSTC in August 1998.

BIPS will enable payers and payees to agree on payment terms and mechanisms and to access multiple bank payment systems. Customers and banks will be able to choose the most cost-effective way to make a payment based on the payer's requirements for cost and speed of settlement.

Although BIPS shows promise, it could suffer from the same difficulties as the SET initiative—a highly complex protocol that delays software availability past the window of opportunity when it could be adopted.

Market Overview

The market for payment system providers is young and volatile. In early 1999, market research organizations have yet to size and segment the market for payment systems, products, and services. Following are descriptions of typical product and service offerings from a variety of suppliers. As is typical in a young market, many of these companies have first-to-market niche products for very narrow aspects of payment handling. Larger, established suppliers license one or more of these components and bundle them together into larger offerings.

Because this market is so new, many of these providers have only started doing business in the last few years and remain privately held companies backed by venture capital funding. This information has been included wherever possible to illustrate the market's scope and development relative to more established markets. Revenue figures reported by public companies also have been included, if available. Given the differences between these types of providers, a comparison of relative market share is not possible.

Just as Internet portal providers such as Excite and Yahoo! have begun offering auction and other specialized services, they now appear poised to enter the payment marketplace as well. In April 1999, Yahoo! announced it would become a channel for electronic bill presentment and payment (EBPP), allowing users to complete a range of financial services transactions via its Web site. Other portal providers likely will follow suit.

ELECTRONIC BILL PRESENTMENT AND PAYMENT

The EBPP market is both immature and complex and is shaped by several factors. EBPP product and service vendors, which include several large legacy players, many partnerships, and some new companies, fulfill multiple roles. Giga reports on the EBPP market, identifying the key suppliers shown in Table 5.

The EBPP marketplace has two key drivers:

- Interest in the market is driven by the enormous cost reductions achieved when paper-based billing eventually transitions to electronic media and transport. Large billers, both in-house and outsource providers, must address a potential disruptive technology that could entirely restructure their industry.

- The market reveals the sharply different intentions of its players: Banks wish to continue processing payments for their customers; billers wish to realize and retain cost savings when moving from paper to electronic bills and remain in immediate contact with their customers; and consolidators would like to insert themselves as a value-added link in the EBPP value chain.

TABLE 5: REPRESENTATIVE EBPP SUPPLIERS

Bill Data Extraction and Transformation		Bill Presentment		Bill Payment	
Software	**Services**	**Software**	**Services**	**Software**	**Services**
@Work	Electronic Data Systems (EDS)	@Work	CheckFree	Edify	CheckFree
Bell & Howell	International Billing Services (IBS)	BlueGill	Electronic Data Systems (EDS)	IBM	CyberCash
BlueGill	IBM	Edify	International Billing Services (IBS)	Maagnum	IBM
edocs	Pitney Bowes	edocs	IBM	Oracle	TransPoint
Electronic Funds & Data (EFD)	Princeton Telecom	Electronic Funds & Data (EFD)	Pitney Bowes	TriSense Software	
IBM		IBM	Princeton Telecom		
Novazen		Just In Time (JIT)	TransPoint		
TriSense Software		Maagnum			
		NCR			
		Netscape			
		Novazen			
		Oracle			

Source: Giga, 1998

The most important factor in this market through the forecast period will be achieving critical mass, or what economists refer to as "network effects." In markets such as EBPP, the value of signing up for EBPP rises as the number of EBPP participants increases.

This situation is true for billers, whose cost savings rise in proportion to the number of electronic customers. It also is true for customers, whose interest in participating will rise when most bills can be received electronically. It is this need for critical mass that encourages the emergence of consolidators.

Bill Data Extraction and Transformation. Product providers are a mix of young startup companies, including @Work, BlueGill, edocs, Novazen, and TriSense Software, and established companies such as Bell & Howell that currently provide paper billing machinery and software and want to adopt new electronic services.

Service providers include International Billing Services (IBS), the largest service bureau for paper and postage billing in the U.S., and Pitney Bowes, its competitor. Along with these traditional service providers are Electronic Data Systems (EDS) and IBM, as global e-business service providers, and Princeton TeleCom, a direct biller now offering billing services to others.

Bill Presentment. Product providers are once again a mix of new—BlueGill, Just In Time (JIT), and others—and old— Edify, IBM, NCR, Oracle, and others. Some providers, such as JIT, Maagnum, NCR, Netscape, and Novazen, aim to serve direct billers, while others such as Oracle support consolidators as well.

Service providers include the most prominent vendors in this space, CheckFree and TransPoint, which have broad e-business agendas that include EBPP. CheckFree and TransPoint are themselves consolidators, while EDS, IBS, and Princeton TeleCom provide outsourcing of bill presentment Web sites on behalf of direct billers.

Bill Payment. Software providers for payment currently are focused on the direct biller market exclusively. CheckFree and CyberCash provide payment services for direct billers, while TransPoint provides payment services only for those enrolled in its consolidation program.

VENDORS

BlueGill Technologies. BlueGill builds software to enable electronic bill presentment and payment (EBPP) systems. Its 1to1Server, a packaged bill presentment product, was released in 1997. In April 1999, BlueGill announced its successor products, the i-Series. The i-Series includes i-Banker, i-Broker, i-Biller, i-Telco, and i-Insurance, each of which works in conjunction with the BlueGill Engine. The BlueGill Engine generally takes as its input legacy billing data of many different kinds, stores this data using an object model, and then reexpresses the data as XML constructs ready for use on the Web. BlueGill deploys its technology in conjunction with service partners such as CheckFree and TransPoint and with technology partners such as IBM and Netscape. Founded in 1996, venture-backed BlueGill is privately held.

CheckFree. CheckFree provides electronic banking services based on the OFX standard. In particular, CheckFree's Web BillPay service provides an online bill payment application for banks and other financial institutions, and its E-Bill service provides bill presentment for billers or consolidators. CheckFree's primary Web BillPay customers are banks that use the application to provide their customers with Web-based online banking services. CheckFree processes 10 million payments per month and serves more than 2.5 million customers. CheckFree's original business was electronic bill payments for consumers using electronic bill management software such as Intuit's Quicken. Founded in 1981, CheckFree became a public corporation in 1995 and reported revenue of $233 million in 1998.

CyberCash. CyberCash provides payment products and services for Internet commerce sites. The initial CyberCash offering was a payment gateway for credit transactions. The newest version of the gateway, CashRegister 3.0, is expected to be released in late 1999. CyberCoin, CyberCash's micropayment product and service, will be phased out beginning in May 1999. Meanwhile, CyberCash is launching PayNow as an EBPP product/service combination to enable direct billing by merchants. Formed in 1994, CyberCash is a public corporation and reported revenue of $12 million in 1998.

edocs. BillDirect is the EBPP software package developed by edocs and marketed to billers in the EBPP marketplace. BillDirect software includes modules for preparing a bill for Web site display and also for preparing e-mail to advise customers their bills are ready. CheckFree and CyberCash payment systems are integrated with BillDirect. Founded in 1997, edocs is a venture-backed, privately held company.

GlobeSet. GlobeSet provides the four products necessary for SET-compliant payment systems: a wallet, a certification authority, a payment gateway, and a merchant server. GlobeSet markets its products, which carry the SET-MARK certification, exclusively through original equipment manufacturers (OEMs). Some OEM partners are system providers such as Compaq, which markets GlobeSet products as a part of its Tandem iTP Payment Solution package. Other OEM partners include financial institutions such as Orient, a Japanese credit-card company, which uses GlobeSet products to make its Auction Market Japan Web site SET-compliant. GlobeSet products are designed for Microsoft Windows NT and UNIX server platforms and also work in conjunction with other Web commerce products such as Microsoft's Site Server 3.0. Founded in 1994, GlobeSet is privately held.

Hewlett-Packard: VeriFone. HP's VeriFone division builds and sells the Integrated Payment System (IPS), a suite of hardware and software products designed to accelerate the development of payment systems. Software is packaged as components focused on specific functionality; a credit authorization component designed to interoperate with American Express, Discover, MasterCard and Visa networks is one example of an IPS component. IPS components fit within VeriFone's E-Services framework, an architecture that integrates existing components and provides a software backplane for new components VeriFone expects to develop in the future. In the hardware area, VeriFone traditionally has been strong in point-of-sale (POS) card-verification systems for restaurant and retail settings. In partnership with Lynk Systems, VeriFone recently announced a low-cost payment terminal and printer, the Omni 3200, which is positioned as a next-generation POS device capable of more complex payment transactions.

IBM. IBM offers two products in the payment marketplace, the IBM Payment Suite and OnDemand, a banking and finance application suite with EBPP capabilities. The IBM Payment Suite consists of four products: a Consumer Wallet, a Payment Server, a Payment Gateway, and a Payment Registry (which is IBM's name for a certification authority). Each component is SET-compliant. The Payment Server (version 1.2) is built around IBM's Multipayment Framework, an architecture for integrating a variety of existing payment methods and accommodating changing payment standards. IBM's framework isolates basic payment system building blocks, such as encryption algorithms, in subsystems called cassettes. IBM's OnDemand is a suite of products designed for billers. In conjunction with BlueGill Technologies, OnDemand is able to redirect selected invoices from the print stream and reformulate these bills for Internet delivery. OnDemand is a broad collection of products including, for example, integration with ImagePlus and Lotus Notes as well as with computer output to laser disk (COLD).

Just In Time. BillCast is the name of Just In Time's product suite, which provides OFX-compliant EBPP packaged applications. Just In Time ascribes to the thin consolidator model for EBPP, and its BillCast OFX Server provides summary information of bills to consolidators. The complementary product, BillCast Presentation Server, provides billing details directly to customers and is intended to run on the merchant's Web site. Just In Time collaborates with AT&T and Intuit to develop products that protect billers' relationships to their customers while allowing consolidators to aggregate customers and billers to achieve critical mass. Founded in 1995, Just In Time is a privately held company with venture and institutional investors.

NetDelivery. NetDelivery positions itself as a technology provider in the electronic delivery management (EDM) business. NetDelivery's EDM approach is called invited push. Based on patented technology, NetDelivery will provide both a consumer browser product called eWizard and a browser for business-to-business commerce called e-Biz. These products will enable customers to register and receive bills on a regular basis. This model of bill delivery differs significantly from competitors that require customers to visit the biller's or a consolidator's site. NetDelivery is partnering with billing companies such as International Billing Services (IBS) to deploy its products. Formed in 1995 and venture-funded, NetDelivery is a privately held company.

Oracle. Oracle provides two products to enable electronic payments, its Payment Server 1.1 and Internet Bill and Pay. Payment Server 1.1 provides integration with traditional payment systems and supports rule-based processing for businesses that want to manage their relationships with payment-processing vendors. Payment Server 1.1 integrates with third-party providers using a system of software cartridges provided by CyberCash, ICVerify, or VeriFone. Internet Bill and Pay was announced in December 1998 in partnership with CheckFree, which contributes its E-Bill services. The product currently is in pilot testing, with initial shipments announced for release by mid-1999. Coupled to Oracle's Financial Services Application suite, Internet Bill and Pay is targeted at large billers. The offering is based on OFX standards. Both the Payment Server and Internet Bill and Pay run in conjunction with Oracle8 and other Oracle packaged software components.

Spyrus/Terisa. With the acquisition of Terisa Systems in 1998, Spyrus extended its suite of software tools to include the SecureWeb Payments toolkit. SecureWeb Payments provides the tools and components for building secure e-business applications, including an industry-standard implementation of SET, a secure key database, a certificate management system, and RSA Data Security's BSafe cryptography engine. (SETCo has chosen SecureWeb Payments as the technical basis for SET certification.) The Spyrus SET wallet 1.0 carries the SET-MARK and is available for Microsoft Windows NT and 95/98 operating systems. Other divisions of Spyrus offer public-key infrastructure toolkits. Privately held Spyrus was formed in 1992 and focuses on providing tools for a variety of security needs, including the construction of SET-compliant payment systems.

TransPoint. TransPoint (previously called MSFDC) is a joint venture of Citigroup, First Data, and Microsoft. TransPoint is a service provider for EBPP. TransPoint intends to differentiate its services from its major competitor, CheckFree, by managing both summary and detailed billing information. TransPoint has announced it will release EBPP services in 1999.

Trintech. PayPurse (a consumer wallet), PayWare (a merchant payment server), and PayGate (a financial services gateway) are the three products marketed by Trintech. PayPurse and PayWare carry the SET-MARK certification, and PayGate's certification approval is pending. Trintech products run in Microsoft Windows NT environments; however, due to a new alliance with Compaq, Trintech announced its intention to port these applications to UNIX. Although it supports the SET payment protocol, Trintech's PayWare merchant application also includes integration aids for accessing relational databases, support for multiple currencies, and interfaces to POS devices. Privately held, Trintech was formed in 1986.

DIGITAL CASH: SMART CARDS

"Smart-card-based digital cash systems will continue to find niche applications in the food, entertainment, education, and transportation markets."

In a recent review of payment technology trends, Giga estimates the combined market for software-based and smart-card-based micropayments was less than 1 percent of all payment transactions in 1998. Giga forecasts growth of smart-card-based transactions to rise as high as 5 percent by 2002, primarily in Europe where smart-card-technology deployment is greater than in other regions of the world. Citing the recent decision by Chase and Citibank to end pilot studies in New York, Giga estimates that mass market adoption in the U.S. may be five to ten years away. Meanwhile, smart-card-based digital cash systems will continue to find niche applications in the food, entertainment, education, and transportation markets.

The next step forward in this market is likely to be driven by a consortium of European smart-card providers. Proton, a card issued in Belgium, the Netherlands, Sweden, Switzerland, and other countries, has 30 million customers. VisaCash and other Visa-related cards reach 22 million additional European customers. Contrast these populations with the Mondex system, which first was announced in 1993 and piloted in 1995. Although Mondex is a mature technology and has been tested around the world, Giga estimates the total number of Mondex card holders at about 150,000 in 1999.

Forecast

Payment-card transactions will remain the dominant payment type throughout the forecast period, with some growth expected in the use of electronic checks.

SSL will remain the most common protocol for secure transmission of financial information over the Web. SET demonstration projects will continue, but uptake will remain slow throughout the forecast period.

Merchants will respond to rising fraud rates by seeking more sophisticated fraud detection techniques rather than shifting to a new transaction protocol.

Electronic bill presentment coupled with direct debit probably will be the method used in most European countries going forward.

Trusted third-party certification services will emerge around the world as governments and businesses invest in more secure infrastructure for payment systems.

REFERENCES

ARTICLES

Aslam, Taimur. Protocols for e-commerce. *Dr. Dobb's Journal*. December 1998: 52.

Bromberek, Jason, Jeetu Patel, and Gautam Desai. Bill presentment and payment hit the Web—organizations seek savings by taking the paperwork out of the billing process. *InformationWeek*. November 16, 1998: 19.

Dalton, Gregory. Online billing flexibility—new Oracle product incorporates technology from Checkfree, CyberCash. *InformationWeek*. December 7, 1998: 38.

Desai, Gautam, Jason Bromberek, and Jeetu Patel. Electronic billing: postage due. *InformationWeek.* November 30, 1998: 73.

Horan, Thomas. Electronic Bill Presentment and Payment: the next step for the e-commerce market. *The Journal of Electronic Commerce,* Vol. 2, No. 1.

Kerstetter, Jim. TransPoint banks on name change, string of deals. *PCWeek.* November 9, 1998: 25.

Radecki, Lawrence J. and John Wenninger. Paying electronic bills electronically. *Current Issues in Economics and Finance,* Vol. 5, No. 1. January 1998.

Reichard, Kevin. E-commerce options. *UNIX Review's Performance Computing.* November 1998: 65.

PERIODICALS, INDUSTRY AND TECHNICAL REPORTS

Agarwal, Rajeev. *Large value payment systems: moving to real-time gross settlement (RTGS).* The Tower Group. November 1998.

Banking on the Internet. Meta Group. July 23, 1998.

Bartels, Andrew. *E-Charge, E-Cash, and E-Check—Internet Electronic Payment.* Giga Information Group. October 27, 1998.

Bartels, Andrew. *Online authentication options: digital certificates.* Giga Information Group. February 19, 1999.

Bartels, Andrew. *The whys and means of online authentication.* Giga Information Group. February 19, 1999.

Beyond Payment Protocols. Meta Group. September 3, 1998.

Burstyn, Paris. *Internet bill presentment for telecoms services: easier said than done?* IDC. December 1998.

Chou, Sylvia. *Internet portals: a threat to financial services institutions?* The Tower Group. November 1998.

DiStephano, Karen M. *Electronic bill payment selection guide.* Faulkner FACCTS. August 1998.

Dooley, Brian J. *The OBI standard.* Faulkner FACCTS. April 1998.

Dooley, Brian J. and Jacqueline Kramer. *Digital cash.* Faulkner FAACTS. August 1998.

Drobik, A. *OBI: global vision but domestic reality.* Garter Group. June 15, 1998.

Kerr, K. *Bill presentment and payment systems: 1999 FI benchmark survey.* Gartner Group. February 26, 1999.

Kerr, K. *MCI's biller-direct electronic billing and payment program.* Gartner Group. February 4, 1999.

Kramer, Jacqueline. *Secure Electronic Transaction (SET) Protocol.* Faulkner FACCTS. August 1998.

Le Tocq, Chris and Steve Young. *SET comparative performance analysis.* (White paper.) Gartner Group. November 2, 1998.

Litan, A. *BAI payments system symposium.* Gartner Group. October 13, 1998.

Litan, A. *E-checks are not in the e-mail—yet.* Gartner Group. November 2, 1998.

Litan, A. *OFX standards stall but e-billing market moves ahead.* Gartner Group. December 30, 1998.

Litan, A. *The different paths of a bill payment transaction.* Gartner Group. September 14, 1998.

Litan, A. *What drives bill presentment and new payment systems?* Gartner Group. August 4, 1998.

Lombardo, D., P. Meehan, G. Phifer, D. Smith, and A. Terhune. *A fresh look at the Internet.* Gartner Group. October 26, 1998.

McCarty, Meredith and Rick Miller. *Behind the scenes of an Internet commerce transaction.* IDC. September 1998.

McQuivey, James, Kate Delhagen, Maria La Tour Kadison, Kip Levin, Alexander Aber, and Carrie Ardito. *Retail's growth spiral.* Forrester Report, Vol. 1, No. 8. November 1998.

McQuivey, James and Michael E. Gazala. *Cyber cash enables one-click buying.* Forrester Brief, Vol. 1, No. 11. August 31, 1998.

Medeiros, David. *Checks: paper or electronic? A new payment mechanism.* The Tower Group. August 1998.

Now presenting...electronic bills. Meta Group. May 15, 1998.

Pang, Albert. *Seismic changes in financial services industry spur strong demand for Internet banking applications.* IDC. January 1999.

Radecki, Lawrence J. and John Wenninger. *Paying electronic bills electronically.* Federal Reserve Bank of New York: Current Issues in Economics and Finance, Vol. 5, No. 1. January 1998.

Robertson, Caroline. *AT&T and HP announce a bridge over the EC gap.* IDC. July 1997.

Rugullies, Erica. *Electronic commerce.* Giga Information Group. October 15, 1998.

Rugullies, Erica. *Topography of electronic bill presentment and payment technologies.* Giga Information Group. December 15, 1998.

Rugullies, Erica and Andrew Bartels. *Options in stored-value "electronic purse" smart cards.* Giga Information Group. November 18, 1998.

Rugullies, Erica. *Status of EBPP in the telecommunications industry.* Giga Information Group. February 17, 1999.

Rugullies, Erica. *Topography of electronic bill presentment and payment technologies.* Giga Information Group. December 15, 1998.

Satterthwaite, R. *Will OBI succeed in transforming procurement?* Gartner Group. April 21, 1998.

Spieler, G. *E-bill presentment: when to outsource customers.* Gartner Group. August 31, 1998.

The check is in the e-mail. Meta Group. October 26, 1998.

The Open Financial Exchange (OFX) specification. Faulkner FACCTS. July 1998.

The technologies of electronic commerce: the integrity of electronic transactions and digital records for tax administration and compliance. (A study prepared for the Electronic Commerce Tax Study Group.) PricewaterhouseCoopers LLP. August 1998.

BOOKS

Grant, Gail L. *Understanding digital signatures.* New York: McGraw-Hill. 1998.

O'Mahony, Donal, Michael Pierce, and Hitesh Tewari. *Electronic payment systems.* Norwood, Mass.: Artech House Inc. 1997.

Patel, Alpesh B. *Trading online.* London: FT Pittman. 1999.

Reference on electronic bill presentment and payment. Doculabs. 1998.

Schneier, Bruce. *Applied cryptography: protocols, algorithms, and source code in C.* (Second edition.) New York: John Wiley and Sons. 1996.

Vartanian, Thomas P., Robert H. Ledig, and Lynn Bruneau. *21st century money, banking, and commerce.* Washington, D.C.: Fried, Frank, Harris, Shriver, and Jacobson. 1998.

URLs OF SELECTED MENTIONED COMPANIES AND ORGANIZATIONS

@Work Technologies www.worktechs.com

Bell & Howell www.bellhowell.com

Electronic Data Systems (EDS) www.eds.com

Electronic Funds and Data (EFD) www.efd.com

Financial Service Technologies Consortium wwww.fstc.org

Integrion Financial Network www.integrion.com

Integrion Financial Network Specification www.bitsinfo.org/ifx/index.htm

International Billing Services www.billing.com

Just In Time Solutions www.justintime.com

Princeton Telecom www.princetontele.com

Tenth Mountain Systems www.tenthmtn.com

World Wide Web Consortium www.w3.org

E-BUSINESS INFRASTRUCTURE

Executive Summary

The specialized e-business platforms, buy- and sell-side packaged e-business applications, and payment and billing systems described in the "E-Business Enabling Technologies" section of the *E-Business Technology Forecast* depend on and make use of an extensive hardware, software, and networking infrastructure. This chapter covers the key technologies that make up this infrastructure.

Although the preceding chapters focus on technologies unique to e-business, the technologies discussed in this chapter have broader applicability. Not every activity that occurs on the Internet is a form of e-business; however, the Internet and the technologies that make it possible have been essential to the rapid growth of e-business during the past five years. This chapter does not attempt to cover every technology drawn on by e-business but rather includes only those technologies directly relevant to it.

The chapter begins with a discussion of the computer equipment used to provide network connectivity and to operate network servers and their clients. Because implementations of the TCP/IP protocol suite are available for virtually every type of computing device, a wide range of computers can serve as server and client devices. Special attention is paid to non-PC clients such as wireless devices, smart cards, and kiosks.

Next, discussion moves to the application programming environments found on the Internet. As the World Wide Web has evolved from a simple mechanism for displaying static pages inside a browser to a platform for sophisticated applications, various techniques have been used to extend the functionality of the basic Web server and browser.

As the range of activities undertaken on the Web has expanded, so too have the demands made on the two protocols that define the Web for additional functionality. Both the HyperText Transport Protocol and the HyperText Markup Language are in the process of evolving. Meanwhile, the institutions that define and manage the Internet are themselves evolving, and there are significant changes underway in the governance and operation of the Domain Name System.

To meet the performance, reliability, and functionality requirements of today's e-business applications, Web sites have evolved from a single HyperText Transport Protocol server to a complex environment that includes multiple specialized servers. Web application servers—a set of HyperText Transport Protocol server products extended to meet the specific needs of transactional applications—play a critical role in this evolution.

The chapter closes with a discussion of the security requirements of e-business applications. Public-key cryptography plays a critical role in allowing secure, authenticated communication between multiple parties across an insecure network such as the Internet. For public-key encryption to be useful, however, it must be surrounded with a public-key infrastructure that utilizes trusted third parties known as certification authorities to verify the legitimacy of each public key and bind it to its owner's identity.

Overview

E-business presupposes a set of supporting technologies, and this chapter focuses on the key technologies that underlie e-business, including the hardware, software, and networking infrastructure that has been essential to its rapid growth. This infrastructure has many elements and layers. A commerce server, for example, is a combination of computer hardware (sometimes more than one physical machine) and software (Web services, application services, and commerce services) using Internet Protocol- (IP-) based networking protocols to communicate with clients over public and private networks by means of the HyperText Transfer Protocol (HTTP) to present content defined in the HyperText Markup Language (HTML).

Today, the Internet is the prominent form of e-business service delivery on public networks. (The word "internet" is a shortened version of "internetwork," or a network of networks. The Internet is the global network of networks accessible to the public.) However, other forms exist for various reasons as well. This discussion focuses on the Internet because of its ubiquity and importance to current forms of e-business solutions. Many observers believe the Internet is helping companies move from their self-contained computing environments of the past to participate in a ubiquitous global network. Meanwhile, the Internet will be improving bandwidth, reliability, quality of service (QoS), and security.

The following sections cover e-business supporting technology from the lower levels—hardware and physical networking standards—to the higher levels—simple interactions between client and server, application programming on the Internet environment, the development of e-business server architectures, and security technologies endemic to e-business.

An intranet is a network that uses a Web browser as a universal applications client and that is accessible only by individuals within a particular enterprise. Functionally, an intranet acts as a private Web partially or wholly blocked from the outside world.

It is commonly believed that the Internet and the Web are one and the same; the terms are mistakenly used interchangeably in the popular media and in many vendors' marketing literature. In reality, the Internet (and intranets) provides a common internetworking framework based on IP, upon which many application services can be built. The Web is merely one of many services that use the Internet, although it is undoubtedly the most visible and the most rapidly evolving. The Web has developed into a collection of applications and content, delivered in the form of "pages" displayed in a browser. Links embedded into these pages connect Web servers around the world. Web pages typically are delivered to the Web browser as HTML documents, which can include text, graphics, editable forms, Java or other client-side applications, animations, and embedded graphics.

Hardware: Network Infrastructure, Server and Client Machines, Smart Cards

Figure 53 on page 171 illustrates the range of communications facilities and devices that connect to the Internet and the kinds of clients and servers connected to the Internet today.

A server is a system that offers services to other computers. Examples include Web servers, e-mail servers, and print servers. A client is a computer that uses the services provided by the server, for example, Web or e-mail clients. Computers can be servers and clients at the same time.

One key feature of IP-based networks is that any computer system that implements the IP suite can connect to the network. By running the appropriate software, such a system then can function as a server, as a client, or as both.

The ease with which new devices can be connected to an IP-based network has been a significant factor in the growth of the e-business platform. Enterprises are in transition from Internet servers and access provided at the individual and department level to enterprise-wide solutions that require higher-level planning and a more substantial and durable infrastructure.

FIGURE 53: POSSIBLE INTERNET CONNECTION METHODS

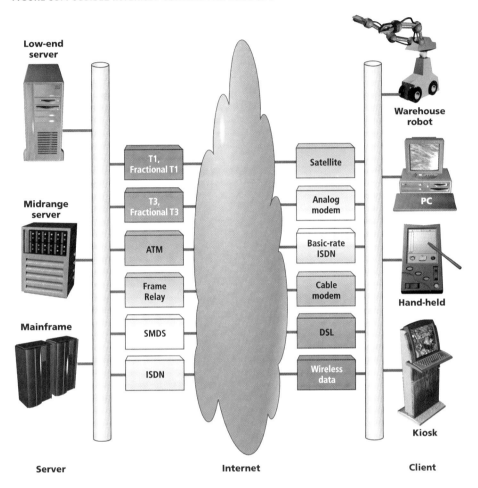

HOW ENTERPRISES CONNECT TO THE INTERNET

Figure 53 shows various technologies in common use for Internet access. Some of the terms refer to packet-switched networks—Frame Relay, Switched Multimegabit Data Service (SMDS), and Asynchronous Transfer Mode (ATM)—and some refer to circuit-switched networks—T1 and T3 (or E1 and E3 in Europe). A connection using Frame Relay, for example, might be provided over a T1 circuit (full or fractional). In addition, Frame Relay, SMDS, and ATM allow a software specification of a maximum guaranteed bandwidth, called the committed information rate (CIR, which usually is lower than the access speed); therefore, CIR means a Frame Relay connection over a T1 line may only guarantee a data rate of 256Kbps if there is congestion but can provide the full capacity of the 1.544Mbps T1 line if bandwidth in the rest of the network is available.

The figure indicates a mix between access methods used primarily by individuals—an analog modem operating at 28.8 or 56Kbps or BRI ISDN, for example—and methods used primarily by businesses and other organizations. There are three types of enterprise Internet usage:

- Access for communication and information purposes as an increasingly strategic part of employees' jobs
- Use of the Internet as a channel for interaction between the business and its customers and suppliers

- Using the Internet and IP-based capabilities as inexpensive substitutes for other network services

Thus, enterprise connections to the Internet handle a combination of outgoing employee access, incoming customer and supplier access, and some use of the Internet as a substitute for other networking solutions. These substitutes include Voice-over-IP (VoIP) instead of traditional voice telephone circuits, or Internet-based virtual private network (VPN) technology (sometimes also called Virtual Public Internet [VPI]) instead of other types of networks.

The Internet is composed of multiple interconnected networks known as autonomous systems. Interior Gateway Protocols (IGPs) such as Hello, Intermediate System to Intermediate System (IS-IS), Open Shortest Path First (OSPF), and Routing Information Protocol (RIP) typically are used within an autonomous system. Exterior Gateway Protocols (EGPs) such as the Border Gateway Protocol (BGP), Border Gateway Protocol version 4 (BGP4), and Exterior Gateway Protocol (EGP) handle the traffic between the autonomous systems.

The oldest routing protocol on the Internet is Routing Information Protocol (RIP), which based its routing decision on a single metric: the number of hops. However, RIP is inadequate to handle today's networks where a choice could exist between multiple hops over fiber-based nodes (fast) or one hop over a single public-switched telephone network (PSTN) node (rather slow). For example, the combined delay introduced by the four fiber-based nodes may be less than the delay introduced by the single PSTN node. RIP's "least number of hops" metric would take the wrong route here if speed is the goal. For this reason, newer routing protocols typically combine various metrics to make their routing decisions.

Engineering the most suitable Internet connection for a particular situation needs to take into account the Internet service provider's (ISP's) architecture, its interconnection with other ISPs through network access points (NAPs) to the Internet backbone (or through private peering arrangements if the ISPs are connected directly to each other), and the organization's requirements with regard to availability, security, and so on. Locating a Web server at the ISP's site may not bring a throughput improvement if it involves interposing one or two routers between the equipment and the customer. The bandwidth and loading of the ISP's connection to a NAP are important to the overall speed of an Internet connection because if this leg is a bottleneck, the average speed of a user's connection will be compromised.

Not all backbone connections of all ISPs have equal performance. Organizations such as Keynote Systems/Baywatch evaluate the performance of backbone providers by measuring times to download a typical Web page. Differences between providers can be substantial, but often they are only a small factor in the performance of a Web site from the visitor's perspective. Other factors such as the speed of the Web server, complexity of the Web pages, time of day, and performance of the visitor's ISP also can have a significant impact. Although a given provider may have a connection that is fast technically, it ultimately may be slower than a (technically) slower connection running at a lower utilization rate. The only realistic way to measure Web server performance is to analyze the Web server's logs to determine how long pages took to download. The increasing importance of the Internet as a factor to conduct business also has given rise to so-called Internet "weather forecasts," where congested areas and links are indicated or predicted.

An autonomous system is a collection of routers under a single technical administrative authority using a common protocol for routing packets.

E-business users can control the quality of their Internet connection by negotiating a service-level agreement (SLA) with their ISP. Typical SLAs for large providers offer 100 percent availability and some average latency on the provider's network, with less-aggressive guarantees for the general Internet. Customers can negotiate for credits for any violation of the agreement.

SERVER HARDWARE

Server hardware for e-business ranges from top-of-the-line mainframe systems to low-end multiprocessing systems that group two to eight commercial chips. Although the technical differences between hardware platforms revolve largely around scalability issues, the common feature among products involves their ability to run server software that implements one or more IP-based services.

Mainframes. Many organizations are interested in using mainframes for e-business because of their centralized administration, superior scalability, and reliability. Mainframes have become more powerful, smaller, and easier to integrate with UNIX and Windows NT. Mainframes also have fallen in price due in part to the move to complementary metal-oxide semiconductor (CMOS) technology, led by IBM in 1994. CMOS technology allows manufacturers to make mainframes that use less energy, run cooler, consume less space, and cost less than the previously dominant emitter-coupled logic (ECL) technology.

Various vendors such as IBM and Interlink now provide full TCP/IP stack implementations for mainframes, which makes them candidates to offer Web-related services. However, many organizations are reluctant to offer direct IP connections to the mainframe for security reasons. Most organizations will shield the mainframe from the Internet by introducing at least a firewall (or even a combination of multiple firewall and intrusion detection systems) and a middleware server.

Midrange. Midrange servers, like mainframes, provide processing capacity through the use of multiple processors. The most common multiprocessor architecture used today is symmetric multiprocessing (SMP), meaning virtually all processors in a machine can perform any task. At the high end of the SMP server spectrum are systems that use a large number of processors with very sophisticated technologies for memory management. Reduced Instruction Set Computing- (RISC-) based servers, which typically run UNIX, tend to be pure SMP machines. Higher-powered Windows NT systems also are based on SMP architecture; they continue to gain in share although still behind UNIX shipments in the midrange. Vendors are competing to improve their interconnect technologies and memory management. IBM's AS/400 also has been a popular midrange machine since its initial offering. IBM has promoted e-business applications on the AS/400e by making it a platform for running Lotus Notes and Domino, offering a Java Virtual Machine (JVM) for the AS/400, and bundling Web server and browser software.

Low-End. Low-end multiprocessing systems typically range from two to eight processors and are most often based on Intel chips. To facilitate the construction of these machines, Intel provides the Standard High Volume (SHV) board, a low-cost multiprocessing motherboard. In 1999 and 2000, a second wave of Intel-based SMP systems, based on a second-generation SHV board, will be offered at about the same prices as the previous generation. Initial models will have four processors, but Intel plans to leverage the eight-way SMP architecture—dubbed Profusion—developed by Corollary (which it acquired in late 1997) as a means to manufacture standard, high-volume eight-way

"Although the technical differences between e-business hardware platforms revolve largely around scalability issues, the common feature among products involves their ability to run server software that implements one or more IP-based services."

Intel PC servers. Intel has announced the Profusion chip set will start shipping by mid-1999. Although versions of UNIX exist for Intel platforms (notably, SCO's UnixWare and SunSoft's Solaris for Intel), these low-end systems largely run Windows NT Server.

See the sidebar "Open-Source Programming" on page 185 for more information.

Linux, the open-source version of UNIX that has received much publicity in recent months, sharply increased its server shipments in 1998 to 750,000 units. The increase bolstered Linux's share of new server operating system (OS) shipments to 17.2 percent, compared with 35.8 percent for Windows NT Server and 17.4 percent for all other UNIX offerings.

CLIENT HARDWARE

Any device running software that allows it to make requests of servers—typically over an IP network—can be a client. Clients are becoming more diverse than just desktop and notebook PCs as IP-based computing becomes more ubiquitous. To support transactions in the field, they are being supplemented by dedicated non-PC clients such as hand-held and other mobile devices, along with embedded devices using TCP/IP as a networking solution.

This variety of devices currently being used as clients has broadened the range of possibilities for e-business. For example, sales representatives now can use a mobile phone or hand-held device to access a central corporate database to retrieve product information from a remote location.

Wireless Devices. The emergence of wireless standards is spurring development of consumer e-business applications for hand-held devices. Smart phones, which combine wireless voice with wireless data and Internet access, are beginning to rival personal digital assistants (PDAs) as a hand-held form-factor. These devices are popular particularly in Europe, where the Global System for Mobile Communications (GSM) standard creates a larger marketplace for a single wireless technology than the U.S., where the market is divided among several competing technologies. The next-generation (sometimes referred to as 3G) Universal Mobile Telecommunications System (UMTS) protocol is planned to in 2002. It eventually could provide 2-Mbps connectivity to hand-held devices. UMTS' combined data and voice functionality is expected to alter the interactive capability of hand-helds significantly.

The adoption of the Wireless Application Protocol (WAP) in April 1998 also has helped define a marketplace. WAP is a specification developed by the Wireless Applications Protocol Forum, whose founding members include Ericsson, Motorola, Nokia, and Unwired Planet. Current Forum members include major wireless handset manufacturers and carriers as well as software and smart card vendors. The WAP 1.0 specification is designed to work across wireless technologies including GSM, Code Division Multiple Access (CDMA), Personal Handyphone System (PHS), and others.

See "Wireless Markup Language (WML)" on page 197 for more information.

WAP is intended to simplify how wireless users access e-mail and voice mail, send and receive faxes, make stock trades, conduct banking transactions, and view Web pages on a wireless terminal's screen. The standard was designed in large part to make it easier for mobile users to view Web pages by defining the Wireless Markup Language (WML), which allows Web sites to tailor the information format to fit the screen of the device. With WAP, these format modifications only have to be made once to be viewed on terminals made by different vendors.

WAP-conformant handsets began to appear on the market in early 1999. Alcatel, France Telecom Mobile, Omnitel, and Sonera (in partnership with Gemplus and Nokia) have announced plans to roll out GSM-based Internet data services during 1999.

Presentation of Internet or database content on a hand-held device presents user-interface challenges: screens are small, backlighting does not overcome the limitations of the low-contrast monochrome displays used in some devices, and existing fonts are hard to read. The amount of data that can be read is limited by the relatively small memory capacities, and the rate at which data can be transferred is restricted by the bandwidth of wireless links combined with poor caching facilities. Most Web sites have been designed to be used with a desktop PC running one of the major browsers, and widespread techniques such as text-on-graphics, client-side execution such as Java, cookies, and frames make many existing Web sites virtually unusable on today's hand-helds.

Several operating systems have been proposed or are being used for hand-held wireless devices. For example, Symbian (a joint venture by Ericsson, Motorola, Nokia, and Psion) represents an attempt to define an operating-system standard that will support the stringent real-time demands of voice traffic. Symbian's Epoch32 operating system product on the smart phone platform competes with Windows CE for mobile phones. Epoch32 eventually will incorporate a JVM, aligning it with Sun, Symbian's strategic partner. Another competitor, 3Com's Palm operating system, may drive a new smart phone to market—the Qualcomm pdQ phone, which combines a cell phone with 3Com's PalmPilot hand-held computer. (The Nokia 9000 is one smart phone that is already on the market; it was released in Europe in 1997 and shipped in the U.S. in November 1998. The Nokia 9000 includes a small keyboard, a Web browser, and a small VGA monitor.)

Microsoft announced its ClearType software in November 1998 as a solution to the font readability problem: By controlling smaller-than-pixel-size regions within the type, Microsoft claims ClearType can improve legibility by 200 to 300 percent in the horizontal axis.

Most approaches to presenting content on hand-helds use summarization to match the small screen area available. 3Com's Web clipping, to be used in its forthcoming Palm VII product, is an example of this approach. Web site developers mark up content to show how it can be summarized, processing is handled by the server, and the client device displays a summary of each page based on this special markup.

Hand-held devices also are emerging as important enterprise clients, and e-business uses for enterprise hand-helds will help promote this platform. Acceptance of hand-helds as serious business tools has been propelled in part by two 1998 software offerings—AvantGo 2.0 and Oracle8i Lite—which synchronize hand-held devices with networked enterprise systems, not just individual PCs. AvantGo 2.0—available for the Palm and Windows CE hand-held operating systems—supports data collection and entry from a hand-held device and synchronization with a server. Oracle8i Lite provides a lightweight PC/notebook/PDA database that combines client and server capabilities by serving as a client for a remote database but also storing records and updates locally. The two products allow a hand-held to synchronize directly with an Oracle database server. Remedy, SAP, Siebel, Sybase, and Vantive also have announced either hand-held products or plans to develop such products.

Vertical-Application Devices. The term vertical-application device (VAD) covers a large number of devices for data collection in the enterprise. The majority of VADs are keypad-based, but other devices use pen input, and many of them have scanners, magnetic-stripe readers, and other data-collection-only input devices.

"Hand-held devices also are emerging as important enterprise clients, and e-business uses for enterprise hand-helds will help promote this platform."

The larger players in the VAD marketplace—Fujitsu Personal Systems, Symbol Technologies, Telxon, and others—historically implemented VADs and the wireless networks that support them as proprietary architectures. Although many devices have migrated from proprietary operating systems to MS-DOS and Windows and will have to respond to competitive pressure from smaller hand-held devices and also from new Internet-based offerings such as DataRover from the General Magic spinoff of the same name. For example, Symbol Technologies concluded an agreement in 1998 to supply a "ruggedized" Palm hand-held as part of its product line.

Kiosks are a natural client for Web-query systems or Web-server-based enterprise systems. There are two different uses of the term "kiosk": a public Web terminal or a dedicated system used, for example, in a retail environment to host a particular application. Touchscreens are the common kiosk interface for retail locations, where the interaction typically may involve selecting a product or product information and then printing out the results to take away. Other types of kiosks generate an order that is sent to the fulfillment systems.

Summit Research Associates estimates there are a few thousand kiosks (which it calls Web Payphones) deployed in public locations in the U.S. A large number of small vendors compete with AT&T, IBM, and NCR in this growing marketplace. The typical Web Payphone-style kiosk for Internet access is a standard PC running Windows 95/NT and enclosed in a rugged, anti-tamper enclosure. Web Payphone-style kiosks use a mouse (or trackball) and keyboard for standard Internet browsing. Special secure browsers may prevent users from downloading files. Web Payphones also need some way to accept user payment, either by means of a card reader or a coin-operated mechanism.

Clients likely will become more special-purpose over time. For example, wearable systems are beginning to come to market. Symbol Technologies manufactures two wearable scanning systems with a bar code scanner that slips on the user's index finger.

SMART CARDS

Smart cards are plastic cards with embedded silicon chips used for the storage and communication of cardholder- or merchant-specific information or for processing transactions that occur between the cards and dedicated terminals.

Smart cards come in a range of formats. The actual chips are embedded in a small plastic carrier module about 1-inch (2.5 centimeters) square. Many GSM mobile telephones use the chip and carrier package alone as a mini-card. Most familiar, however, are the credit-card-sized cards with the distinctive gold contacts on the front. This form-factor must be inserted into a special reader (known as a smart-card acceptance device) to function. Another variant is the contactless card, with which communication with the reader is established using a radio frequency link.

Common applications for smart cards are found in the health care, telecommunications, transit, and financial services industries; used as access keys to buildings or networks; and for information storage. In Europe, smart cards are used as token cards (France Telecom), offline debit cards (Carte Bleu in France), and stored-value cards (Belgium's Proton card and Denmark's Danmønt). GSM phones use subscriber identification modules (SIMs): microprocessor smart cards that are inserted into the phone to identify the subscriber, execute encryption algorithms, store cardholder data, and so on. Increased capacity GSM SIMs can serve as platforms for a range of digital services, including Internet access, bill payment, and electronic wallet (which allows digital cash to be sent into and out of the handsets).

Token cards for telecommunications are prepaid smart cards commonly used in Africa, Asia, and Europe to pay for some telecommunications services. France Telecom was the first to convert coin telephone users to cards. Telephone cards were issued with a varying number of units written into the chip, which allowed the phone itself to read and decrement the chip based on the distance and the duration of the call. Periodically, the phone sends the units upstream to a central server at France Telecom for settlement.

The U.S. continues to lag behind the rest of the world in the adoption of smart card technology for payments because of existing inexpensive and widely available communications networks that can be used for credit-/debit- card authorization and because of the lack of a centralized banking authority to mandate adoption. Numerous smart-card pilot projects have failed to reveal compelling applications that cannot be implemented with the existing infrastructure of magnetic stripe cards. Like any client device, the advantage would lie with smart cards if applications were found that require or take advantage of the processing power to be found on the smart card itself or if multiple applications can be consolidated onto a single card.

Security may well be such an application. The security needs of e-business benefit from storing encryption keys and performing encryption and decryption operations on a dedicated hardware device. This security capability is more portable and safer on a smart card than a desktop machine, and the combination of portability and computing ability would be a unique advantage for the smart card. According to Microsoft, Windows 2000 will allow users to log in using a smart card.

See "Security Requirements for E-Business" on page 209 for more information.

Microsoft's Smart Cards for Windows and Sun's JavaCard are among the attempts to create an application standard for smart cards that would make it easier to develop multi-application smart cards. (See the *Technology Forecast* for more information on other potential standards.)

E-Business Platform Application Programming

As e-business moves from the static display of company or product information (sometimes referred to as "brochureware") to more interactive and customer-oriented exchanges, application programming becomes indispensable on both the server and client sides of the network. Applications can produce unique Web pages in real time based on a combination of information from the user and information stored on the server side, and can allow users to interact with applications running on a Web server or other enterprise server.

Figure 54 on page 178 illustrates the construction of a dynamic Web page for a specific user. The server relies on a cookie stored on the client's machine to identify the user. The example includes programming languages and environments on the client and server sides of the e-business platform. The example shows a dynamic HTML page being constructed for a user, based on the user's profile, as well as database lookup and application scripting on server and client sides.

FORMS

A form is an HTML construct that defines graphical user interface (GUI) user-interaction objects—fields, checkboxes, pop-up lists, radio buttons—together with a method for using HTTP to transfer form information from client to server. Forms still are the workhorses of user interaction on the Internet.

Compared with what users are accustomed to on other GUI platforms, interaction with Web-based HTML forms seems clumsy and unintuitive. A user must fill out and submit an entire form before the information contained in the form can be validated. (HTML itself provides no means of validation, although client-side scripting languages such as JavaScript or JScript can provide this function.) Because the page must be regenerated by the server and then sent completely back to the user's browser each time a user interacts with a form, a delay may occur between a submission and the response from the server. One motive for application development for the client side has been to compensate for some of the limitations of forms. HTML 4.0 addresses some of these problems.

See "HTML" on page 193 for more information.

FIGURE 54: CONSTRUCTION OF A DYNAMIC WEB PAGE

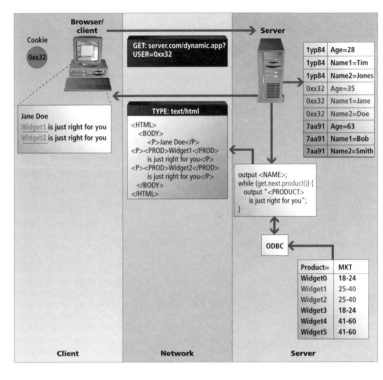

Many U.S. government agencies, formal international standards organizations, Internet-specific groups, and private business are involved with creating new technical standards for the Internet.

INTERNET ENGINEERING TASK FORCE (IETF)

The IETF is perhaps the most important standards body developing Internet technology; its hundreds of sequentially numbered request for comment (RFC) documents cover key technologies such as IP and Internet addressing, e-mail, file transfer, network news protocols, and security. Most work of IETF is handled through mailing lists for dozens of specific work groups, although regular meetings are held during the year.

OTHER INTERNET BODIES

- The Internet Society (ISOC)—The umbrella group comprised of individuals and organizations active in Internet-related activities.

- The Internet Architecture Board (IAB)—Defines the Internet protocols and standards.

- The Internet Engineering Steering Group (IESG)—Responsible for the technical and administrative management of IETF activities and the Internet standards process.

- The Internet Research Task Force (IRTF)—Works with IAB to research long-term developments and technologies for the Internet.

- The Internet Assigned Numbers Authority (IANA)—The central coordinator for the assignment of unique parameters such as TCP ports or protocol types. IANA is being replaced by ICANN

IAB, IESG, and IANA are chartered by ISOC.

WORLD WIDE WEB CONSORTIUM (W3C)

W3C was founded in October 1994 and is led by Tim Berners-Lee, creator of the Web. W3C plays a central role in evolving the Web-specific software standards and languages. W3C writes proposals to enhance core technologies such as HTML, XML, and SMIL.

NATIONAL SCIENCE FOUNDATION (NSF)

The National Science Foundation (NSF) is involved in funding many aspects of basic science and engineering research; it is an independent agency of the U.S. government, established by the National Science Foundation Act of 1950. The NSF Directorate for Computer and Information Science and Engineering (CISE) has a division entitled Advanced Networking Infrastructure and Research (ANIR), whose work includes the Next Generation Internet program, the Very High-Speed Backbone Network Service (vBNS), and other programs to connect researchers and educators to information resources, computational resources, and special facilities. ANIR funds up to $5 million per year for research and pilot projects addressing "unresolved Internet-related areas of discovery and development."

NETWORK SOLUTIONS INC. (NSI)

NSI is a publicly traded company largely owned by Science Applications International Corp. (SAIC), a high-technology research and engineering company. Since 1993, NSI has been the registrar for .com, .net, .org, .gov, and .edu top-level Internet domains. NSI's status as the sole registrar is in the process of changing. ■

PROGRAMMING AND SCRIPTING LANGUAGES

Various development languages are used for writing e-business platform applications. Although some languages historically have been "client" or "server" languages, the trend is to find the same languages used in both environments.

A server can do more than send static content. It also can cause a browser or other client to execute a plug-in or helper application. Another option is to send a program in some scripting language directly to the browser. These programs—sometimes called applets or active content—are interpreted by code in the client. Applets can range in complexity from simple animation add-ons to sophisticated graphical user interface (GUI) functionality to handling business logic in the client.

The three most common script or interpreted languages for the Internet are Java, Java-Script, and VBScript, which resembles Visual Basic. Applet languages are designed to be platform-independent and can be processed by a Web browser running on any client operating system as long as the browser understands that language.

Scripts written in client-side scripting languages are embedded directly in the HTML document downloaded to the client. The script can be run by several events, such as in response to user actions or automatically when download completes.

Java. Java, developed by Sun, is an object-oriented language. It can be used either to develop Internet applets or as a general-purpose application development language. A Java program is written to run on a hypothetical computer known as a Java Virtual Machine (JVM); any operating system or application that implements a JVM can run a Java program. For a Web browser to execute Java applications, a JVM must be included with the Web browser (as is the case for the browsers running on Microsoft Windows or the Apple Macintosh) or be included in the operating system itself (as is the case for IBM's OS/2 Warp and Sun's Solaris). However, Microsoft's extensions to its Windows implementation of Java limit the portability of any applications developed on its platform because Java applets created with these extensions will not run on non-Windows versions of the JVM. (With such extensions, the language cannot be considered Java, according to Sun's license agreement for Java. A 1999 U.S. federal court ruling requires Microsoft to distribute a fully Java-compliant version worldwide.)

Java Applets. The Java language was designed for use in applets, code objects that are transmitted over a network for execution on a remote machine. Two key objectives in designing an applet language are providing security (a malicious applet cannot damage a remote host) and platform independence (the applet can run on any supported system).

Java applets enforce security in several ways, two of which are built into the language. The first aspect checks the Java program for internal integrity and ensures it has been compiled correctly. The second aspect initially referred to the fact that when a Java applet was running, it could be forced to execute in a constrained execution environment (known as the "sandbox"). In this environment, the applet is barred from a range of activities such as writing data to the local disk or deleting files. (By enforcing the sandbox restrictions, a user can execute a Java program with confidence that it cannot damage the local system.)

In response to some of the limitations of the original Java security model, Sun has begun to redo the Java security model. The first enhancement to the Java Development Kit (JDK 1.1) provides for signed applets that contain the creator's digital signature to help determine whether they can go beyond the sandbox security model used by JDK 1.0. Trusted applets could read or write to local storage. JDK 1.2, which shipped in December 1998, includes a new security model that replaces the sandbox; instead, a flexible

"Although some development languages historically have been 'client' or 'server' languages, the trend is to find the same languages used in both environments."

permissions scheme allows users to assign specific capabilities to each applet. The Java Protected Domains Security Model allows administrators to assign capabilities to applets being downloaded across a network, based on their source as verified by a digital signature. Those that are not signed still are executed within the original sandbox model. JDK 1.2 also allows companies to create cryptography extensions to Java applications using technology licensed from RSA Data Security Inc. (RSADSI).

JavaScript. JavaScript is a scripting language developed by Netscape to provide simple client-side applications such as form-validation code. Despite the similarity of their names, JavaScript has no relationship to Sun's Java, although the two languages look similar and work well together. JavaScript has no security model and typically is distributed to the client as part of an HTML page. Netscape also has introduced a server-side version for use with its HTTP servers. Netscape browsers have included a JavaScript interpreter since version 2.0.

JScript. JScript is Microsoft's implementation of JavaScript. It is not compatible directly with JavaScript, although with care, it is possible to write code that will executive in both JavaScript and JScript. Like JavaScript, JScript is both a client- and server-side language. A JScript interpreter has been included in all versions of Microsoft's Internet Explorer since the 3.0 release.

VBScript. VBScript, developed by Microsoft, is a scripting language based on a subset of the Microsoft Visual Basic for Applications (VBA) language. A VBScript interpreter has been included in all versions of Microsoft's Internet Explorer since the 3.0 release as well as in Microsoft servers. Because VBScript is limited to Microsoft Web browsers, it is employed more commonly in controlled environments such as intranets where the restriction to Internet Explorer is less of an issue. The VBScript interpreter can be disabled by the user for security reasons. Often, corporate policies may mandate that client-side execution is disabled, and such policies may be enforced by overriding the user's browser configuration or by removing any scripting language code with a firewall-based filter before delivering the HTML page to the user's desktop browser.

C++. Designed at AT&T Bell Laboratories in the early 1980s, C++ is a general-purpose language based on extending the C language with native support for objects, classes, and inheritance. C++ has been an important language for development of commercial desktop application programs and general programming tasks on UNIX systems, slowly replacing C over the course of the mid-1990s. The existence of disparate application frameworks and the fact that a C++ standard was adopted only in 1998, however, mean there still are incompatibilities between C++ implementations on different platforms, limiting code portability.

Perl. Perl (Practical Extraction and Report Language) is an interpreted language with sophisticated features for manipulating text and accessing network resources. Perl provides a mix of power and flexibility for writing Web scripts, and is building a following as a general-purpose language for UNIX application development. A CGI program developed as a Perl script on a Windows NT server can be transferred to a UNIX server, where it runs without modification. This portability makes Perl an asset comparable with the benefits of Java.

Perl has intrinsic support for network APIs (TCP/IP sockets), text manipulation, and database access. Perl is provided as freely available C source code and as ready-to-run interpreters on most UNIX platforms. Versions also are available for Windows 95/98/NT, OS/2, and the Macintosh.

See "Server-Side Scripting Languages" on page 184 for more information about Perl.

ActiveX. ActiveX is another client-side applications language. ActiveX is a method for creating custom controls under Microsoft's Windows 95/98/NT operating systems. Based on Microsoft's Common Object Model (COM) technology, ActiveX objects are not complete applications; rather, they are pieces of code—dependent upon the ActiveX support built into Windows—that add functionality to Web pages. Unlike Java programs, which are limited in scope to functions available in their JVM, ActiveX objects can utilize any Windows function. It has been argued that this feature also is a liability, however. A Java applet can be confined within the JVM, but a malicious or "buggy" ActiveX program can have free access to the client workstation.

Although ActiveX objects commonly exist only on browsers running under Windows, Software AG's product, EntireX, extends the ActiveX component standard to platforms such as OS/390, AIX, HP-UX, Linux, and Sun Solaris.

CLIENT SOFTWARE ISSUES

One of the main problems in e-business application design is whether the application should be designed to use only the capabilities common to nearly all browsers or to take advantage of more advanced features that are not available uniformly. If advanced features are required, then access can be restricted to those users who have the right software, or it can be made possible for users to obtain the necessary software easily. In either case, there is an additional problem when the user population is split among different platforms, such as Windows, Macintosh, and UNIX. There are a number of possible approaches:

- The e-business site adapts to the capabilities of a particular user. For example, it may select dynamically whether to use frames. This selection may be automatic if the site can identify the capabilities of the browser.

- The e-business site requires the user to have particular software installed, such as an animation plug-in, commerce module, or particular version of a browser. This solution is appropriate particularly in closed user communities, where a single organization has substantial influence over the users (such as an intranet). Adobe Acrobat is one example of a file format that commerce sites can count on users having access to the plug-in.

- The e-business site looks best when viewed with particular software, such as a particular browser version. It may or may not look as good with other software. If one or two types of client software have a dominant market share among the targeted user base, this may be an acceptable system.

- The e-business site is usable with a basic client that just renders HTML tables and forms. If the client supports client-side execution, graphics, frames, and other enhancements, then the user has an enriched experience. The site makes no attempt to identify the type of browser being used because this task is difficult and even when successful does not indicate what capabilities of the browser are enabled—for example, Java—or even the screen resolution. Instead, the site "gracefully degrades" its usability and additional functionality along with reduced client capability until only the most basic site functions are left. Asking users to choose is not an effective option because it requires them to make a decision about matters that they may not understand.

It is possible to take advantage of new features when they become available as commerce sites gain experience with customers and as the software evolves. At one time, for example, few users had browsers capable of rendering tables in HTML; now, most

"One of the main problems in e-business application design is whether the application should be designed to use only the capabilities common to nearly all browsers or take advantage of more advanced features that are not available uniformly."

installed browsers can do so. Therefore, a choice that was appropriate at one time may not be appropriate as the available software changes.

One of the key advantages of moving functionality to the desktop via specialized client software is interactivity. Because the software is running directly on the user's computer, a very high-bandwidth, low-latency channel is available between the user and the application. This connection permits the use of highly interactive metaphors, such as drag-and-drop, that would be impossible for a purely server-based implementation.

However, as mentioned previously, most client software efforts have not been terribly successful to date. There are several disadvantages of client software for commerce:

- *Security*—The security technology for Java applets primarily is designed to protect the desktop computer and its user from hostile software. ActiveX provides full access to Windows APIs and therefore provides no security. Neither Java nor ActiveX does much to protect a distributed application from a hostile user or untrustworthy client computer. Any use of client software for Internet commerce must be evaluated carefully to ensure that errors, accidental or malicious, in the operation of the client software cannot damage the integrity of the application.

- *Universality*—Until client technologies such as Java are available universally, requiring client capabilities may only serve to reduce the audience for an e-business application. If the user does not have the equipment or environment for the client software, that user cannot use the application. In addition, if the user must take special action such as installing a plug-in or control, it may discourage use of the server application.

- *Reliability*—Many of the potential benefits for client software require that a persistent state must be maintained on the client computer. This setup can cause problems in usability and reliability, however. If the user habitually uses several computers—an office desktop and a laptop, for example—the stored state on the two computers may be incomplete and incompatible. If the user's computer crashes, the stored state may be lost. It may not be adequate to depend on the user for backup of application-critical information.

- *Versioning*—Even if everyone had a Java-capable browser and companies trusted the security model enough to enable it, not everyone would be running the same version of the JVM. This situation leaves developers with a dilemma: develop for an old version that everyone can use, or develop for the latest version and accept a smaller base of users. The same tradeoff exists for any client-side execution system.

When it is used, client-side software in a business-to-consumer environment can provide several kinds of functions:

- *Receipt and coupon storage*—The desktop is a natural place to store Internet commerce purchase receipts and coupons. (For example, coupon Web sites such as `Valuepage.com` let consumers print out a bar-coded shopping list good for discounts at thousands of participating supermarkets. Other sites, such as `supercoops.com`, offer the equivalent of direct-mail coupons, allowing shoppers to search for local coupons or for coupons in particular categories similar to those they might receive in the postal mail. Although most coupon Web sites are not conducting actual transactions, and therefore might not be considered Internet shopping per se, the category is one of the fastest-growing in the e-business space, according to Jupiter Communications.)

- *Payment credentials and applications*—Some Internet payment protocols, such as SET, require a client-side software wallet to function. Others, such as entering a credit-card number into a secure HTML form, can benefit from desktop software that could, for example, automatically enter such information into the form. Also, some applications use cookies as a storage mechanism.

- *Shopping cart*—Shopping cart functionality may be placed at the transaction engine, for cross-store purchasing; at the catalog server, for complex pricing; and at the user desktop, for maximum interactivity. With client software, drag-and-drop item selection can be implemented as well as highly interactive pricing calculations and order modification.

- *User profile*—User profile information, from the shipping address to preferences in colors and styles, is a natural candidate for client storage. By keeping such information at the client, it can be used across multiple Internet sites and potentially kept more private.

See "Secure Electronic Transaction" on page 157 for more information about SET. See "Maintaining State and User Activity in HTTP" on page 191 for more information on cookies.

Some examples of client software for commerce are wallets, such as those built by CyberCash, IBM, JavaSoft, VeriFone, and others. These applications store user payment credentials for SET and similar protocols and also may play a role in receipt storage.

SERVER-SIDE APPLICATION PROGRAMMING

On the server-side, the basic way application programs generate dynamic content that is sent to clients is in the form of an HTML page. (XML and plug-ins are other ways to send content.) These server-side applications may be simple scripts or complex programs that interact with order-entry and customer-relations systems, request stock-ticker data from other Web servers, and so on. They also may interact with other systems belonging to trading partners.

Common Gateway Interface. Common Gateway Interface (CGI) was the original specification for interfacing scripts and programs to an HTTP server. It still is widely used, particularly on UNIX platforms. CGI specifies how clients ask HTTP servers to run a program, how HTTP servers activate the program and pass client parameters to it, and how programs send responses back to the client. CGI programs can be written in any programming language supported on the platform. In practice, interpreted scripting languages such as Perl are used widely for writing CGI programs.

See "Perl" on page 180 for more information.

CGI's primary disadvantage is that each invocation of a CGI program means a new process creation on the server, a relatively slow and resource-intensive task. CGI programming also requires more programming skill than environments that embed server-parsed script code in HTML documents. Several initiatives address these shortcomings. The mod_perl project embeds a Perl interpreter into Apache, thereby avoiding the process-startup overhead. Perl's CGI.pm module greatly simplifies the task of CGI programming, although it does not approach the simplicity of other environments.

Alternatives to CGI. The shortcomings of CGI, even on the UNIX platform, have led to the creation of alternative server-side programming technologies.

Microsoft and Netscape each have developed an interface for directly linking applications to their respective HTTP server products (rather than creating new processes to run a separate program as in CGI). Running the application in the same process space as the HTTP server itself avoids the overhead associated with creating a new process, thus significantly improving performance. (If the application crashes, however, so does the HTTP server; therefore, it may be advisable to run an application on a separate application server rather than in the HTTP process space.)

- *Domino Server Application Programming Interface (DSAPI)*—Included in release 5 of Lotus' Domino (Domino R5), it allows developers to customize secure access from browsers, build a single sign-on utility, and build extensions.

- *Internet Server Application Programming Interface (ISAPI)*—A Windows-only specification from Microsoft. Applications are built as dynamic-link libraries (DLLs) that run in the same process space as an HTTP server.

- *Netscape Server Application Programming Interface (NSAPI)*—Netscape's mechanism for connecting application programs with an HTTP server. As with ISAPI, NSAPI applications run in the same process space as the HTTP server. All of Netscape's HTTP servers support NSAPI, which runs on several variants of UNIX as well as on Windows NT.

- *Java servlets*— JavaSoft's Java Servlet API provides a method for Java programs running under a JVM to share process space with a Web server. Servlets can run on Java-capable HTTP servers such as IBM's Internet Connection Server, Lotus' Domino Go, O'Reilly's Website Professional, Sun's Java Web server, and the World Wide Web Consortium's Jigsaw Web server. The Servlet API also can run via the use of an adapter on almost any Web server, including Microsoft's Internet Information Server and Netscape's Enterprise Server.

SERVER-SIDE SCRIPTING LANGUAGES

Both JavaScript and VBScript are used as scripting languages on the server side as well as on the client. Both languages have server-side extensions for database access and other specific requirements. Perl currently is the most widely used scripting language because of its portability, its suitability for systems administration and text processing, and the vast array of extension modules.

See "Perl" on page 180 for more information.

Active Server Pages. Microsoft's server-side scripting environment is called Active Server Pages (ASP). ASP comes as a part of the Internet Information Server (IIS) on Windows NT, and a commercial package is available from Chili!Soft to run ASP on Web servers from multiple vendors.

Like its competitor environments—CGI programming and the use of third-party products such as Allaire Cold Fusion or Netscape LiveWire—ASP allows a Web page author to combine HTML, scripting languages, and activation of other software objects on a single Web page. In ASP, VBScript is the default scripting language; however, ASP allows developers to use JScript (Microsoft's implementation of JavaScript) and (with plug-ins) Perl and REXX. Several scripting languages can be mixed on a single page.

ASP also contains a set of built-in objects for developers. The Request object, for example, encapsulates the data sent to the server by a user response to an HTML form. Developers can invoke any ActiveX object, thus allowing access to ODBC-compliant databases through the Data Access Object (DAO) interfaces. Like other scripting environments, ASP allows for a quicker develop-test-revise cycle than CGI programming. As with other server-side approaches that run in the same process space as the Web server, there is no execution penalty for starting up ASP applications, but ASPs themselves place a greater overhead on the server than pure HTML documents. The controls that interact with the ASP can be either client- or server-side. ASP also includes functionality based on server-side include (SSI), for example, including HTML documents within HTML documents.

COMPONENT-BASED PROGRAMMING

Substantial application programming for e-business is just beginning. Despite the success of packaged applications within enterprise computing as a whole, there will be a large amount of custom programming in the e-business area for some time to come, and it is here that application development technologies such as component-based programming or distributed objects will be needed, used, stressed, refined, and developed.

The widely shared vision of Internet platform computing involves an evolution over the next few years to distributed component-based systems whose elements dynamically invoke the services of other components that provide the capabilities needed for a given task. Migrating to software components and distributed objects will improve flexibility, scalability, and robustness. Application functionality can be changed by modifying individual objects without requiring changes to the rest of the application code. Robustness, scalability, and performance can be improved by changing (in some cases, dynamically) the assignment of specific objects to specific servers for execution.

Basing development on components also can deliver some level of interoperability. These objects can exist on virtually any server platform because object middleware includes the flexibility needed to support heterogeneous environments. Making robust and important functionality provided by existing enterprise applications available as software components (a process sometimes known as "encapsulation") preserves the existing investment in this software and allows distributed computing to encompass these existing applications. Furthermore, component-based development offers the

"There will be a large amount of custom programming in the e-business area for some time to come, and it is here that application development technologies such as component-based programming or distributed objects will be needed, used, stressed, refined, and developed."

OPEN-SOURCE PROGRAMMING

Open-source software (OSS) is software made available in source code form at no cost to developers. According to the Open Source Organization, such software must be licensed for free redistribution without payment of a royalty or other fee for its sale. Only software that complies with the organization's definition and licensing terms is allowed to use the Open Source trademark (www.opensource.org).

In theory, OSS benefits from a large distributed group of volunteers working with the source code, fixing bugs, and adding features. The best fixes are selected by an owner or leader and incorporated into the ongoing product. Because the group is large and the source code is available for scrutiny, bugs are found and fixed easily. Because several solutions may be found separately, the best fix is picked, improving the quality of the code.

Aside from the coders, a large body of volun-

teers writes documentation and provides expert, timely, and free support via the Internet.

The publicity surrounding the Linux operating system, an OSS version of UNIX, brought questions of open-source development methods to the fore during 1998. Many industry players, including Compaq, HP, IBM (DB2, Lotus, and Tivoli), Oracle, and Sun have announced plans to supply ports of their software to Linux, and IDC estimates that Linux had a 17 percent share of the new server operating system shipments at the end of 1998, compared with 36 percent for Microsoft's Windows NT and 24 percent for Novell's NetWare.

The most widely used programs on the Internet—those for delivering e-mail, distributing discussion groups, serving DNS queries, activating Web pages, and serving Web pages—already are OSS. These programs include the Apache Web server, BIND, Perl, and Sendmail.

In addition, IBM announced in late 1998 that it was releasing the source code for Secure Mailer, a candidate to replace sendmail as a ubiquitous e-mail server. Netscape's browser has been available as an OSS product at mozilla.org for some months, and it is claimed that the code base has been improved in several significant ways that Netscape plans to incorporate into the next commercial release of the browser.

Successful OSS products may become fragmented in time, however, especially after their development leaders no longer are available. Linux and Perl have identifiable leaders, and what would happen in the event of their leaders being unable to continue the work is unclear.

OSS also may suffer the same problems as conventional software development when projects scale. The source code for Linux is still only about 10 percent the size of commercial UNIX releases. ■

potential to change and customize applications more easily by adding or modifying components. Some of this modification can be accomplished dynamically by adding new or more powerful components.

Therefore, companies with these needs increasingly are looking to distributed objects to allow global access to information resources while hiding platform and database heterogeneity. A method gaining increasing popularity in this context is the use of object request brokers (ORBs), which are generic middleware layers for connecting distributed software components. These products allow software components to interact across networks by locating the appropriate objects and brokering the communications. However, the process of developing applications using distributed objects still is complex today. Furthermore, the existence of competing ORB standards, such as Microsoft's COM/Distributed COM (DCOM) and the Object Management Group's Common Object Request Broker Architecture (CORBA), has tended to slow the adoption of object technology.

Basic Web Interactions

Figure 55 illustrates the technology that underlies the process of browsing and downloading. This section covers the basic technology for interactions between client and server on the Internet: the HTTP protocol, HTML and its descendents, and how various kinds of files are sent across the Internet and decoded at the client end. Figure 55 illustrates a typical exchange where a client requests a Web page and the server returns it.

FIGURE 55: INTERNET BROWSING AND DOWNLOADING

Section A of Figure 55 shows a file being displayed by the browser. Section B of Figure 55 shows that file being downloaded to disk.

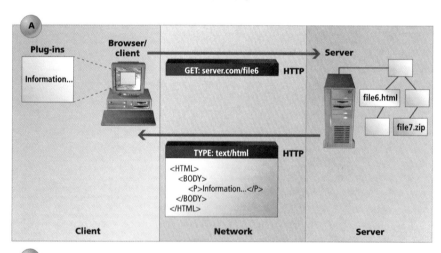

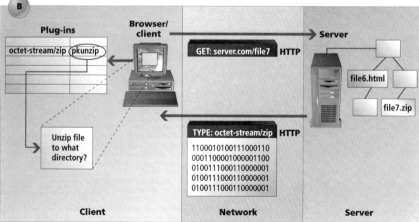

The HTTP protocol defines the messages that can be exchanged between a Web server and a Web client. The server needs to interpret uniform resource locators (URLs) and other data contained in the request sent to it by the client. The client needs to interpret HTML files and other types of files sent to it by the server. Many browser clients also include other functionality to handle Internet e-mail, newsgroups, and file transfer using the File Transfer Protocol (FTP).

URLs AND DOMAIN NAMES

Every device on the Internet has an IP address, which is a unique set of digits identifying the device (for example, `199.95.73.144` is the "dotted quad" address for PricewaterhouseCoopers' Web site). Although computers work well with numeric IP addresses, humans do not. Domain names that use a word (such as `www.pwcglobal.com`) rather than a number format are easier to remember, and these are mapped to IP addresses by the computer. The mapping is done via the Domain Name Service, a service that resides on systems distributed hierarchically through the Internet.

A "dot address," also known as "dotted quad" or "dotted decimal notation," is a 32-bit IP address expressed as four decimal numbers, each in the range 0 to 255.

Domain names consist of a series of names separated by dots that refer to progressively larger parts of the total domain name space as they are read from left to right. The last (rightmost) part of the domain is known as the top-level domain. The most common top-level domain is `.com` for commercial business in the U.S.; other U.S.-managed top-level domains are `.edu` for educational institutions, `.gov` for the U.S. federal government (formerly, this name also was given out to nonfederal government entities), `.mil` for the military, `.org` (initially) for nonprofit organizations, and `.net` (also initially) for institutions related to the management or administration of the Internet.

Internationally, each country is allocated a two-letter top-level domain based on the International Organization for Standardization (ISO) country code specification ISO-3166; for example, `.ca` for Canada, `.fr` for France, and `.de` for Germany. (The U.S. has been issued the top-level domain `.us`, but it is used primarily by local government agencies and school districts.) Administration of names within each of these domains usually is performed by a nonprofit organization (called a network information center [NIC]) in each country. All unused two-letter top-level domain codes are reserved for future ISO-3166 country-code allocations.

The country-specific top-level domains have not been used consistently. For example, because of the Internet's start in the U.S., `.us` usually is not added; instead, the absence of a specific country implies U.S. origin. As use of the Internet has grown outside the U.S., some believe names such as `.com` should become `.com.us` to eliminate this built-in assumption, just as `.com.au` and `.com.mx` tell people they are doing business with a company in Australia or Mexico, respectively. For example, companies in the United Kingdom and New Zealand use the `.co.uk` and `.co.nz` domains, while their governments use `.gov.uk` and `.govt.nz`. Alternatively, because existing top-level domains already are used by multinational organizations headquartered anywhere in the world, some people believe these names should remain available for global assignment.

Controversy has arisen over who should be in charge of registration and administration of domain names on the Internet, the relationship between trademarks and domain names, the assignment of names requested by more than one person or organization, and the creation of new top-level domain names. The number of organizations involved in registration and in the decision-making process about the future of domain names has increased significantly, and participants now include businesses, service providers, governments, nonprofit organizations, and standards bodies.

Computing IP Addresses from Domain Names

Domain names must be resolved into numeric IP addresses to allow communication; this transformation is done invisibly to the user by network protocol software. Originally, all Internet-connected systems maintained a list, called the HOSTS file, of all host names and corresponding IP addresses on the Internet. Due to the growth and volatility of the Internet, the HOSTS system stopped being viable in the early 1980s. It was replaced by the Domain Name System (DNS), a distributed database that stores domain names and their associated IP addresses and that can be queried by network protocol software. Most Internet service providers (ISPs) and many companies maintain DNS servers, which store the DNS information for a particular set of domains. The servers also cache recently used domain names and their IP addresses in a local look-up cache. If a request arrives to resolve a domain name that is not in the cache, the request is forwarded to other DNS servers, which either resolve the address or pass the request up the chain until the request reaches the domain's top-level DNS server.

In October 1998, the U.S. government and Network Solutions (which has administered .com domain names since 1993) began phasing in a shared registration system in March 1999, with full implementation expected by June 1999. The Internet Corporation for Assigned Names and Numbers (ICANN), a nonprofit body formed by the Internet Assigned Numbers Authority (IANA), was put in charge of overseeing this privatization by an agreement with the U.S. Department of Commerce concluded in November 1998. ICANN announced its approval for five organizations—America Online (AOL), the France Telecom, Internet Council of Registrars (CORE, a Geneva-based trade group), Melbourne IT, and Register.com—to compete with Network Solutions. Following a test period scheduled to conclude in June 1999, the right to register domains likely will be extended to 29 additional companies. Although Network Solutions charges $70 per name for 2 years of registration, competing registrars will be free to set their own prices. Each new registrar will maintain a mirror site of Network Solutions' database, updating records simultaneously across all mirror sites. Competing registrars will pay $9 per name annually to Network Solutions for its role as the centralized registry.

The direction that a new domain naming system will take is still undetermined. ICANN faces challenges in several areas:

Domain Names and Trademarks. Although domain names are employed as a user-friendly version of numeric IP addresses, the names have commercial value in themselves similar to easily recognizable or heavily promoted phone numbers. Domain name registration in the top-level domains of countries where a company is doing business also helps prevent others from using the company's trademark in their domain names. Most customers recognize second-level domain names, which are frequently company or organization names, such as "ibm" in ibm.com.

However, the issue is more complex because there can be only a single site with a given name in the .com domain, although multiple companies can use the same trademarked name (if they are distinguished by type of product or by geography). Thus, there may be multiple legitimate claimants to a given domain name.

The current domain name system allows "cybersquatters" to buy up domain names and then resell them for a substantial profit to their namesakes. However, recent court rulings against cybersquatters have helped protect the legitimate owners of domain names. The practice of pirating domain names also is impossible in countries such as

---

IPv4 AND IPv6

The Internet Protocol (IP), a connectionless network protocol for packet-switched networks, is the Layer 3 (network layer) protocol of the Internet. IPv6 (previously called next-generation IP, or IPng) is a backward-compatible extension of the current version of IP, IPv4. IPv6 is designed to solve problems brought on by the success of the Internet (such as running out of IP addresses and address space in router tables), adds features such as security, and may guarantee real-time services similar to quality of service (QoS).

In IPv4, no mechanism is specified for allowing packets to be delivered with con-

sistent QoS in terms of bandwidth and packet delay, which is a requirement for reliable, high-quality delivery of multimedia content in real time as well as real-time device-control applications.

Future versions of IP, such as IPv6, will enhance these QoS features; however, until IPv6 is implemented, streaming multimedia will remain a challenge for the Internet.

Increased Internet usage and the allocation of many of the available IP addresses have created a need for increased addressing capacity. IPv4 uses a 32-bit number to form an address, which can offer about 4 billion

distinct network addresses. In comparison, IPv6 uses 128-bit addresses, which offers a theoretical maximum of 340 trillion, trillion, trillion hosts (or 3.4×10^{38}). (In practice, because of the way IP addresses are allocated, the actual number of addresses available for use is significantly less than these numbers suggest.)

IPv6 was deployed on an experimental basis across part of the Internet, known as the 6Bone, in 1998. However, it will take time for the disparate networks that compose the Internet to upgrade to the new IPv6 protocol, and it may never be deployed as widely as originally expected. ■

the Netherlands where all domain name requests are relayed to a central chamber of commerce for adjudication. Similar controls exist in other countries as well. A workable domain name system needs to be efficient and fair while meshing domain name selection with the existing infrastructure for establishing and protecting trademarks.

The increasing pressure on the .com namespace has led companies to look elsewhere for their domain names. To this end, the tiny Pacific nations of Tuvalu and Niue have been selling their domain namespace of .tv and .nu, respectively. Most countries require users of their domain names to maintain some type of presence in the host country, but Tuvalu and Niue are waving this requirement. Both new domains are attractive commercially, and companies are beginning to take advantage of these new domain names.

New Top-Level Domain Names. The International Ad Hoc Committee (IAHC) was established to study the issue of top-level domain names, and it proposed a plan to increase the number of top-level domains. The plan was ratified in Geneva in May 1997 by 80 organizations, but not by the U.S. government. The plan called for an unlimited number of organizations to act as domain-name registrars and for seven new generic top-level domain names (gTLDs). However, given the other changes occurring in the governance of the domain name system, implementation of these gTLDs currently is on hold. (See Table 6.)

TABLE 6: NEW GENERIC TOP-LEVEL DOMAIN NAMES

Domain Name	Designation
.firm	Businesses
.store	Businesses offering goods for sale
.web	Web-related sites
.art	Cultural and entertainment
.rec	Recreational activities
.info	Information services
.nom	Personal sites

IAHC subsequently was replaced by the Interim Policy Oversight Committee (IPOC). Formed to administer the original IAHC proposal, IPOC governs worldwide registration for the new gTLDs and runs a nonprofit association in Switzerland. Under that plan, the World Intellectual Property Organization would moderate trademark disputes over domain names. One potential problem is that multiple gTLDs may be confusing if different organizations can register a given name in different domains (if vacation.com, vacation.store, and vacation.firm were registered by different organizations, for example).

HTTP

An HTTP transaction consists of a server and client sending one another messages. Each message contains a request or response statement, a header with information about the client or server, and various optional fields containing data.

If a user requests the page "example.html" from www.pwcglobal.com, for example, the client browser generates an HTTP message whose method is GET (because the client is requesting to get a resource) and whose extra data is "example.html." The client sends this HTTP message to the http daemon (a program listening for HTTP messages) at www.pwcglobal.com.

The server, when it receives the message, authenticates the browser to see whether the user has rights to access this server. (Public Web sites allow anyone to access them.) If so, the server searches to determine whether the requested resource exists. The server then constructs a return message. The response statement begins with an HTTP header that describes the HTTP version the response will take and the status of the client's request. This status is defined in a three-digit code. Codes in the range 200–299 mean the request was successful, as in "200 OK." Codes in the range 300–399 mean redirection, for example, a page that has been relocated temporarily. The range 400–499 means an error on the part of the client, for example, "401 Not Authorized" or "404 Not Found." Codes in the range 500–599 mean an error on the part of the server.

The message's header section describes the data that follows, including its content type (such as human-readable text, HTML document, graphic file, or a binary file designed to be saved on disk or to be sent to a certain plug-in extension or helper application) and the amount of data in bytes. The data itself follows the header.

HTTP 1.0, the current version of HTTP in use on most of the Internet, will send only one resource per message exchange. For example, if an HTML document contains text and 10 embedded graphic images, it will take 11 specific exchanges to build that document at the browser: The first will contain the basic HTML text and then the browser must request the 10 graphics individually. This is not an efficient process, because establishing a connection may take some time. It would be more efficient—and (because of the way TCP works) produce a faster response time to the user—to send the entire set of resources in the context of one exchange.

In November 1998, IETF released a sixth draft of HTTP/1.1. HTTP/1.1, as it is developing, addresses many of these issues. In particular, HTTP/1.1 addresses the need for persistent connections, thus eliminating the requirement for browsers and Web servers to initiate and terminate numerous TCP connections when transmitting complex Web pages. Under HTTP/1.1, the server connection can remain open while a server sends all resources that compose a Web page. The server optionally may log the transaction as well. HTTP/1.1 currently is implemented in the latest Web servers and browsers from Microsoft, Netscape, and other major vendors.

The HTTP protocol continues to develop. The HTTP next generation (HTTP-NG) project, initiated by the World Wide Web Consortium (W3C) in April 1998, will address four basic weaknesses of HTTP/1.1:

- **Complexity**—Although HTTP/1.1 provides many interesting features, it does not provide a clean framework for defining their interaction. This deficit has resulted in the large and complex HTTP specification.

- **Poor extensibility**—Acknowledging a large number of proposed extensions as part of the core protocol has stretched HTTP/1.1. The interactions between the extensions are complex at best, often unspecified, or even broken.

- **Lack of generality**—Many applications and services are being deployed on the Web that are not, in fact, retrieval of documents. Some applications using HTTP would be deployed more appropriately as applications of a distributed object system.

- **Poor scalability**—At the time the HTTP/1.0 protocol was designed, Web traffic still represented a very low fraction of Internet traffic, and therefore, the scalability of the protocol was less important than it is today. Caching and connection management have improved HTTP/1.1, but the protocol overhead still can be further improved in terms of processing and network efficiency.

In November 1998, Phase I of the HTTP-NG project began to wind down, with W3C handing off the detailed development of protocols to an IETF Working Group. The group has established a series of milestones for delivering parts of the specification, with a target completion date of May 2000.

The basic design approach to the new work is to separate the HTTP protocol into three layers:

- **Message transport**—The lowest layer focuses on transporting messages without concern about their contents. The concept of a message transport will be added on top of transport protocols such as TCP or User Datagram Protocol (UDP). The proposed WebMux filter would combine several transport services (such as batching, pipelining, chunking, and multiplexing messages to deliver them more efficiently) and would work with lower-level transports such as TCP.

- **Remote invocation**—The middle layer implements a generalized request/response messaging protocol that is separate from higher-level application-specific services. The generic model will allow clients to invoke operations on resources resident on a server without regard to the specific nature of the services. The services offered at this layer overlap with functionality supplied in CORBA, DCOM, or Java Remote Method Invocation (RMI); therefore, part of the work of defining this layer involves integration with those efforts.

- **Web application**—At this layer, the visible methods (that is, commands) of the existing HTTP protocol (such as GET, HEAD, and PUT), as well as services such as content negotiation, caching, and access authentication will be implemented as application-specific services that use the lower layers. HTTP thus would become one of a possible set of Web applications using the new message transport and remote invocation layers.

Maintaining State and User Activity in HTTP. HTTP 1.1 is a stateless protocol, meaning HTTP does not require (or permit) the server to retain any information about the history of its transactions with a given client. Whenever the client requests an additional resource, the entire process begins anew. The advantage of this approach is that HTTP servers can work quickly, without needing to track sessions or clients from one transaction to the next. The disadvantage is that the server cannot remember what it has just told a client; therefore, techniques such as "cookies" or hidden fields must be used to allow the server or server-side scripts to track a user's status.

Many e-business applications need to maintain state information. Even filling out a multipage form is impossible to implement using the HTTP protocol unless some extra measures are adopted for transferring the information from one page of the form to the next. Without some way to preserve state information, the server would not associate the second page of a form with the information from the first page. Instead, each interaction would begin from the beginning.

There are two aspects to state: session management, where the server and client can maintain the relevant information about the current interaction, and user identification, where the same user is recognized on future sessions at that Web site.

A cookie is a block of data that a Web server stores on a client system. When a user returns to a Web site, the browser sends a copy of the cookie back to the server. Cookies are used to identify users, to instruct the server to send a customized version of the requested Web page, to submit account information for the user, and for other administrative purposes.

Cookies are stored on the user's computer. If a server creates a cookie the first time a user visits a site, the server can keep track of both session and user state information by retrieving the cookie on subsequent site hits. Cookies do not need to contain state information (such as user purchases or preferences); they usually are simply identifiers that reference user information stored on the server side.

The major weakness of cookies is that users, out of concern for privacy or security issues, may disable cookies in their Web browsers, thus defeating any attempt to save state information. Cookies also suffer from being tied to a specific browser copy—if a user has multiple computers, then the cookies are available only on the physical machine they were created on.

Other schemes—coding a special session identifier into each URL the browser sends after establishing a session with a site or using hidden tags on each HTML page written to the user's browser—do not suffer from this problem, but these schemes can keep only session, not user, state information. If a user is obliged to log into the Web site with a user name and password, then this method provides the most effective means of session management. However, this method likely will discourage use of public-access Web sites because no casual user will wish to establish a log-in before browsing the site.

The classic measurement of Web site activity is the "hit," or one HTTP transaction. Because each Web page usually consists of more than one resource, fetching a single page typically results in recording multiple hits. For each hit, the HTTP protocol delivers information about the date and time of the hit as well as the IP address of the client requesting the hit. Most HTTP servers keep detailed logs of every hit, which form the basis for higher-level statistics. One of the most useful of these statistics is the page view or how many times a particular page was seen by a visitor. Sequences of page views become paths, which detail the pages a visitor saw and indicate how much time was spent on each page. It often is possible to log the page from which a given user came to a Web site, the last page visited before leaving, and even the text typed in at a search engine to find the Web site. However, Web site visitor analysis has many exceptions, assumptions, and estimates inherent in the reporting process, and, like all mass-collected statistics, these must be understood fully to understand the data.

"An IP address is not really adequate to identify a particular computer, let alone the person using it. Many software manufacturers and e-business merchants, however, would like to be able to identify clients uniquely."

The only HTTP information about the identity of a user comes from the IP address of the client, which is included in each interchange. By connecting all the contiguous hits with the same IP address, Web site analysis software can attempt to create a picture of each user's path through the site. However, the IP address is not really adequate to identify a particular computer (as discussed below), let alone the person using it. Many software manufacturers and e-business merchants, however, would like to be able to identify clients uniquely.

No unique mapping exists between IP addresses and client machines, however. Many dial-in clients are assigned a dynamic IP address by their ISP when they connect. (The same situation is true for business users who are assigned an IP address when their computers start up.) This IP address changes each time the client connects, and the same address may be assigned to more than one client in sequence. Identifying a machine with a dynamic IP address could lead to false identity.

Fundamental identification numbers on clients could be used to establish identity reliably. For example, Intel has introduced a 96-bit processor ID in the Pentium III chip. In response to protests from privacy advocates, however, Intel has agreed to have the ID function turned off by default. Some security flaws already have been found in the chip, however; for example, it has been demonstrated that an ActiveX control can turn the ID function back on. With the function turned back on, a site can access users' machines and "steal" a chip's ID number to track users' activities without their knowledge.

HTML

HTML is a document description language derived from SGML that consists of text and fixed tags. Tags describe the attributes of the text and other content and are used by clients to determine how to display the text or perform other manipulations. Each version of HTML has added new tags, which then must be implemented by all clients. A tag is enclosed in "<" and ">" symbols, such as **<B>** to indicate the text that follows the tag must be bold. The corresponding **</B>** end tag indicates the bold is turned off. Not all tags require end tags, for example, the **<HR>** tag, which defines a horizontal rule. Tags often can be given parameters; for example, **<HR WIDTH="50%">** instructs the browser to display a horizontal rule of 50 percent of the screen width. If a user clicks any Web page and chooses View Source from the context menu, the underlying HTML code which the user's browser parses to produce the Web page will be displayed. A complete HTML document begins with **<HTML>** and ends with **</HTML>**.

HTML is in transition from version 3.2 to the current version, 4.0. HTML 4.0 is implemented in all popular Web browsers and was approved as a W3C standard in April 1998. While this new version of HTML is being rolled out, work already is beginning on the next generation of HTML, which will be reimplemented as an application of eXtensible Markup Language (XML). Part of this effort will be to define a core set of tags for marking up headings, paragraphs, lists, and so forth and then to define collections of special-purpose tag sets for applications such as forms, tables, graphics, multimedia, and so on. The W3C Working Group overseeing this effort plans to complete its specification work by mid-2000.

Major features of HTML 4.0 are cascading style sheets (CSSs) and what often is called Dynamic HTML (DHTML), although this term is not used by the W3C.

Cascading Style Sheets. CSSs are used by Web page designers in conjunction with HTML to specify consistent structure and layout across multiple HTML documents. A CSS can be stored in an external file so a single style sheet can be referenced by multiple HTML documents or across an entire Web site. If a style sheet is modified, those modifications affect all HTML documents that reference the style sheet; each HTML document does not need to be changed individually.

The use of CSSs has other benefits. Because basic HTML markup commands can be used to format text only in very rudimentary ways, it has become common to create images of text to control fonts and colors. These images typically are created as separate graphics files (such as Graphics Interchange Format [GIF] files) and then downloaded to the Web browser as needed for display. A CSS can replace a GIF file and display the same image, but the CSS file typically will be much smaller than the GIF file, allowing the contents to be downloaded more quickly, thus improving performance. Another significant advantage of CSS is it allows Web operators to change the entire look and feel of a site by editing a single file—if every page refers to a given CSS for its font sizes, paragraph formatting, colors, and spacing, then only one file needs to be changed for the entire site to change. This process is in contrast to non-CSS sites, where pages either must be generated dynamically, which increases server load, or must be individually or mass-edited with a program.

See "Client Software Issues" on page 181 for more information.

The major drawback of CSS has been its implementation in client software. The version-4 browsers from Microsoft and Netscape partially support CSS and do so differently, which makes designing Web sites with CSS problematic and may negate the advantages to a large extent.

A CSS defined by the page designer can be overridden by a special CSS defined by the user. For example, a user can specify a CSS optimized for their particular device (WebTV, hand-held device, PC, and so on). Also, a visually impaired user could specify a larger font size than the one originally specified.

In May 1998, the W3C released the CSS2 specification, which includes features ranging from new positioning properties that control layout to more effective presentation of multilingual documents, including writing direction, font styles, and quoting conventions. CSS2 also adds features specifically targeted at displaying XML documents.

Dynamic HTML (DHTML). DHTML is a combination of HTML, style sheets, and scripts that allows Web pages to be updated in response to actions taken by the user, without the need to reconnect to the Web server to download a new version of the page. For example, data in a table could be resorted at the user's request, or new visual elements (such as a pop-up text box) could appear when the mouse is positioned over a particular point on the page.

DHTML works by bringing together scripting languages and the HTML tags on a page. All the elements of a Web page—from text to tables to graphic images to drop-down lists—are classed as objects that have properties such as size, content, location, and fonts. These properties can be modified by scripting languages in response to user actions without having to reload the page from the server.

These capabilities give the Web page designer control over how an HTML page appears in the user's browser window; for example, the designer can specify the exact position where a graphical object should appear.

In addition, Web pages created with DHTML can have contents that change automatically without action by the user, for example, by having a graphic element move across the page or perform special effects such as animation or morphing.

Because these kinds of actions can be carried out by a DHTML-enabled browser, they utilize the processing power of the client computer. This process eliminates the load on the HTTP server and network connections that would occur if it were necessary to send the browser a new version of the page each time the appearance is updated. It also gives the user a faster response by eliminating the latency imposed by a roundtrip network exchange between the browser and server.

DHTML is not an official standard of the W3C, and Microsoft and Netscape have included their own incompatible versions of DHTML features in Internet Explorer 4.0 and Netscape Communicator 5.0, respectively. The versions differ in some details of the scripting language (JScript versus JavaScript) and in some details of the object model (how scripts refer to elements on the HTML page when manipulating them dynamically). Although the differences are not large from a technical point of view, they have made the creation of browser-independent HTML pages very difficult. This difficulty, in turn, has tended to limit the adoption of DHTML in mainstream Web design.

The W3C directed its standards work in this area to the adoption of the Document Object Model (DOM) Level 1 in October 1998. DOM defines a standard method for referring to elements on the HTML page so different kinds of DHTML will work without needing to have separate versions of the code for specific browsers.

Other new elements in HTML 4.0 include the following:

- Major changes to the way tables are displayed (important because tables are a major formatting element in HTML). HTML 4.0 supports the ability to align tabular columns on designated characters such as ".", the ability to display large tables incrementally, support for horizontally and vertically scrollable tables with fixed headers, and other enhancements.

- Adoption of ISO 10646 as the character set for HTML, thus supporting international character sets and writing direction. Additionally, HTML 4.0 provides support for target media such as Braille and character-based terminals via style sheets.

- Improvements in forms, including the ability to provide direct keyboard access to form fields, the option to make specific form fields read-only, tools to enable the browser to provide basic field validation, and the ability to add author-defined buttons to a form. (HTML 3.2 only allowed two button functions, for submitting and resetting a form, although scripting languages were able to extend this basic functionality.)

- Formal adoption of a new `<object>` tag, which allows all categories of embedded data objects—including images, embedded HTML documents, Java or ActiveX applets, and JavaScript objects—to be processed with one tag rather than with specific tags for each object type. The `<object>` tag is extensible and can handle any object type, whether specifically defined in HTML 4.0 or not.

XML

XML is a meta language for describing data so it can be interpreted and manipulated in more intelligent ways, such as being processed by applications resident on desktops or servers, as opposed to being displayed just by a browser, which is what HTML enables. An XML document outwardly resembles an HTML document but with new field tags that describe the structure of its content, unlike HTML, which only describes how the document should be displayed. Figure 56 on page 196 shows a commented sample XML document. XML was adopted as a standard by the W3C in February 1998.

XML and HTML were both developed as subsets of the Standard Generalized Markup Language (SGML), but, unlike HTML, which is a fixed language, XML can generate new special-purpose languages for specific applications. In Figure 56 on page 196, a new XML "language" for describing purchase orders is defined and then used to record a specific purchase order. (Obviously, a real purchase-order language would contain much more detail than this example.)

XML as a Data-Structuring Language. XML is designed to provide structure to semi-structured or unstructured (and usually, although not necessarily, textual) data, the kinds of data that abound on the Internet and e-business settings. XML, like SGML, describes structure. In other words, an XML tag does not lead directly to a specific behavior. Both devices and applications can handle the same XML tag in different ways.

Data Type Descriptors. The XML language can be defined by a data type descriptor (DTD), which declares what kinds of tags can be present in a valid instance of the language and how the tags are related. In the simple XML example in Figure 56 on page 196, the DTD declares the valid purchase order needs a date and one or more items and may contain an account number. It also declares an item needs to contain an item number, a description, and a quantity.

This document defines the data in a purchase order, including a Document Type Definition (DTD) that describes the acceptable data, followed by sample data that can be verified against the DTD for syntactic correctness.

Note: Comments in blue are not part of the document.

FIGURE 56: A SAMPLE XML DOCUMENT

```
<?XML version="1.0" ?>
<!DOCTYPE purchases [

a "Purchases" document consists of 0 or more purchases
<!ELEMENT main (purchase)*>

a purchase must have a date, may have an account, and one or more items
<!ELEMENT purchase (date,account?,item+)>

a date and an account number can be any string of characters
<!ELEMENT date (#PCDATA)>
<!ELEMENT account (#PCDATA)>

an item must have a number, description, and quantity
<!ELEMENT item ((itemno,itemdes,quantity)|#PCDATA)*>

<!ELEMENT itemno (#PCDATA)>
<!ELEMENT itemdes (#PCDATA)>
<!ELEMENT quantity (#PCDATA)>
]>
the actual purchase order begins here
<main>
<purchase>
<date> 11/15/1998 </date>
<account> Smith </account>
<item>
<itemno> 12345 </itemno>
<itemdes> Muffler for 57 Chevy </itemdes>
<quantity> 1 </quantity>
</item>
<item>
<itemno> 12346 </itemno>
<itemdes> Muffler Bracket for 57 Chevy </itemdes>
<quantity> 2 </quantity>
</item>
</purchase>
</main>
```

Comparing an XML structure to its DTD allows an application to check the validity of the data. Transmitting an XML document together with its DTD is a form of self-describing data definition, although a DTD only prescribes the structure of an XML document, not the meaning. The DTD in this example has no way to express the requirement that a purchase order date be a valid date, much less a sensible one. The DTD in the above example would admit “DOG” as a valid date; a more elaborate definition could require a date to have the “number slash number slash number” appearance of a date.

XML special-purpose languages may be used to represent the following:

- ***Tabular data***—On any Web page in which tables of information are presented, users want to be able to manipulate a table by changing its appearance, re-sorting it, or switching to different views of various data. Users also want to be able to import data from the table into other applications. The HTML tags (**<table>** and so forth) used for tables are not rich enough for this purpose. There is no HTML tag, for example, to denote the column on which a table is sorted or even to denote the idea that a table can be sorted.

- *Electronic Data Interchange (EDI)*—EDI today uses extensive tagging of data for interchange between businesses. Many analysts expect XML languages to be used to reimplement existing EDI standards. There already are XML encapsulations of existing X12 tag sets (a simple one-to-one mapping connects an X12 tag with an equivalent in XML). (Note that XML cannot define the meaning of data, only its structure; therefore, the primary benefit it offers over existing EDI standards is convergence on a common syntax.)

- *Content tagging*—Tagging content with XML tags is a natural way to categorize information for distribution to different groups of subscribers. Microsoft's Channel Definition Format (CDF) is an application of XML where a Web site developer uses CDF tags to define what pages on the site are to be displayed as channels, which icons to display for each channel, what the update schedules are, and so on. A CDF file specifies the Web page that a user will view if that channel is selected and the subpages that can be selected from the main channel page. The CDF file resides on the Web server; a user who selects a channel actually is specifying the URL of the CDF file. Currently, CDF is used only by Internet Explorer. Content tagging also is used in formats such as Open Financial Exchange (OFX), and Synchronized Multimedia Integration Language (SMIL).

- *Wireless Markup Language (WML)*—One XML-based markup language, WML, is intended for use in specifying content and user interfaces for mobile wireless devices such as cellular phones and pagers. It is designed to create Web pages that can be viewed effectively despite the limitations of these devices, which include small screen size, limited input capabilities, limited memory and computational resources, and narrowband network connectivity.

XML and HTML. XML is not a replacement for HTML. HTML is a specific presentation or formatting language for content on the Web. XML is a specification for generating new languages. HTML could be rewritten or redefined as an XML language (and the W3C's Extensible HTML [XHTML] project is trying to accomplish precisely that goal); however, it does not make sense to speak of XML replacing HTML. XML processors will be implemented internally in browsers as a way to display XML marked-up content. However, XML processors will be needed in other e-business components as well.

WEB SERVERS

The most widely used Web server software on publicly accessible Web sites is Apache. (See Table 7.)

TABLE 7: LEADING PUBLICLY ACCESSIBLE WEB SERVERS (BY NUMBER OF WEB SITES)

Server	Number of Sites (as of April 1999)	Percent of Sites Surveyed
Apache	2,832,119	56%
Microsoft-IIS	1,164,132	23%
AOL (Netscape)-Enterprise	253,660	5%
Rapidsite	94,808	2%
WebSitePro	79,615	2%
thttpd	66,211	1%
Stronghold	64,491	1%

See "Evolution and Future of Electronic Data Interchange" on page 120 for more information.

X12, an Accredited Standards Committee (ASC) of the American National Standards Institute (ANSI), created the primary North American standard for defining EDI transactions. The standard specifies the vocabulary (dictionary) and format for e-business transactions.

See "Web Browsers" on page 201 for more information on XML support in Web browsers.

TABLE 7: LEADING PUBLICLY ACCESSIBLE WEB SERVERS (BY NUMBER OF WEB SITES) (CONTINUED)

Server	Number of Sites (as of April 1999)	Percent of Sites Surveyed
WebSTAR	53,985	1%
Zeus	51,969	1%
NCSA	40,823	1%

Source: Netcraft's Web Server Survey, 1999

In terms of new units shipped in 1997 for Internet and intranet contexts, the leading servers are from Microsoft, AOL (Netscape), and IBM. (See Table 8.)

TABLE 8: LEADING WEB SERVERS (INCLUDING INTRANETS) BY UNITS SHIPPED: 1997

Note: Because Microsoft's IIS Web server is bundled with Windows NT Server, the number of units in use is difficult to estimate.

Server	Internet (in thousands)	Intranet (in thousands)	Total (in thousands)	Market Share
Microsoft	247	974	1,221	38%
AOL (Netscape)	292	682	974	31%
IBM/Lotus	186	424	610	19%
Apache	239	42	281	9%
All others	56	43	99	3%
TOTALS	1,020	2,165	3,185	100%

Source: Zona Research, 1998

AOL's (Netscape's) Enterprise Server. AOL's Enterprise Server 3.6, introduced in January 1998, offers security, content management, search capabilities, and application development options. A key differentiator of Enterprise Server is the many ways it offers to develop customer applications, including Netscape's Web Application Interface (WAI) and Netscape API (NSAPI), CGI, and Java. WAI augments NSAPI and takes advantage of both NSAPI and CGI interfaces. WAI applications can be developed in a variety of programming languages, including C, C++, or Java. Unlike CGI scripts, a WAI application does not have to be restarted with each request, thus improving performance. Extra connection support to applications is provided through LiveWire and CORBA objects. Enterprise Server also has extensive database-access support, with Open Database Connectivity (ODBC), Java Database Connectivity (JDBC), and native drivers for IBM's DB2, Informix, Microsoft's SQL Server, Oracle, and Sybase. (Note that Microsoft's Internet Information Server offers all the foregoing database access support as well.)

Versions of Enterprise Server 3.6 are available from Netscape for Windows NT, Sun Solaris, HP-UX, IBM AIX, SGI IRIX, and Compaq (Digital) UNIX.

Apache Project's Apache Web Server. Apache's Web Server—in use by about half of all publicly accessible Web servers worldwide—is distributed free by the Apache Project. The Apache Project is a group of volunteers who have collaborated on creating a free Web server that is distributed with source code. Their work is based on a Web server designed by Rob McCool at the National Center for Supercomputing Applications (NCSA) at the University of Illinois.

The Apache Web Server is available compiled for Windows 95/98/NT and in source code for various UNIX systems that can be modified and recompiled by developers. Apache is supported by user manuals, an extensive Web site, and discussions by many knowledgeable experts in Usenet newsgroups.

In June 1998, IBM announced it would begin shipping the Apache HTTP server with its WebSphere Application Server. WebSphere is IBM's Java-based Web application server. In addition, IBM announced it is a full participant in the Apache HTTP Server Project.

The latest version, Apache 1.3, was released in 1998 and includes support for HTTP/1.1, CGI server-side scripting, virtual hosts, and SSI. Apache also can function as an HTTP and FTP proxy, has an API set of custom extensions, and includes search engine functionality. Many plug-in modules have been created that extend Apache's base functionality, for example, integration with the Perl scripting language to avoid the CGI process-startup overhead (mod_perl), Java integration, and database connectivity. For reasons related to U.S. government export restrictions, Apache does not include support for SSL. A commercial version of Apache called Stronghold does support SSL, and technical support is available.

See "Secure Sockets Layer" on page 145 for more information.

IBM's Domino Go Webserver. IBM's Domino Go Webserver 4.6.1 is a stand-alone version of the server engine included with Lotus Domino groupware software. It is available in two versions: a basic package for Windows 95/98/NT, AIX, OS/2 Warp Server, Solaris, HP-UX, and OS/390; and a Domino Go Webserver Pro package for Windows 95/98/NT only, which adds site management, authoring tools, advanced database connectivity, and other development tools.

In December 1998, IBM announced it was discontinuing development and support for the Domino Go Webserver product. Webserver functionality will be repackaged under the IBM HTTP Server brand, and IBM will continue to bundle it with other Lotus Domino products and IBM's WebSphere application server line. Two variations currently are available:

- IBM HTTP Server powered by Apache (based on the Apache HTTP Server), which runs on AIX, Solaris, and Windows NT
- IBM HTTP Server based on the technology used in Lotus Domino Go Webserver, which runs on OS/390 and AS/400

Microsoft's Internet Information Server. Microsoft's Internet Information Server (IIS) 4.0 was introduced in 1997 as part of a free option pack for Windows NT 4.0. The core component of IIS 4.0 is a Web server, but it also includes a basic news server and an e-mail server. IIS supports SSL on all three components, and ships with a digital certificate server. IIS' search engine is Microsoft Index Server, a component that allows users to search in several languages for HTML documents and non-HTML document formats such as Excel, PDF, and Word. IIS has a wide array of server-side programming options: It supports CGI, Java servlets, and Microsoft's Internet Server Application Program Interface (ISAPI), which is similar in function to CGI but without the process-starting overhead. IIS' Active Server Pages system allows scripting language code to be embedded into a standard HTML page, thereby creating dynamic pages without using CGI. Languages supported include ASP, JScript, Perl, and VBScript.

See "Active Server Pages" on page 184 for more information.

IIS 4.0 is attractive to many sites running Windows NT Server because it is free and because it is tightly integrated into Microsoft's Windows NT domain security system. IIS 4.0 has one major limitation, however: It is available only for Windows NT 4.0 or later.

SERVING MULTIMEDIA CONTENT

To say audio or video data is "streamed" means it is being played or displayed as it is being sent. (Nonstreaming data has to be sent in its entirety to the client before playback can begin.) This process requires the data be transmitted at least at the same rate it is intended to be played back at a client workstation and that the latency of the transmission not change significantly during the playback.

Streaming multimedia has many advantages over nonstreaming multimedia. Playback can be started very quickly. Storage space is not needed on the client, beyond a limited amount used to buffer the transmission against slight transmission delays. A streaming multimedia server can tailor the data it transmits to the available bandwidth and to the playback capabilities of the client workstation. Also, if a viewer changes his or her mind after the first few seconds and cancels the playback, the network has not wasted resources by downloading the entire file.

The two leading vendors in the Internet streaming multimedia market are RealNetworks and Microsoft. Both vendors' products provide protocols that attempt to enable the delivery of broadcast-quality multimedia over existing IP networks. According to RealNetworks, approximately 85 percent of Web pages serving streaming multimedia are using RealNetworks' servers. RealNetworks' newest high-end streaming media server software, RealSystem G2, builds on the company's existing audio and video compression technology. RealSystem G2 implements multiple formats for multimedia content, including Microsoft's Active Streaming Format, the proposed IETF standard Real-time Streaming Format, Synchronized Multimedia Integration Language (SMIL), and Apple's QuickTime. In April 1999, RealNetworks signed an agreement to acquire Xing Technology, a developer of MP3 digital audio software.

Version 3.0 of Microsoft's NetShow server offers several new technologies that bring it closer to RealNetworks' functionality. The NetShow Server was the first to offer on-the-fly scaling (Microsoft calls it intelligent streaming), which lets the video stream's frame rate and quality adjust dynamically to changing line conditions. When combined with Microsoft's newly redesigned Media Player, NetShow Server enables video watermarks, an advertising banner bar, and a title bar, which can be customized by the publisher— all potential branding opportunities for content providers. Two other features are NetShow Indexer, which can mark a media file so users can jump to predefined points using Media Player controls, and TAG author (the Temporal Annotation Generator from Digital Renaissance), which interleaves still images with streaming audio. RealNetworks' RealServer G2 offers a similar feature to TAG, which the company calls SmartStream.

MULTICASTING

Delivery of the same data to many recipients without sending it separately to each recipient—often called "multicasting"—has many uses that will be important to the growth of e-business.

Multicasting involves the broadcasting of a message from one host to many specific hosts in a one-to-many relationship. Multicast-capable routers are responsible for forwarding the transmission to all the networks (and only the networks) where someone has signed up to receive the multicast. (This setup contrasts with broadcasting, which sends a message to everyone on a network or network segment.) Thus, implementing multicast on the Internet requires changes to the router software. Today, most broadcast content on the Web actually is being sent separately to individual recipients, which does not make optimal use of network bandwidth.

"Today, most broadcast content on the Web actually is being sent separately to individual recipients, which does not make optimal use of network bandwidth."

Several protocols are being implemented for IP multicasting, including upgrades to IP itself. For example, some of the changes in IPv6 will support different forms of addressing for unicast (point-to-point communications—the majority of today's traffic), anycast (communications with the closest member of a device group), and multicast.

See the sidebar "IPv4 and IPv6" on page 188 for more information.

WEB BROWSERS

The desktop Web browser market is dominated by Microsoft's Internet Explorer (IE) and Netscape's Navigator. IE 5.0 was released for various Windows and UNIX platforms in March 1999, with a Macintosh release scheduled for mid-1999. IE 5.0 contains many usability enhancements such as a Search Assistant wizard to improve searching by inexperienced users, page-rendering speedups, and an AutoComplete tool that suggests ways to complete partially typed Web site names, and search queries based on intelligent analysis of previous user selections. IE 5.0 inaugurates XML support, including some integration with CSS. Perhaps most important for the enterprise, the Internet Explorer Administration Kit (IEAK) allows an administrator to control many aspects of browser configuration and appearance such as proxy servers, security settings, and default pages. Internet Explorer can be configured to check for updates to the central configuration, further reducing the support overhead.

AOL's (Netscape's) Communicator 4.5, the current version, already has some support for enterprise browser configuration management via the Mission Control Desktop application. Current feature descriptions for Seamonkey (the code name for Communicator 5.0) seem to focus on areas similar to IE 5.0: improved search and organization of information and better and faster page display. The current code base (used for both versions 4.5 and 5.0) contains support for displaying XML pages using CSS. AOL expects Communicator 5.0 to be released by mid-1999.

CLIENTS: MIME TYPES AND FILE TYPES

The HTTP protocol contains a field for specifying the MIME type associated with a file. MIME is an acronym for Multipurpose Internet Mail Extensions, an Internet e-mail standard that includes a scheme for classifying types of content (text, images, and so on). Clients receiving an HTTP message can inspect the MIME type and determine how to display, process, or manage the associated content.

All current browsers can interpret several formats natively, including plain ASCII text (to display within the browser's window), HTML text, and several common graphics file formats such as GIF and JPEG.

If the file format is not understood by the browser, the browser then will look to see whether an installed plug-in extension or helper application has registered this format as one that it supports; if so, the browser then launches the plug-in or helper and passes the data to it. If no plug-in or helper can process this data, the browser typically prompts the user with a dialog box that indicates the data cannot be understood. The dialog box presents the user with the choice to save the file onto disk or to cancel the request.

A plug-in application actually is an extension to the code of the Web browser itself; a helper application is a separate client-side program that can be launched by the Web browser. The first time a browser encounters a file type it cannot process, a user needs to download and install the appropriate plug-in or helper application; however, on subsequent interactions after downloading, the auxiliary program is invoked automatically from the browser.

Plug-in and helper application developers often distribute their client-side software at no charge; in some cases, a premium product for playback is sold relatively inexpensively. (The basic client is free because the developers' goal is to build market share by

See "Serving Multimedia Content" on page 200 for more information on streaming multimedia.

ensuring that as wide an audience as possible can understand their data.) Their revenue is derived from licensing the server-side application that creates data for the plug-in or helper. For example, a popular helper application is RealPlayer, a streaming-audio and streaming-video player freely available from RealNetworks that has become the de facto standard for transmitting voice, video clips, and music over the Internet. RealNetworks derives its revenue from several developer and server products, including the RealPublisher software to encode data into the format used by RealPlayer, and the RealServer, which runs as an optional service on HTTP servers and boosts the delivery performance of the streamed audio and video. Table 9 lists some common MIME types.

TABLE 9: COMMON MIME TYPES

MIME Type	Common File Suffix(es) for this Type	File Description/Plug-in or Helper Application
application/futuresplash	.spl	Shockwave Flash Object
application/octet-stream	.exe, .bin	Generic application/prompt user to save or run
application/pdf	.pdf	Acrobat file/Adobe Acrobat Reader
application/x-cdf	.cdf	Channel Definition File
application/x-x509-ca-cert	.crt	Security Certificate/browser
application/zip	.zip	Zip file/PKunzip, WinZip
audio/mid	.mid	MIDI file/audio player
audio/x-pn-realaudio	.ra	RealAudio file/multimedia player
image/gif	.gif	GIF image file/browser
image/jpeg	.jpg, .jpeg, .jpe	JPEG photograph/browser
message/rfc822	.eml	E-mail message/mail reader
text/html	.htm, .html	HTML file/browser
text/plain	.txt	Ordinary text/browser
video/mpeg	.mpeg	MPEG video file/multimedia player
video/quicktime	.mov	QuickTime video-file/multimedia player
video/x-ms-asf	.asf	Advanced Streaming Format/multimedia player

File Downloading. Internet activity includes the transfer of files without interpretation by the client. Files can be transferred using HTTP or the older File Transfer Protocol (FTP).

The manual process of downloading an installable file (usually compressed in some archive format), unpacking it, and running an installer, if any, is difficult for many users. The trend is to use special installers—plug-ins, helper applications, or full-blown custom clients—rather than leaving the details of downloading up to users.

E-Business Web Site Architectures

As e-business applications have become more sophisticated and the volume of transactions they handle has increased, the technology architecture of e-business Web sites has evolved, and will continue to do so. A key aspect of this evolution has been the movement away from the use of a single Web server to perform multiple functions, in favor of a more complex architecture with multiple servers, each playing a distinct role. Not only does this evolution provide the scalability needed for the e-business site to handle a larger workload, it also provides the transactional integrity, application reliability, and Web site fault-tolerance needed for e-business applications.

Figure 57 illustrates this concept by depicting the variety of servers that might be used in a high-end Web site to meet the requirement for higher transaction volumes and connectivity to external databases. The figure shows an HTTP server acting as the front end to the Web site, accepting incoming connections from Web browsers and routing them to other servers that handle specialized application logic (such as the personalization logic shown here) and manage transactions with an external database management system (DBMS).

FIGURE 57: SERVER ARCHITECTURE IN TRANSITION

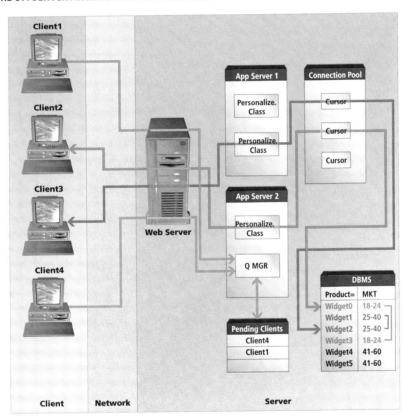

APPLICATION SERVERS AS MULTITIER ARCHITECTURES

The emerging e-business architecture—with a browser on the client, an HTTP server and a (possibly separate) application server, and a database server—is an extension to the three-tier architecture used in client/server computing.

In the classic three-tier model, a separate application server tier is interposed between the database server and the client. Centralizing application logic on a server (or a group of servers) eliminates the need to install and maintain it on all client PCs and tune them for performance, thus easing application deployment and management. Furthermore, because the application logic has been moved off the client, less processing power is required on the desktop. In addition, it is easier to support heterogeneous client devices (such as a mixture of Windows-based PCs and Macintoshes) because only a presentation layer needs to be present on the client. Application performance also can be improved by moving the execution of application logic from the database server onto separate application servers, which can be replicated for greater scalability.

In a typical e-business application, this classic three-tier model is modified in several ways. The client software typically is a browser, possibly enhanced by a helper application or downloadable applet (rather than an application-specific piece of client software permanently installed on the client machine). Therefore, heterogeneous client devices can be supported and the need for software to be installed and maintained on the clients eliminated. Also, if the client software is restricted to the browser itself (without the use of a helper application or downloadable applet), then only the presentation layer of our application runs on the client.

Second, the three-tier model has now been extended to a multitier model. In particular, there may be three (or more) types of servers used to operate the Web site, as illustrated in Figure 57 on page 203. These include the front-end HTTP server that accepts incoming connection requests, the Web application servers that execute various parts of the application logic, and the database servers used to manage the application's data.

> *"The requirement for an e-business application to access data from multiple existing sources and functionality from existing enterprise applications often leads to complex architectures."*

The use of multiple tiers of servers often is a consequence of the increasing heterogeneity of platforms used in corporate computing. Enterprise data may be stored in data repositories tied to mainframe applications as well as in a variety of different relational database management systems (RDBMSs). The requirement for an e-business application to access data from multiple existing sources and functionality from existing enterprise applications often leads to complex architectures. In the most complex e-business applications, multiple application servers may be accessing multiple database servers (sometimes running RDBMS products from different vendors) while being accessed by a variety of clients that might include dumb terminals, Web browsers running on a range of platforms, desktop PCs or UNIX workstations running client-specific software, mobile devices, and even other servers.

WEB APPLICATION SERVERS

Web application servers are products that enhance the basic HTTP server functionality with special-purpose features that make them better equipped to handle the requirements of transactional applications. They commonly are used to host the application logic of an e-business or other Web application, connecting on the one hand to the front-end HTTP server that handles incoming client connections and on the other hand to the back-end database that manages the application's data.

Web application servers typically provide the following set of interrelated features:

- *Transaction Processing (TP) monitor*—Manages the interaction between the application logic and an external DBMS in order to provide the so-called "ACID properties" necessary for reliable transactions (discussed below in detail).

- *Database connection pooling*—Improves application performance by managing a pool of threads on the database server to which application clients can connect, thus avoiding the overhead of creating a new thread for each client connection.

- *Load balancing*—Provides a mechanism for assigning incoming client requests to one of multiple application servers (typically whichever one is least heavily loaded at a given point in time).

- *Fault tolerance*—Provides for a particular client request to be reassigned from one server to another, in a way that is transparent to the user, if the first server fails because of hardware or software problems.

An application server is not the same thing as an e-business server, which refers to a Web server that provides prebuilt e-business functionality (such as catalog, shopping cart, payments, and customer service). An application server may be the platform on which an e-business server runs, but it generally does not include any e-business functionality out of the box, and the applications which it hosts are not necessarily e-business applications as defined in this book.

See "Commerce Platforms" on page 61 for more information on e-commerce servers.

Application servers provide well-tuned functional modules, resulting in faster response time for the kinds of high-transaction, fault-tolerant systems needed for e-business. In a typical e-business site, a single front-end HTTP server can call on multiple application servers that implement various parts of the site's application logic.

A large number of application server vendors had arisen in 1997 and early 1998, with each product fulfilling some specific roles but none covering all the bases. The end of 1998 saw a rapid consolidation of application server providers. AOL's acquisition of Netscape (which included an arrangement for Sun to control Netscape's server business, including application servers), BEA's acquisition of WebLogic, and Sun's acquisition of NetDynamics leaves only BEA, IBM, Microsoft, Oracle, and Sun/Netscape as all-around vendors of application servers, with a large field of smaller vendors (such as Bluestone, Intertop, and SilverStream) with less-comprehensive offerings looking for acquirers or other kinds of partnerships.

The application server performs several e-business functions simultaneously, as discussed below.

CONNECTIONS TO DBMSs

Initially, the Web was a mechanism for displaying static HTML pages—that is, pages that had been created with some sort of authoring tool and were stored in the Web server's file system. In this original model, the only information the Web server could present to the browser was one of these prebuilt pages.

However, developing an entire Web site that consists of static HTML pages is inefficient, particularly when many of the pages will be similar, and where the unique content of each page is best managed by a database rather than being stored as a static page image. (This situation is true particularly for an e-business site's catalog, where each catalog page displayed to the user will have a similar appearance, and where the catalog data itself is best stored in a database.) Furthermore, much of the information that needs to be incorporated into e-business Web pages is already stored in the databases used by other enterprise applications (such as an order-entry system), or needs to be "live" data that reflects ongoing changes (such as the level of inventory for a particular product). However, this functionality comes at a cost: Generating each page dynamically at the time it is displayed requires more processing power on the Web site than merely displaying static pages.

It did not take long for site developers to realize the benefits of allowing the Web server to access the data stored in RDBMSs and other applications. Initially, this access was accomplished through low-level mechanisms such as CGI. Today, Web servers (including application servers) typically include various interfaces that can access RDBMSs directly. For example, they can make ODBC calls, allowing them to access databases that include ODBC interfaces (a category including all the leading RDBMS products). The database may be running on the same hardware as the server itself or on a separate

See "Common Gateway Interface" on page 183 for more information on CGI.

database server accessible over a network. A new standard, Java Database Connectivity (JDBC), is designed to allow Java applications running on a server to access RDBMS servers directly. Some database vendors, such as Informix, Oracle, and Sybase, already are shipping JDBC drivers with their products, and the other major vendors are expected to follow suit. For example, Oracle features JDBC drivers in its Oracle8i DBMS (released in December 1998) and HiT Software announced direct JDBC connectivity to IBM's DB2 in January 1999.

Although it is possible to establish database connections directly from an HTTP server to a DBMS using these interfaces, it is not desirable to do so for any but the smallest e-business applications. Setting up a database connections involves significant processing overhead, and it is not feasible to do so for each HTTP message from a client. Instead, on sites with higher transaction levels, application servers that implement connection pooling typically are used to connect an e-business application to the DBMS.

In addition to performance, there are other reasons to host the HTTP server and the DBMS server on physically different machines. Having the database on a different server from the HTTP server—one that cannot be accessed directly from outside the organization's firewall—provides an additional layer of security to protect the integrity of the database. In some cases, the HTTP server physically may not even belong to the enterprise but reside on an ISP's premises. Furthermore, HTTP software is less reliable than DBMS software, and may cause the entire system to hang or need to be rebooted if it fails. Finally, because an HTTP server does not maintain state, it is far less critical to the enterprise, and recovery is easier than recovering a failed DBMS server.

APPLICATION SERVERS AS TP MONITORS

TP monitors are a type of middleware that provides transactional integrity and improve performance for high-performance applications. The DBMS connection-pooling provided by an application server (discussed previously) is part of the functionality of a classic TP monitor product (such as BEA's Tuxedo or IBM's CISC).

In addition to enhancing performance, TP monitors handle provide transactional integrity. A transaction is a sequence of computer operations—typically involving database reads and writes—all of which must be completed successfully to leave the database in a consistent state. A system that provides transactional integrity must guarantee what are called ACID properties, where the ACID acronym stands for atomicity, consistency, isolation, and durability.

- *Atomicity*—Means each transaction executes completely or not at all and leaves no partial results. This capability is true even after a system crash and recovery (part of the durability requirement). It also is true for concurrent transactions (a side effect of the isolation guarantee, explained later).

- *Consistency*—Means each completed transaction moves the system from one consistent state to another consistent state. For example, consider a consistency requirement that assets equal liabilities plus equity. Executing a transaction that records the purchase of a computer using a purchase order would violate the consistency requirement if only the increase in assets was recorded (for example, if the database server crashed at that stage in the operation); to guarantee consistency of the database, the corresponding increase in liabilities must be recorded or the increase in assets "rolled back" (that is, reversed).

- *Isolation*—Means each transaction executes as if it were running alone, even though transactions are run concurrently to improve performance. For example, if one transaction transfers money from one account to another, a different transaction is not allowed to view an intermediate result where one of the balances has changed but not the other. Such a transaction (viewing a result that was never true in fact) might make an improper decision. It might refuse credit to the account holder or even make a change to the data by fining the account holder for falling under a minimum total balance. Almost all DBMSs guarantee this isolation property by locking data items they access, following a paradigm known as two-phase locking.

- **Durability**—Means after a transaction is complete, the results that have been committed will not be lost because of a system or storage failure (processor or disk crash). As the DBMS makes updates to the database, it writes a transaction log (to a different storage medium than the database itself) that will allow it to undo those changes if the transaction should later fail for some reason (possibly because of a system crash) or to redo those changes in case the transaction succeeded without all the updates getting saved prior to the crash.

APPLICATION SERVERS AS DEVELOPMENT ENVIRONMENTS

It is becoming common for application servers to provide support for design, prototyping, development, testing, and deployment of applications. Indeed, differences between application server products in terms of which development facilities are built in and which third-party tools can be used is an important criterion enterprises use in determining which vendor's application server to adopt. The power of its application development facilities and the prevalence of Microsoft-platform programming skills have been attractive features of Windows NT-based servers.

The migration toward Java and component programming is one of the motivating factors for the tendency to add an application development environment to the server. Because they are created with an object-oriented language, Java applications gain considerable leverage from vendor-supplied class libraries or component frameworks. Enterprises standardizing on Java as a development language for e-business applications need Java development tools that work well with the component frameworks supplied by their application server vendor. It is this need for tools that work well with their frameworks that drives application server vendors to include development environments with their products. For example, development environments such as Bluestone's Sapphire/Web, IBM's Visual Age, Microsoft's Visual J++, and Oracle's AppBuilder are becoming integrated more tightly with those companies' application servers.

APPLICATION SERVERS AS MIDDLEWARE PLATFORMS AND OBJECT MANAGERS

Middleware is a generic term used to describe software that "sits in the middle" and connects different parts of an application. It includes several specific types of products. In addition to DBMS access and TP monitor middleware, these groups include the following:

- **Remote procedure calls (RPCs)**—Allow an application running on one computer system to call a procedure that executes on another system in a synchronous fashion. The RPC middleware provides an API the programmer uses to initiate and respond to the procedure call in the client and server applications; run-time RPC code provided by the middleware vendor manages the details of transferring the calls across the network.

- **Message-oriented middleware (MOM)**—Provides interapplication communication, typically on an asynchronous basis, using message queues. The MOM software provides an API the programmer uses to submit messages to the queue and receive them from the queue in the client and server applications; then at run

"Differences between application server products in terms of which development facilities are built in and which third-party tools can be used is an important criterion enterprises use in determining which vendor's application server to adopt."

time, it manages the details of ensuring reliable delivery as the messages are transferred between the applications.

- **_Distributed object middleware_**—Extends the basic model of object-oriented programming, where self-contained objects send messages to each other to invoke services, by allowing objects to be used across a network of distributed systems.

Both RPC and MOM middleware can be used to connect different applications running on the same computer system (which is how this software originally was used) or running on separate systems connected by a network.

Existing middleware vendors are transitioning into the application server marketplace. For example, BEA's M3 product combines a Java-based object request broker (ORB) with a TP monitor based on its Tuxedo product. Released in June 1998, M3 implements Enterprise JavaBeans, the Java Transaction Service, and the Java Transaction API. It is designed for building distributed applications for the enterprise in Java. In addition, BEA's late-1998 acquisition of WebLogic, a supplier of Java application servers, cemented its commitment to the application server arena.

XML and Middleware. One of XML's many promises is generating middleware interchange languages that would create a standardized way of describing the application and data interfaces provided by middleware products. Because XML is a meta language, new XML-based languages for a broad variety of middleware applications are easy to imagine. It is important to understand, however, that XML in itself does not provide any middleware functionality but only gives developers a consistent method for describing the interfaces and data on which the middleware software is acting.

See "XML" on page 195 for more information.

In January 1999, Bluestone announced extensive support for XML in its Sapphire/Universal Business Server and Developer products. Developer provides facilities for defining XML DTDs either statically or dynamically. Then, DTDs are deployed in what Bluestone calls content generators, which can map data on interchange and display formats.

Other application server vendors are developing middleware for use with XML. For example, Object Design's announcement of its XML-based Excelon data server in November 1998 is part of its new XML infrastructure, which allows XML data to be stored in a middleware cache where the company says it can be manipulated more fully than in a relational database.

Security

Security is critical because it provides the technologies, policies, and infrastructure that permit e-business transactions between parties (who may not have a preexisting business relationship) to occur over a global public network with confidence that the parties are who they claim to be, and that the contents of the transaction have not been intercepted or altered.

The field of security is a tradeoff between protection on the one hand and functionality, performance, and ease-of-use on the other hand. Making a system more secure inevitably slows performance and makes it harder to accomplish some tasks. In an e-business context, there also is a tradeoff between security (especially authentication) and privacy. However, without the protection offered by security, many individuals and companies would not transact business over the Web.

It is difficult to cover the broad field of security in sufficient detail in a single section of a chapter. Therefore, a detailed discussion of security topics such as firewalls, gateways, and bastion networks has not been attempted here. (See the *Technology Forecast* for full coverage of these topics.)

SECURITY REQUIREMENTS FOR E-BUSINESS

Security technology is called upon to perform several functions in e-business transactions: authentication, confidentiality, secure delivery, privacy, and nonrepudiation.

Customer Authentication. The merchant needs to establish that customers are who they say they are, at least in the sense that they are authorized to approve purchases. For example, if a customer uses a credit-card number, the merchant needs to establish that the customer is an authorized user of the card.

Merchant Authentication. The customer needs to establish that merchants are who they say they are.

Confidentiality and Secure Delivery. The main confidentiality concerns in e-business, as in other business interactions, focus on what the vendor or merchant does with customer information once it is provided and how the system protects confidential information. Proper use of confidential data is more important (and more difficult) than simply encrypting information as it crosses networks.

In addition, the customer and the merchant need to ensure that private information (merchant prices, customer credit-card numbers, and so on) can be transferred securely from one to the other. Each party needs to be certain the information will not be intercepted, viewed, or maliciously tampered with.

Mutual Privacy. The customer and merchant need to ensure private information will remain private once it arrives at its destination. Credit-card numbers and other customer information need to be stored securely at the merchant's site, and the customer and merchant need to agree on how the merchant is allowed to use the information. Merchants and customers need to agree on how merchant information such as prices and availabilities will be used by the customer, including situations where the customer is a software agent or robot.

Security technologies offer an electronic means—digital signatures—to verify that each party agreed to whatever arrangements are adopted. It is possible to use SET to accomplish a transaction without revealing certain information (such as credit-card numbers) to the merchant.

Nonrepudiation. The customer and merchant need to be certain neither party can repudiate an agreement once it is agreed to. Security technologies can prevent parties to an agreement from claiming they were not the ones who signed the agreement. Nonperformance of an agreement still needs to be handled by the legal system.

AUTHENTICATION

Authentication means establishing an association between an interaction or message and a person (or, more properly, a "principal" because authentications increasingly will involve agents or other proxies as well as human users, and frequently, it is not the particular user but an institutional capability that is implied in an authentication).

Authentication methods are based on something users know (such as a password), something users have (such as security tokens or smart cards), or something users are (biometrics). Two-factor authentication—using two of the foregoing methods—provides a higher level of security than simple authentication and is gaining ground rapidly

See "Secure Sockets Layer" on page 145 for more information on authentication.

within the corporate world. In general, the sophistication of the authentication process should be related directly to the level of business risk associated with an unauthorized disclosure or modification of the data being protected.

CONFIDENTIALITY

Confidentiality ensures the privacy of a transaction or message. The credit-card information that authenticates a purchase over the Internet must be concealed from third parties during transmission and while in storage on the merchant sites.

Confidentiality on computer systems normally is obtained by restricting access to the data, and requiring some form of authentication for access. Confidentiality over public networks is obtained by encrypting the data.

An encryption algorithm transforms plain text into a coded equivalent, known as the cipher text, for transmission or storage. The coded text subsequently is decoded (decrypted) at the receiving end and restored to plain text. The encryption algorithm uses a key, which is a binary number typically from 40 to 128 bits in length for symmetric (single-key) systems or 512 to 2,048 bits or more for asymmetric (public-key) systems. The data is "locked" for sending by using the bits in the key to transform the data bits mathematically. At the receiving end, the key is used to unscramble the data, restoring it to its original form.

The effort required to decode the unusable scrambled bits into the original data without knowledge of the key—known as "breaking" or "cracking" the encryption—typically is a function of the complexity of the algorithm and the length of the keys. The longer the key, the harder it is to decode the encrypted message through "brute force" (that is, by trying each possible password until the proper one is found).

Two types of algorithms are in use today: shared single-key (also known as "secret-key" or symmetric-key) and public-key (or asymmetric-key).

Shared Single-Key. In the shared single-key method, the same key is used to encrypt and decrypt the message. However, this method requires that the sender and recipient both have the same key and that no one else does. Transmitting the key over the same insecure channel as the encrypted message is not acceptable, so a secure out-of-band communications method is required. (Even more critical to such an exchange is a pre-existing relationship between the two parties that creates a secure context within which the secret-key can be exchanged.) Moreover, each pair of parties requires a unique key. The number of keys increases rapidly as the number of transactors grows.

"Out-of-band" refers to the part of a communication sent by a separate and independent channel from that used for the rest of the communication.

The most commonly used symmetric-key algorithms are the Data Encryption Standard (DES), the International Data Encryption Algorithm (IDEA), or Triple-DES.

Public-Key. Public-key encryption is based on two keys: one to encrypt the message and another to decrypt it. The algorithm is not symmetric, so knowing the public encryption key is no help in being able to decrypt a message (thus, this technique sometimes is referred to as asymmetric-key). Users wanting to receive confidential information can freely announce their public key, which then is used by the sender to encrypt data to be sent to them. (Typically, public keys are stored in a publicly accessible standardized directory.) The data can be decrypted only by the holder of the corresponding private key.

One great advantage of a public-key over a private-key algorithm is that using a public-key algorithm eliminates the complexity of handling the large number of secret-key pairs needed for single-key algorithms; however, it requires a process to ensure the public keys are authentic and really belong to their announced owner. The problem of managing a large number of public keys and making them widely available (yet easily revoked by their owners' certificate issuers if the corresponding private-key has been compromised) is the primary challenge that needs to be addressed.

Despite these drawbacks, interest in and use of key cryptography continues to grow rapidly because of its potential to facilitate electronic commerce using the Internet, in particular because it does not require an out-of-band process for secure exchange of private keys before sending encrypted messages.

The most commonly used public-key mathematical algorithm, which is based on the difficulty of factoring large numbers, was invented by Ron Rivest, Adi Shamir, and Leonard Adelman at MIT and published in 1978. This algorithm, known as RSA (for its inventors), is covered by a patent in the U.S. that expires in the year 2000.

A specific assessment of the security of 512-bit RSA keys shows that in 1998, a single key could be cracked for less than $1 million in cost and 8 months of effort. With the advent of new factoring algorithms and distributed computing, 512-bit keys no longer provide sufficient security and should not be used. Starting in 1999, RSADSI's recommended key sizes are 768 bits for personal use; 1,024 bits for corporate use; and 2,048 bits for extremely valuable keys such as the key of a certification authority. RSADSI expects a 768-bit key to be secure until the year 2004. Recommended key length schedules are published on RSADSI's Web site on a regular basis.

One drawback of public-key algorithms is that they are considerably slower to execute than symmetric-key algorithms. Therefore, a document often is encrypted with a symmetric-key algorithm using a randomly generated symmetric-key. The encrypted document then is "hashed," producing a unique signature from the document, which is much smaller than the document.

"Interest in and the use of key cryptography continues to grow rapidly because of its potential to facilitate electronic commerce using the Internet."

DIGITAL SIGNATURES

Digital signatures allow the receiver of a digitally signed electronic message to authenticate the sender and verify the integrity of the message. Most important, digital signatures are difficult to counterfeit and easy to verify, making them superior even to handwritten signatures.

A digital signature is established by creating a message digest of an electronic communication, which then is encrypted with the sender's private key using a asymmetric encryption (a public-key algorithm). (A message digest is a condensed text string distilled from the contents of a text message.)

A recipient who has the sender's public key can verify that the digest was encrypted using the corresponding private key and thus determine whether the communication has been altered since the digest was generated.

Because the public-key encryption algorithm ensures that only the public key can decrypt a digest encrypted with the corresponding private key, this process establishes that only the holder of the private key could have created the digitally signed message.

Digital signatures by themselves do not provide functions such as nonrepudiation. They merely prove that a given message came from the holder of a given private key—not even that the holder of the key is who he or she purports to be. Proof that the signer of the message really is who he or she claims to be is supplied by a certification authority, which checks the credentials of the key holder before signing the holder's public key with the certification authority's certificate.

Secure hash functions most often are used to produce the message digest. It is computation-

ally (or at least economically) infeasible for an attacker to find modifications to the input data that would generate a hash value identical to the original. Therefore, if someone sends a file and a hash value generated from the file, and if the recipient runs the same hash algorithm and gets the same result, both parties can be nearly certain the file was received intact.

Examples of a secure hash function include MD5 and SHA-1. MD5 is a public-domain standard for generating 128-bit cryptographic checksums. SHA-1 is a hashing function for generating 160-bit cryptographic checksums. Developed as part of the Digital Signature Standard (DSS) by the U.S. Department of Commerce and the National Institute of Standards and Technology, SHA-1 performs an advanced form of a checksum on all data received. ■

Both the symmetric key and the hash then are encrypted with the sender's private key and the recipient's public key in a digital envelope. The message and envelope then are sent. Although this approach is complex, it ensures the following:

- The quicker symmetric-key algorithm is used for the bulk of the encryption

- The shared secret, the symmetric key itself, is transmitted securely using public-key encryption

- The message could have been encrypted only by the sender using the sender's private key because it can be decrypted with the sender's public key

- The message can be decrypted only by the recipient (because it was encrypted using the recipient's public key and thus can be decrypted only with the recipient's private key)

- Sending the hash verifies the message has not been tampered with, otherwise a different hash result will be produced when the hash algorithm is run on the decrypted message

INTEGRITY

Ensuring data integrity protects transactions or messages from being altered or destroyed, either maliciously (as the result of a third-party or a dishonest first or second party) or by accident.

See the sidebar "Digital Signatures" on page 211 for more about secure hash algorithms.

The essential technique for ensuring data integrity is to compute a "checksum" by performing a mathematical operation on the data that produces a result that meets several criteria: It must be computed uniquely from the data (so that if the data are modified, the result will be different); irreversible (so that the data cannot be reconstituted from the code); and reproducible (so that any time the same computation is performed on the data the same result is achieved). This process is performed by a secure hashing algorithm such as Secure Hash Algorithm-1 (SHA-1) or Message Digest 5 (MD5).

THE CHANGING ENTERPRISE SECURITY PICTURE

Until recently, security in the enterprise has been a matter of thoroughly executing on rather basic techniques and precautions. In an e-business world, this picture needs to change. E-business requires that enterprises provide access to their systems not only to employees but to suppliers, customers, and everyone that they do, or potentially do, business with. This access also allows competitors possible access to the enterprise's information—a concern that must be considered. Two aspects of security in particular stand out as candidates for rapid change:

- *Public-key infrastructure (PKI)*—An infrastructure is required because every user of public-key cryptography has a key that is freely distributed, and storage of these keys is a major problem. A PKI provides the means by which public keys can be managed on a secure basis for use by widely distributed users or systems.

- *Networking security*—Allowing secure communications to take place over the Internet requires rapid development of solutions for securing public IP-network traffic, including VPNs.

Public-Key Infrastructure. A PKI is the underlying technical and institutional framework that allows public-key encryption technology to be deployed widely. Such services are provided by government agencies (postal authorities), by technology providers such as GTE or VeriSign (a spinoff of RSADSI), by service providers using a product such as Nortel's Entrust, or by a third party such as a financial service provider with an established network and a reputation for trustworthiness. A financial services provider such as a bank could underwrite any identity certificates that it issues (just like a credit card), thereby making financial transactions more attractive to end users and merchants. Supported applications could include secure e-mail, payment protocols, electronic checks, EDI, IP network security (IPSec), electronic forms, and digitally signed documents. Products currently are available from a variety of vendors, including Entrust, GTE, Motorola, and VeriSign.

Integral to a PKI are a means of authentication and encryption, secure directory services, secure interoperation of directory servers and client access to directories, and the Simple Distributed Security Infrastructure (SDSI, a system that uses public-key cryptography combined with mechanisms for defining groups and group membership certificates).

A PKI is designed to solve the problem of trustworthiness. Who will vouch in a trustworthy fashion that a public key claimed to belong to A in fact belongs to A? Or, who will vouch for A's assertion that his key represents authorization from some corporate or government entity?

Certification Authorities. Certification authorities address the PKI problem by supplying authentication as a service from a trusted third party. The certification authority vouches for the authenticity of a public key either by storing it in a centralized, online database or by distributing it with a certificate, which is basically a copy of the user's public key that has been digitally signed by the certification authority. An enterprise may operate its own certification authority.

A certificate is similar to an identity card with a notary seal on it. It is valid for a stated period of time and is subject to cancellation by being included on a certificate revocation list (CRL). CRLs basically are "hot lists" that identify certificates that have been withdrawn, canceled, or compromised or that should not be trusted for other specified reasons.

Commercial certification authorities such as Deutsche Telekom, Entrust, GTE, IBM, and VeriSign are endeavoring to fill the need for certification authority services in electronic commerce. VeriSign, for example, issues and manages several levels of digital IDs, differentiated by the level of assurance or trust associated with the ID. The assurance level typically is dependent on the level of diligence the certification authority applies to establishing the relationship between an individual or entity and its public key. VeriSign and other vendors already have begun to issue "branded" certificates on behalf of banks and other companies and institutions. For example, VeriSign provided its E-Commerce Solutions and Global Server IDs to the Sumitomo Bank, which then issued its own branded certificates to its Internet banking customers worldwide in June 1998.

One question customers ask about commercial certification authorities is how trustworthy they are. There has been some tendency for governmental authorities to step into the certification authority role. Some postal authorities outside the U.S. are assuming the role of certification authority. Canada, for example, is in the process of establishing a national PKI. The U.K. is in the process of establishing a national certification authority with the help of VeriSign, as is France. However, other countries, such as Japan and South Korea, are opening the certification authority market to private industry, much in the same model as the U.S.

Banks have weighed in as certification authorities as well. Eight global financial institutions (ABN AMRO, Bank of America, Bankers Trust, Barclays, Chase Manhattan, Citibank, Deutsche Bank, and HypoVereinsbank) formed a certification authority services provider called Global Trust Enterprises in December 1998. Global Trust Enterprise expects to have offerings in place by late 1999 and will use CertCo's PKI technology.

The American Bar Association (ABA) also has taken a keen interest in certification authorities. In June 1998, the ABA's Information Security Committee met to discuss its 100-page Certificate Authority Evaluation Guidelines, the first step in defining what a certification authority is and does. The document seeks to define the issues of trust in a certification authority. The ABA is working with international groups such as the European Union (EU) and the United Nations Commission on International Trade Law to reach international agreement on the legal implications of a certification authority. Within a X.509 directory record, the lawyers want to place a stamp or a URL link guaranteeing that the certification authority certifying that public key has been audited and approved. To receive the stamp, a certification authority will have to pass a Statement of Auditing Standards Evaluation. The ABA, through a third-party company such as Science Applications International Corp. (SAIC), proposes to look at areas such as key retention, what constitutes trustworthy personnel, how users should protect their private keys, what types of notices and disclosures should be in place, and methodologies for identification. VeriSign, for example, already has met the ABA's criteria.

A general shortcoming of the certification authority business model is that enterprise certificate users increasingly want to issue and manage their own certificates. PKI product vendors such as Baltimore Technologies, Entrust, and Xcert International already are entering the enterprise certification authority market, but they must overcome a perception that their offerings are too complex. (Baltimore Technologies was acquired by Zergo Holdings in January 1999; the new company operates under the Baltimore name.) On the other hand, certification authority service providers such as GTE and VeriSign have reacted to enterprise reluctance to outsource PKI completely by offering comanaged PKI solutions.

SECURE EXTRANET SERVICES OVER THE INTERNET

A VPN is a wide area communications network operated by a common carrier that provides what appears to be dedicated lines when used, but that actually consists of backbone trunks shared among all customers in a public network. Essentially, a VPN allows a private network to be configured within a public network.

"The relentless demands that encryption/decryption in real time place on processor cycles implies that hardware solutions will be attractive alternatives to software solutions."

With increasing use of the Internet has come rising interest in using the Internet for private network functions. Currently, four standards are being used: IPSec, Point-to-Point Tunneling Protocol (PPTP), Layer 2 Forwarding (L2F), and Layer 2 Tunneling Protocol (L2TP). IPSec was posted as an Internet Draft by IETF in November 1998, and another round of draft specifications is expected to be released by IETF's IPSec Working Group in 1999.

VPN products and services became hot news in late 1998. A variety of vendors appeared, and many firewall or other server products were repositioned with VPN capability. The relentless demands that encryption/decryption in real time place on processor cycles implies that hardware solutions such as VPN-capable routers and switches or cryptography accelerators (add-in boards with cryptographic coprocessors) will be attractive alternatives to software solutions. In January 1999, for example, Cisco Systems announced a suite of VPN-capable products by enhancing its IOS operating system for VPN support, adding IPSec accelerators to its high-end router lines, and adding VPN service-level agreement monitoring services.

However, putting VPN encryption functionality on routers or switches can create bottlenecks in those devices and limit their ability to handle increased traffic. An alternative way to create scalable VPNs may be to continue to use separate devices for encryption.

On the service front, GTE Internetworking announced its VPN Advantage service in December 1998. Using IPSec, VPN Advantage will offer PKI support for device and user authentication and built-in service-level guarantees of 99.9 percent availability and roundtrip latencies of 125 milliseconds or less for dedicated VPNs. AT&T, IXC Communications, MCI WorldCom's UUNet Technologies, and Qwest Communications all have announced plans to offer Internet-based VPN services some time in 1999.

For companies that require a secure operating environment across a globally distributed network, a new architecture comes from TriStrata Security Systems. A central security server authenticates users and provides them with single-use shared private keys for encryption of all data transmissions, including messages, documents, and multimedia. The encryption method relies on the Vernam cipher, an extremely fast technique. The current version of its product is capable of encrypting 50Mbps on a 200MHz Pentium Pro. The TriStrata Enterprise Security Server (TESS) can issue "permits" containing the access signatures at 2,000 transactions per second on a comparable machine. This low overhead makes it practical to grant each individual user's access to any given block of data from a TESS at the time of decryption by connecting to the TESS over a network. This setup allows centralized control and instant revocation of any user's access to any given data, a feature not available in other security architectures.

Advantages of the TriStrata architecture include self-escrowing of keys, secure logging of all access signature uses anywhere in the network, replication of TESS servers for scalability, and fast, strong encryption of all communication, built into the operating system at the most fundamental level, namely, the device drivers. One disadvantage of the system is the size of the pads used to generate keys, which makes distribution and storage of them problematic for small-memory-capacity devices such as smart cards. Version 2.0 of the TESS suite, composed of the Windows NT-based TriStrata Secure Operating System and TESS (implemented using Windows NT, secure e-mail, Document Security System [DSS], and the API toolkit), began shipping in June 1998, adding capabilities such as router control and video stream encryption. Pricewaterhouse-Coopers is TriStrata's first implementation partner.

Market Overview

This section devotes particular attention to the speed with which users connect to the Internet because that will be an increasingly important determinant of their ability to participate in e-business transactions. (See the *Technology Forecast* for market overviews on other technologies and market share data on their respective vendors.)

ENTERPRISE INTERNET CONNECTIONS

According to IDC, 53 percent of corporate Internet access in 1997 was via 28.8K and 56K dial-up modems as compared with 32.5 percent in 1998. This situation represents a shift in 1998 toward leased line, Integrated Services Digital Network (ISDN), and Frame Relay, in that order. (See Figure 58 on page 216.) (Note that the 1997 IDC data mixed basic-rate ISDN and primary-rate ISDN together, blurring an important distinction.) This shift also reflects a change from individual or small-scale access solutions to enterprise-wide or location-wide solutions.

CONSUMER AND SMALL-TO-MIDSIZED ENTERPRISE INTERNET CONNECTIONS

Consumer Internet connection technologies also are changing rapidly. Table 10 on page 216 projects which technologies consumers use and will use for Internet access. Broadband access—cable modem, digital subscriber line (xDSL), and satellite—will grow rapidly but will not affect the basic scenario of consumers predominantly using dial-up analog modems for Internet access (although they will migrate to 56K modems

FIGURE 58: REPRESENTATIVE INTERNET ACCESS TECHNOLOGIES FOR U.S. ENTERPRISES: 1998

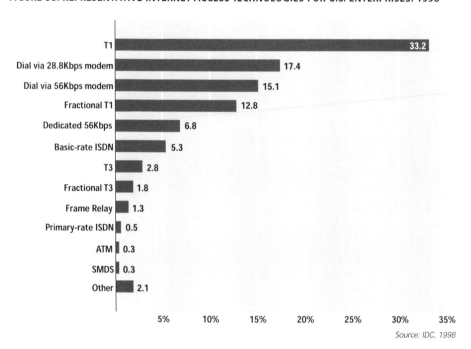

Source: IDC, 1998

during the forecast period). Active e-business customers will be heavily over-repre-sented in the ranks of the higher-speed access technologies because they are the most likely to purchase high-speed access.

TABLE 10: WORLDWIDE INSTALLED BASE OF HOME-BASED INTERNET CONNECTIVITY METHODS

Technology	1998		1999		2000		2001		2002	
	Installed Base (in millions)	Market Share	Installed Base (in millions)	Market Share	Installed Base (in millions)	Market Share	Installed Base (in millions)	Market Share	Installed Base (in millions)	Market Share
Analog modem	55.39	90.8%	69.39	85.7%	79.53	79.5%	87.56	73%	93.53	66.8%
Cable modem	0.57	0.9%	2.12	2.6%	4.25	4.3%	7.26	6.1%	10.76	7.7%
xDSL	0.05	0.1%	0.35	0.4%	1.10	1.1%	3.10	2.6%	6.20	4.4%
ISDN	4.89	8.0%	8.99	11.1%	14.87	14.9%	21.53	17.9%	28.61	20.4%
Wireless data	0.10	0.2%	0.15	0.2%	0.25	0.3%	0.55	0.5%	0.90	0.6%
TOTALS	61	100%	81	100%	100	100%	120	100%	140	100%

Source: IDC, 1999

Note that the data in Table 10 relates only to home PCs with Internet or remote access connectivity. It indicates analog modems will remain the easiest and most pervasive method of home PC connectivity. Large capital investments to upgrade the cable infra-structure will result in high growth of cable modem sales. xDSL sales to the home will lag cable modem sales, particularly between 1999–2000, due to slow rollouts by incumbent carriers.

Strong growth is expected for ISDN, cable modems, and xDSL during the forecast period. The ISDN projections in Table 10 are somewhat surprising from a U.S. stand-point, where ISDN is being eclipsed rapidly by broadband technologies. The ISDN projections reflect IDC's analysis of rapid ISDN growth in Western Europe and Japan. Wireless data remains a niche solution but is likely to grow steadily due to the introduction of new data services in GSM networks from 1999 onwards. Analog modems remain the dominant solution in terms of installed base and throughout the forecast period.

The cable modem has a cost advantage over xDSL technologies in the consumer marketplace, where cable plant is widespread (although xDSL service prices have been dropping in early 1999). The adoption of the Data Over Cable Service Interface Specification (DOCSIS), which permits interoperation of competing cable modem products, is expected to increase cable modem deployments quickly.

Various forms of xDSL technology can provide high-speed service (more than 100 times faster than today's analog modems) using existing copper lines. These asymmetric xDSL technologies incorporate tradeoffs between the length of the loop and the speed of service. Distance limitations of around 12,000 feet between customers and central offices make xDSL most viable in metropolitan areas or in densely populated countries.

DirecPC from Hughes offers satellite-based Internet access and data delivery service at 400Kbps downstream. Upstream access by users is via modem or other landline connection through their ISPs. At least two satellite-based broadband data systems—Sky-Bridge and Teledesic—are in the deployment stage. Both systems have an asymmetric bandwidth similar to Asymmetric Digital Subscriber Line (ADSL) and cable modems, where a much higher rate is available going to the subscriber than coming back from the subscriber, although Teledesic will have a fully symmetrical option with a special broadband terminal. Neither of these systems is scheduled to be operational before 2001.

Terrestrial wireless services such as Multichannel Multipoint Distribution Service (MMDS) and Local Multipoint Distribution Service (LMDS) have some promise as technologies for consumer and small to midsized enterprises (SME) Internet access, but thus far they show negligible market penetration. MMDS is used primarily for video distribution, and widespread LMDS service offerings are not expected before late 1999. Both technologies need a "line of sight" path from transmitter to receiver and have limited transmission ranges (particularly LMDS).

It is too soon to say which of the broadband technologies will dominate in the consumer arena. Some analysts suggest that each technology will find a niche or niches where it best serves market needs.

WEB BROWSERS

Microsoft has gained near market-share parity with Netscape. According to Zona Research, Netscape's share of the browser market has dropped from a high of 87 percent in April 1996 to 54 percent in July 1998, while Microsoft has grown from 2 percent market share to 45 percent during the same period.

In the enterprise, Zona surveys indicate 60 percent of browsers were a Netscape product as of 1998. The 63 percent of survey respondents who had a corporate browser policy were split fairly evenly between Netscape and Microsoft.

REFERENCES

ARTICLES

World Wide Web Consortium. Web security: a matter of trust. *World Wide Web Journal.* Summer 1997. (Special issue).

PERIODICALS, INDUSTRY AND TECHNICAL REPORTS

Acly, Ed. *Businessware market makers: past, present, and future.* IDC. July 1998.

Acly, Ed. *Businessware: uniting the business to deliver greater customer value.* IDC. December 1998.

Acly, Ed. *IBM fortifies its WebSphere product family: a simpler message promises a more powerful solution.* IDC. October 1998.

Acly, Ed. *Level 8 focuses on its Microsoft partnership: opening windows of opportunity for a Win-Win relationship.* IDC. September 1998.

Acly, Ed. *Middleware: 1998 worldwide markets and trends.* IDC. May 1998.

Acly, Ed. *WebLogic acquired by BEA Systems: a Web application server converges with distributed transaction processing middleware.* IDC. November 1998.

Chaki, Abhi. *Consumer broadband market: five-year outlook.* Jupiter Communications. January 1999.

Christiansen, Chris and Roseann Day. *Adoption of information security technology in the enterprise.* IDC. August 1998.

Dahlquist, Katrina and Randy Giusto. *Beyond today's boundaries: the evolving portable PC platform.* IDC. October 1998.

Germanow, Abner H. and Roseann Day. *Encryption software: market and trends.* IDC. December 1998.

Germanow, Abner H. and Chris Christiansen. *The 1998 Internet security survey.* IDC. December 1998.

Graham, Stephen D. and Michael O'Neil. *Partnering on the electronic frontier: staking your ground in e-commerce.* IDC. November 1998.

Grant, Gail. *Internet business models.* CommerceNet (Research Report 98-26). November 1998.

House, Jill, Randy Giusto, and Diana Hwang. *Jupiter: not for many moons.* IDC. November 1998.

Hwang, Diana, Jill House, and Randy Giusto. *Biweekly update: December 21, 1998/January 4, 1999.* IDC. January 1999.

Hwang, Diana, et al. *It's a small, small world: worldwide smart hand-held devices market review and forecast, 1998–2002.* IDC. November 1998.

Hwang, Diana. *Technology road map of smart hand-held devices.* IDC. June 1998.

IEEE Internet Computing (bimonthly). IEEE Computer Society.

Llewellyn, Gareth. *What is a trusted third party anyway?* CommerceNet (Information Bulletin 98-23). November 1998.

Machefsy, Ira. *A total economic impact analysis of two PKI vendors: Entrust and VeriSign.* Giga Information Group. September 1998.

Mason, R. Paul, et al. *Internet infrastructure software: 1997–2002.* IDC. December 1998.

McAteer, Seamus. *Internet appliances: non-PC access devices ride Internet standards wave.* Jupiter Communications. October 1998.

McClure, Steve. *Is JINI genius or just Java RMI au jus?* IDC. September 1998.

Oleson, Thomas D. *What emerging technologies warrant IS attention today?* IDC. September 1998.

Owen, Eric and Melanie Posey. *Impact of the Internet on corporate WANs in Europe and the U.S.* IDC. May 1998.

Pang, Albert, et al. *Sun scores big: an analysis of the AOL/Netscape and Sun alliance.* IDC. December 1998.

Peterson, William, Jean S. Bozman, and Dan Kusnetzky. *Operating environments review and forecast, 1997–2002.* IDC. December 1998.

Posey, Melanie. *Frame Relay market share assessment and forecast, 1997–2002.* IDC. December 1998.

Posey, Melanie. *1998 WAN manager survey.* IDC. November 1998.

Randolph, Bob and Ed Acly. *Transaction processing software: 1998 worldwide markets and trends.* IDC. June 1998.

Sheppard, Gregory. *Modem and remote access system semiconductors and application markets.* Dataquest. September 1998.

World Intellectual Property Organization. *The management of Internet names and addresses: intellectual property issues.* WIPO Interim Report. December 1998.

BOOKS

Dowd, Kevin. *Getting connected: the Internet at 56K and up.* Sebastopol, Calif.: O'Reilly. 1996.

Ghosh, Anup K. *E-commerce security: weak links, best defenses.* New York: John Wiley & Sons. 1998.

Grant, Gail L. *Understanding digital signatures.* New York: McGraw-Hill. 1998.

Minoli, Daniel and Emma Minoli. *Web commerce technology handbook.* New York: McGraw-Hill. 1997.

Naik, Dilip. *Internet standards and protocols: the professional desktop reference.* Redmond, Wash.: Microsoft Press. 1998.

Oppliger, Rolf. *Internet and intranet security.* Boston: Artech House. 1998.

Orfali, Robert, Dan Harkey, and Jeri Edwards. *Client/server survival guide.* New York: John Wiley & Sons. 1999.

Orfali, Robert, Dan Harkey, and Jeri Edwards. *The essential distributed objects survival guide.* New York: John Wiley & Sons. 1995.

URLs OF SELECTED MENTIONED COMPANIES AND ORGANIZATIONS

American Bar Association www.abanet.org

American National Standards Institute www.ansi.org

AT&T Bell Labs portal.research.bell-labs.com/geninfo/

BEA/WebLogic weblogic.beasys.com

Comprehensive Perl Archive Network www.perl.com/CPAN

Critical Path www.cp.net

Ebizmart (division of CPU Micromart) www.ebizmart.com

Generic Top Level Domain Memorandum of Understanding www.gtld-mou.org

International Ad Hoc Committee www.IAHC.org

Internet Architecture Board www.iab.org

Internet Assigned Numbers Authority www.iana.org

Internet Engineering Steering Group www.ietf.org/iesg.html

Internet Engineering Task Force www.ietf.org

Internet Research Task Force www.irtf.org

Internet Society www.isoc.org

IXC Communications www.ixc-comm.com

National Center for Supercomputing Applications www.ncsa.uiuc.edu

National Science Foundation www.nsf.gov

Network Solutions Inc. www.networksolutions.com

Netcraft Ltd. www.netcraft.com

Open Source Initiative opensource.org

The Risks Digest catless.ncl.ac.uk/risks

World Intellectual Property Organization www.wipo.int

World Wide Web Consortium www.w3.org

E-BUSINESS OVERVIEW	4	Charles Schwab's Online Accounts and Trades Completed
	4	E*Trade's Online Accounts and Trades Completed
	10	Users and Devices on the Web Worldwide
	11	The European Online Population
	11	PCs Connected to the Internet Worldwide
	12	Japanese Online Service Penetration: 1996–2000
	14	Japanese Internet Commerce Market: 1996–2002
	14	Worldwide Commerce on the Web
	15	Global versus U.S. Internet Commerce
	16	U.S. Business-to-Business Internet Commerce Revenue by Industry
	16	Growth in Internet Host Computers and Major E-Commerce Developments
	17	Worldwide Business-to-Business E-Business Revenue
	18	Worldwide Business-to-Consumer E-Business Revenue
	21	The Internet Makes the World Smaller
	24	Customer E-Mail Response Architecture
E-BUSINESS ENABLING TECHNOLOGIES	52	Overview of a Basic Internet E-Business Architecture
	53	Overview of a Multitier Internet E-Business Architecture
	60	How Taxware's Sales Tax Software Interfaces with the Commerce Server
	62	IBM's Net.Commerce Products
	64	Microsoft's Commerce Server Structure and Components
	65	Oracle's Internet Commerce Server
	67	BroadVision's One-to-One Commerce
	69	Inex's Commerce Court
	70	Intershop's Merchant Edition
	71	InterWorld's Commerce Exchange
	73	Technical Architecture of the Pandesic E-Business Solution
	84	Brightware's Advice Agent Architecture
	94	Brightware's Contact Center
	95	eGain's Email Management System
	99	OBI 1.0 Purchasing Process
	101	Worldwide Internet Commerce Applications Market: 1998–2003
	101	Top Business-to-Business Internet Commerce Applications Vendors: 1998
	102	Top Business-to-Consumer Internet Commerce Applications Vendors: 1998

102	Sell-Side Software Market: 1998–2003
103	Top Sell-Side Software Vendors: 1998
103	Worldwide Web-Based Procurement Software Sales
104	Future Purchasing Criteria for Web-Procurement Software
111	Application Integration Hierarchy
112	Approaches to Application Integration
119	SAP's Internet Transaction Server
124	The EDI Process Using a Value-Added Network
127	OFX Billing and Payment Process
128	OFX Bill Presentment in XML Notation
132	Architecture of an EAI System
135	Worldwide EDI Services Revenue by Provider: 1997
136	EAI Software Revenue Growth: 1998–2001
144	Typical Payment-Card Processing
145	Eavesdropping on Internet Transactions
146	SSL Prohibits Eavesdropping, Not Masquerading
147	Typical Check Payment Processing
150	Cash-and-Transfer Model for Electronic Checks
150	Lockbox Model for Electronic Checks

E-BUSINESS SUPPORTING TECHNOLOGIES

171	Possible Internet Connection Methods
178	Construction of a Dynamic Web Page
186	Internet Browsing and Downloading
196	A Sample XML Document
203	Server Architecture in Transition
216	Representative Internet Access Technologies for U.S. Enterprises: 1998

E-BUSINESS ENABLING TECHNOLOGIES

115	ERP/Application Server Integration Solutions
122	ANSI X12 EDI Transaction Sets
157	SSL versus SET
159	C-SET versus e-COMM
162	Representative EBPP Suppliers

E-BUSINESS SUPPORTING TECHNOLOGIES

189	New Generic Top-Level Domain Names
197	Leading Publicly Accessible Web Servers
198	Leading Web Servers (Including Intranets) by Units Shipped: 1997
202	Common MIME Types
216	Worldwide Installed Base of Home-Based Internet Connectivity Methods

SYMBOLS

@Work 163

NUMERICS

3Com Corp.
Palm 175
Palm VII 175
pdQ phone 175
Web clipping 175

A

ABN AMRO Bank N.V. 6, 213
ACH
for automated clearing-house
transactions 139
vs. electronic checks 151
ACID
for atomicity, consistency,
isolation, and durability
components 206
definition 206
Actinic Software Ltd.
Actinic Catalog 55
Active Software Inc.
ActiveWorks 132
server integration solutions 116
ActiveX 68, 117, 181, 184
Acuity Corp.
WebCenter 93
Adobe Systems Inc. 85
Advantis 135
advertising
advertising-based e-business 32
World Wide Web 30
affinity programs 56
Agency.com 30
**Alcatel Alsthom Compagnie
Generale d'Electricité SA** 174
algorithms
asymmetric key 210
encryption 211
public-key 210
shared single-key 210
symmetric-key 210, 211
Allaire Corp.
Cold Fusion 184
Amazon.com Inc. 16, 22, 27, 31
American Airlines Inc.
SABRE 23
American Bar Association 214
American Express Co. 97, 157, 164
Ameritrade Holding Corp. 37
ANIR 178
for Advanced Networking
Infrastructure and Research
ANSI 122
for American National Standards
Institute

AOL
for America Online Inc.
Netscape API 198
Netscape Application Server 116
Netscape BuyerXpert 78
Netscape CommerceXpert 72,
78
Netscape Communications
Corp. 50, 97, 100, 101, 134,
162, 163, 205
Netscape Communicator 194, 201
Netscape Enterprise Server 75,
81, 184, 197, 198
Netscape JavaScript 180, 194
Netscape LiveWire 184
Netscape MerchantXpert 72
Netscape Navigator 16, 36, 201
Netscape server 198
Netscape SSL 145
Netscape Web Application
Interface 198
NSAPI 184
PersonaLogic 58
Apache Project
Apache Web Server 197, 198
Stronghold 197, 199
API
for application programming
interface
and e-business 36
BAPI 119
definition 115
DSAPI 184
ISAPI 184
NSAPI 184
Apple
for Apple Computer Inc.
Apple WebObjects 115
Macintosh 179
QuickTime 200
applets
definition 179
Java 179
languages 179
application servers
development environments 207
ERP 115
market 205
middleware 208
multitier architectures 203
TP monitors 206
Web 204
Aptex Software Inc.
SelectResponse 93
Ariba Technologies Inc.
Ariba.com 18
Operating Resource Manage-
ment System 18, 78

Art Technology Group Inc.
Dynamo 83
ASC X12 122
for Accredited Standards
Committee X12
Aspect Development
Aspect CSM Catalog
Management 56
AT&T Corp.
AT&T Universal Card Services
100
Easylink 135
InteractiveAnswers 96
ATM 171
for Asynchronous Transfer
Mode
AtomFilms.com 28
auctions
Dutch 33
extranet-based 34
market 34
overview 33
products 34
reverse 33
software 80
technologies 79
vendors 81
Yankee 33
**Australia and New Zealand Banking
Group Ltd.** 75
authentication
definition 125, 209
methods 209
overview 209
payment technologies 140
PKI 213
Autobytel.com Inc. 17, 20
Automotive Industry Action Group
125
Automotive Network eXchange 15

B

Baan Co. N.V.
Baan IV 117
E-Enterprise 117
back-office systems
commerce servers 61
ERP 114
Baltimore Technologies Ltd.
see Zergo Holdings
bandwidth
pipes 172
BankAmerica Corp. 6, 158, 161, 213
Bankers Roundtable 160
Bankers Trust Corp. 6, 213

banking
    certification authorities 213
    consumer mortgages 20
    customers 15
    debit cards vs. electronic checks
        144
    e-business 6, 50
    e-business assets 6
    e-business effects 6
    OFX 160
    online 3
    online market 103
    payment cards 143
    security 6
    SET 157
    smart cards 177
    Web-based 4
**Banking Industry Technology
    Secretariat** 160
BAPI 118, 119
    for business API
Barclays PLC 6, 213
BEA Systems Inc.
    BEA Connector Series 116
    M3 208
    Tuxedo 68, 206
    WebLogic 205, 208
Bell & Howell Co. 163
Best Buy 10
BIPS 161
    for Bank Internet Payment
        System
Blue Martini Software Inc.
    Blue Martini E-Merchandising
        System 56
BlueGill Technologies Inc. 163, 164
Bluestone Software Inc.
    Bluestone 115
    Sapphire/Universal Business
        Server and Developer 208
    Sapphire/Web 207
BMG Entertainment 29
Brightware Inc.
    Advice Agent 84
    Contact Center 94
BroadVision Inc.
    One-to-One Commerce 66
    One-to-One Enterprise 84
    One-to-One Financial 73
Brokat Infosystems AG
    Twister 74
browsers
    market 217
    plug-in 201
    technologies 201
buy-side applications
    approval workflow 76
    components 76
    example of 76

forecast 105
    interface to suppliers 77
    management and reporting
        tools 77
    market 103
    multisupplier catalog 76
    packaged 76
    technologies 76
    user profiles 82
    vendors 78
    workflow system 77

C

C++ programming language
    overview 180
cable modems 217
Calico Commerce Inc.
    eSales Suite 57
call centers
    IP telephony 96
**Canadian Imperial Bank of
    Commerce** 100
CarPrices.com 17
Carte Bleu 176
Catalog City Inc. 25, 26
catalogs
    aggregation 25
    buy-side 76
    categories 55
    content 54
    customization 54
    inventory status 54
    multisupplier 76
    one-stop Web sites 18
    overview 52, 53
    scope 55
    searching 54
    technologies 53, 54, 55
    vendors 55, 56
CDMA 174
    for Code Division Multiple
        Access
CDnow Inc. 30
CertCo Inc. 6, 213
certification authority
    definition 6
    legal standards 214
CGI 63, 183
    for Common Gateway Interface
chargebacks
    definition 158
Charles Schwab & Co. Inc. 37
Chase Manhattan Bank N.A. 6, 158,
    161, 166, 213
CheckFree Corp.
    OFX 130, 160
    Web BillPay 163
Chemdex Corp. 35

Chemical Industry Data Exchange
    126
Circuit City Stores Inc. 10
circuits
    T1 171
    T3 171
Cisco Systems Inc. 3, 16, 26, 214
CISE 178
    for Computer and Information
        Science and Engineering
Citibank N.A. 6, 73, 75, 161, 166, 213
Citigroup Inc. 165
Clarify Inc. 132, 133
Clarus Corp.
    Clarus E-Procurement 78
ClearCommerce Corp. 60
client/server computing
    definition 174
    kiosks 176
    MIME 201
    overview 174
    payment credentials and
        applications 183
    queuing 120
    receipt and coupon storage 182
    server-side 183
    shopping cart 183
    software issues 181, 183
    three-tier architecture 203
    user profile 183
    wallets 183
    World Wide Web interactions
        186
CNET Inc. 85
Cognos Corp. 68
collaborative filtering 82
COM
    for Component Object Model
    DCOM 52, 61
    e-mail 87
Commerce One Inc.
    BuySite 78
    MarketSite 18
commerce platforms
    example of 64
    overview 61
    vendors 61
CommerceNet Ltd.
    OBI 97
    XML Exchange 128
**Common Electronic Purse
    Specification** 161
**Commonwealth of Pennsylvania
    Department of General Services**
    80

Compaq Computer Corp.
Compaq@Home 10
Digital UNIX 198
OSS 185
Tandem iTP Payment Solution 164

configurators
definition 57
technologies 57
vendors 57

ConnectInc.com
MarketStream 2.0 67

cookies
definition 29, 82, 191
overview 192
weakness 192

CORBA 52, 61
for Common Object Request Broker Architecture

CoreStates Financial Corp. 122

Council of Government Information Systems 13

CRM
for customer relationship management
case-based 83
collaborative filtering 82
e-business 2, 38
IP telephony 96
market 23
overview 114
personalization 81, 82
rules-based 83
user profiles 81
vendors 83

CrossWorlds Software Inc.
Customer Interaction 133
ERP Interaction 133
Supply Chain Interaction 133

cryptography
hash 211

CSP 32, 69
for commerce service provider

CSS
for cascading style sheet
benefits 193
challenges 194

customer service
automating 23
e-business 23
e-mail responses 24
World Wide Web 23

CyberCash Inc.
bill payment 162, 163
CashRegister 3.0 164
CyberCoin 164
OTP 100
PayNow 164
wallets 183

CyberSource Corp. 61

D

Danmønt 176
databases
searching 54
DBMS
for database management system
Web connections 205
DCOM 52, 61
for Distributed COM
Dell Computer Corp. 16, 19, 27
DES 210
for Data Encryption Standard
Deutsche Bank AG 6, 213
DHL International Ltd. 8
DHTML 68, 193, 194
for Dynamic HTML
digital cash
market 156, 166
micropayments 155
overview 154, 155, 156
requirements 155
smart cards 155
digital signatures
overview 211
DNS 188
for Domain Name System
DOCSIS 217
for Data Over Cable Service Interface Specification
DOM 195
for Document Object Model
domain names
overview 187, 189
top-level 187, 189
trademarks 188
dot address 187
DSAPI 184
for Domino Server Application Programming Interface
DSL 217
for Digital Subscriber Line
DSS 211
for Digital Signature Standard
DTD 116, 195
for data type descriptor

E

E*Trade Group Inc. 4, 37
e2 Software Corp.
SalesOffice 56
EAI
for enterprise application integration
advantages 130
architecture 132

componentization 131
connectors 132
data transformation engine 132
definition 109
integration 131
market 136
middleware 130
overview 113
package 132
rules engine 132
technologies 130, 131
transport system 132
vendors 132, 133
eBay Inc. 33, 79
EBPP
for electronic bill presentment and payment
biller direct 153
consolidator 153
invited push 154
market 154, 162, 163
steps 154
vendors 162
e-business
advantages 3, 5, 18, 19, 20, 21
advertising-based 32
and the Web 2
APIs 36
application integration 109, 110
application programming 177
application servers 205
architectures 203
assemble-to-order products 26
auctions 33
authentication 27
automotive industry 15, 17
banking 6
brand perceptions 22
brochureware 177
build-to-order 9, 19
business event processing 110
business-to-business 6, 17, 22, 27, 33, 49
business-to-consumer 18, 22, 23, 27
buyer vs. seller 2
competition 5
competition focus 8
configurator 26
connectivity between applications 110
consumer mortgage 20
convenience 25, 26
coordination 18, 19, 20
costs 2, 3, 6
customer service 23, 24
customer-centric 2
definition 1
enabled by the Web 36, 37

engineer-to-order products 26
entertainment and media
     industry 28
ERP 7, 114
euro 22
European online population 11
film industry 28
financial services 6, 152
financial services providers 4
forms 177
globalization 21, 22
government systems 12
hand-held computing 175
HTTP 191
human resource systems 25
impact 17, 39
in inventory management 19
infomediaries 34, 35, 39
infrastructure 170, 173
integration 110, 112
integration hierarchy 111
international 11, 12, 21, 22
international acceptance 6
Internet 35, 36, 37
Internet costs 3
Internet-native business models
     32, 33, 34
logistics 8, 9
market 9, 11, 13, 15, 215
models 31
MRO 5
music industry 29
networking 36
one-stop exchanges 18
online brokerage 3, 4, 6
overview 1, 169, 170
payment systems 152
payment technologies 142, 143,
     147
personalization 27, 31
pricing 22, 26
print industry 28
procurement 5, 8
programming languages 179
real estate model 32
sales costs 3
sales process 3
security 6, 208, 209, 210, 211
server architectures 204
SET 158
ship-to-order products 26
site capabilities 49
specialized client software 182
summary 38, 39
supply chain management 7
three-tier model 204
transactions 1
travel Web sites 19
user profiles 30

uses of 1
value proposition 18
virtual storefront 3
vs. in-person selling 2
vs. other media 2
World Wide Web 35, 36, 37
e-business systems
affinity programs 56
architecture 52
auction-based selling 79
backbone 114
background 50
bid systems 80
business-to-business 50, 54, 55,
     97, 101
business-to-consumer 50, 102,
     130
buy-side 50
buy-side applications 77
buy-side packaged applications
     76
catalogs 53, 55, 56, 76
collaborative filtering 82
commerce platforms 61
components 50
configurators 57
customer relationships 81, 82
databases 54
distribution 60
EDI 113
e-mail 87, 88
ERP 109, 114, 134
evolutionary path 51
exchanges 80
forecast 104
initiatives 97
integration 52
market 100, 103
marketplace 50
merchandising 56
OBI 97
OTP 100
overview 51
payment systems 60
repositories 128
searching 54
sell-side 50, 65, 66
shipping 59
shopping carts 58
simple 51
software 50
storefront components 52
summary 49
tax calculation 58, 59
telephony 96
tools 51
vendors 59, 61, 66, 78, 81, 83, 93,
     96

see also auctions, buy-side
     applications, marketplaces,
     selling systems, sell-side
     applications, storefront
     systems
e-COMM
     vs. Europay C-SET 159
EDI
     for electronic data interchange
     advantages 121
     application protocols 129
     audit trails 126
     background 121
     challenges 125
     costs 5, 123, 125
     data formats 123
     definition 120
     e-business 5
     EDIFACT 122
     end-to-end capability 122
     extranets 135
     forecast 137
     frameworks 131
     Internet 121, 137
     market 134, 135
     overview 109, 113
     processing 123
     queuing 120
     revenue 135
     security 120, 125
     standards 122, 125, 126
     trading partners 120
     traditional 120, 121, 122, 125, 126
     transaction sets 122, 129
     trends 120
     value-added network 124
     VANs 124, 125, 135
     Web-based 122
     XML 120, 126, 127, 129, 130, 137, 197
EDIFACT 122, 126
     for Electronic Data Interchange
     for Administration,
     Commerce and Transport
Edify Corp. 74, 75, 103, 162, 163
edocs Inc.
     BillDirect 164
     bill data extraction 163
EDS Corp. 153, 163
     for Electronic Data Services
EFT 154
     for electronic funds transfer
eFusion Inc.
     eBridge 97
     IP Push to Talk 96
eGain Communications Corp.
     Email Management System 94,
     95
EJBs 116
     for Enterprise JavaBeans

Elcom Systems Inc.
PECOS Procurement Manager
78
electronic checks
cash and transfer 148, 150
lockbox 149, 150
overview 147
reducing float 151
vs. ACH 151
Electronic Funds & Data Corp. 162
electronic wallets 156
Electronics Industry Data Exchange 126
E-Loan Inc. 6, 20
e-mail
challenges 24, 87
customer response 24
customer-facing 87
customer-facing packages 88
initial routing 90
knowledge base 92
management and reporting tools 92
managing message workflow 91
market 104
MIME 201
payment cards 143
receiving and categorizing 89, 90
responding to 91
technologies 93
vendors 93
vs. Web forms 88
EMI 29
encryption
algorithms 210
breaking 210
checksum 212
locked data 210
overview 210
public-key 210
recommended key sizes 211
SET 159
shared single-key 210
SSL 139
technologies 211
VPN 214
Energy Marketplace 80
Engage Technologies Inc.
ProfileServer 4.0 84
enterprise computing
EAI 130
forecast 136
hand-held 175
market 134, 136, 215, 216
middleware 111, 130
security 212, 213
summary 109
VADs 175

Entrust Technologies Ltd. 214
ErgoTech International Inc.
WebLeader E-Mailroom 94
Ericsson Inc.
IP Telephony Solution for Carriers 97
PhoneDoubler 97
Symbian 175
WAP 174
Web procurement 5
ERP
for enterprise resource planning
application servers 115
BAPIs 119
business-partner integration 115
customer relationship management 7
devices 137
EAI 130
e-business 7, 114
forecast 104, 136
human resources 114
linking e-business servers 115
market 134, 136
overview 112
strategies 112
suites 112
technologies 113
vendors 117, 132, 133
Web access 136
Web interface vs. application-specific 114
Web-enabling 114
Web-extension 114
see also EAI, EDI, XML
EU 214
for European Union
euro
e-business 6, 22
Europay C-SET
vs. e-COMM 159
Europay International SA 100
European Union
Privacy Directive 85
Excite Inc. 30
extranets 135
Extricity Software Inc.
Alliance Process Manager 133

F

FairMarket Inc. 34
FAQ 24
for frequently asked question
FastParts Inc. 34, 80
Federal Express Corp. 8, 68
FEDI
for financial electronic data interchange
benefits 152

model 153
Financial Services Technology Consortium 161
First Data Corp.
TransPoint 165
First Virtual Holdings Inc. 81
Fisher Technology Group Inc.
Corner Stone 78
FIX Organization 130
Fleet Financial Group Inc.
storefronts@fleet 6
float
definition 151
Ford Motor Co. 5
Frame Relay 171
framework
definition 131
France Telecom Inc. 176
France Telecom Mobile 174
FreeMarkets OnLine Inc. 80
Frontec Group 132
AMTrix 133
FTP 202
for File Transfer Protocol
Fujitsu Ltd. 100
Fujitsu Personal Systems Inc. 176
Fulcrum Technologies Inc.
SearchServer and Search Builder 70
Future of Advertising Stakeholders 30

G

Gas Industry Standards Board 125
GCA 128
for Graphic Communications Association
Gemplus S.C.A. 174
General Electric Co. 3
General Electric Information Services Inc.
EDI 134
TradeWeb 135
General Magic Inc.
DataRover 176
General Motors Co.
GM BuyPower 17
Genesys Telecommunications Laboratories Inc.
Adante 93
giros
definition 141
Global Trust Enterprise 6, 213
GlobeSet Inc. 158, 164
Greenwood Trust Co.
Discover 164
GSM 174
for Global System for Mobile Communications

GTE Service Corp. 151, 212, 213, 214, 215
gTLD 189
    for generic top-level domain
        name
GUI 177
    for graphical user interface

H
HAHT Software Inc.
    HAHTsite 116
hand-held computing
    devices 175
    Internet 175
    smart phones 174
    VADs 176
Harbinger Corp.
    Knowbility 56
    Premenos Templar 135
    Trusted Link Enterprise 135
hash
    definition 211
Hitachi Ltd. 100
HP
    for Hewlett-Packard Co.
    HP-UX 75, 119, 199
    Integrated Payment System 164
    VeriFone 68, 81, 100, 158, 164, 165,
       183
    VeriFone E-Services 164
    VeriFone vPOS SET 70
HTML
    for HyperText Markup Language
    4.0 features 195
    CSSs 193, 194
    DHTML 68, 194
    forms 177
    overview 193
    vs. XML 197
HTTP
    for HyperText Transport
       Protocol
    hits 192
    HTTP-NG 190
    MIME 201
    overview 170
    server 204, 206
    session management 191
    technologies 190, 191, 192
    user activity 192
    user identification 191
    vertical layers 191
Huffman coding
    definition 129
Hughes Network Systems Inc.
    DirecPC 217
Huntington Bancshares Inc. 75
HypoVereinsbank AG 6, 213

I
i2 Technologies Inc.
    Global Logistics Manager 7
IAB 178
    for Internet Architecture Board
IAHC 189
    for International Ad Hoc
       Committee
IANA 188
    for Internet Assigned Numbers
       Authority
IBM
    for International Business
       Machines Corp.
    AIX 119, 199
    AS/400 173
    CISC 206
    CMOS 173
    DB2 94, 185, 206
    Domino Go Webserver 199
    Domino R5 184
    IBM Global Service 62
    IBM HTTP 199
    IBM WebSphere 116
    Interactive Financial Service 75
    Internet Connection Server 184
    Lotus 185
    Lotus Domino 116, 173, 199
    Lotus Domino Go 184
    Lotus Notes 94, 173
    Lotus server 198
    MQ Integrator 133
    MQSeries 68, 120, 132, 133
    Multipayment Framework 164
    Net.Commerce PRO 61, 62, 63
    Net.Commerce START 68
    OnDemand 164
    OS/2 Warp 179, 199
    OS/390 68, 199
    Payment Suite 164
    San Francisco Project 131
    Secure Mailer 185
    Tibco Rendezvous 121
    Tivoli 185
    Visual Age 207
    WebSphere Application Server
       199
    WebSphere Application Server
       Advanced Edition 68
    WebSphere Performance Pack
       68
IBS 163
    for International Billing Services
iCat Corp.
    Electronic Commerce Suite 3.0
       Professional Edition 68
    see also Intel Corp.

ICE 85
    for Information and Content
       Exchange
ICOMS 60
    for Internet Commerce Services
       Corp.
ICVerify Inc. 165
IDEA 210
    for International Data
       Encryption Algorithm
IESG 178
    for Internet Engineering Steering
       Group
IETF
    for Internet Engineering Task
       Force
    overview 178
    Real-time Streaming Format
       200
    SSL 146
    standards 97
iFilm.net 28
IFX 161
    for Interactive Financial
       Exchange
IGP 172
    for Interior Gateway Protocol
IIS 199
    for Internet Information Server
INEX Corp.
    Commerce Court 69
Inference Corp. 88
infomediaries 33, 34
InformationWeek 7
Informix Software Inc. 68, 75
Ingram Micro Inc.
    Auction Block 81, 34
integration
    application integration 110, 112
    application servers 115
    business integration 111
    business processes 112
    connectivity 110
    definition 110
    EAI 130, 131
    event processing 110
    levels 110
    overview 110
    subscription methods 121
    technologies 111
    types of 110
Integrion Financial Network LLC
    Gold standard 127, 160, 161
Intel Corp.
    Corollary 173
    iCat Corp. 68
    Pentium III 192
    Profusion 174
    SHV 173

Intelisys Electronic Commerce LLC
IEC-Enterprise 78
Interdepartmental Information System For The Citizen 12
International Billing Services 163, 165
Internet
access methods 171
advertising 30
auctions 79
background 172
bid systems 80
business categories 50
commerce applications 51, 100
connection market 215
connection methods 171, 172
connection technologies 216
definition 170
direct marketing 32
domain names 178, 187
downloading files 186, 202
e-business 32, 35, 36, 37
e-business systems 51
EDI 121, 137
enterprise usage 171
evolution 16
global vs. U.S. commerce market 15
globalization 21
hand-held computing 175
HOSTS file 188
IEFT 178
infrastructure 170
international users 9, 11
Japanese commerce market 10, 12, 14
MIME 201
multimedia 188
networking 171
organizations 178
payment cards 143
personalization 81
platform computing 185
routing protocols 172
security 125, 214
streaming 200
telephony 95, 96
text chats 96
total users 9
unsecure transactions 145
URLs 187
weather forecasts 172
Web Payphones 176
Internet Corporation for Assigned Names and Numbers 188
Internet Purchasing Roundtable 97

Intershop Communications Inc.
cartridge family 70
Intershop Merchant Edition 3.0 70
InterWorld Corp.
Commerce Exchange 70, 71
intranets
buy-side applications 76
human resources 114
Intuit Inc.
OFX 129, 160
Quicken 160
IP
for Internet Protocol
addresses 188, 192
IPv4 188
IPv6 188, 201
multicasting 200
networks 170
telephony 96
VoIP 172
IPOC 189
for Interim Policy Oversight Committee
IPSec 15, 214
for IP Security
IRTF 178
for Internet Research Task Force
ISAPI 184
for Internet Server application programming interface
ISDN 171
for Integrated Services Digital Network
ISDN-BRI 171
for ISDN-basic rate interface
ISO
for International Organization for Standardization
ISOC 178
for Internet Society
ISP 69
for Internet service provider
ISV 131
for independent software vendor
IT
for information technology
e-business 1
IXC Communications Inc. 215

J
J Sainsbury PLC 5
J.D. Edwards and Co.
OneWorld 117
Japanese Ministry of Posts and Telecommunications 9
Java
applets 179
application servers 207

e-mail 87
Enterprise JavaBeans 63, 116
Java Protected Domains Security Model 180
JavaScript 180
JDBC 206
JDK 179
JRE 58
JScript 177, 180
JVM 173, 179, 181
overview 179
servlets 184
JDBC 206
for Java Database Connectivity
see also Java
JDK 179
for Java Development Kit
see also Java
JRE 58
for Java Runtime Environment
see also Java
Just In Time Solutions Inc.
BillCast 165
bill presentment 162
JVM 173
for Java Virtual Machine
see also Java

K
Kana Communications Inc.
auto response e-mail 88
Customer Messaging System 94
Kenan Systems Corp. 132
Keynote Systems
Baywatch 172
kiosks
technologies 176
Web Payphones 176

L
L2F 214
for Layer 2 Forwarding
L2TP 214
for Layer 2 Tunneling Protocol
Lending Tree Inc. 6, 20
Linux 174, 185
LMDS 217
for Local Multipoint Distribution Service
Lynk Systems Inc. 164

M
Maagnum 162, 163
mainframes 173
Manugistics Group Inc. 7, 133

marketplaces
  auctions 79
  bid systems 80
  exchanges 80
  overview 50
  shopping carts 58
  technologies 50
MasterCard International Inc. 100,
  139, 141, 157, 158, 164
**Matrix Information and Directory
  Services Inc.**
  Internet Weather Report 36
MCI WorldCom Inc.
  Click'nConnect 96
  UUNet Technologies 215
MD5 211
  for Message Digest 5
Mellon Bank Corp. 158
Mercado Software Inc.
  Catalog Builder 56
Mercantec Inc.
  SoftCart 71
message broker
  subscription methods 121
MeTechnology AG
  Me/4 74
MFG Pro 133
Microsoft Corp.
  Active Server Pages 63, 184
  Active Streaming Format 200
  ActiveX 117, 181
  CarPoint 17
  ClearType 175
  COM 61, 93, 181
  Commerce Server 64
  Commercial Internet System 69
  Complete Commerce 72
  Firefly Network 85
  Firefly Passport 27, 85
  IIS 199
  Internet Explorer 180, 194, 201
  Internet Information Server 184,
    197, 199
  JScript 180, 184, 194
  Media Player 200
  MSMQ 120
  NetShow 3.0 200
  OFX 160
  Outlook 94
  P3P 85
  Site Server 3.0 164
  Site Server Commerce Edition
    63, 69, 73
  Slate 28
  smart cards for Windows 177
  SQL Server 94
  TransPoint 165
  VBScript 180
  Visual Basic 180

  Visual Basic for Applications 180
  Visual J++ 207
  Win32 95
  Windows 176, 179, 181, 199
  Windows CE 175
  Windows NT 164, 165
  Windows NT Server 174, 207
middleware
  application servers 208
  definition 110, 207
  distributed object 208
  EAI 130
  market 136
  product types 207
  TP monitors 206
  XML 129, 208
MIME
  for Multipurpose Internet Mail
    Extensions
  types 202
MMDS 217
  for Multichannel Multipoint
    Distribution Service
Moai Technologies Inc.
  LiveExchange 81
modems
  cable 217
MOM 111, 120, 207
  for message-oriented
    middleware
Mondex International Ltd. 100, 166
Moore's Law 36
Motorola Inc.
  PKI 213
  Symbian 175
  WAP 174
MP3
  for MPEG Audio Layer 3
  definition 29
MPEG 29
  for Motion Pictures Experts
    Group
MRO
  for maintenance, repair, and
    operations
  e-business 5
multicasting
  definition 200
MultiLogic Inc. 85
multimedia
  bandwidth 188
  technologies 200
Mustang Software Inc.
  Internet Message Center 95

N

NACHA 152
  for National Automated Clearing
    House Association

**National Association of Theater
  Owners** 28
**National Computerization Agency
  of Korea** 13
National Semiconductor Corp. 97
NCR Corp. 162, 163, 176
NCSA 198
  for National Center for Super-
    computing Applications
NEON Inc. 133
  for New Era of Networks Inc.
Net Perceptions Inc.
  Realtime Recommendation
    Engine 85
NetDelivery Corp.
  e-Biz 165
  eWizard 165
NetDynamics Inc.
  see Sun Microsystems Inc.
Netscape Communications Corp.
  see AOL
Netweave Corp.
  Netweave DS 120
network infrastructure
  IP-based networks 170
  connecting to the Internet 171
Network Solutions Inc. 178, 188
New England Circuit Sales Inc. 35
Nokia Mobile Phones Inc.
  Nokia 9000 175
  Symbian 175
  WAP 174
Nortel
  Entrust 212
Novazen Inc. 163
Novell Inc.
  NetWare 185
Novus Services Inc.
  Discover 157
NSAPI 184
  for Netscape Server application
    programming interface
NSF
  for National Science Foundation
  overview 178

O

O'Reilly and Associates Inc.
  Website Professional 184
OAGI
  for Open Applications Group
    Inc.
  XML 116
Oberon Software Inc.
  Prospero 133
OBI
  for Open Buying on the Internet
  architecture 98
  overview 97

purchasing process 99
security 98
version 1.1 98
OBI Consortium 97
Object Design Inc.
Excelon 208
ODBC 68, 94
for Open Database Connectivity
OECD 5, 31
for Organization for Economic
Cooperation and
Development
Office Depot Inc. 10, 97
OFX 127, 129, 156, 160
for Open Financial Exchange
technologies
Omnitel Inc. 174
Onsale Inc. 33, 79
Open Group 97
Open Market Inc.
Folio 60
LiveCommerce 72
market 102, 134
OBI 97
OM-Transact 60, 72
OpenSite Technologies Inc.
OpenSite Auction 4.0 81
operating systems
AIX 119
hand-held computing 175
HP-UX 75
Linux 185
Solaris 119
OPS 85
for Open Profiling Standard
Oracle Corp.
AppBuilder 207
AvantGo 2.0 175
Financial Services Application
165
Internet Bill and Pay 165
Internet Commerce Server 1.1
64
Oracle Applications 11 117
Oracle Field Sales Online 117
Oracle Strategic Procurement
117
Oracle7 94
Oracle8 94, 165
Oracle8i 117, 206
Oracle8i Lite 175
Payment Server 1.1 165
ORB 186
for object request broker
Orient Corp.
Auction Market Japan 164
OSS 185
for open-source software

OTP 100
for Open Trading Protocol
out-of-band 210

P

P3P 84, 85
for Platform for Privacy
Preferences
Pandesic LLC
Pandesic 72
payment cards
debit cards vs. electronic checks
144
electronic wallets 156
overview 143, 145
technologies 143
typical processing 144
payment technologies
automated clearing-house 142
check 141
credit transfer 141
debit transfer 141
definition 140
design issues 142, 143
digital cash 154, 155, 156
EBPP 152
e-business 142, 143, 147
electronic bill presentation 151,
152, 154
electronic checks 147, 149
electronic wallets 156
forecast 166
key issues 140
market 161, 162, 163, 164, 165
overview 60, 140
payment card 141, 143, 145
requirements 140
RTGS 142
smart cards 155
standards 156
summary 139
traditional methods 141
types of 139
typical electronic check process
147
typical scenario 143, 147
wire transfer 142
Paymentech 60
PDA
for personal digital assistant
ERP 137
PeerLogic Inc.
Pipes 121
PeopleSoft Inc.
EAI market 136
PeopleSoft Business Network 118
strategies 117
Supply Chain Collaborator 115

Perl
for Practical Extraction and
Report Language
Comprehensive Perl Archive
Network 219
overview 180
Persistence Software Inc.
PowerTier Web Server 116
PHS 174
for Personal Handyphone
System
PING 36
for Packet Internet Groper
definition
Pitney Bowes Inc. 163
Pivotal Software Inc. 132
PKI
for public-key infrastructure
challenges 213
overview 212
supported applications 213
Platform for Privacy Preferences 29
PPTP 214
for Point-to-Point Tunneling
Protocol
Preview Systems Inc. 60
Priceline.com Inc. 33
PricewaterhouseCoopers LLP 11, 187,
215
Princeton TeleCom Corp. 163
Principal Financial Group 75
procurement
overview 8
programming
C++ 180
component-based 185
e-business applications 177
Java 179
JavaScript 180
languages 179
objects 185
open-source 174, 185
Perl 180, 185
server-side 183
protocols
ATM 171
FTP 202
HTML 193
HTTP 187, 189, 190
OFX 160
PPTP 214
RIP 172
SET 147, 148, 149, 157
SMDS 171
SSL 145
UMTS 174
XML 195
see also standards

Proton 166, 176
PSINet Inc.
    Intranet 135
Psion PLC
    Symbian 175

Q
QoS 188
    for quality of service
Qualcomm Inc.
    pdQ phone 175
queuing systems
    forecast 137
    overview 120
    publish-and-subscribe
        products 121
    vendors 120
Qwest Communications
    International Inc. 215

R
Rainbow Technologies Inc. 159
Rapidsite Inc. 197
Rational Software Inc. 68
RDBMS 64, 75
    for relational database
        management system
RealNetworks Inc.
    RealPlayer 202
    RealPublisher 202
    RealServer 202
    RealSystem G2 200
Recording Industry Association of
    America 29
Red Sky Interactive 30
Remedy Corp. 175
repudiation
    definition 140
Requisite Technology Inc.
    BugsEye 56
Revnet Systems Inc.
    UnityMail 56
RFC 146, 178
    for request for comment
RIP 172
    for Routing Information
        Protocol
RISC 173
    for Reduced Instruction Set
        Computing
Royal Bank of Scotland Group PLC
    122
RPC
    for remote procedure call
    definition 207
    ERP integration 110

RSADSI
    for RSA Data Security Inc.
    BSafe 165
    recommended key length 211
    with JDK 180
RTGS 142
    for real-time gross settlement

S
SABRE Group
    EasySABRE 23
    Travelocity 23
Salon 28
SAP AG
    for Systeme Anwendung
        Produkte AG
    ABAP 119
    BAPIs 119, 131,
    Business-to-Business
        Procurement 115
    IDoc and ALE 133
    Internet Application
        Components 118, 119
    Internet Transaction Server 119
    R/3 9, 63, 73, 116, 118
    R/3 Release 4.0 119
    Remote Function Calls 120
Science Applications International
    Corp.
    Network Solutions Inc. 178
    certification authority 214
SCM
    for supply chain management
    overview 114
SCO Inc.
    for Santa Cruz Operation Inc.
    UnixWare 174
scripting
    applets 179
    DHTML 194
    languages 179, 184
    Perl 184
SDSI 213
    for Simple Distributed Security
        Infrastructure
searching
    features 55
Secure Digital Music Initiative 29
Secure Electronic Transaction LLC
    158
security
    authentication 209
    branded certificates 213
    certification authority 6, 213
    commerce 182
    confidentiality 209, 210
    customer authentication 209
    data integrity 212
    digital certificates 29

    digital signatures 211
    e-business 6, 208, 209, 210, 211
    EDI 120, 125
    enterprise-level 212, 213
    Internet 125, 214
    IPSec 15
    MD5 211
    merchant authentication 209
    mutual privacy 209
    networking 212
    nonrepudiation 209
    SET 60, 61, 148, 149, 159
    smart cards 177
    SSL 60, 61, 145
    technologies 209
    VANs 124
Security First National Bank 75, 103
Security First Technologies Corp.
    Virtual Financial Manager 75
Selectica Inc.
    ACE Enterprise 58
selling systems
    catalogs 53
    cross-selling 54
    searching 54
    up-selling 54
sell-side applications
    entry-level packages 66
    forecast 104
    high-end packages 66
    market 102, 103
    overview 65
    serendipity control 85
    vendors 66, 67, 68, 70, 71, 72, 73,
        74, 75, 87
    vertical market packages 73
servers
    application 205, 207
    architectures 202
    DNS 188
    e-business 61
    e-business server 170, 205
    HTTP 206
    low-end systems 173
    mainframes 173
    midrange 173
    multiple tiers 204
    operating systems 185
    queuing 120
    transitions 203
    UNIX-based 173
    Web 51, 197, 198, 204
SET
    for Secure Electronic
        Transaction
    alternatives 159
    background 157, 158
    concerns 159
    electronic wallets 156

overview 148, 149
payment systems 60, 165
performance 159
platforms 61,
prospects 158
SET-MARK 158
technologies 157, 158
typical transaction 149
vs. SSL 147
SET Consortium 157
SFA 114
for sales force automation
SGI
for Silicon Graphics Inc.
IRIX 198
SGML 160, 195
for Standard Generalized
Markup Language
Shenzen Power 11
shipping 59
shopping carts 58
SHV 173
for Standard High Volume
Siebel Systems Inc.
EAI market 136
Siebel 99 86, 87
Silicon Graphics Inc.
see SGI
SkyBridge LP 217
smart cards
acceptance device 176
definition 176
formats 176
market 166, 176, 177
overview 176
payment cards 141, 143
security 177
stored-value 155
technologies 176
token cards 176
SMDS 171
for Switched Multimegabit Data
Service
SMIL 200
for Synchronized Multimedia
Integration Language
SMP 173
for symmetric multiprocessing
SMTP 89
for Simple Mail Transfer
Protocol
**Society for Worldwide Interbank
Financial Transactions** 142
Software AG
EntireX 181
Sonera Technologies 174
Sony Corporation of America 29
Southern California Gas Co. 80

Sprint Communications Corp.
Give Me A Call 96
VANs 135
Spyrus Inc.
SecureWeb Payments 165
SET wallet 1.0 165
Terisa Systems 165
SSL
for Secure Sockets Layer
disadvantages 145
eavesdropping 146
forecast 166
liability 145
limitations 145, 146
overview 145
trusted third-party 147
version 2.0 146
version 3.0 146
vs. SET 157
**Standard Product and Service
Classifications** 55
standards
ASC X12 97, 122
CDMA 174
CGI 183
DES 210
e-COMM 159
EDI 122, 125
EDIFACT 122
Europay C-SET 159
GSM 174
Internet EDI 125
IPSec 214
IPv4 188
IPv6 188, 201
ISAPI 184
MIME 201
OBI 97, 98
OFX 160
OTP 100
payment technologies 156
SET 148, 149, 157
VPN 214
WAP 174
XML 195
see also protocols
Sterling Commerce Inc.
Commerce Now 135
Gentran 78
market 101
storefront systems
commerce server products 66
vendors 66
Suite Software
DOME 121
Sun Microsystems Inc.
Java 179, 184
Java Servlet API 184
JavaCard 177

JavaSoft 183
NetDynamics Inc. 119, 205
OTP 100
Solaris 119
SunSoft Solaris 174, 179, 199
see also Netscape
Communications Corp.
SupplyWorks Inc. 97
Sybase Inc.
Sybase SQL Anywhere 5.5 68
Symbian Ltd.
Epoch32 175
Symbol Technologies Inc. 176

T

TanData Corp.
Progistics CS 73
Progistics Merchant 59
tax calculation software 58, 60
Taxware International Inc. 59, 68, 73
TCP/IP
overview 35
telcos 70
for telecommunications
providers
telecommunications
e-business 35
vendors 96
Teledesic Corp. 217
telephony
vendors 96
Web-based customer service 95
Telxon Corp. 176
Tenth Mountain Systems Inc. 158
Texcel Systems Inc. 129
Time-Warner Inc. 29
TLS 146
for Transport Layer Security
TP 206
for transaction processing
TPA 123
for Trade Partner Agreement
**Trade'ex Electronic Commerce
Systems Inc.**
MetalSite 18, 33
procurement 79
The Plastics Network 18
transaction
definition 206
transmission media
cable modems 217
xDSL 217
TransPoint LLC 162, 163, 165
see also First Data Corp. and
Microsoft Corp.
Trilogy Software Inc.
Selling Chain Suite 58

Trintech Group
>   PayGate 165
>   PayPurse 165
>   PayWare 165
>   SETCo 158
TriSense Software Ltd. 163
TriStrata Security Systems Inc.
>   TriStrata Enterprise Security
>   Server 215
True Software Inc. 81
TRUSTe Trustmark 84
TSI International Software Ltd.
>   Mercator 68, 116
Tuxedo/T 75

U

U.S. Department of Defense 151
U.S. Department of the Treasury 161
U.S. National Security Agency 161
U.S. Postal Service 161
UMTS 174
>   *for* Universal Mobile Telecom-
>   munications System
UN/ECE 122
>   *for* United Nations Economic
>   Commission for Europe
United Music Group 29
**United Nations Commission on
    International Trade Law** 214
Universal Card Services Corp. 100
UNIX
>   Linux 174, 185
>   servers 173
Unwired Planet Inc. 174
UPS 9, 59, 68
>   *for* United Parcel Service of
>   America
URL
>   *for* uniform resource locator
>   overview 187

V

VAD
>   *for* vertical-application device
>   definition 175
>   overview 176
VAN
>   *for* value-added network
>   audit trails 126
>   costs 125
>   EDI 121, 124, 125
>   FEDI 152
>   forecast 137
>   Internet 126
>   procurement 5
>   security 124, 125

>   technologies 124
>   vendors 135
Vantive Corp.
>   EAI market 136
>   Vantive 8 87
vBNS 178
>   *for* Very High-Speed Backbone
>   Network Service
Vector Quantization Format 29
VeriSign Inc. 212, 213, 214
Vignette Corp.
>   StoryServer 4.0 85
>   Syndication Server 86
Visa International Inc.
>   and SET 157, 158
>   OTP 100
>   payment cards 141
>   standards 139
>   VisaCash 166
Vitria Technology Inc.
>   BusinessWare 133
VoIP 172
>   *for* Voice-over-IP
VPN
>   *for* virtual private network
>   definition 214
>   overview 214
>   standards 214
>   vs. VoIP 172
VRML 68
>   *for* Virtual Reality Modeling
>   Language

W

W3C
>   *for* World Wide Web Consortium
>   Jigsaw Web server 184
Wachovia Corp. 75
WAP 174
>   *for* Wireless Application Protocol
Web forms 88, 89
Web-based customer service
>   forecast 105
webMethods Inc. 129
WebVision Inc.
>   WEBtropolis 81
Wells Fargo and Co. 100, 158, 161
**Wireless Applications Protocol
    Forum** 174
wireless communications
>   market 217
>   overview 174
>   VADs 176
WML 197
>   *for* Wireless Markup Language
World Economic Forum 11
World Wide Web
>   advertising 30
>   application servers 204

>   automotive industry 17
>   banking 6
>   collecting user profiles 192
>   commerce 14
>   customer service 23
>   domain names 187, 188
>   downloading files 202
>   e-business 35, 36, 37
>   e-business systems 1, 50
>   ERP access 136
>   evolution 16
>   impact 38
>   interaction 186, 187, 188, 189, 190,
>   191, 192, 194, 195, 201
>   interactive devices 137
>   IP addresses 188
>   mindshare 32
>   online brokerage 3
>   page construction 178
>   sales costs 3
>   servers 51, 197
>   subscription-based sites 32
>   total users 9
>   URLs 187
>   user devices 10
>   user income 14
>   Web forms 88
>   Web Payphones 176
>   Web-based ERP 114
WorldPay PLC 70

X

X12 126
Xcert International Inc. 214
XML
>   *for* eXtensible Markup Language
>   advantages 128
>   and HTML 193
>   business languages 129
>   challenges 127
>   content tagging 197
>   data representation 196
>   data-structuring 195
>   DTD 195, 196
>   EDI 120, 126, 128, 129, 137, 197
>   efficiency 129
>   examples 127
>   forecast 137
>   market 130, 136
>   metadata 128
>   middleware 129, 208
>   OAGI 116
>   OBI 98
>   overview 195
>   sample document 196
>   tabular data 196
>   trends 130
>   vs. HTML 197
>   WML 197

XML Solutions LLC 128
XQL 129
for eXtensible Query Language

Y
Yahoo! Inc. 22

Z
Zergo Holdings PLC
Baltimore Technologies Ltd. 214
Zeus 198

PricewaterhouseCoopers *E-BUSINESS TECHNOLOGY FORECAST:*
READER SURVEY

We are interested in your feedback on the PricewaterhouseCoopers *E-Business Technology Forecast*. We would appreciate a few minutes of your time to fill out this questionnaire after you have had a chance to review the *E-Business Technology Forecast*. Please mail to the address on the back or fax to +1-650-321-5543.

1. For what purposes have you used the *E-Business Technology Forecast*?

__ to prepare for a presentation or client meeting   __ as a general technology reference
__ for strategic technology advice   __ as a technology implementation guide
__ for marketing/competitive products information   __ other: ....

2. Does the *E-Business Technology Forecast* meet your needs? (circle one)

Yes, always   Most of the time   Sometimes yes, sometimes no   Usually not   Never

3. Can you easily find the topics you are looking for?

Yes, always   Most of the time   Sometimes yes, sometimes no   Usually not   Never

4. Is the depth of coverage appropriate for the topics?

More information than I need   Just right   Less information than I need   Too superficial

5. How do you rate the organization of the individual sections (Executive Summary, Technology, Market Overview, Forecast, References)?

Excellent   Good   OK   Confusing

6. How do you rate the overall organization of the *E-Business Technology Forecast*?

Excellent   Good   OK   Confusing

7. Chapter names you particularly liked: ....

8. Chapter names you particularly disliked: ....

9. Are there additional topics that should be covered in the *E-Business Technology Forecast*?

10. Other suggestions for improving the *E-Business Technology Forecast*:

Optional: Name ....

Company ....

Address ....

....

Phone ....

Technology Forecast
PricewaterhouseCoopers Technology Centre
68 Willow Road
Menlo Park, CA 94025-3669
U.S.A.

IIIlııılıılIIIıııılılılıııılIıllıııllıılıılııllııl